QUESTIONING OUR KNOWLEDGE

THE QUEST FOR REALITY AND SIGNIFICANCE

Book 1 – BEING TRULY HUMAN:
    The Limits of our Worth, Power, Freedom and Destiny

Book 2 – FINDING ULTIMATE REALITY:
    In Search of the Best Answers to the Biggest Questions

Book 3 – QUESTIONING OUR KNOWLEDGE:
    Can we Know What we Need to Know?

Book 4 – DOING WHAT'S RIGHT:
    Whose System of Ethics is Good Enough?

Book 5 – CLAIMING TO ANSWER:
    How One Person Became the Response to our Deepest Questions

Book 6 – SUFFERING LIFE'S PAIN:
    Facing the Problems of Moral and Natural Evil

BOOK 3

QUESTIONING OUR KNOWLEDGE

CAN WE KNOW WHAT WE NEED TO KNOW?

DAVID GOODING
JOHN LENNOX

Myrtlefield House
Belfast, Northern Ireland

David Gooding and John Lennox have asserted their right under the Copyright, Designs and Patents Act, 1988, to be identified as Authors of this work.

Questioning Our Knowledge: Can we Know What we Need to Know?
Book 3, The Quest for Reality and Significance
Copyright © Myrtlefield Trust, 2019

All rights reserved. No part of this publication may be reproduced, stored in a retrieval system, or transmitted, in any form or by any means, electronic, mechanical, photocopying, recording or otherwise, without the prior permission of the publisher or a license permitting restricted copying. In the UK such licenses are issued by the Copyright Licensing Agency Ltd., Barnard's Inn, 86 Fetter Lane, London, EC4A 1EN, UK.

All Scripture quotations, unless otherwise indicated, are taken from The Holy Bible, English Standard Version, copyright © 2001 by Crossway Bibles, a division of Good News Publishers. Used by permission. All rights reserved. Italics within Scripture quotations indicate emphasis added. Scripture quotations marked (our trans.) are as translated by David Gooding. Foreign language quotations marked (our trans.) are as translated by John Lennox.

Cover design: Frank Gutbrod.
Interior design and composition: Sharon VanLoozenoord.

Published by The Myrtlefield Trust
PO Box 2216
Belfast, N. Ireland, BT1 9YR
w: www.myrtlefieldhouse.com
e: info@myrtlefieldhouse.com

ISBN: 978-1-912721-10-8 (hbk.)
ISBN: 978-1-912721-11-5 (pbk.)
ISBN: 978-1-912721-12-2 (PDF)
ISBN: 978-1-912721-13-9 (Kindle)
ISBN: 978-1-912721-14-6 (EPUB without DRM)
ISBN: 978-1-912721-30-6 (box set)

23 22 21 20 19   10 9 8 7 6 5 4 3 2

DEDICATED TO OUR YOUNGER FELLOW STUDENTS,

REMEMBERING THAT WE WERE ONCE STUDENTS—AND STILL ARE

CONTENTS

BOOK 3: QUESTIONING OUR KNOWLEDGE

CAN WE KNOW WHAT WE NEED TO KNOW?

Series Preface   xi

Analytical Outline   xv

Series Introduction   1

HOW DO WE KNOW ANYTHING?

1. **How We Perceive the World**   43
2. **False Alternatives at the Extremes**   67
3. **The Epistemology of Immanuel Kant**   101
4. **Reason and Faith**   135

WHAT IS TRUTH?

5. **In Search of Truth**   159
6. **Particular Truths and Ultimate Truth**   181
7. **The Biblical View of Truth**   197
8. **Truth on Trial**   213

POSTMODERNISM

9. **Postmodernism, Philosophy and Literature**   231
10. **Postmodernism and Science**   271

Appendix: The Scientific Endeavour   287

Series Bibliography   323

Study Questions for Teachers and Students   355

Scripture Index   373

General Index   375

ILLUSTRATIONS

I.1. A Rose   5
I.2. The School of Athens by Raphael   10–11
I.3. On the Origin of Species (1859) by Charles Darwin   27
I.4. A Touchstone   32
I.5. An Apple   35
Ap.1. Benzene Molecule   290
Ap.2. Model T Ford Motor Car   307
Ap.3. Milky Way Galaxy   318–19

SERIES PREFACE

The average student has a problem—many problems in fact, but one in particular. No longer a child, he or she is entering adult life and facing the torrent of change that adult independence brings. It can be exhilarating but sometimes also frightening to have to stand on one's own feet, to decide for oneself how to live, what career to follow, what goals to aim at and what values and principles to adopt.

How are such decisions to be made? Clearly much thought is needed and increasing knowledge and experience will help. But leave these basic decisions too long and there is a danger of simply drifting through life and missing out on the character-forming process of thinking through one's own worldview. For that is what is needed: a coherent framework that will give to life a true perspective and satisfying values and goals. To form such a worldview for oneself, particularly at a time when society's traditional ideas and values are being radically questioned, can be a very daunting task for anyone, not least university students. After all, worldviews are normally composed of many elements drawn from, among other sources, science, philosophy, literature, history and religion; and a student cannot be expected to be an expert in any one of them, let alone in all of them (indeed, is anyone of us?).

Nevertheless we do not have to wait for the accumulated wisdom of life's later years to see what life's major issues are; and once we grasp what they are, it is that much easier to make informed and wise decisions of every kind. It is as a contribution to that end that the authors offer this series of books to their younger fellow students. We intend that each book will stand on its own while also contributing to the fuller picture provided by the whole series.

So we begin by laying out the issues at stake in an extended introduction that overviews the fundamental questions to be asked, key voices to be listened to, and why the meaning and nature of ultimate reality matter to each one of us. For it is inevitable that each one of us will, at some time and at some level, have to wrestle with the fundamental questions of our existence. Are we meant to be here, or is it really by accident that we are? In what sense, if any, do we matter, or are we simply rather insignificant specks inhabiting an insubstantial corner of our galaxy? Is there a purpose in it all? And if indeed it does matter, where would we find reliable answers to these questions?

In Book 1, *Being Truly Human*, we consider questions surrounding the value of humans. Besides thinking about human freedom and the dangerous way it is often devalued, we consider the nature and basis of morality and how other moralities compare with one another. For any discussion of the freedom humans have to choose raises the question of the power we wield over other humans and also over nature, sometimes with disastrous consequences. What should guide our use of power? What, if anything, should limit our choices, and to what extent can our choices keep us from fulfilling our full potential and destiny?

The realities of these issues bring before us another problem. It is not the case that, having developed a worldview, life will unfold before us automatically and with no new choices. Quite the opposite. All of us from childhood onward are increasingly faced with the practical necessity of making ethical decisions about right and wrong, fairness and injustice, truth and falsity. Such decisions not only affect our individual relationships with people in our immediate circle: eventually they play their part in developing the social and moral tone of each nation and, indeed, of the world. We need, therefore, all the help we can get in learning how to make truly ethical decisions.

But ethical theory inevitably makes us ask what is the ultimate authority behind ethics. Who or what has the authority to tell us: you ought to do this, or you ought not to do that? If we cannot answer that question satisfactorily, the ethical theory we are following lacks a sufficiently solid and effective base. Ultimately, the answer to this question unavoidably leads us to the wider philosophical question: how are we related to the universe of which we form a part? What is the nature of ultimate reality? Is there a creator who made us and built into us our moral awareness, and requires us to live according to his laws? Or, are human beings the product of mindless, amoral forces that care nothing about ethics, so that as a human race we are left to make up our own ethical rules as best we can, and try to get as much general agreement to them as we can manage, either by persuasion or even, regretfully, by force?

For this reason, we have devoted Book 2, *Finding Ultimate Reality*, to a discussion of Ultimate Reality; and for comparison we have selected views and beliefs drawn from various parts of the world and from different centuries: the Indian philosophy of Shankara; the natural and moral philosophies of the ancient Greeks, with one example of Greek mysticism; modern atheism and naturalism; and finally, Christian theism.

The perusal of such widely differing views, however, naturally provokes further questions: how can we know which of them, if any, is true? And what is truth anyway? Is there such a thing as absolute truth? And how should we recognise it, even if we encountered it? That, of course, raises the fundamental question that affects not only scientific and philosophical theories, but our day-to-day experience as well: how do we know anything?

The part of philosophy that deals with these questions is known as epistemology, and to it we devote Book 3, *Questioning Our Knowledge*. Here we pay special attention to a theory that has found wide popularity in recent times, namely, postmodernism. We pay close attention to it, because if it were true (and we think it isn't) it would seriously affect not only ethics, but science and the interpretation of literature.

When it comes to deciding what are the basic ethical principles that all should universally follow we should observe that we are not the first generation on earth to have thought about this question. Book 4, *Doing What's Right*, therefore, presents a selection of notable but diverse ethical theories, so that we may profit from their insights that are of permanent value; and, at the same time, discern what, if any, are their weaknesses, or even fallacies.

But any serious consideration of humankind's ethical behaviour will eventually raise another practical problem. As Aristotle observed long ago, ethics can tell us what we ought to do; but by itself it gives us no adequate power to do it. It is the indisputable fact that, even when we know that something is ethically right and that it is our duty to do it, we fail to do it; and contrariwise, when we know something is wrong and should not be done, we nonetheless go and do it. Why is that? Unless we can find an answer to this problem, ethical theory—of whatever kind—will prove ultimately ineffective, because it is impractical.

Therefore, it seemed to us that it would be seriously deficient to deal with ethics simply as a philosophy that tells us what ethical standards we ought to attain to in life. Our human plight is that, even when we know that something is wrong, we go and do it anyway. How can we overcome this universal weakness?

Jesus Christ, whose emphasis on ethical teaching is unmistakable, and in some respects unparalleled, nevertheless insisted that ethical teaching is ineffective unless it is preceded by a spiritual rebirth (see Gospel of John 3). But this brings us into the area of religion, and many people find that difficult. What right has religion to talk about ethics, they say, when religion has been the cause of so many wars, and still leads to much violence? But the same is true of political philosophies—and it does not stop us thinking about politics.

Then there are many religions, and they all claim to offer their adherents help to fulfil their ethical duties. How can we know if they are true, and that they offer real hope? It seems to us that, in order to know whether the help a religion offers is real or not, one would have to practise that religion and discover it by experience. We, the authors of this book, are Christians, and we would regard it as impertinent of us to try to describe what other religions mean to their adherents. Therefore, in Book 5, *Claiming to Answer*, we confine ourselves to stating why we think the claims of the Christian gospel are valid, and the help it offers real.

However, talk of God raises an obvious and very poignant problem: how can there be a God who cares for justice, when, apparently, he makes no attempt to put a stop to the injustices that ravage our world? And how can it be thought that there is an all-loving, all-powerful, and all-wise creator when so many people suffer such bad things, inflicted on them not just by man's cruelty but by natural disasters and disease? These are certainly difficult questions. It is the purpose of Book 6, *Suffering Life's Pain*, to discuss these difficulties and to consider possible solutions.

It only remains to point out that every section and subsection of the book is provided with questions, both to help understanding of the subject matter and to encourage the widest possible discussion and debate.

DAVID GOODING
JOHN LENNOX

ANALYTICAL OUTLINE

SERIES INTRODUCTION 1

The shaping of a worldview for a life full of choices 3

Why we need a worldview 3

Asking the fundamental questions 9

   First fundamental worldview question: *what lies behind the observable universe?* 12

   Second fundamental worldview question: *how did our world come into existence, how has it developed, and how has it come to be populated with such an amazing variety of life?* 13

   Third fundamental worldview question: *what are human beings? where do their rationality and moral sense come from? what are their hopes for the future, and what, if anything, happens to them after death?* 14

   The fundamental difference between the two groups of answers 15

Voices to be listened to 16

   The voice of intuition 17

   The voice of science 18

   The voice of philosophy 20

   The voice of history 22

   The voice of divine self-revelation 24

The meaning of reality 29

What is the nature of ultimate reality? 34

   Ourselves as individuals 34

   Our status in the world 35

   Our origin 36

   Our purpose 36

   Our search 38

Our aim 39

PART 1. HOW DO WE KNOW ANYTHING? 41

CHAPTER 1. HOW WE PERCEIVE THE WORLD 43

How do we know anything? 45

   The limitations of sense perception 45

   The role of epistemology 46

   A second-order discipline 47

   The rise of scepticism 48

   Forms of scepticism 50

      Socrates 50

      Pyrrho (4th–3rd century BC); Sextus Empiricus (AD *c.*200) 50

   Examples of extreme scepticism 52

      René Descartes (1596–1650) 52

      The 'brain in a vat' analogy 54

         Thinking more about brains in vats 56

      What then qualifies as knowledge? 57

How do we perceive the external world? 57

   Defining perception 58

   The case for the Representative Theory of Perception 59

      Hallucinations 59

      Mirages 60

      Perceptual error 60

      Perspectival relativity 60

   Evaluation 60

      Hallucinations 61

      Mirages 62

      Perceptual error 62

      Perspectival relativity 63

   A thought experiment 63

Final thoughts on the Representative Theory of Perception 64

CHAPTER 2. FALSE ALTERNATIVES AT THE EXTREMES 67

Middle ground? 69

Idealism and realism 69
Idealism 69
Realism 70

Knowledge is subjective and knowledge is objective 72
Bringing the issue of subjectivity into focus 73
Man, the knower, as Subject 73
The objective reality of the universe 74

Rationalism and empiricism 75
The historical context of the debate 76
The dispute between rationalism and empiricism 78
Locke's epistemological theory 78
The validation of ideas 79
An evaluation of Locke's epistemology 80
Leibniz's criticism of Locke 81
A serious weakness in Locke's epistemology 81
Evaluation of Locke's snowball 84
Evaluation of Locke's theory about colour 84
Topic for debate: Is the greenness in the grass? 86

David Hume's epistemology 89
Hume's philosophy of mind 89
Question 1 – How do we grasp spoken information? 91
Question 2 – What am I myself? 92
Question 3 – What causes things? 94
Evaluation of Hume's billiard balls 96

CHAPTER 3. THE EPISTEMOLOGY OF IMMANUEL KANT 101

Kant's metaphysics 103
Kant's distinction between pure reason and practical reason 104
Knowing God 107
Denying knowledge to make room for faith 109
Kant's Copernican revolution 110
Kant's scientific background 110
William Harvey and the circulation of the blood 110
Newton's theory of gravitation 111
Kant's objections to Hume's philosophy 113
Sound principles and specific knowledge 113
Kant's aims in writing the *Critique* 114
The irony of Kant's Copernican revolution 117

Kant's basic principles of a priori synthetic knowledge 117
First Principle: The possibility of a priori synthetic knowledge 117
Analytic propositions 118
Synthetic propositions 118
Kant's contention 119
The proposition 'Everything which happens has its cause' 119
Arithmetical propositions 119
All geometrical propositions 120
Second Principle: The transcendental aesthetic 121
Evaluation of the transcendental aesthetic 122
Third Principle: The transcendental analytic: pure concepts of the understanding 123

The limits of knowability according
to Kant 124
   Epistemology 125
      An example: The rainbow 125
   Psychology 127
      Practical reason and the soul 128
   Cosmology and theology 130
      The argument from causation and the argument from design 131
      Kant's objection to the argument from design 132
      Kant's objections to the argument from causation 130
   A critique of Kant's 'Critique' 133

CHAPTER 4. REASON AND FAITH 135

A fourth false alternative 137
   The limitations of pure reason 138
   Human reason did not create the universe 139
   Reason's underlying authority 140

The nature of theism's faith 142
   God's self-revelation through creation 144
      The points raised by Romans 1:19–21 144
   The false charge that men have invented God 145
   Basic beliefs 148

Objections and answers 149
   Some reasons why people are not aware of God 149
      The problem of evil and suffering 149
      A basic antagonism to God and to the idea of God 150
      Suppression by peer pressure 150
      Atrophy 151
      Fear 151
   The Bible's major storyline 151

      The original false turn that humanity took in relation to God 153
      Conditions for knowing God 154
      The test of genuine knowledge of God 154

PART 2. WHAT IS TRUTH? 157

CHAPTER 5. IN SEARCH OF TRUTH 159

What we are looking for 161
   Our ambivalent attitude to truth 161

Objections and rejections 163
   Objections to the idea of universal objective truth 163
      Reason 1 – The limitations of language 163
      Reason 2 – The limitations of knowledge 163
      Reason 3 – The arrogance of so-called objective truth 164
      Reason 4 – Objective truth enslaves 164
      Reason 5 – Claims to objective truth are elitist and undemocratic 164
   Some underlying reasons for this rejection of objective truth 164
      The past enforcement of ideologies and religions by sheer power 164
      The globalisation of knowledge 165

Long-term consequences of the devaluation of objective truth 166

Conventionalism 169

The definition of truth 170
   The correspondence theory of truth 170
      Aristotle's view of truth 170
      Bertrand Russell's view 172
      The need to distinguish between objective facts and subjective feelings 173

An objection to the correspondence theory 173
The subjective element in knowing the truth 175
The coherence theory of truth 175
Evaluation of the coherence theory 176
The pragmatic theory of truth 178
Questions remain 179

CHAPTER 6. PARTICULAR TRUTHS AND ULTIMATE TRUTH 181

Truth at different levels 183
Different kinds of truth? 184
Historical truths 186

Historicism and the truth about everything 187
The urge to know the whole story 188
The historicism of Hegel and Marx 191
Hegel's basic premise 192
Hegel's philosophy of freedom 193
Marx's historicism 196
A final comment on Hegel and Marx 196

CHAPTER 7. THE BIBLICAL VIEW OF TRUTH 197

A preliminary word study 199
Truth as correspondence of words with the facts 200
Genesis 42:16 200
John 4:17-18 200
Truth as correspondence of deeds and words 200
1 John 3:17 200
Galatians 2:13-14 201
Genesis 32:9-10 201
Truth as coherence 201
Mark 14:56-59 201
Pragmatic truth 201
1 Thessalonians 2:13 201
Truth and true as openness and honesty 202
Matthew 22:16-17 202
Mark 5:33 202
Truth as integrity 202
Exodus 18:21-22 202
Jeremiah 9:3-6 202
Zechariah 8:16-17 203
Truth and true as what is real and genuine 203
John 17:3 203
1 Thessalonians 1:9 203
True as what is real and eternal 203
John 6:27, 32 203
Truth as what is ontologically real 204
John 4:22-24 204
True as what is the real thing as distinct from its symbol 204
Hebrews 8:1-2 204

Different ways of expressing truth 205
Poetic truth or truth expressed through poetry 205
Propositional truth 206
Truths expressed in precise legal language 207
Existential truth 208
Revealed truth 208
Creation 208
The gospel 209
Christ is himself the truth 210

CHAPTER 8. TRUTH ON TRIAL 213

Coming to face the truth 215

The trial of Christ 216
The background to the trial 217
The trial: first phase—Pilate discovers the truth 218

The arrest (John at 18:1–11) 218
The first formal session of the court (John 18:28–32) 219
Pilate's first interview with Christ (John 18:33–38) 219
A test for truth (John 18:38–40) 221
An interval for reflection 222
The trial: second phase—Pilate discovers his own responsibility 222
Pilate's first attempt to release Christ (John 19:1–6) 223
The priests' next move (John 19:7–8) 223
Pilate's second interview with Christ (19:9–11) 224
Pilate's final attempts to release Christ (John 19:12–15) 226
Questions arising 226

PART 3. POSTMODERNISM 229

CHAPTER 9. POSTMODERNISM, PHILOSOPHY AND LITERATURE 231

Introduction 233

Literary criticism's search for truth 233
Postmodernism's relation to modernism 234
Derrida's position in the history and practice of literary criticism 236
Some basic principles of Derrida's theory of literary criticism 237

Prohibition of appeal to the intended meaning of the author 237

Limits to the intentional fallacy 240
Exaggerations of reader-response criticism 241
Example 1 – Robert Crosman 242
Example 2 – Stanley Fish 244

The denial of metaphysics 245

Logocentrism 246
The Stoic understanding of 'logos' 247
The Christian understanding of 'logos' 247
Derrida's rejection of 'logos' 247
Presence 248
The inescapability of metaphysics 250

The assertion that writing precedes speech and that signification creates meaning 251

A possible interpretation of Derrida's meaning 253
Fitting the idea that signification creates meaning 254
The idea is not original to Derrida 255
Conventionalism 256
Conventionalism's first denial 256
1. A word can denote something that does not exist, and never did exist, in the world 257
2. Different meanings for the same word in different time periods 257
3. Sometimes a word contains an evaluation 257
Animals and plants 258
Physical things 258
Conventionalism's second denial 259
The laws of mathematics 260
The basic universal moral laws 261
Conventionalism's third denial 261

The denial that words have any intrinsic meaning 262

Deconstruction 263

On deconstruction 264
The first object of its negative, subversive criticism 264
The other object of its negative, subversive criticism 265
Its revolutionary opposition to all power and privilege 265

What deconstructionists propose to put in the place of traditional literary criticism 265

The trouble with deconstructionism's demolition of all traditional literary criticism 266

Deconstruction theory refuses to have its own principles applied to itself 266

Deconstructionism's self-imposed inability to help anyone appreciate any literary text 267

Derrida's ideal writing 267

What he rejects 268

What he accepts and aims at 268

Concluding comment on Derrida 268

CHAPTER 10. POSTMODERNISM AND SCIENCE 271

Just another story? 273

An overreaction to modernism 275

A response to postmodernism: is science a social construct? 276

Postmodernism's confusion of categories 277

Postmodernism's overestimate of the subjectivity of science 278

The Sokal affair 280

The universe is not an intellectual construct 283

Conclusion: The intellectual incoherence of the postmodernist illusion 284

APPENDIX: THE SCIENTIFIC ENDEAVOUR 287

The clear voice of science 289

Scientific method 290

Observation and experimentation 291

Data, patterns, relationships and hypotheses 291

Induction 293

The role of deduction 296

Competing hypotheses can cover the same data 298

Falsifiability 301

Repeatability and abduction 302

Explaining explanations 305

Levels of explanation 305

Reductionism 309

Basic operational presuppositions 313

Observation is dependent on theory 314

Knowledge cannot be gained without making certain assumptions to start with 315

Gaining knowledge involves trusting our senses and other people 316

Gaining scientific knowledge involves belief in the rational intelligibility of the universe 317

Operating within the reigning paradigms 319

Further reading 321

QUESTIONING OUR KNOWLEDGE

SERIES INTRODUCTION

Our worldview . . . includes our views, however ill or well thought out, right or wrong, about the hard yet fascinating questions of existence and life: What am I to make of the universe? Where did it come from? Who am I? Where did I come from? How do I know things? Do I have any significance? Do I have any duty?

THE SHAPING OF A WORLDVIEW FOR A LIFE FULL OF CHOICES

In this introductory section we are going to consider the need for each one of us to construct his or her own worldview. We shall discuss what a worldview is and why it is necessary to form one; and we shall enquire as to what voices we must listen to as we construct our worldview. As we set out to examine how we understand the world, we are also trying to discover whether we can know the ultimate truth about reality. So each of the subjects in this series will bring us back to the twin questions of what is real and why it matters whether we know what is real. We will, therefore, need to ask as we conclude this introductory section what we mean by 'reality' and then to ask: what is the nature of ultimate reality?[1]

WHY WE NEED A WORLDVIEW

There is a tendency in our modern world for education to become a matter of increasing specialisation. The vast increase of knowledge during the past century means that unless we specialise in this or that topic it is very difficult to keep up with, and grasp the significance of, the ever-increasing flood of new discoveries. In one sense this is to be welcomed because it is the result of something that in itself is one of the marvels of our modern world, namely, the fantastic progress of science and technology.

But while that is so, it is good to remind ourselves that true education has a much wider objective than this. If, for instance, we are to understand the progress of our modern world, we must see it against

---

[1] Please note this Introduction is the same for each book in the series, except for the final section—Our Aim.

the background of the traditions we have inherited from the past and that will mean that we need to have a good grasp of history.

Sometimes we forget that ancient philosophers faced and thought deeply about the basic philosophical principles that underlie all science and came up with answers from which we can still profit. If we forget this, we might spend a lot of time and effort thinking through the same problems and not coming up with as good answers as they did.

Moreover, the role of education is surely to try and understand how all the various fields of knowledge and experience in life fit together. To understand a grand painting one needs to see the picture as a whole and understand the interrelationship of all its details and not simply concentrate on one of its features.

Moreover, while we rightly insist on the objectivity of science we must not forget that it is we who are doing the science. And therefore, sooner or later, we must come to ask how we ourselves fit into the universe that we are studying. We must not allow ourselves to become so engrossed in our material world and its related technologies that we neglect our fellow human beings; for they, as we shall later see, are more important than the rest of the universe put together.[2] The study of ourselves and our fellow human beings will, of course, take more than a knowledge of science. It will involve the worlds of philosophy, sociology, literature, art, music, history and much more besides.

Educationally, therefore, it is an important thing to remember—and a thrilling thing to discover—the interrelation and the unity of all knowledge. Take, for example, what it means to know what a rose is: *What is the truth about a rose?*

To answer the question adequately, we shall have to consult a whole array of people. First the scientists. We begin with the *botanists*, who are constantly compiling and revising lists of all the known plants and flowers in the world and then classifying them in terms of families and groups. They help us to appreciate our rose by telling us what family it belongs to and what are its distinctive features.

Next, the *plant breeders* and *gardeners* will inform us of the history of our particular rose, how it was bred from other kinds, and the conditions under which its sort can best be cultivated.

---

[2] Especially in Book 1 of this series, *Being Truly Human*.

FIGURE I.1. A Rose.

In William Shakespeare's play *Romeo and Juliet*, the beloved dismisses the fact that her lover is from the rival house of Montague, invoking the beauty of one of the best known and most favourite flowers in the world: 'What's in a name? that which we call a rose / By any other name would smell as sweet'.

Reproduced with permission of ©iStock/OGphoto.

Then, the *chemists*, *biochemists*, *biologists* and *geneticists* will tell us about the chemical and biochemical constituents of our rose and the bewildering complexities of its cells, those micro-miniaturised factories which embody mechanisms more complicated than any built by human beings, and yet so tiny that we need highly specialised equipment to see them. They will tell us about the vast coded database of genetic information which the cell factories use in order to produce the building blocks of the rose. They will describe, among a host of other things, the processes by which the rose lives: how it photosynthesises sunlight into sugar-borne energy and the mechanisms by which it is pollinated and propagated.

After that, the *physicists* and *cosmologists* will tell us that the chemicals of which our rose is composed are made up of atoms which themselves are built from various particles like electrons, protons and neutrons. They will give us their account of where the basic material in the universe comes from and how it was formed. If we ask how such knowledge helps us to understand roses, the cosmologists may well point out that our earth is the only planet in our solar system that is able to grow roses! In that respect, as in a multitude of other respects, our planet is very special—and that is surely something to be wondered at.

But when the botanists, plant breeders, gardeners, chemists, biochemists, physicists and cosmologists have told us all they can, and it is a great deal which would fill many volumes, even then many of us will feel that they will scarcely have begun to tell us the truth about roses. Indeed, they have not explained what perhaps most of us would think is the most important thing about roses: the beauty of their form, colour and fragrance.

Now here is a very significant thing: scientists can explain the astonishing complexity of the mechanisms which lie behind our senses of vision and smell that enable us to see roses and detect their scent. But we don't need to ask the scientists whether we ought to consider roses beautiful or not: we can see and smell that for ourselves! We perceive this by *intuition*. We just look at the rose and we can at once see that it is beautiful. We do not need anyone to tell us that it is beautiful. If anyone were so foolish as to suggest that because science cannot measure beauty, therefore beauty does not exist, we should simply say: 'Don't be silly.'

But the perception of beauty does not rest on our own intuition alone. We could also consult the *artists*. With their highly developed sense of colour, light and form, they will help us to perceive a depth and intensity of beauty in a rose that otherwise we might miss. They can educate our eyes.

Likewise, there are the *poets*. They, with their finely honed ability as word artists, will use imagery, metaphor, allusion, rhythm and rhyme to help us formulate and articulate the feelings we experience when we look at roses, feelings that otherwise might remain vague and difficult to express.

Finally, if we wanted to pursue this matter of the beauty of a rose deeper still, we could talk to the *philosophers*, especially experts in aesthetics. For each of us, perceiving that a rose is beautiful is a highly subjective experience, something that we see and feel at a deep level inside ourselves. Nevertheless, when we show a rose to other people, we expect them too to agree that it is beautiful. They usually have no difficulty in doing so.

From this it would seem that, though the appreciation of beauty is a highly subjective experience, yet we observe:

1. there are some objective criteria for deciding what is beautiful and what is not;
2. there is in each person an inbuilt aesthetic sense, a capacity for perceiving beauty; and
3. where some people cannot, or will not, see beauty, in, say, a

rose, or will even prefer ugliness, it must be that their internal capacity for seeing beauty is defective or damaged in some way, as, for instance, by colour blindness or defective shape recognition, or through some psychological disorder (like, for instance, people who revel in cruelty, rather than in kindness).

Now by this time we may think that we have exhausted the truth about roses; but of course we haven't. We have thought about the scientific explanation of roses. We have then considered the value we place on them, their beauty and what they mean to us. But precisely because they have meaning and value, they raise another group of questions about the moral, ethical and eventually spiritual significance of what we do with them. Consider, for instance, the following situations:

First, a woman has used what little spare money she had to buy some roses. She likes roses intensely and wants to keep them as long as she can. But a poor neighbour of hers is sick, and she gets a strong feeling that she ought to give at least some of these roses to her sick neighbour. So now she has two conflicting instincts within her:

1. an instinct of self-interest: a strong desire to keep the roses for herself, and
2. an instinctive sense of duty: she ought to love her neighbour as herself, and therefore give her roses to her neighbour.

Questions arise. Where do these instincts come from? And how shall she decide between them? Some might argue that her selfish desire to keep the roses is simply the expression of the blind, but powerful, basic driving force of evolution: self-propagation. But the altruistic sense of duty to help her neighbour at the expense of loss to herself—where does that come from? Why ought she to obey it? She has a further problem: she must decide one way or the other. She cannot wait for scientists or philosophers, or indeed anyone else, to help her. She has to commit herself to some course of action. How and on what grounds should she decide between the two competing urges?

Second, a man likes roses, but he has no money to buy them. He sees that he could steal roses from someone else's garden in such a way that he could be certain that he would never be found out. Would it be wrong to steal them? If neither the owner of the roses, nor the police, nor the courts would ever find out that he stole them, why shouldn't he steal them? Who has the right to say that it is wrong to steal?

Third, a man repeatedly gives bunches of roses to a woman whose husband is abroad on business. The suspicion is that he is giving her roses in order to tempt her to be disloyal to her husband. That would be adultery. Is adultery wrong? Always wrong? Who has the right to say so?

Now to answer questions like these in the first, second, and third situations thoroughly and adequately we must ask and answer the most fundamental questions that we can ask about roses (and indeed about anything else).

Where do roses come from? We human beings did not create them (and are still far from being able to create anything like them). Is there a God who designed and created them? Is he their ultimate owner, who has the right to lay down the rules as to how we should use them?

Or did roses simply evolve out of eternally existing inorganic matter, without any plan or purpose behind them, and without any ultimate owner to lay down the rules as to how they ought to be used? And if so, is the individual himself free to do what he likes, so long as no one finds out?

So far, then, we have been answering the simple question 'What is the truth about a rose?' and we have found that to answer it adequately we have had to draw on, not one source of knowledge, like science or literature, but on many. Even the consideration of roses has led to deep and fundamental questions about the world beyond the roses.

It is our answers to these questions which combine to shape the framework into which we fit all of our knowledge of other things. That framework, which consists of those ideas, conscious or unconscious, which all of us have about the basic nature of the world and of ourselves and of society, is called our worldview. It includes our views, however ill or well thought out, right or wrong, about the hard yet fascinating questions of existence and life: What am I to make of the universe? Where did it come from? Who am I? Where did I come from? How do I know things? Do I have any significance? Do I have any duty? Our worldview is the big picture into which we fit everything else. It is the lens through which we look to try to make sense of the world.

> Our worldview is the big picture into which we fit everything else. It is the lens through which we look to try to make sense of the world.

ASKING THE FUNDAMENTAL QUESTIONS

'He who will succeed', said Aristotle, 'must ask the right questions'; and so, when it comes to forming a worldview, must we.

It is at least comforting to know that we are not the first people to have asked such questions. Many others have done so in the past (and continue to do so in the present). That means they have done some of the work for us! In order to profit from their thinking and experience, it will be helpful for us to collect some of those fundamental questions which have been and are on practically everybody's list. We shall then ask why these particular questions have been thought to be important. After that we shall briefly survey some of the varied answers that have been given, before we tackle the task of forming our own answers. So let's get down to compiling a list of 'worldview questions'. First of all there are questions about the universe in general and about our home planet Earth in particular.

The Greeks were the first people in Europe to ask scientific questions about what the earth and the universe are made of, and how they work. It would appear that they asked their questions for no other reason than sheer intellectual curiosity. Their research was, as we would nowadays describe it, disinterested. They were not at first concerned with any technology that might result from it. Theirs was pure, not applied, science. We pause to point out that it is still a very healthy thing for any educational system to maintain a place for pure science in its curriculum and to foster an attitude of intellectual curiosity for its own sake.

But we cannot afford to limit ourselves to pure science (and even less to technology, marvellous though it is). Centuries ago Socrates perceived that. He was initially curious about the universe, but gradually came to feel that studying how human beings ought to behave

QUESTIONING OUR KNOWLEDGE

SERIES INTRODUCTION

FIGURE I.2. *The School of Athens* by Raphael.

Italian Renaissance artist Raphael likely painted the fresco *Scuola di Atene* (The School of Athens), representing Philosophy, between 1509 and 1511 for the Vatican. Many interpreters believe the hand gestures of the central figures, Plato and Aristotle, and the books each is holding respectively, *Timaeus* and *Nicomachean Ethics*, indicate two approaches to metaphysics. A number of other great ancient Greek philosophers are featured by Raphael in this painting, including Socrates (eighth figure to the left of Plato).

Reproduced from Wikimedia Commons.

was far more important than finding out what the moon was made of. He therefore abandoned physics and immersed himself in moral philosophy.

On the other hand, the leaders of the major philosophical schools in ancient Greece came to see that you could not form an adequate doctrine of human moral behaviour without understanding how human beings are related both to their cosmic environment and to the powers and principles that control the universe. In this they were surely right, which brings us to what was and still is the first fundamental question.[3]

First fundamental worldview question

What lies behind the observable universe? Physics has taught us that things are not quite what they seem to be. A wooden table, which looks solid, turns out to be composed of atoms bound together by powerful forces which operate in the otherwise empty space between them. Each atom turns out also to be mostly empty space and can be modelled from one point of view as a nucleus surrounded by orbiting electrons. The nucleus only occupies about one billionth of the space of the atom. Split the nucleus and we find protons and neutrons. They turn out to be composed of even stranger quarks and gluons. Are these the basic building blocks of matter, or are there other even more mysterious elementary building blocks to be found? That is one of the exciting quests of modern physics. And even as the search goes on, another question keeps nagging: what lies behind basic matter anyway?

The answers that are given to this question fall roughly into two groups: those that suggest that there is nothing 'behind' the basic matter of the universe, and those that maintain that there certainly is something.

Group A. There is nothing but matter. It is the prime reality, being self-existent and eternal. It is not dependent on anything or on anyone. It is blind and purposeless; nevertheless it has within it the power to develop and organise itself—

---

[3] See Book 4: *Doing What's Right*.

still blindly and purposelessly—into all the variety of matter and life that we see in the universe today. This is the philosophy of materialism.

Group B. Behind matter, which had a beginning, stands some uncreated self-existent, creative Intelligence; or, as Jews and Muslims would say, God; and Christians, the God and Father of the Lord Jesus Christ. This God upholds the universe, interacts with it, but is not part of it. He is spirit, not matter. The universe exists as an expression of his mind and for the purpose of fulfilling his will. This is the philosophy of theism.

Second fundamental worldview question

This leads us to our second fundamental worldview question, which is in three parts: *how did our world come into existence, how has it developed, and how has it come to be populated with such an amazing variety of life?*

Again, answers to these questions tend to fall into two groups:

Group A. Inanimate matter itself, without any antecedent design or purpose, formed into that conglomerate which became the earth and then in some way (not yet observed or understood) as a result of its own inherent properties and powers by spontaneous generation spawned life. The initial lowly life forms then gradually evolved into the present vast variety of life through the natural processes of mutation and natural selection, mechanisms likewise without any design or purpose. There is, therefore, no ultimate rational purpose behind either the existence of the universe, or of earth and its inhabitants.

Group B. The universe, the solar system and planet Earth have been designed and precision engineered to make it possible for life to exist on earth. The astonishing complexity of living systems, and the awesome sophistication of their mechanisms, point in the same direction.

It is not difficult to see what different implications the two radically different views have for human significance and behaviour.

Third fundamental worldview question

The third fundamental worldview question comes, again, as a set of related questions with the answers commonly given to central ideas falling into two groups: *What are human beings? Where do their rationality and moral sense come from? What are their hopes for the future, and what, if anything, happens to them after death?*

Group A. *Human nature.* Human beings are nothing but matter. They have no spirit and their powers of rational thought have arisen out of mindless matter by non-rational processes.

Morality. Man's sense of morality and duty arise solely out of social interactions between him and his fellow humans.

Human rights. Human beings have no inherent, natural rights, but only those that are granted by society or the government of the day.

Purpose in life. Man makes his own purpose.

The future. The utopia dreamed of and longed for will be brought about, either by the irresistible outworking of the forces inherent in matter and/or history; or, alternatively, as human beings learn to direct and control the biological processes of evolution itself.

Death and beyond. Death for each individual means total extinction. Nothing survives.

Group B. *Human nature.* Human beings are created by God, indeed in the image of God (according, at least, to Judaism, Christianity and Islam). Human beings' powers of rationality are derived from the divine 'Logos' through whom they were created.

Morality. Their moral sense arises from certain 'laws of God' implanted in them by their Creator.

Human rights. They have certain inalienable rights which all other human beings and governments must respect, simply because they are creatures of God, created in God's image.

Purpose in life. Their main purpose in life is to enjoy fellowship with God and to serve God, and likewise to serve their fellow creatures for their Creator's sake.

The future. The utopia they long for is not a dream, but a sure hope based on the Creator's plan for the redemption of humankind and of the world.

Death and beyond. Death does not mean extinction. Human beings, after death, will be held accountable to God. Their ultimate state will eventually be, either to be with God in total fellowship in heaven; or to be excluded from his presence.

These, very broadly speaking, are the questions that people have asked through the whole of recorded history, and a brief survey of some of the answers that have been, and still are, given to them.

The fundamental difference between the two groups of answers

Now it is obvious that the two groups of answers given above are diametrically opposed; but we ought to pause here to make sure that we have understood what exactly the nature and cause of the opposition is. If we were not thinking carefully, we might jump to the conclusion that the answers in the A-groups are those given by science, while the answers in the B-groups are those given by religion. But that would be a fundamental misunderstanding of the situation. It is true that the majority of scientists today would agree with the answers given in the A-groups; but there is a growing number of scientists who would agree with the answers given in the B-groups. It is not therefore a conflict between science and religion. It is a difference in the basic philosophies which determine the interpretation of the evidence which science provides. Atheists will interpret that evidence in one way; theists (or pantheists) will interpret it in another.

This is understandable. No scientist comes to the task of doing research with a mind completely free of presuppositions. The atheist does research on the presupposition that there is no God. That is his basic philosophy, his worldview. He claims that he can explain everything without God. He will sometimes say that he cannot imagine what kind of scientific evidence there could possibly be for the existence of God; and not surprisingly he tends not to find any.

The theist, on the other hand, starts by believing in God and finds in his scientific discoveries abundant—overwhelming, he would say—evidence of God's hand in the sophisticated design and mechanisms of the universe.

> We pick up ideas, beliefs and attitudes from our family and society, often without realising that we have done so, and without recognising how these largely unconscious influences and presuppositions control our reactions to the questions with which life faces us.

It all comes down, then, to the importance of recognising what worldview we start with. Some of us, who have never yet thought deeply about these things, may feel that we have no worldview, and that we come to life's questions in general, and science in particular, with a completely open mind. But that is unlikely to be so. We pick up ideas, beliefs and attitudes from our family and society, often without realising that we have done so, and without recognising how these largely unconscious influences and presuppositions control our reactions to the questions with which life faces us. Hence the importance of consciously thinking through our worldview and of adjusting it where necessary to take account of the evidence available.

In that process, then, we certainly must listen to science and allow it to critique where necessary and to amend our presuppositions. But to form an adequate worldview we shall need to listen to many other voices as well.

VOICES TO BE LISTENED TO

So far, then, we have been surveying some worldview questions and various answers that have been, and still are, given to them. Now we must face these questions ourselves, and begin to come to our own decisions about them.

Our worldview must be our own, in the sense that we have personally thought it through and adopted it of our own free will. No one has the right to impose his or her worldview on us by force. The days are rightly gone when the church could force Galileo to deny what science had plainly taught him. Gone, too, for the most part, are the days when the State could force an atheistic worldview on people on pain of prison and even death. Human rights demand that people should be free to hold and to propagate by reasoned argument whatever worldview they believe in—so long, of course, that their view does not injure other people. We, the authors of this book, hold a theistic worldview. But we shall not attempt to force our view down anybody's throat. We come from a tradition whose basic principle is 'Let everyone be persuaded in his own mind.'

So we must all make up our own minds and form our own worldview. In the process of doing so there are a number of voices that we must listen to.

The voice of intuition

The first voice we must listen to is intuition. There are things in life that we see and know, not as the result of lengthy philosophical reasoning, nor as a result of rigorous scientific experimentation, but by direct, instinctive intuition. We 'see' that a rose is beautiful. We instinctively 'know' that child abuse is wrong. A scientist can sometimes 'see' what the solution to a problem is going to be even before he has worked out the scientific technique that will eventually provide formal proof of it.

A few scientists and philosophers still try to persuade us that the laws of cause and effect operating in the human brain are completely deterministic so that our decisions are predetermined: real choice is not possible. But, say what they will, we ourselves intuitively know that we do have the ability to make a free choice, whether, say, to read a book, or to go for a walk, whether to tell the truth or to tell a lie. We know we are free to take either course of action, and everyone else knows it too, and acts accordingly. This freedom is such a part of our innate concept of human dignity and value that we (for the most part) insist on being treated as responsible human beings and on treating others as such. For that reason, if we commit a crime, the magistrate will first enquire (*a*) if, when we committed the crime, we knew we were doing wrong; and (*b*) whether or not we were acting under duress. The answer to these questions will determine the verdict.

We must, therefore, give due attention to intuition, and not allow ourselves to be persuaded by pseudo-intellectual arguments to deny (or affirm) what we intuitively know to be true (or false).

On the other hand, intuition has its limits. It can be mistaken. When ancient scientists first suggested that the world was a sphere, even some otherwise great thinkers rejected the idea. They intuitively felt that it was absurd to think that there were human beings on the opposite side of the earth to us, walking 'upside-down', their feet pointed towards our feet (hence the term 'antipodean') and their heads hanging perilously down into empty space! But intuition had misled them. The scientists who believed in a spherical earth were right, intuition was wrong.

The lesson is that we need both intuition and science, acting as checks and balances, the one on the other.

The voice of science

Science speaks to our modern world with a very powerful and authoritative voice. It can proudly point to a string of scintillating theoretical breakthroughs which have spawned an almost endless array of technological spin-offs: from the invention of the light bulb to virtual-reality environments; from the wheel to the moon-landing vehicle; from the discovery of aspirin and antibiotics to the cracking of the genetic code; from the vacuum cleaner to the smartphone; from the abacus to the parallel computer; from the bicycle to the self-driving car. The benefits that come from these achievements of science are self-evident, and they both excite our admiration and give to science an immense credibility.

Yet for many people the voice of science has a certain ambivalence about it. For the achievements of science are not invariably used for the good of humanity. Indeed, in the past century science has produced the most hideously efficient weapons of destruction that the world has ever seen. The laser that is used to restore vision to the eye can be used to guide missiles with deadly efficiency. This development has led in recent times to a strong anti-scientific reaction.

This is understandable; but we need to guard against the obvious fallacy of blaming science for the misuse made of its discoveries. The blame for the devastation caused by the atomic bomb, for instance, does not chiefly lie with the scientists who discovered the possibility of atomic fission and fusion, but with the politicians who for reasons of global conquest insisted on the discoveries being used for the making of weapons of mass destruction.

Science, in itself, is morally neutral. Indeed, as scientists who are Christians would say, it is a form of the worship of God through the reverent study of his handiwork and is by all means to be encouraged. It is for that reason that James Clerk Maxwell, the nineteenth-century Scottish physicist who discovered the famous equations governing electromagnetic waves which are now called after him, put the following quotation from the Hebrew Psalms above the door of the Cavendish Laboratory in Cambridge where it still stands: 'The works of the LORD are great, sought out of all them that have pleasure therein' (Ps 111:2).

We must distinguish, of course, between science as a method of investigation and individual scientists who actually do the investigation. We must also distinguish between the facts which they establish beyond (reasonable) doubt and the tentative hypotheses and theories which they construct on the basis of their initial observations and experiments, and which they use to guide their subsequent research.

These distinctions are important because scientists sometimes mistake their tentative theories for proven fact, and in their teaching of students and in their public lectures promulgate as established fact what has never actually been proved. It can also happen that scientists advance a tentative theory which catches the attention of the media who then put it across to the public with so much hype that the impression is given that the theory has been established beyond question.

> Scientists sometimes mistake their tentative theories for proven fact, and in their teaching of students and in their public lectures promulgate as established fact what has never actually been proved.

Then again, we need to remember the proper limits of science. As we discovered when talking about the beauty of roses, there are things which science, strictly so called, cannot and should not be expected to explain.

Sometimes some scientists forget this, and damage the reputation of science by making wildly exaggerated claims for it. The famous mathematician and philosopher Bertrand Russell, for instance, once wrote: 'Whatever knowledge is attainable, must be attained by scientific methods; and what science cannot discover, mankind cannot know.'[4] Nobel laureate Sir Peter Medawar had a saner and more realistic view of science. He wrote:

> There is no quicker way for a scientist to bring discredit upon himself and on his profession than roundly to declare—particularly when no declaration of any kind is called for—that science knows or soon will know the answers to all questions worth asking, and that the questions that do not admit a scientific answer are in some way nonquestions or 'pseudoquestions' that only simpletons ask and only the gullible profess to be able to answer.[5]

Medawar says elsewhere: 'The existence of a limit to science is, however, made clear by its inability to answer childlike elementary questions having to do with first and last things—questions such as "How did everything begin?"; "What are we all here for?"; "What is the point of living?"' He adds that it is to imaginative literature and religion that we must turn for answers to such questions.[6]

However, when we have said all that should be said about the limits of science, the voice of science is still one of the most important voices to which we must listen in forming our worldview. We cannot, of course, all be experts in science. But when the experts report their findings to students in other disciplines or to the general public, as they increasingly do, we all must listen to them; listen as critically as we listen to experts in other fields. But we must listen.[7]

The voice of philosophy

The next voice we must listen to is the voice of philosophy. To some people the very thought of philosophy is daunting; but actually any-

---

[4] Russell, *Religion and Science*, 243.
[5] Medawar, *Advice to a Young Scientist*, 31.
[6] Medawar, *Limits of Science*, 59–60.
[7] Those who wish to study the topic further are directed to the Appendix in this book: 'The Scientific Endeavour', and to the books by John Lennox noted there.

one who seriously attempts to investigate the truth of any statement is already thinking philosophically. Eminent philosopher Anthony Kenny writes:

> Philosophy is exciting because it is the broadest of all disciplines, exploring the basic concepts which run through all our talking and thinking on any topic whatever. Moreover, it can be undertaken without any special preliminary training or instruction; anyone can do philosophy who is willing to think hard and follow a line of reasoning.[8]

Whether we realise it or not, the way we think and reason owes a great deal to philosophy—we have already listened to its voice!

Philosophy has a number of very positive benefits to confer on us. First and foremost is the shining example of men and women who have refused to go through life unthinkingly adopting whatever happened to be the majority view at the time. Socrates said that the unexamined life is not worth living. These men and women were determined to use all their intellectual powers to try to understand what the universe was made of, how it worked, what man's place in it was, what the essence of human nature was, why we human beings so frequently do wrong and so damage ourselves and society; what could help us to avoid doing wrong; and what our chief goal in life should be, our *summum bonum* (Latin for 'chief good'). Their zeal to discover the truth and then to live by it should encourage—perhaps even shame—us to follow their example.

Secondly, it was in their search for the truth that philosophers from Socrates, Plato, and Aristotle onwards discovered the need for, and the rules of, rigorous logical thinking. The benefit of this to humanity is incalculable, in that it enables us to learn to think straight, to expose the presuppositions that lie sometimes unnoticed behind even our scientific experiments and theories, to unpick the assumptions that lurk in the formulation and expressions of our opinions, to point to fallacies in our argumentation, to detect instances of circular reasoning, and so on.

However, philosophy, just like science, has its proper limits. It cannot tell us what axioms or fundamental assumptions we should

---

[8] Kenny, *Brief History of Western Philosophy*, xi.

adopt; but it can and will help us to see if the belief system which we build on those axioms is logically consistent.

There is yet a third benefit to be gained from philosophy. The history of philosophy shows that, of all the many different philosophical systems, or worldviews, that have been built up by rigorous philosophers on the basis of human reasoning alone, none has proved convincing to all other philosophers, let alone to the general public. None has achieved permanence, a fact which can seem very frustrating. But perhaps the frustration is not altogether bad in that it might lead us to ask whether there could just be another source of information without which human reason alone is by definition inadequate. And if our very frustration with philosophy for having seemed at first to promise so much satisfaction, and then in the end to have delivered so little, disposes us to look around for that other source of information, even our frustration could turn out to be a supreme benefit.

The voice of history

Yet another voice to which we must listen is the voice of history. We are fortunate indeed to be living so far on in the course of human history as we do. Already in the first century AD a simple form of jet propulsion was described by Hero of Alexandria. But technology at that time knew no means of harnessing that discovery to any worthwhile practical purpose. Eighteen hundred years were to pass before scientists discovered a way of making jet engines powerful enough to be fitted to aircraft.

When in the 1950s and 1960s scientists, working on the basis of a discovery of Albert Einstein's, argued that it would be possible to make laser beams, and then actually made them, many people mockingly said that lasers were a solution to a non-existent problem, because no one could think of a practical use to which they could be put. History has proved the critics wrong and justified the pure scientists (if pure science needs any justification!).

In other cases history has taught the opposite lesson. At one point the phlogiston theory of combustion came to be almost universally accepted. History eventually proved it wrong.

Fanatical religious sects (in spite, be it said, of the explicit prohibition of the Bible) have from time to time predicted that the end of the world would take place at such-and-such a time in such-and-such a place. History has invariably proved them wrong.

In the last century, the philosophical system known as logical positivism arose like a meteor and seemed set to dominate the philosophical landscape, superseding all other systems. But history discovered its fatal flaw, namely that it was based on a verification principle which allowed only two kinds of meaningful statement: *analytic* (a statement which is true by definition, that is a tautology like 'a vixen is a female fox'), or *synthetic* (a statement which is capable of verification by experiment, like 'water is composed of hydrogen and oxygen'). Thus all metaphysical statements were dismissed as meaningless! But, as philosopher Karl Popper famously pointed out, the Verification Principle itself is neither analytic nor synthetic and so is meaningless! Logical positivism is therefore self-refuting. Professor Nicholas Fotion, in his article on the topic in *The Oxford Companion to Philosophy*, says: 'By the late 1960s it became obvious that the movement had pretty much run its course.'[9]

Earlier still, Marx, basing himself on Hegel, applied his dialectical materialism first to matter and then to history. He claimed to have discovered a law in the workings of social and political history that would irresistibly lead to the establishment of a utopia on earth; and millions gave their lives to help forward this process. The verdict has been that history seems not to know any such irresistible law.

History has also delivered a devastating verdict on the Nazi theory of the supremacy of the Aryan races, which, it was promised, would lead to a new world order.

History, then, is a very valuable, if sometimes very disconcerting, adjudicator of our ideas and systems of thought. We should certainly pay serious heed to its lessons and be grateful for them.

But there is another reason why we should listen to history. It introduces us to the men and women who have proved to be world leaders of thought and whose influence is still a live force among us today. Among them, of course, is Jesus Christ. He was rejected, as we know, by his contemporaries and executed. But, then, so was Socrates. Socrates' influence has lived on; but Christ's influence has been and still is infinitely greater than that of Socrates, or of any other world leader.

---

[9] Fotion, 'Logical Positivism'.

It would be very strange if we listened, as we do, to Socrates, Plato, Aristotle, Hume, Kant, Marx and Einstein, and neglected or refused to listen to Christ. The numerous (and some very early) manuscripts of the New Testament make available to us an authentic record of his teaching. Only extreme prejudice would dismiss him without first listening to what he says.

> History introduces us to the men and women who have proved to be world leaders of thought and whose influence is still a live force among us today. . . . It would be very strange if we listened, as we do, to Socrates, Plato, Aristotle, Hume, Kant, Marx and Einstein, and neglected or refused to listen to Christ.

The voice of divine self-revelation

The final voice that claims the right to be heard is a voice which runs persistently through history and refuses to be silenced in claiming that there is another source of information beyond that which intuition, scientific research and philosophical reasoning can provide. That voice is the voice of divine self-revelation. The claim is that the Creator, whose existence and power can be intuitively perceived through his created works, has not otherwise remained silent and aloof. In the course of the centuries he has spoken into our world through his prophets and supremely through Jesus Christ.

Of course, atheists will say that for them this claim seems to be the stuff of fairy tales; and atheistic scientists will object that there is no scientific evidence for the existence of a creator (indeed, they may well claim that assuming the existence of a creator destroys the foundation of true scientific methodology—for more of that see this book's Appendix); and that, therefore, the idea that we could have direct information from the creator himself is conceptually absurd. This reaction is, of course, perfectly consistent with the basic assumption of atheism.

However, apparent conceptual absurdity is not proof positive that something is not possible, or even true. Remember what we noticed earlier, that many leading thinkers, when they first encountered the suggestion that the earth was not flat but spherical, rejected it out of hand because of the conceptual absurdities to which they imagined it led.

In the second century AD a certain Lucian of Samosata decided to debunk what he thought to be fanciful speculations of the early scientists and the grotesque traveller's tales of so-called explorers. He wrote a book which, with his tongue in his cheek, he called *Vera historia* (A True Story). In it he told how he had travelled through space to the moon. He discovered that the moon-dwellers had a special kind of mirror by means of which they could see what people were doing on earth. They also possessed something like a well shaft by means of which they could even hear what people on earth were saying. His prose was sober enough, as if he were writing factual history. But he expected his readers to see that the very conceptual absurdity of what he claimed to have seen meant that these things were impossible and would forever remain so.

Unknown to him, however, the forces and materials already existed in nature, which, when mankind learned to harness them, would send some astronauts into orbit round the moon, land others on the moon, and make possible radio and television communication between the moon and the earth!

We should remember, too, that atomic radiation and radio frequency emissions from distant galaxies were not invented by scientists in recent decades. They were there all the time, though invisible and undetected and not believed in nor even thought of for centuries; but they were not discovered until comparatively recent times, when brilliant scientists conceived the possibility that, against all popular expectation, such phenomena might exist. They looked for them, and found them.

Is it then, after all, so conceptually absurd to think that our human intellect and rationality come not from mindless matter through the agency of impersonal unthinking forces, but from a higher personal intellect and reason?

An old, but still valid, analogy will help us at this point. If we ask about a particular motor car: 'Where did this motor car begin?' one answer would be, 'It began on the production lines of such-and-such a factory and was put together by humans and robots.'

Another, deeper-level, answer would be: 'It had its beginning in the mineral from which its constituent parts were made.'

But in the prime sense of beginning, the motor car, of which this particular motor car is a specimen, had its beginning, not in the factory, nor in its basic materials, but in something altogether different: in the intelligent mind of a person, that is, of its inventor. We know this, of course, by history and by experience; but we also know it intuitively: it is self-evidently true.

Millions of people likewise have felt, and still do feel, that what Christ and his prophets say about the 'beginning' of our human rationality is similarly self-evidently true: 'In the beginning was the Logos, and the Logos was with God, and the Logos was God. . . . All things were made by him . . .' (John 1:1-2, our trans.). That is, at any rate, a far more likely story than that our human intelligence and rationality sprang originally out of mindless matter, by accidental permutations, selected by unthinking nature.

Now the term 'Logos' means both rationality and the expression of that rationality through intelligible communication. If that rational intelligence is God and personal, and we humans are endowed by him with personhood and intelligence, then it is far from being absurd to think that the divine Logos, whose very nature and function it is to be the expression and communicator of that intelligence, should communicate with us. On the contrary, to deny a priori the possibility of divine revelation and to shut one's ears in advance to what Jesus Christ has to say, before listening to his teaching to see if it is, or is not, self-evidently true, is not the true scientific attitude, which is to keep an open mind and explore any reasonable avenue to truth.[10]

Moreover, the fear that to assume the existence of a creator God would undermine true scientific methodology is contradicted by the sheer facts of history. Sir Francis Bacon (1561–1626), widely regarded as the father of the modern scientific method, believed that God had revealed himself in two great Books, the Book of Nature and the Book of God's Word, the Bible. In his famous *Advancement of Learning* (1605), Bacon wrote: 'Let no man . . . think or maintain, that a man can search too far, or be too well studied in the book of God's word, or in the book of God's works; divinity or philosophy; but rather let men endeavour an endless progress or proficience in both.'[11] It is this quotation which Charles Darwin chose to put at the front of *On the Origin of Species* (1859).

---

[10] For the fuller treatment of these questions and related topics, see Book 5 in this series, *Claiming to Answer*.
[11] Bacon, *Advancement of Learning*, 8.

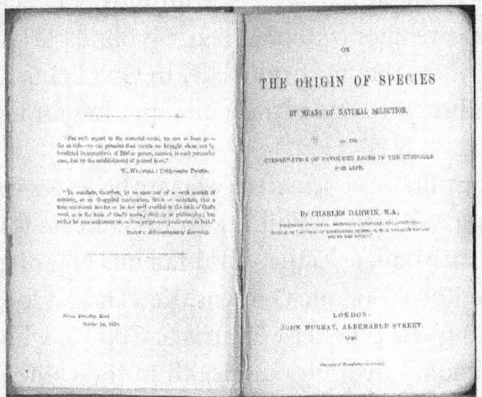

FIGURE I.3.
On the Origin of Species (1859) by Charles Darwin.

One of the book epigraphs Charles Darwin selected for his magnum opus is from Francis Bacon's *Advancement of Learning* (1605).

Reproduced from Dennis O'Neil.

Historians of science point out that it was this theistic 'Two-Book' view which was largely responsible for the meteoric rise of science beginning in the sixteenth century. C. S. Lewis refers to a statement by one of the most eminent historians of all time, Sir Alfred North Whitehead, and says: 'Professor Whitehead points out that centuries of belief in a God who combined "the personal energy of Jehovah" with "the rationality of a Greek philosopher" first produced that firm expectation of systematic order which rendered possible the birth of modern science. Men became scientific because they expected Law in Nature and they expected Law in Nature because they believed in a Legislator.'[12] In other words, theism was the cradle of science. Indeed, far from thinking that the idea of a creator was conceptually absurd, most of the great leaders of science in that period did believe in a creator.

Johannes Kepler	1571–1630	Celestial mechanics
Blaise Pascal	1623–62	Hydrostatics
Robert Boyle	1627–91	Chemistry, Gas dynamics
Isaac Newton	1642–1727	Mathematics, Optics, Dynamics
Michael Faraday	1791–1867	Magnetism
Charles Babbage	1791–1871	Computer science
Gregor Mendel	1822–84	Genetics
Louis Pasteur	1822–95	Bacteriology
Lord Kelvin	1824–1907	Thermodynamics
James Clerk Maxwell	1831–79	Electrodynamics, Thermodynamics

[12] Lewis, *Miracles*, 110.

All of these famous men would have agreed with Einstein: 'Science without religion is lame, religion without science is blind.'[13] History shows us very clearly, then, that far from belief in God being a hindrance to science, it has provided one of the main impulses for its development.

Still today there are many first-rate scientists who are believers in God. For example, Professor William D. Phillips, Nobel laureate for Physics 1997, is an active Christian, as is the world-famous botanist and former Director of the Royal Botanic Gardens, Kew in London, Sir Ghillean Prance, and so is the geneticist Francis S. Collins, who was the Director of the National Institutes of Health in the United States who gained recognition for his leadership of the international Human Genome Project which culminated in 2003 with the completion of a finished sequence of human DNA.[14]

But with many people another objection arises: if one is not sure that God even exists, would it not be unscientific to go looking for evidence for God's existence? Surely not. Take the late Professor Carl Sagan and the Search for Extra Terrestrial Intelligence (the SETI project), which he promoted. Sagan was a famous astronomer, but when he began this search he had no hard-and-fast proven facts to go on. He proceeded simply on the basis of a hypothesis. If intelligent life has evolved on earth, then it would be possible, perhaps even likely, that it would have developed on other suitable planets elsewhere in the universe. He had no guarantee that it was so, or that he would find it, even if it existed. But even so both he and NASA (the National Aeronautics and Space Administration) thought it worth spending great effort, time and considerable sums of money to employ radio telescopes to listen to remote galaxies for evidence of intelligent life elsewhere in the universe.

Why, then, should it be thought any less scientific to look for an intelligent creator, especially when there is evidence that the universe bears the imprint of his mind? The only valid excuse for not seeking for God would be the possession of convincing evidence that God does not, and could not, exist. No one has such proof.

But for many people divine revelation seems, nonetheless, an utter

---

[13] Einstein, 'Science and Religion'.
[14] The list could go on, as any Internet search for 'Christians in science' will show.

impossibility, for they have the impression that science has outgrown the cradle in which it was born and somehow proved that there is no God after all. For that reason, we examine in greater detail in the Appendix to this book what science is, what it means to be truly scientific in outlook, what science has and has not proved, and some of the fallacious ways in which science is commonly misunderstood. Here we must consider even larger questions about reality.

> The only valid excuse for not seeking for God would be the possession of convincing evidence that God does not, and could not, exist. No one has such proof.

THE MEANING OF REALITY

One of the central questions we are setting out to examine is: can we know the ultimate truth about reality? Before we consider different aspects of reality, we need to determine what we mean by 'reality'. For that purpose let's start with the way we use the term in ordinary, everyday language. After that we can move on to consider its use at higher levels.

In everyday language the noun 'reality', the adjective 'real', and the adverb 'really' have several different connotations according to the contexts in which they are used. Let's think about some examples.

First, in some situations the opposite of 'real' is 'imaginary' or 'illusory'. So, for instance, a thirsty traveller in the Sahara may see in the distance what looks to him like an oasis with water and palm trees, when in fact there is no oasis there at all. What he thinks he sees is a mirage, an optical illusion. The oasis is not real, we say; it does not actually exist.[15] Similarly a patient, having been injected with powerful drugs in the course of a serious operation, may upon waking up from the anaesthetic suffer hallucinations, and imagine she sees all kinds of weird creatures stalking round her room. But if we say, as we do, that these things which she imagines she sees, are not real, we

---

[15] Mirages occur 'when sharp differences in temperature and therefore in density develop between thin layers of air at and immediately above the ground. This causes light to be bent, or refracted, as it travels through one layer to the next. . . . During the day, when a warm layer occurs next to the ground, objects near the horizon often appear to be reflected in flat surfaces, such as beaches, deserts, roads and water. This produces the shimmering, floating images which are commonly observed on very hot days.' *Oxford Reference Encyclopaedia*, 913.

mean that they do not in actual fact exist. We could argue, of course, that something is going on in the patient's brain, and she is experiencing impressions similar to those she would have received if the weird creatures had been real. Her impressions, then, are real in the sense that they exist in her brain; but they do not correspond with the external reality that the patient supposes is creating these sense impressions. The mechanisms of her brain are presenting her with a false picture: the weird creatures do not exist. She is not seeing *them*. They are not real. On the basis of examples like this (the traveller and the patient) some philosophers have argued that none of us can ever be sure that the sense impressions which we think we receive from the external world are true representations of the external world, and not illusions. We consider their arguments in detail in Book 3 in this series, *Questioning Our Knowledge*, dealing with epistemology and related matters.

To sum up so far, then: neither the traveller nor the patient was perceiving external reality as it really was. But the reasons for their failure were different: with the traveller it was an external illusion (possibly reinforced by his thirst) that made him misread reality and imagine there was a real oasis there, when there wasn't. With the patient there was nothing unusual in the appearance of her room to cause her disordered perception. The difficulty was altogether internal to her. The drugs had distorted the perception mechanisms of her brain.

From these two examples we can learn some practical lessons:

1. It is important for us all to question from time to time whether what we unthinkingly take to be reality is in fact reality.
2. In cases like these it is external reality that has to be the standard by which we judge whether our sense perceptions are true or not.
3. Setting people free from their internal subjective misperceptions will depend on getting them, by some means or other, to face and perceive the external, objective reality.

Second, in other situations the opposite of 'real', in everyday language, is 'counterfeit', 'spurious', 'fraudulent'. So if we describe a piece of metal as being 'real gold', we mean that it is genuine gold, and not something such as brass that looks like gold, but isn't. The practical importance of being able to discern the difference between what is real in this sense and what is spurious or counterfeit, can easily be illustrated.

Take coinage, for instance. In past centuries, when coins were made (or supposed to be made) of real gold, or real silver, fraudsters would often adulterate the coinage by mixing inferior metal with gold or silver. Buyers or sellers, if they had no means of testing whether the coins they were offered were genuine, and of full value, or not, could easily be cheated.

Similarly, in our modern world counterfeiters print false bank notes and surreptitiously get them into circulation. Eventually, when the fraud is discovered, banks and traders refuse the spurious bank notes, with the result that innocent people are left with worthless pieces of paper.

Or, again, a dishonest jeweller might show a rich woman a necklace made, according to him, of valuable gems; and the rich, but unsuspecting, woman might pay a large price for it, only to discover later on that the gems were not real: they were imitations, made of a kind of glass called paste, or strass.

Conversely, an elderly woman might take her necklace, made of real gems, to a jeweller and offer to sell it to him in order to get some money to maintain herself in her old age. But the unscrupulous jeweller might make out that the gems were not as valuable as she thought: they were imitations, made of paste; and by this deceit he would persuade the reluctant woman to sell him the necklace for a much lesser price than it was worth.

Once more it will be instructive to study the underlying principles at work in these examples, because later on, when we come to study reality at a higher level, they could provide us with helpful analogies and thought models.[16]

Notice, then, that these last three examples involve significantly different principles from those that were operating in the two which we studied earlier. The oasis and the weird creatures were not real, because they did not actually exist in the external world. But the spurious coins, the fraudulent bank notes, and the genuine and the

---

[16] See especially in Book 2: *Finding Ultimate Reality*.

imitation gems, all existed in the external world. In that sense, therefore, they were all real, part of the external reality, actual pieces of matter.

What, then, was the trouble with them? It was that the fraudsters had claimed for the coins and the bank notes a value and a buying power that they did not actually possess; and in the case of the two necklaces the unscrupulous jewellers had on both occasions misrepresented the nature of the matter of which the gems were composed.

The question arises: how can people avoid being taken in by such spurious claims and misrepresentations of matter? It is not difficult to see how questions like this will become important when we come to consider the matter of the universe and its properties.

In modern, as in ancient, times, to test whether an object is made of pure gold or not, use is made of a black, fine-grained, siliceous stone, called a touchstone. When pure gold is rubbed on this touchstone, it leaves behind on the stone streaks of a certain character; whereas objects made of adulterated gold, or of some baser metal, will leave behind streaks of a different character.

FIGURE I.4. A Touchstone.

First mentioned by Theophrastus (c.372–c.287 BC) in his treatise *On Stone*, touchstones are tablets of finely grained black stones used to assay or estimate the proportion of gold or silver in a sample of metal. Traces of gold can be seen on the stone.

Reproduced from Mauro Cateb/Flickr.

In the ancient world merchants would always carry a touchstone with them; but even so it would require considerable knowledge and expertise to interpret the test correctly. When it comes to bank notes and gems, the imitations may be so cleverly made that only an expert could tell the difference between the real thing and the false. In that case non-experts, like ourselves, would have to depend on the judgments of experts.

But what are we to do when the experts disagree? How do we

decide which experts to trust? Is there any kind of touchstone that ordinary people can use on the experts themselves, or at least on their interpretations?

There is one more situation worth investigating at this point before we begin our main study.

Third, when we are confronted with what purports to be an account of something that happened in the past and of the causes that led to its happening, we rightly ask questions: 'Did this event really take place? Did it take place in the way that this account says it did? Was the alleged cause the real cause?' The difficulty with things that happened in the past is that we cannot get them to repeat themselves in the present, and watch them happening all over again in our laboratories. We have therefore to search out and study what evidence is available and then decide which interpretation of the evidence best explains what actually happened.

This, of course, is no unusual situation to be in. Detectives, seeking to solve a murder mystery and to discover the real criminal, are constantly in this situation; and this is what historians and archaeologists and palaeontologists do all the time. But mistakes can be made in handling and interpreting the evidence. For instance, in 1980 a man and his wife were camping in the Australian outback, when a dingo (an Australian wild dog) suddenly attacked and killed their little child. When, however, the police investigated the matter, they did not believe the parents' story; they alleged that the woman herself had actually killed the child. The courts found her guilty and she was duly sentenced. But new evidence was discovered that corroborated the parents' story, and proved that it really was a dingo that killed the infant. The couple was not fully and finally exonerated until 2012.

Does this kind of case mean, then, that we cannot ever be certain that any historical event really happened? Or that we can never be sure as to its real causes? Of course not! It is beyond all doubt that, for instance, Napoleon invaded Russia, and that Genghis Khan besieged Beijing (then called Zhongdu). The question is, as we considered earlier: what kind of evidence must we have in order to be sure that a historical event really happened?

But enough of these preliminary exercises. It is time now to take our first step towards answering the question: can we know the ultimate truth about reality?

WHAT IS THE NATURE OF ULTIMATE REALITY?

We have thought about the meaning of reality in various practical situations in daily life. Now we must begin to consider reality at the higher levels of our own individual existence, and that of our fellow human beings, and eventually that of the whole universe.

Ourselves as individuals

Let's start with ourselves as individuals. We know we exist. We do not have to engage in lengthy philosophical discussion before we can be certain that we exist. We know it intuitively. Indeed, we cannot logically deny it. If I were to claim 'I do not exist', I would, by stating my claim, refute it. A non-existent person cannot make any claim. If I didn't exist, I couldn't even say 'I do not exist', since I have to exist in order to make the claim. I cannot, therefore, logically affirm my own non-existence.[17]

There are other things too which we know about ourselves by intuition.

First, we are self-conscious, that is, we are aware of ourselves as separate individuals. I know I am not my brother, or my sister, or my next-door neighbour. I was born of my parents; but I am not just an extension of my father and mother. I am a separate individual, a human being in my own right. My will is not a continuation of their will, such that, if they will something, I automatically will the same thing. My will is my own.

My will may be conditioned by many past experiences, most of which have now passed into my subconscious memory. My will may well be pressurised by many internal desires or fears, and by external circumstances. But whatever philosophers of the determinist school may say, we know in our heart of hearts that we have the power of choice. Our wills, in that sense, are free. If they weren't, no one could ever be held to be guilty for doing wrong, or praised for doing right.

Second, *we are also intuitively aware of ourselves as persons, intrinsically different from, and superior to, non-personal things.* It is

---

[17] We call this law of logic the law of non-affirmability.

not a question of size, but of mind and personality. A mountain may be large, but it is mindless and impersonal. It is composed of non-rational matter. We are aware of the mountain; it is not aware of us. It is not aware of itself. It neither loves nor hates, neither anticipates nor reflects, has no hopes nor fears. Non-rational though it is, if it became a volcano, it might well destroy us, though we are rational beings. Yet we should not conclude from the fact that simply because such impersonal, non-rational matter is larger and more powerful that it is therefore a higher form of existence than personal, rational human beings. But it poignantly raises the question: what, then, is the status of our human existence in this material world and universe?

Our status in the world

We know that we did not always exist. We can remember being little children. We have watched ourselves growing up to full manhood and womanhood. We have also observed that sooner or later people die, and the unthinking earth, unknowingly, becomes their grave. What then is the significance of the individual human person, and of his or her comparatively short life on earth?

Some think that it is Mankind, the human race as a whole, that is the significant phenomenon: the individual counts for very little. On this view, the human race is like a great fruit tree. Each year it produces a large crop of apples. All of them are more or less alike. None is of any particular significance as an individual. Everyone is

FIGURE I.5. An Apple.

Apple trees take four to five years to produce their first fruit, and it takes the energy from 50 leaves to produce one apple. Archaeologists have found evidence that humans have been enjoying apples since before recorded history.

Reproduced with permission of ©iStock/ChrisBoswell.

destined for a very short life before, like the rest of the crop, it is consumed and forgotten; and so makes room for next year's crop. The tree itself lives on, producing crops year after year, in a seemingly endless cycle of birth, growth and disappearance. On this view then, the tree is the permanent, significant phenomenon; any one individual apple is of comparatively little value.

Our origin

But this view of the individual in relation to the race, does not get us to the root of our question; for the human race too did not always exist, but had a beginning, and so did the universe itself. This, therefore, only pushes the question one stage further back: to what ultimately do the human race as a whole, and the universe itself, owe their existence? What is the Great Reality behind the non-rational matter of the universe and behind us rational, personal, individual members of the human race?

Before we begin to survey the answers that have been given to this question over the centuries, we should notice that though science can point towards an answer, it cannot finally give us a complete answer. That is not because there is something wrong with science; the difficulty lies in the nature of things. The most widely accepted scientific theory nowadays (but not the only one) is that the universe came into being at the so-called Big Bang. But the theory tells us that here we encounter a singularity, that is, a point at which the laws of physics all break down. If that is true, it follows that science by itself cannot give a scientific account of what lay before, and led to, the Big Bang, and thus to the universe, and eventually to ourselves as individual human beings.

Our purpose

The fact that science cannot answer these questions does not mean, of course, that they are pseudo-questions and not worth asking. Adam Schaff, the Polish Marxist philosopher, long ago observed:

> What is the meaning of life? What is man's place in the universe? It seems difficult to express oneself scientifically on such

hazy topics. And yet if one should assert ten times over that these are typical pseudo-problems, *problems would remain*.[18]

Yes, surely problems would remain; and they are life's most important questions. Suppose by the help of science we could come to know everything about every atom, every molecule, every cell, every electrical current, every mechanism in our body and brain. How much further forward should we be? We should now know what we are made of, and how we work. But we should still not know what we are made for.

Suppose for analogy's sake we woke up one morning to find a new, empty jeep parked outside our house, with our name written on it, by some anonymous donor, specifying that it was for our use. Scientists could describe every atom and molecule it was made of. Engineers could explain how it worked, and that it was designed for transporting people. It was obviously intended, therefore, to go places. But where? Neither science as such, nor engineering as such, could tell us where we were meant to drive the jeep to. Should we not then need to discover who the anonymous donor was, and whether the jeep was ours to do what we liked with, answerable to nobody, or whether the jeep had been given to us on permanent loan by its maker and owner with the expectation that we should consult the donor's intentions, follow the rules in the driver's handbook, and in the end be answerable to the donor for how we had used it?

That surely is the situation we find ourselves in as human beings. We are equipped with a magnificent piece of physical and biological engineering, that is, our body and brain; and we are in the driver's seat, behind the steering wheel. But we did not make ourselves, nor the 'machine' we are in charge of. Must we not ask what our relationship is to whatever we owe our existence to? After all, what if it turned out to be that we owe our existence not to an impersonal what but to a personal who?

To some the latter possibility is instinctively unattractive if not frightening; they would prefer

> Must we not ask what our relationship is to whatever we owe our existence to? After all, what if it turned out to be that we owe our existence not to an impersonal what but to a personal who?

---

[18] Schaff, *Philosophy of Man*, 34 (emphasis added).

to think that they owe their existence to impersonal material, forces and processes. But then that view induces in some who hold it its own peculiar *angst*. Scientist Jacob Bronowski (1908–74) confessed to a deep instinctive longing, not simply to exist, but to be a recognisably distinct individual, and not just one among millions of otherwise undifferentiated human beings:

> When I say that I want to be myself, I mean as the existentialist does that I want to be free to be myself. This implies that I want to be rid of constraints (inner as well as outward constraints) in order to act in unexpected ways. Yet I do not mean that I want to act either at random or unpredictably. It is not in these senses that I want to be free, but in the sense that I want to be allowed to be different from others. I want to follow my own way—but I want it to be a way recognisably my own, and not zig-zag. And I want people to recognise it: I want them to say, 'How characteristic!'[19]

Yet at the same time he confessed that certain interpretations of science roused in him a fear that undermined his confidence:

> This is where the fulcrum of our fears lies: that man as a species and we as thinking men, will be shown to be no more than a machinery of atoms. We pay lip service to the vital life of the amoeba and the cheese mite; but what we are defending is the human claim to have a complex of will and thoughts and emotions—to have a mind....
>
> The crisis of confidence... springs from each man's wish to be a mind and a person, in face of the nagging fear that he is a mechanism. The central question I ask is this: Can man be both a machine and a self?[20]

Our Search

And so we come back to our original question; but now we clearly notice that it is a double question: not merely to what or to whom

---

[19] Bronowski, *Identity of Man*, 14–5.
[20] Bronowski, *Identity of Man*, 7–9.

does humanity as a whole owe its existence, but what is the status of the individual human being in relation to the race as a whole and to the uncountable myriads of individual phenomena that go to make up the universe? Or, we might ask it another way: what is our significance within the reality in which we find ourselves? This is the ultimate question hanging over every one of our lives, whether we seek answers or we don't. The answers we have for it will affect our thinking in every significant area of life.

These, then, are not merely academic questions irrelevant to practical living. They lie at the heart of life itself; and naturally in the course of the centuries notable answers to them have been given, many of which are held still today around the world.

If we are to try to understand something of the seriously held views of our fellow human beings, we must try to understand their views and the reasons for which they hold them. But just here we must sound a warning that will be necessary to repeat again in the course of these books: those who start out seriously enquiring for truth will find that at however lowly a level they start, they will not be logically able to resist asking what the Ultimate Truth about everything is!

In the spirit of truthfulness and honesty, then, let us say directly that we, the authors of this book, are Christians. We do not pretend to be indifferent guides; we commend to you wholeheartedly the answers we have discovered and will tell you why we think the claims of the Christian gospel are valid, and the help it offers real. This does not, however, preclude the possibility of our approaching other views in a spirit of honesty and fairness. We hope that those who do not share our views will approach them in the same spirit. We can ask nothing more as we set out together on this quest—in search of reality and significance.

OUR AIM

Our small contribution to this quest is set out in the 6 volumes of this series. In this, the third book in the series, we consider the fundamental question that affects not only scientific and philosophical theories, but our day-to-day experience as well: how do we know anything?

The part of philosophy that deals with this question is known as epistemology, and our first four chapters consider some of its major problems, key thinkers and big ideas. We take the following four chapters to look at the question of how we should define truth and whether there is any such thing as absolute truth. Among the many voices we listen to, we let the Bible speak for itself, as we look at the various facets of truth it addresses. We also look in some detail at the trial of Jesus Christ and its significance for the question of knowing the truth. Finally, in our last two chapters, we pay close attention to postmodernism, both its theory and its potential to affect ethics, science and the interpretation of literature.

HOW DO WE KNOW ANYTHING?

CHAPTER 1

HOW WE PERCEIVE THE WORLD

Epistemology starts by asking how, and by what means, and to what extent, we can gain not just opinion but true and certain knowledge of the world of things around us. And in that connection it asks if we can know for certain whether the world of human beings and things owes its existence to a Creator; and if so, can we know what he is like?

HOW DO WE KNOW ANYTHING?

It might well seem a silly question to ask: 'How do we know anything?' when in fact we all know that we know ten thousand and one things and run our daily lives on the basis of knowing them. We know that the world is full of *material* things like houses and chairs, rocks and rivers, vegetables and machines. We know *intangible* things like 3 × 3 = 9, and the laws of logic and that other people have minds as we ourselves have. We know *historical* things, such as that Caesar Augustus was emperor at Rome, and that Hitler never succeeded in capturing St. Petersburg. We instinctively know some *moral* truths, such as that it is wrong to torture children; and we know from experience that not everybody is honest and tells the truth. We even know *hypothetical* things, such as what would happen if we were to drive a car at 120 kph straight into a solid stone wall.

All these things and hundreds more besides, we feel we know so well that we do not necessarily stop to think how we know them, or whether we are justified in claiming to know them. We not only know these things but we believe them to the extent that we are prepared to commit ourselves to acting on the basis of this knowledge. Life would become impossible if we didn't. Why, then, should we bother to discuss *how* we know things? And why should we be called upon to justify our claim to know them?

The limitations of sense perception

Some easy examples will help. For centuries the vast majority of people believed that the earth was stationary and that the sun went round the earth. As far as people's sense perceptions were concerned, no one felt that the earth was rotating about 1,600 kph and carrying its inhabitants round the sun at 108,000 kph (no one *feels* it even now). Their senses told them that the earth was immobile; but their senses misled them.

Sight can mislead us. Travellers in a desert sometimes see ahead what they interpret as an oasis with water and palm trees; but when they arrive at the spot, there is nothing there but sand. What they saw was a mirage.[1] How, then, can we be certain that our sense perception of the external world is normally reliable?

If, in reaction to this, we try to ignore our senses and rely solely on reason to get to know the world around us, we shall soon discover that reason too has its limits. If you are sitting in your room, reason cannot tell you whether or not there is a red car parked out of sight round the corner in the next street. To find that out you will have to go and look—and trust your senses! In cases like this, reason cannot begin to work until it has got some factual evidence to work on.

At another level, we all know that juries have sometimes reached wrong verdicts, acquitting the guilty, or condemning the innocent. Let's assume that in these cases they did their best to understand the propositions put before them, and honestly believed that their verdicts were true. But obviously, sincere belief was not enough to guarantee they were true. How and by what tests could they rightly have been expected to justify their belief? Could they ever have been certain that their belief was true? In some countries the standard set to juries is that a guilty verdict should be beyond reasonable doubt! Does it matter if juries can never be absolutely certain that their verdicts are true?

The role of epistemology

The term epistemology comes from two Greek words: *epistēmē*—'knowledge', and *logos*—'science', or 'study'. It is the name given to that branch of philosophy that is concerned not with what we do believe but with what we are justified in believing.

It starts by asking how, and by what means, and to what extent, we can gain not just opinion but true and certain knowledge of the world of things around us. And in that connection it asks if we can know for certain whether the world of human beings and things owes its existence to a Creator; and if so, can we know what he is like?

---

[1] For a discussion of this and similar illusions refer to the Series Introduction.

Epistemology also invites us to consider how far our prejudices, values and even our methods of scientific investigation limit or even distort the impressions we receive.

Quantum physicists tell us that the very means they must use to investigate elementary particles so affects those particles that the scientist cannot simultaneously determine both the location and the velocity of any one particle. It is also well known that a scientist's personal worldview can affect the interpretation he places on the results of his experiments, and on the theories he forms (see Appendix: 'The Scientific Endeavour').

Epistemology, then, is devoted to challenging our claims to sure and certain knowledge.

A second-order discipline

It is probably true to say that epistemology is one of the biggest, most complicated, and therefore most disputed, fields of philosophy. Certainly at its advanced levels it becomes intensely technical. In this chapter we shall investigate some, at least, of the major theories and positions that have been, and still are, held in this field. We can do no more than that in our limited space; but we hope to do enough to whet people's interest to take up the subject themselves and to investigate it further.

It is only when we have discovered and learned many things, that epistemology will invite us rationally to justify our beliefs and to explain how we know these things to be true.

This much, however, we should understand right from the start: epistemology is a second-order, and not a first-order, discipline. That is to say, we do not first have to understand, still less to solve, all the problems that epistemology raises, before we can usefully begin the fascinating task of understanding the world around us, and of making valid discoveries about ultimate reality and how we are related to it. It is only when we have discovered and learned many things, that epistemology will invite us rationally to justify our beliefs and to explain how we know these things to be true. In other words epistemology does not lay down how we should go about discovering new knowledge. It invites us to test the knowledge that we believe we have discovered to see if it is true knowledge.

Look at the progress of life itself. A baby is born with an instinctive urge to get to know and understand itself and the world around it. Watch a baby grab hold of its foot, bring it to its mouth, and so begin to discover that this thing, whatever it is, is a part of itself. Listen to a child interminably asking 'Why this? Why that?' It is, in fact, astonishing how much a child has learned by the time it is five (without having studied the abstract theories of epistemology about how we can justify our claim to know anything!). Much of what it has learned, moreover, will prove to be permanently valid, though from time to time, of course, critical reflection will rightly modify, or even eliminate, some of its beliefs.

Similarly at the other extreme, it would be a methodological mistake for scientists to regard epistemology as a first-order discipline, and to feel that, before they may rightly attempt to make any discovery, they must first solve by abstract reasoning epistemology's theoretical question 'How can we have any true perception of the external world?' Instead they adopt what epistemologist Edmund Husserl (1859–1938) described and commended as the proper standpoint for scientists to take, the 'dogmatic standpoint' as he called it:

> The right attitude to take in the *pre-philosophical*, and, in a good sense, *dogmatic* sphere of inquiry, to which all empirical sciences (but not these alone) belong, is in full consciousness *to discard all scepticism together with all 'natural philosophy' and 'theory of knowledge'*, and find the data of knowledge there where they actually face you, whatever difficulties epistemological reflection may *subsequently* raise concerning the possibility of such data being there.[2]

SCEPTICISM

The rise of scepticism

As far as Europe is concerned it was some of the early Greek philosophers who first became aware that there are questions to be asked about the means we have to get to know the world around us. And so

---

[2] *Ideas*, 95 f., emphasis in original.

epistemology was born. However, it was not long after that that scepticism raised its head. Now the Greek verb *skeptomai*, from which the noun scepticism is derived, basically means 'to investigate carefully', or 'to examine critically'; but the noun 'scepticism' came eventually to denote the philosophical attitude that claims that nothing at all can be known for certain. The best we can achieve is to have more or less right opinions about the practical concerns of life; but beyond that we must reserve our judgment.

It came about this way. At first the early Greek thinkers studied the universe as they saw it and tried to work out what it was made of and how it worked.[3] It did not occur to them to question that they had direct apprehension of the world around them. They took it for granted that the world was what it appeared to them to be. Their aim was to probe beneath its surface and discover the basic substance or substances of which it was made, and the processes that kept it working together as one harmonious whole.

But then, one of them, Heraclitus, came up with the theory that the universe is held together in tension by an alternating flux between equal and opposite forces. Heat is presently overcome by cold, and cold eventually by heat, and so on, thus maintaining an equilibrium. That means, as he saw it, that everything is constantly changing. How, then, other philosophers, like Plato, asked, can you have full and certain knowledge of anything in the world, if that thing, and the world itself, is constantly (even if imperceptibly) changing? All you can have is a more or less right opinion about it.

Parmenides, by contrast, maintained that change is an illusion. Our senses tell us that change is everywhere taking place; but our senses, he said, deceive us. Reason, so he claimed, proves that change is impossible. We must, therefore, if we would have true knowledge of the world, trust reason and not our senses.

Difficulties arose with contrasting views like these. Schools of philosophy were formed, and each maintained that its theory was the only right one, claimed to prove it by a long string of arguments and taught it to its students as dogma.

Almost inevitably this conflict of rival dogmas led to scepticism

---

[3] For further discussion of all of the Greek thinkers mentioned, see Book 2 in this series: *Finding Ultimate Reality*, Ch. 2.

among other philosophers. It is an epistemological stance still advocated by some thinkers today.

Scepticism comes in various strengths, from mild and limited, to strong and extreme. As we consider some of those forms, we should observe, among other things, their motivation.

Socrates (470–399 BC)

Later members of Plato's Academy held that Socrates himself was a sceptic, because he went about questioning prominent people in the city who thought they knew the answers to life's big questions, such as what is justice, and courage, etc. He soon was able to expose the fact that their claim to knowledge was invalid; but when they rounded on him and asked him what the answers were, he would reply that he didn't know either. The result was that he publicly embarrassed many prominent 'experts' and demolished generally accepted, but unthought-out, beliefs. Unfortunately, some young men at the time got the impression that the role of philosophy was simply to debunk traditional moral beliefs, without putting anything else in their place.

That, in fact, was the last thing Socrates intended to do. Apollo's oracle at Delphi had declared him to be the wisest man on earth; and he had taken that to mean that his wisdom lay in the fact that he knew that he did not know, whereas others thought they did know when they didn't. But Socrates did not rejoice in his ignorance, or suppose that life's great questions were necessarily unanswerable, and make that an excuse for not continuing vigorously to seek the truth. His awareness of his own ignorance acted for him as a spur to seek the truth; and he hoped that when he showed other people that their current beliefs were not true, the shock of their demonstrated ignorance would act as a similar spur to them. His scepticism, therefore, if we may call it so, was of a very healthy kind. All of us need a dose of it from time to time in order to challenge our invalid beliefs and to spur us to seek the truth.

> Socrates did not rejoice in his ignorance, or suppose that life's great questions were necessarily unanswerable, and make that an excuse for not continuing vigorously to seek the truth. His awareness of his own ignorance acted for him as a spur to seek the truth.

Pyrrho (4th–3rd century BC); Sextus Empiricus (AD c.200)

Pyrrho was the first representative of so-called Pyrrhonian scepticism. Amid the welter of contemporary philosophical theories he argued that the reasons in favour of a belief are never better than those against—hence he refused to commit himself to any positive belief.

Centuries later Sextus Empiricus wrote a number of works detailing the historical development of this school of scepticism. He compiled a long series of arguments, arranged formally in groups, that his adherents could then have ready to hand to justify their scepticism, by presenting on each occasion contradictory claims about the same subject. Let's take a couple of examples.

The same tower, they pointed out, that from a distance looks round, will from near at hand look square. In other words the same faculty of sight that claimed the tower to be round, now claims it to be square. From this they deduced that you cannot trust eyesight.

Or take human sacrifice to the gods. The Scythians argued that it was right; the Greeks that it was wrong. In other words moral arguments of similar (so they claimed) strength could be used to support directly opposite views.

We need not stop to critique the arguments they used to support their form of scepticism. The interesting thing to notice here is what they aimed to achieve by their scepticism, namely, a state of unperturbedness, happiness and peace of mind—what the Greeks called *ataraxia*. It was not that this blissful state of mind was simply the natural result of their philosophical thinking. It was that they deliberately designed their process of thinking to make sure it achieved this result. That process was in three stages:

Stage 1   *antithesis*: that is, the deliberate collection and presentation of contradictory claims about any one and the same subject.

Stage 2   *epochē*: that is, suspension of judgment, on the grounds that, the arguments for and against being of equal strength, it was impossible rationally to decide which was right.

Stage 3   *ataraxia*: unperturbedness, peace of mind. One is then freed from dogmatism and can live peacefully in the world, following one's own inclinations and fitting in with the laws and customs of any society one happens to be living in.

It is to be feared that many people still in our modern world practise this same kind of scepticism, and do so for the same reason. Thinking seriously about life's big questions and deciding rationally between different worldviews can be hard work; and if it means questioning the generally accepted but unthought-out views of contemporary society, it can unsettle one's peace of mind. Many people, therefore, take up the sceptic's stance and so justify their refusal to think about life's big questions. But it is the coward's way out.

On the other hand, some serious modern philosophers, whom no one would ever think of charging with cowardice, have come to the conclusion after vigorous thinking that some form of partial (if not complete) scepticism is unavoidable.

René Descartes (1596–1650)

Descartes has a reputation for extreme, if not obsessive, doubt and scepticism, but it is not really deserved. His great masterpiece, *Meditations on First Philosophy* (published in 1641), sets out the core of his philosophical system. In the Synopsis to that work he wrote:

> The purpose of my arguments is not that they prove what they establish—that there really is a world and that human beings have bodies and so on—since no one has ever seriously doubted these things.[4]

To understand, then, the famous passages in which he describes his doubts, we must see them against his background. As a boy he was thoroughly trained in the dogmatic scholastic philosophy of the time, about which he later wrote:

> I observed with regard to philosophy that despite being cultivated for many centuries by the best minds, it contained no point which was not disputed and hence doubtful.[5]

---

[4] Cited in Cottingham, 'Descartes', 202.
[5] *Discourse*, part 1, cited in Cottingham, 'Descartes', 201.

From the title of this work (*Discourse on the Method of Rightly Conducting Reason and Reaching the Truth in the Sciences*) we can at once see that Descartes' predominant interest was in science, rather than in philosophy strictly so-called. For him the precision of mathematical reasoning was more attractive, and yielded more certain results, than philosophical argument had hitherto achieved. He confesses:

> those long chains, composed of very simple and easy reasonings, which geometers customarily use to arrive at their most difficult demonstrations, gave me occasion to suppose that all the things which fall within the scope of human knowledge are interconnected in the same way.[6]

His book *Le Monde* ('The World', or 'The Universe'), composed in the early 1630s, dealt with physics and cosmology. In it he abandoned the centuries long Aristotelian tradition that from the moon upwards the motion of the heavenly bodies was divinely perfect, whereas sublunary motion was imperfect. He held that the matter of the universe was the same throughout, and obeyed uniform physical laws. He therefore offered a comprehensive explanation of the universe based on simple mechanical principles.[7]

His project, however, of explaining the workings of the universe on the basis of strictly logical mathematical and mechanical principles, naturally ran up against the difficulties posed by the vague and often misleading impressions of the external world that we receive through our senses (like the straight stick that in water appears bent). Descartes therefore set himself to the task of leading the mind away from the senses, since, as he puts it:

> the senses deceive from time to time, and it is prudent never to trust wholly those who have deceived us even once.[8]

Even so he concedes, that in spite of the fact that visual appearances may mislead us, in many situations doubt would be absurd. For instance, he observed that no argument, however strong, based on the supposed unreliability of the senses, could cause him to doubt

---

[6] *Discourse*, part 2, cited in Cottingham, 'Descartes', 201.
[7] In his time such views were dangerous; and on hearing of Galileo's condemnation he withdrew his book from publication.
[8] *Meditations*, Meditation 1, cited in Cottingham, 'Descartes', 202.

that he was at that moment sitting by the fire holding a piece of paper in his hands.

It was at that point, then, and in pursuit of doubting all that could reasonably—and unreasonably—be doubted, in order to find and establish a ground of knowledge that could not possibly be doubted, that he set about conjuring up doubts in what he called their most 'hyperbolical', or exaggerated form.

He began by admitting that 'there are no certain marks to distinguish being awake from being asleep'; and that therefore, though he believed he was sitting by his fireside, he might in fact be in bed dreaming that he was sitting by his fireside.

From that he proceeded to raise radical doubts about whole classes of external objects and ended up by deliberately imagining the possibility that he was being systematically deceived by a malicious demon bent on tricking him in every possible way. Perhaps, he says, 'the sky, the earth, colours, shapes, sounds and all external things' are nothing but 'the delusions of dreams which he has devised to ensnare my judgment'.[9]

His thought experiment was severe; but at last he reached a firm foundation for certain, indubitable knowledge: he could not doubt that he was doubting! And if he was doubting, then he existed, for if he didn't exist he couldn't doubt. He expressed that certainty in a phrase that has since become famous: '*Cogito, ergo sum*', 'I am thinking, therefore I exist'.

Descartes recognised, of course, that certainty attained on this basis was but temporary: he could be sure of his existence only as long as he was doubting. But starting from this small glimpse of certainty, he endeavoured to construct a whole system of reliable knowledge. Its ultimate guarantee was the existence and character of God who would not allow his creature to be demonically deceived as to the reality of God and his creation.

The 'brain in a vat' analogy

A modern form of extreme scepticism substitutes for Descartes' 'evil demon' argument, the so-called 'brain-in-a-vat' argument. This al-

---

[9] 'Descartes', 202.

leges that what I have hitherto taken for granted to be my genuine experience of the external world would be no different if the actual fact was that my brain had been removed from my body, placed in a vat of nutrients, and wired up to a computer that was providing me with a coherent sequence of nevertheless misleading experiences. In that case, the sceptic points out, any evidence I might appeal to, any argument I might use, to prove I was not a brain in a vat, could have been planted in my brain by the computer. How then, the sceptic asks, can you prove your brain is not in fact in some such analogous condition? 'Unless you can prove it', he adds, 'your claims to have genuine, day-to-day knowledge of the external world are illegitimate. And (he asserts as a parting shot) you have no hope of proving it.'

Commenting on this, and other sceptical arguments Professor C. J. Hookway remarks:

> Of course, such challenges have no role in our ordinary practice of making and defending views: if we were to invoke them, we would appear silly or mad.[10]

Quite so. Most people would agree. But Hookway continues:

> But the significance of this is unclear: it might be a sign that these sceptical doubts are unnatural or improper, that the legitimacy of our beliefs is not affected by our ignoring them. If that is correct, then we could safely avoid any engagement with arguments in the sceptical canon.[11]

Once more, many people would agree that such sceptical arguments are unnatural and improper. But Hookway himself seems to regard scepticism as unanswerable:

> If, on the other hand, it simply reflects the ways in which we cope practically with the fact that scepticism is unanswerable (by ignoring it), then it would be evasion of responsibility to ignore sceptical arguments . . . Several contemporary philosophers, notably Barry Stroud, suspect that scepticism may be unavoidable.[12]

---

[10] 'Scepticism', 795.
[11] 'Scepticism', 795.
[12] 'Scepticism'.

Hilary Putnam, on the other hand, has argued that a brain in a vat could not even formulate the thought that it is one.[13]

More deserves to be said, at least from a practical point of view, about the 'brain-in-a-vat' analogy. I am a human being with a human brain. So is the sceptic. He suggests that my human brain might be like a brain in a vat, wired up to a computer that is constantly feeding my brain with misleading experiences. Well, if my human brain is like that, so is his: for what ground has he for thinking that his brain is different from mine? And if his brain too is wired up to a computer that is feeding it with false experiences, then his very suggestion that I should regard my brain as being in a vat comes from a similarly deceptive computer. In other words, if I, for the sake of argument, accept his hypothetical analogy, I must conclude that his proposed analogy itself comes from a deceptive source and is perverse, and that he cannot prove it is not. Why should I believe it? Any further discussion would be useless.

These deceptive computers in the sceptic's analogy, that feed our human brains with false ideas, what or whom do they represent? In real life computers have to be programmed by intelligent beings. Who is supposed to have programmed the computers in the sceptic's analogy?

And then there is another point. These deceptive computers in the sceptic's analogy, that feed our human brains with false ideas, what or whom do they represent? In real life computers have to be programmed by intelligent beings. Who is supposed to have programmed the computers in the sceptic's analogy?

There is, of course, no need to push the details of the analogy beyond what it was intended to illustrate. But if there were any truth in the analogy as a whole, it would spell the end of all philosophical, scientific and practical reason.

But the analogy is useful, for it drives us to decide what, in real life, is the source and status of human rationality. If human rationality is the gift of God, the Creator, and is used in true dependence on him, then we can be sure it is an essentially good, healthy and reli-

---

[13] *Reason, Truth and History*, Ch. 1.

able instrument. But if we start out with the assumption that there is no God and that human rationality is the product of mindless forces and that it must not allow the existence of God any place in its presuppositions, then we must not be surprised if extreme scepticism uses its powers of reason ultimately to argue that human rationality is invalid and deceptive.

What then qualifies as knowledge?

The philosopher G. E. Moore (1873–1958) was impatient with sceptical arguments that we could not know for certain that there is an external world. Holding up his hands before him, he affirmed his knowledge that he had two hands, and, since hands were objects in the external world, he concluded that there was an external world.

According to C. J. Hookway,[14] some philosophers admire Moore's robust claim that our knowledge that there is an external world is direct, instinctive and incorrigible: it needs no defence. Others have criticised it. At the level of everyday practical life, they admit, it needs no defence; but at the philosophical level it does. But that raises the question of the relation of philosophy to daily life. Is it really so, that we have no right to be certain that there is an everyday external world until philosophy has proved that there either is, or isn't?

Wittgenstein[15] stated that the certainty of the existence of the external world stood fast for him as it did for Moore. His criticism of Moore was that Moore should not have called his certainty knowledge. However, it is difficult to think that no one has the right to claim to know, for example, that the sun exists until philosophy has first proved it does.

HOW WE PERCEIVE THE EXTERNAL WORLD

By 'external world' we mean, of course, the objective world around us: the world of people, things, events and facts. That being so, the common sense answer to the question 'how do we perceive the external

---

[14] 'Scepticism'.
[15] *On Certainty*, para. 151.

world?' would be 'through our senses: sight, hearing, touch, taste and smell; and then by study and classification of the information with which the external world provides us through those senses'.

But, as usual, to the philosopher things are not quite so simple. Philosophers seek to understand the actual process that is going on when we perceive something in the external world; and even at this primary level there is already a difference of opinion.

Direct Realism and the Representative Theory of Perception

At one extreme in the debate stands Naive, or, Direct Realism. It asserts that under normal conditions we have direct perception of the external world. I see a tree, for instance, and I perceive its existence and its qualities simply by looking directly at it, touching it, smelling it even.

At the other extreme in the debate stands the Representative Theory of Perception. It asserts that we never perceive a tree, or anything else, directly. When we look at a tree, what happens is that our minds receive certain subjective impressions or representations of the tree; and it is these subjective representations—sense-data as they are called—that we directly and most immediately perceive, not the objective tree itself. And it is on these sense-data that we depend for our knowledge of the tree. Some philosophers who espouse this theory liken it to watching a football match, not directly, but on a television screen, but this theory does not claim that we are necessarily conscious of these subjective sense-data, as we would be of a television screen, or that we formally infer from the sense-data the existence and the features of the tree. But nonetheless it maintains that this is what is really happening; what we perceive are simply these subjective sense-data, not the tree itself, and our knowledge of the tree is built on them.

The implication of this theory should now be clear: if it were true, we could never check the accuracy of our subjective impressions of the objective world against the objective world itself, because however much we studied the objective world we would never perceive it itself, but only some subjective impression of it. We might decide that one set of sense-data were better than another (though by what standard should we judge?); but we could never be sure that any set of sense-data represented the objective reality with complete accuracy.

Defining perception

Before we try to understand the two extremes in the debate and to assess their comparative value, we ought to decide what is meant by 'perception', because it seems to be used in different senses in different contexts.

Sometimes it is used as though it meant no more than 'seeing', even when 'seeing' is being used in its basic visual sense:

'The doctor saw the telltale signs that the body had been poisoned.'

'The doctor perceived the telltale signs that . . .'

But often 'perception' implies a simultaneous gathering of information from an observation that 'seeing' does not necessarily imply. So it would make sense to say 'He saw his wife dressed up in this strange clothing, but did not realise that it was his wife'; but it would not make sense to say 'He perceived his wife dressed up in this strange clothing but did not realise that it was his wife.' 'Perceiving' his wife here means recognising that it was his wife.

Again, there is a difference between seeing an event and seeing a fact about that event. One can see a robbery taking place without necessarily realising that it is a robbery. But one cannot say, coherently, 'I saw the fact that a robbery was taking place, but I did not realise that it was a robbery.' When it comes to observing facts, then, 'seeing' and 'perceiving' carry the same implication of understanding.

The word 'perceive' can also be used of seeing through or past obstacles or outward appearances and catching sight of the reality behind them. So behind what you at first thought was foliage, you might perceive a camouflaged soldier.

In our discussion of the Representative Theory of Perception (hereafter referred to by the initials RTP) we must from time to time ask ourselves in what sense the term 'perception' is being used.

The case for the Representative Theory of Perception

The case for RTP is built largely on the claim that it can explain illusionary experiences better than Direct Realism can.

Hallucinations

During some illnesses, or through drug taking, people can experience hallucinations. They may see a red, white and blue polka-dotted snake coming at them through a hole in their bedroom wall and be convinced that it is real, though of course it is non-existent. RTP alleges that Direct Realism cannot account for this type of experience, for Direct Realism claims that we have direct visual perception of the external objective world. If, then, that were so, how could it ever explain how anyone could see a red, white and blue polka-dotted snake, when such things don't exist in the external world?

RTP claims that it can explain this state of affairs.

Neither in hallucination nor in genuine vision is the observer directly perceiving the objective reality of the external world. In both cases what the observer is directly aware of is the subjective sense-data in his own brain. The difference is that in genuine vision the cause of the sense-data is an objective reality, outside of the viewer, whereas in hallucination the cause of the sense-data is some subjective disturbance in the observer's brain, drugs in the bloodstream or psychological maladjustment. Since RTP can explain what Direct Realism cannot, so the argument goes, RTP must be correct.

During some illnesses, or through drug taking, people can experience hallucinations. They may see a red, white and blue polka-dotted snake coming at them through a hole in their bedroom wall and be convinced that it is real, though of course it is non-existent.

Mirages

Travelling on a long, straight road in the heat of summer, many people have on occasions seen ahead what looked to them like a large sheet of water. Arriving at the spot, they have found no water there. The fact is, they have simply seen a mirage. On this basis RTP claims that when they saw the water ahead, they could not have been directly perceiving objective reality. Direct Realism, therefore, it is alleged, must be wrong in this case.

Perceptual error

A straight stick, dipped in water, will appear bent, though it is not. According to RTP, you could not have been in direct perceptual contact with the stick when it appeared bent. Direct Realism is wrong again, so it seems.

Perspectival relativity

Looked at directly from above, a square table will appear square. Stand at one corner, and look diagonally across to the other corner, and the table will appear to be rhomboid. But the table cannot objectively have both shapes. Therefore, Direct Realism's theory that we have direct perceptual contact with objective reality, must have been wrong on one of these occasions; and if on this one occasion, how can we be sure that it will not be wrong on hundreds of other occasions as well?

Evaluation of the Representative Theory of Perception

If these, then, are the main arguments in favour of RTP, how cogent are they? Let's review them.

Hallucinations

No one, not even extreme naïve realists, would deny that our visual mechanisms can, at times, be distorted through drugs or illness. All would admit that the sufferer who sees a red, white and blue polka-dotted snake in an hallucination is not in direct visual contact with an objective reality. But to generalise on the basis of that exceptional experience in illness, and claim that even in health one could never have direct perception of reality, would be a non sequitur.

Moreover, if someone claimed to be seeing a red, white and blue polka-dotted snake, anyone else would know he was hallucinating, because no such coloured snakes exist. But suppose someone in an hallucination says he sees a brown rabbit sitting on the carpet. In that case, according to RTP, his sense-data would be exactly the same as they would be if there were an actual brown rabbit sitting on the carpet. Then by sight alone he could never discover the difference between a rabbit seen in hallucination and a real one since the sense-data would be the same. But there is one thing he could do, if he were willing. He could stretch out his two hands and touch, or even grab, the real rabbit. But never with his real hands could he touch the hallucinated rabbit.

This reminds us that we have, not one but, five senses and that we can check the information we receive from one sense against the information received through another. Moreover, each of our senses can at times provide us with information unexpectedly, and therefore before reason has had time to take it in and digest it. But that is not always so. Reason often works along with our senses and uses them as a team of instruments to discover what it wants to know. Reason, thinking sight has been careless, can direct the eyes to look again in order to obtain more exact and detailed information. Reason in a blind man can order his fingers to make direct contact with an object; and then reason cooperates with the sense of touch to discover whether the object is rough or smooth, round or square, hot or cold, etc. It is a mistake, then, to concentrate too much on visual perception, and to treat reason as some second, delayed stage in the process of perception.

Mirages

In the Series Introduction at the start of this book we considered the difference between hallucinations and mirages, and found that in the case of a mirage it would not be true to say that we are not visually in contact with objective reality. A woman seeing what to her looks like a sheet of water on the road ahead is actually observing a real objective atmospheric phenomenon. Admittedly she misinterprets what she sees; but the phenomenon itself is real enough. When she gets to the point in the road where she thought she saw water, the atmospheric phenomenon will have disappeared, and all she will see is the bare road. She may not understand what it was that caused her to think she saw water; but she will have witnessed, whether she realises it or not, an instance of the refraction of light in certain atmospheric conditions and its effects in the external world.

Perceptual error

The example of a straight stick that appears bent when a part of it is submerged in water, has been quoted thousands of times down the centuries. It is perhaps surprising to find philosophers still quoting it in support of RTP, when scientists have long since shown what causes the stick to look bent in water. When a light-wave crosses the boundary between one transparent medium (like air) and another (like water), it changes speed. Moreover if the wave strikes the water at an oblique angle, one end of it has entered the water and has reduced speed, while the other end is still outside the water and travelling at normal speed. The result is that the wave's direction is bent, a phenomenon called the refraction of light. And that is why a straight stick, partly submerged in water, will look straight outside the water but bent inside.

We have no need to dwell further on the details of the phenomenon; but for our purposes, we should recall from our physics books the experiments by which the scientists discovered refraction: they guided a beam of light through the air, then through another medium like glass, set at an oblique angle. They measured the difference in the speed of the light and measured the extent of the bending of the light wave, and with the help of trigonometry worked out the refractive index.

The point is this: what will RTP say about all this investigation of the behaviour of light? Did the scientists conduct it all without any direct objective perception of light, simply by perceiving the subjective sense-data inside their own heads?

Perspectival relativity

The fact that a square table looks rhomboid when viewed from one corner need deceive no one, whatever his or her sense-data. We can measure the angles at the corners of the table and thus know it is square; and common sense will tell us that a wooden table does not change its shape by being looked at from a different angle. Nor does it prove that we never have direct perception of the table. How could we measure the angles of the table if we could not see directly enough to position the protractor in the right place and read off the angles? And obviously we must read off the angles before they can become a sense-datum in our heads! Moreover, the phenomenon of perspectival reality is so well known that it deceives no thinking person. Astronomers take it for granted: they will explain the appearance of some object in the sky by saying, for instance, that it is in fact a spiral galaxy that we are looking at edge-on, and therefore cannot actually see that it is spiral in form.

A thought experiment

Until now we have been studying instances of visual perception, because it is to cases of apparently misleading visual perception that RTP appeals to support its theory. But, as we have said, to concentrate solely on visual perception could be a mistake. In addition to our five senses we have reason and memory; and often two or more senses can be applied together, and memory and reason can join them simultaneously to achieve direct and correct perception. Let's do a mental experiment to show this is so.

Suppose we stand in the middle of a straight railway track. As we look along the track, the two rails will appear to converge in the distance, until we can no longer distinguish them. At that moment our sense-data will record that they have coalesced.

Presently a train comes up behind us. We step out of the way and the train goes by. As it recedes into the distance, the train will appear to get smaller, and according to RTP our sense-data duly record an ever diminishing train.

But now reason and memory come into play. Reason tells us that locomotives cannot get smaller just by travelling (unless its speed approaches that of light!), and memory of trains we have travelled on reminds us that trains don't get smaller as they proceed. So now, although our visual perception sees the train getting smaller, we actually know that it is the same size as when it passed us. That means that as we watch the train reach the distant point where the rails look as if they coalesced (and still look so in our sense-data) we can use the known size of the locomotive as a distant means of measuring the distance between the two rails at that point, and know with total confidence that the rails, in spite of appearance, are the same distance apart there as where we stand.

All this is going on in our heads simultaneously. Initial visual perception suggested the rails were coalescing. Now visual perception allows us to see what happens when the train reaches the point of apparent coalescence; and we see that the train does not come to a halt but keeps going; and reason simultaneously perceives with absolute certainty that the rails cannot have coalesced but are as far apart as usual. In other words, it is not necessarily always true that vision produces subjective sense-data that reason subsequently turns into valid concepts. In a knowledgeable person reason and memory can work alongside of vision to help achieve true perception of objective reality.

Final thoughts on the Representative Theory of Perception

Commenting on the RTP, philosopher Roger Scruton remarks:

> it seems to say that we perceive physical objects only by perceiving something else, namely, the idea or image that represents them. But then, how do we perceive that idea or image? Surely we shall need another idea, which represents it to consciousness, if we are to *perceive* it? But now we are embarked on an infinite regress. Wait a minute, comes the reply; I didn't say that we perceive mental representations as we perceive physical objects. On the contrary, we perceive the representations *directly*, the objects only *indirectly*. But what does that mean? Presumably this: while I can make mistakes about the physical object, I cannot make mistakes about the representation, which is, for me, immediately incorrigible, self-intimating—part of what is 'given' to consciousness. But in that case, why say that I *perceive* it at all? Perception is a way of *finding things out*; it implies a separation between the thing perceiving and the thing perceived, and with that separation comes the possibility of error. To deny the possibility of error is to deny the separation. The mental representation is not perceived at all; it is simply *part* of me. Put it another way: the mental representation *is* the perception. In which case the contrast between direct and indirect perception collapses. We *do* perceive physical objects, and perceive them directly. . . . And we perceive physical objects by *having* representational experiences.[16]

In other words there is no third intermediate and quasi-independent thing called sense-data between our perception and objects in the external world. The sense-data, or representations, are our perception of the external world; and that perception of the world is direct.

---

[16] *Modern Philosophy*, 333.

That does not mean that direct perception is never mistaken. The fact is that when it comes to using our senses to gain information about the external, objective world, humankind has had to learn to use its five senses correctly, and interpret their information correctly; and each one of us individually has to do likewise. A youth may hear a musical sound, as sound waves enter his ear and then his brain, and yet misjudge from what musical instrument it comes. Experience, sight, instruction, memory will all be necessary before he can immediately recognise from what instrument the sound comes. But that doesn't mean that he didn't originally hear the sound directly. A person recently blinded will need to develop an increasingly sensitive touch in order to read Braille. And since light behaves as we now know it does, we have to learn to see and how to gather correct information from eyesight. From time to time, moreover, we misinterpret what we see, hear, touch, taste and smell, and we have to learn to use our senses with greater discernment. But none of this means that we cannot have direct perception of anything at all in the external world.

CHAPTER 2

FALSE ALTERNATIVES AT THE EXTREMES

As to those *impressions*, which arise from the *senses*, their ultimate cause is, in my opinion, perfectly inexplicable by human reason, and it will always be impossible to decide with certainty, whether they arise immediately from the object, or are produced by the creative power of the mind, or are derived from the author of our being.

—David Hume, *A Treatise of Human Nature*

MIDDLE GROUND?

We cannot study epistemology long without discovering that several of the debates that have arisen in this area of philosophy each present us with two extreme positions and invite us to choose between them. Here are some of those extremes:

    I. Idealism and realism
   II. Knowledge is subjective and knowledge is objective
  III. Rationalism and empiricism
  IV. Reason and faith

In this chapter we will consider I and II and spend longer on III, especially as it pertains to John Locke and David Hume. Our next chapter will be given over to Immanuel Kant's contribution to epistemology, and we will give the following chapter over to IV.

Common sense might at once suggest that, as so often in life, the truth lies neither at one extreme nor the other, but somewhere in the middle. In the course of history, however, and to this present day, great minds have aligned themselves firmly with one extreme or the other; and if we are going to understand the history of human thought, and the seriously held views of our fellow human beings round the world, we must try to understand what views they hold and the reasons for which they hold them.

IDEALISM AND REALISM

First, let's consider the meaning of the terms.

Idealism

What it is not. In everyday life an ideal is a concept of perfection, of a maximum good, of the best of all possible situations, be it private and personal, or public and political. 'Ideal behaviour' is the best behaviour one can imagine, to which we all aspire, even though in practice we all fall short of it. Idealism in this context, therefore, denotes the attitude that pursues perfection even though it often has to tolerate, and put up with, non-ideal realities. But this is *not* what idealism means in epistemology.

What it is. Idealism is a metaphysical theory about the nature of reality. It asserts that what is real is in some way confined to, or at least related to, the contents of our minds.[1]

An extreme form of idealism was adopted by the Irish philosopher George Berkeley (1685–1753). He held that things exist only as they are perceived by us (or by God): they have no existence independently of our perceiving them.[2]

Realism

Realism stands at the opposite end of the spectrum to idealism, though nowadays perhaps no one stands at either extreme. It would be better, therefore, to explain the difference this way: to assert that our knowledge of things is largely mind-dependent is to move in the idealist direction; to assert that something is somehow mind-independent is to move in the realist direction.

Obviously, it would be silly to maintain that everything is in every way independent of minds: it is, for instance, through our minds that we perceive pain. If there were no minds there would be no pain. On the other hand, most people would agree that if every mind in the whole world forgot that the Andromeda galaxy existed, and never thought of it again, it would not cease to exist. Not everything, then, is in every way dependent on minds.

Again, when it comes to our perception of things, it is obvious that all the information we can gather about reality is mediated to us through our minds. The amount of knowledge, therefore, that we can receive and understand is limited by the powers and concepts

---

[1] We should not confuse Plato's Theory of 'Forms', or 'Ideas' (see Book 2: *Finding Ultimate Reality*, Ch. 2) with Idealism. Plato held that the Ideas, or Forms, exist eternally independent of us and of our minds.

[2] Berkeley was actually an empiricist in the tradition of John Locke, whom we shall discuss presently. But, incongruously enough, Berkeley was a metaphysical idealist, and denied the existence of matter.

of our mind. At the same time, when we put questions to external reality in our effort to discover what reality is like, the answers are provided by that reality itself. Nicholas Rescher (b. 1928), who calls himself a pragmatic idealist, expresses it thus:

> Perhaps the strongest argument favouring idealism is that any characterisation of the real that we can devise is bound to be a mind-constructed one: *our* only access to information about what the real is through the mediation of mind. What seems right about idealism is inherent in the fact that in investigating the real we are clearly constrained to use our own concepts to address our own issues; we can only learn about the real in our own terms of reference. But what seems right about realism is that the answers to the questions we put to the real are provided by reality itself—whatever the answers may be, they are substantially what they are because it is reality itself that determines them to be that way. Mind proposes but reality disposes.³

A realist, on the other hand, would wish to qualify Rescher's remarks. It is certainly true to a large extent that 'in investigating the real we are clearly constrained to use our own concepts'. But it is equally important in investigating the real, that we do not, consciously or unconsciously, come to regard our own concepts as the fixed criteria by which we judge reality.

In the course of the last century, radically new scientific understanding of reality has come about. Realists, like Einstein, have started from the assumption that the universe has its own inherent intelligibility independent of us, whether we eventually discover and understand it, or not. They were prepared, therefore, not to rest content with the concepts of classical Newtonian physics, but to open their minds to possible

> Realists, like Einstein, have started from the assumption that the universe has its own inherent intelligibility independent of us, whether we eventually discover and understand it, or not.

higher levels of reality's own deep-lying structures and to grasp them, not so much by laborious deductive reasoning based on their already formed concepts, but initially by direct intuition. The result has been

---

³ 'Idealism', 429. In this article Rescher lists eight different forms of idealism.

a vast increase in our knowledge and understanding, an invigorating challenge to envisage counter-intuitive states of affairs, and also an awe-inspiring awareness that reality has still greater depths of intelligibility that for the time being go beyond our cognitive powers and imagination.

Rescher is certainly right to emphasise the fact that when we put our questions to reality, it is reality itself that provides the answers, and therefore we must always be prepared to submit our minds to reality. But it is by listening to, and learning more about, reality that we also come to know what are the right and sensible kinds of questions to put to it.

The ancients conceived of the earth as being flat and immobile. They therefore asked what happened to the sun when it sank below the edge of the earth every night. Did it go out, and then get reborn every morning? Or did it travel beneath the earth and come up in the east at daybreak? Their questions were unanswerable on the basis of their fundamental concepts. Better observation of the astronomical reality led them to abandon their former concepts, in favour of better theories. They were then in a position to put more suitable questions to reality.

KNOWLEDGE IS SUBJECTIVE
AND KNOWLEDGE IS OBJECTIVE

Once again, let us start by defining the terms.

The noun *subject*, in many languages, is used in different senses. It can denote, for instance, a subject that we study at school, like chemistry or literature. Or we can use it of the subject, that is, the topic, of a conversation.

In grammar and syntax, however, subject has an almost opposite meaning. In the sentence, 'Maria is reading a book', 'Maria', we say, is the *subject* of the verb: she is the one who is doing the reading. 'The book', by contrast, is the *object* of the verb, the thing that suffers the action of the verb, that undergoes the reading.

If as a potter I make a vase, then I am the subject who does the making, the vase is the object that is made. Moreover, as the subject I bring my creative powers of intellect and aesthetic sense to bear upon the basic material, clay, and create something new and beautiful. In that process I am the one who is active; the clay is passive.

It is in this sense that we shall be using the term *subject* in this part of our study. The issue at stake will be as follows: in getting to know and understand the world around us, are we just passive learners on whose mind the universe imposes and impresses its objective facts that we must accept and submit to? Or, are we active and creative subjects? And is it so that the only significance that the universe has is what we give it by our own creative thought?

Bringing the issue of subjectivity into focus

This is an issue that pervades the whole of the voluminous writings of Nicolai Alexandrovitch Berdyaev (1874–1948). He reacted very strongly against the views of the English philosopher John Locke (1632–1704), the father of English empiricism. Locke, as we shall see in our next section, held that our minds are like a blank piece of paper on which the external world makes its impressions. We have no direct perception of the external world. It is only when that world has made its impressions on our mind and provided it with sense-data, that our intellect can begin to deduce from them their significance. The external world is our teacher; it supplies the facts that we submissively accept and try to understand.

Berdyaev would have none of this; he felt it robbed man of his freedom and status. To Berdyaev man is the great Subject. It is his creative spirit that perceives, if not creates, the significance of the objective, or, to use his word, the 'objectified', world of matter. It is man that decides, and gives to the world, its meaning.

Man, the knower, as Subject

One can agree with Berdyaev, to this extent at least, that when it comes to getting to know the world and indeed to the administration of it, man is not a passive object that simply receives the impressions that the world makes upon him. He is a subject who can take the initiative.

We can see that in the advance of science. Röntgen, Madam Curie and Rutherford did not sit around waiting for the atom to disclose its inner structures to them. They took the initiative, creatively thought up ingenious experiments in order to make the atom yield up its secrets, and then made use of the most sophisticated mathematics to interpret them.

That said, however, it would be an unbalanced view so to emphasise man as Subject, as to belittle, or even to denigrate, the objective reality and proper dignity of the universe.

The objective reality of the universe

If man is the Subject who knows, it surely follows that his knowledge, to be genuine, requires some genuine Object, so that it can be knowledge of something. Moreover, if that knowledge is to be worthwhile having, the Object of that knowledge must exist and have its own inherent value. A man's knowledge, moreover, that was not genuine knowledge of a real object, would be subjective in the bad sense of that term.

Moreover, if we start off with the value judgment that the creation of matter and of the universe was some kind of a 'fall', we are bound to come up with a false evaluation of the universe, and of its Creator. There is, however, a centuries-long tradition that regards the material universe as an unfortunate state brought about by the mixing of the World Soul or Spirit with matter by some minor deity. We meet this view in Hinduism and Neoplatonism, and it has been repeated by a succession of mystical thinkers.[4] In this view true knowledge is to penetrate beyond matter, not to its inner structure and workings, but to the World Spirit of which it is a passing illusory embodiment. It is to this existentialist, mystical view that Berdyaev seems to have been inclined:

> To the existential philosophy of spirit the natural material world is a fall, it is the product of objectification, self-alienation within existence. But the *form* of the human body and the *expression* of the eyes belong to the spiritual personality and are not opposed to spirit.[5]

This view of the world is not that of the Bible. According to the Bible the creation of the material world was not a fall, not a 'self-es-

---

[4] See Book 2 in this series for an analysis of this view in Hinduism (Ch. 1) and Neoplatonism (Ch. 2).

[5] *Beginning and End*, 104, emphasis added.

trangement and an exteriorization of spirit by which it is ejected into the external'.[6] That is an old Gnostic view of matter. The creation of the objective material world was God's deliberate action, an expression of his mind; and the result he pronounced 'very good' (Gen 1:31).

Nor was the human spirit eternally existent, and part of the World Spirit, that has emanated out of God and temporarily been imprisoned in matter, as Hinduism and Gnosticism teach. According to the Bible, man's spirit and intelligence were created by God out of nothing, just as the universe was. Man's spirit is not part of God. Though created and constantly maintained by God, and though constantly pointing away from itself to its Creator, Nature has its own, God-given (if limited), objective autonomy, value and significance. Its autonomy, then, and inherent value are not to be devalued by a false spirituality. It is not true that if you looked deeply into the created universe you would eventually come across the uncreated Spirit of God, as a substratum of matter.

This means that if we would get to know and understand the universe around us, subjects though we are, and capable of creative thinking, we must humbly submit our minds to the objective reality of the universe, as science constantly does, and let the universe teach us God-created facts about itself; and the truth of our discoveries must always be tested, not against our subjective judgment, but against Nature's objective facts.[7]

RATIONALISM AND EMPIRICISM

To understand the debate between Rationalism and Empiricism we must, of course, begin by defining the terms. Rationalism comes from the Latin word *ratio*, which means, among other things, 'reason'. Empiricism is based on the Greek word *empeiria* which means 'experience'. Merely to say that, however, will scarcely explain why, in the context of man's attempt to understand the universe and his place in it, there ever arose a debate between reason and experience. Why should anyone ever have thought that reason and experience were in

---

[6] Berdyaev, *Beginning and End*, 87.
[7] It should be noticed that Berdyaev fully approved of the scientific study of the universe, though he was strongly, and rightly, opposed to materialism (*Beginning and End*, 86–8).

any way opposed to each other? Is it not common sense to view them rather as partners in the noble shared adventure of getting to know the majestic reality of the universe?

Unfortunately, the early rationalists and the early empiricists have often been represented as being members of two opposite camps that shared little common ground. In actual fact, that is far from the truth. The early rationalists did not deny that experience of objective reality was absolutely necessary. If we can have no experience of the universe, reason has nothing to work on and explain. And the empiricists for their part freely admitted that reason plays, and must play, an essential part in the interpreting and understanding of our experience of the external world.

What then was the difference between so-called rationalists and so-called empiricists? To put it simply for the moment—though we shall need to explain this 'explanation' more fully later on—it was a question of the relative importance of reason and experience in the attempt to understand the universe. Rationalists tended to give the priority to reason; empiricists tended to give the priority to experience. Even so, we shall not fully understand this debate and the emotions that it continues to excite right up to the present time, unless we first briefly investigate the historical context in which it arose in modern Europe.

The historical context of the debate

The debate surged into prominence as a result of the intellectual movement known as the Enlightenment, which began in the seventeenth century. Its motivation and moving spirit were eventually described by Immanuel Kant as the

> emergence of man from his self-imposed infancy. Infancy is the inability to use one's reason without the guidance of another. It is self-imposed, when it depends on a deficiency, not of reason, but of the resolve and courage to use it without external guidance. Thus the watchword of the enlightenment is: *Sapere aude!* Have the courage to use your own reason.[8]

---

[8] See 'Beantwortung der Frage', 35.

In consequence the Enlightenment has come to be known as 'the Age of Reason'. Too long, it was felt, people had through lack of courage allowed themselves to behave like infants and to accept views and beliefs imposed on them by the authority of church and state. Now they were at last emerging from intellectual infancy into mature adulthood, unafraid to form and hold views and beliefs that they had arrived at by their own powers of reason.

Certainly education in the schools and universities of Europe at the time was long overdue for reform; and men like Galileo Galilei (1564–1642) and Isaac Newton (1642–1727) broke free from the outmoded abstract cosmological theorizings of Plato and Aristotle and began empirically with open minds to investigate the actual God-created objective realities of the universe.

Plato, for instance, with his dualistic thought, had divided epistemology into two distinct areas: the Intelligible World of the eternally unchanging Forms, of which we could hope to achieve genuine knowledge, and the Sensible World, where everything is changing, of which we can have only more or less right opinion.

Aristotle's dualistic cosmology likewise sharply distinguished between celestial mechanics and terrestrial mechanics. For him ideal and perfect movement was circular, and such movement was to be seen in the celestial realm from the moon upwards. But below the moon movement was rectilinear, and thus an instance of the imperfections of the sublunary realm. The moon also was thought to have a soul, in the sense of having its own source of motion.

But then Galileo pointed his telescope to the sky and observed craters on the moon, spots on the face of the sun and the phases of Venus. So now technology showed that from the moon upwards all was not in Aristotle's sense 'perfect'.

Then Newton discovered the law of universal gravitation and gave it mathematical expression. Aristotle's dualistic cosmology, therefore, was shown not to be true. The universe was one, and the law of gravitation applied everywhere. The same intelligibility marked the whole universe, and all was open to be investigated by human intelligence.

One can understand, therefore, how these brilliant successes of 'rational' empiricism—as distinct from the authoritarian dogma of traditional philosophy—transformed people's attitudes to the acquirement of knowledge of the universe. No longer were they to be dependent on abstract philosophy, or natural theology. Now reason, and human reason at that, was to be the ultimate source of all knowledge and the judge of its truth. Not that they were all atheists: Descartes, Locke and Leibniz (1646–1716) were theists. Newton was a deist, but anti-religion Spinoza (1632–77) was a pantheist. David Hume (1711–76) was an atheist, and Immanuel Kant (1724–1804) a believer in God, in the immortal soul and in the life to come.

The dispute between rationalism and empiricism

But simply making reason supreme did not solve all the problems of epistemology. After all, if reason was going to *explain* the universe, reason was obliged to admit right from the start that abstract reasoning did not, and could not, *create* the universe. It would need first to get to know the facts about the universe before it could begin to study and explain them. How then did you get to know the facts?

Locke's epistemological theory

Locke's view, which he expounded at great length in his famous work *An Essay Concerning Human Understanding* (dated 1689), was that all our knowledge of the world is a posteriori, that is, it comes *after*, and derives *from*, experience. He rejected the rationalist theory that we start with primary, self-evident, notions, which somehow are implanted in our minds at birth—innate ideas as they have come to be called—which we know even before we start to study the external world and which we then use in order to analyse the world and subject it to our understanding.[9] At birth, he maintained, our minds are like a blank piece of paper, void of any letters, and without any ideas.[10] From where, then, does the mind receive all the necessary materials for reason to work on and turn into knowledge? 'To this I answer,' says Locke 'in one word, from *experience*. In that all our knowledge is founded; and from that it ultimately derives itself.'[11]

He then goes on to explain that our knowledge, from which all our ideas spring, is fed by two fountains:

---

[9] See *An Essay Concerning Human Understanding* 1.2.1.
[10] A 'tabula rasa'.
[11] See *Essay* 2.1.2 ff.

1. *our senses*. Objects in the external world affect our senses, and those senses convey to the mind distinct perceptions of these external objects, and so we come by the ideas we have of yellow, white, heat, cold, soft, hard, bitter, sweet, etc.
2. *the operations of our own minds*. These furnish the understanding with another set of ideas which we could not get from external objects, namely, perception, thinking, doubting, believing, reasoning, knowing, willing and all the different actings of our own minds.[12]

Locke, then, did not deny or despise the role of reason. Without reason we could never perceive the significance of the ideas received by our senses. He did not deny what rationalists like Descartes and Leibniz claimed, that it is by reason that we perceive the laws of logic (e.g. that A cannot be the same as non-A, and that an external angle of a triangle equals the sum of the opposite two angles). What he did claim, however, in contrast to the rationalists, was that these logical powers of reasoning are not implanted in a child at birth: they simply develop in a child as it grows up and learns to reflect on the numerous ideas with which the senses have furnished its mind.[13] Nor did he deny the validity of abstract thought, as we can see from his remarks about the validation of ideas.

The validation of ideas

According to Locke, abstract truths of, say, mathematics, require no validation beyond their logical coherence. The reason for that is that their 'archetypes', as he called them, are internal to the mind. They do not pretend to have 'substance', that is, they do not claim to be objects that actually exist in the external material world. The mind lays down their axioms and by logical deduction builds up its theorems. Whether the formal system thus constructed can be shown to be consistent with external reality or not is irrelevant to the validity of the system. It did not claim to represent anything in the external world. The only validation required is to demonstrate the logical coherence of the system. If however it were claimed that this system did represent some actual state of affairs in the external world, then its validity would depend on

---

[12] See *Essay* 2.1.2–4.
[13] See *Essay* 2.1.6 ff.

its being tested against this external reality. Similarly, all the concepts we arrive at by reasoned reflection on the sense-impressions made on our minds by objects in the external world must be checked for their validity against those objects themselves.[14]

An evaluation of Locke's epistemology

We can safely say, therefore, that the difference in epistemology between empiricist Locke and rationalists like Descartes does not amount to very much. Each agreed that both reason and experience have their part to play in our acquirement of knowledge. Their main disagreement was over whether or not human beings are born with certain innate ideas in their minds.

(a) Both agreed that unborn infants have simple 'thoughts' and 'ideas', such as pains and sensations of warmth. Neither held that infants had profound philosophical thoughts.

(b) Both agreed that it was capacity for thought—not necessarily actual thinking—that distinguished human beings from animals.[15]

(c) Both agreed that assent to certain mathematical propositions (such as 3 + 2 = 5), or to logical laws (such as it is impossible for the same thing to exist and simultaneously not to exist), does not depend on experience. But Locke argued that a person must first go through a process of learning before he grasped these ideas. Descartes maintained that these ideas were innate; but he would admit that many people consciously assent to them only after laborious thinking.

(d) Locke maintained that innate concepts without experience would be insufficient to account for the phenomena of human knowledge. Descartes put it the other way round:

---

[14] An interesting example of these principles is to be seen in the work of the Russian mathematician Nikolai Ivanovich Lobachevski and others. By sheer abstract mathematical reasoning they independently discovered non-Euclidean geometry. Logically coherent in itself, their theory did not attract widespread interest until it was discovered that actual space-time has the features of non-Euclidean geometry.

[15] See Book 1: *Being Truly Human*, Ch. 3 for Noam Chomsky's view that human babies are born, not of course with a ready-made language, but with an inborn language faculty that allows them to learn whatever language their society speaks and to understand the logical concepts which its grammar and syntax express.

experience without an element of innate concepts would be insufficient to account for what we know.

The difference is not so very great, after all.[16]

Leibniz's criticism of Locke

Leibniz is famous because, among other things, independently of Newton he invented the infinitesimal calculus. In epistemology he was a rationalist and criticised Locke's theories more severely than we have just done. He insisted on the absolute distinction between what he called necessary truth and contingent truth. A necessary truth is something that is true in all possible worlds; its contrary is impossible. A contingent truth is something whose contrary could have been possible. So 2 + 3 = 5 is a necessary truth. It would be true in all possible worlds. Its contrary is impossible. On the other hand, 'Wellington beat Napoleon at the battle of Waterloo' is a contingent truth. Though that is what in fact happened, and therefore is now unalterably so, it could have been different. It is not logically inconceivable that Napoleon could have defeated Wellington.

Leibniz held, then, that knowledge of necessary truths is a priori knowledge. Its propositions are seen to be, not only true, but necessarily true, independently of any experience. That is because, so he held, the soul right from the start contains the sources of various concepts and doctrines. In other words the concepts and doctrines are innate.

Leibniz, therefore, disagreed strongly with Locke's idea that at birth a child's mind is like a blank piece of white paper, and that all that is eventually written on it comes from experience, and that abstract reasoning can reflect only on what experience has provided. On the basis of experience, Leibniz argued, Locke might show that something was true; but he could never show that something must be necessarily true. Only innate concepts could do that.

A serious weakness in Locke's epistemology

We need not stay to adjudicate between Leibniz and Locke, because before we leave Locke we must notice a weakness in his epistemology that has had a long-lasting and unfortunate effect on some of his successors.

---

[16] See the detailed discussion in Kenny, *Brief History of Western Philosophy*, 208–12.

In the first place he seems to have taught an early form of the Representative Theory of Perception, the difficulties of which we discussed in Chapter 1. According to Locke the steps in the process of our coming to know objects in the external world are:

1. The objects affect our senses.
2. Our senses convey into the mind what nowadays would be called sense-data, but which Locke called perceptions, or ideas, of these objects.
3. Our mind brings its own powers of thought to bear upon these perceptions, or ideas, and thus comes to understand them.[17]

Then Locke turns his attention to what it is in external objects that has the power to cause the sense-impressions, and thus the ideas, in our minds. Whatever it is that has this power he calls a *quality* of the external object. As an example, he cites a snowball. It has the power 'to produce in us the ideas of white, cold and round [shape]'. The power in the snowball that produces these ideas in us, he calls 'qualities' in the snowball.[18]

Next, however, he divides these qualities in external objects into two groups:

1. *Original or primary qualities.* These are: solidity, extension, figure (shape), motion, or rest, and number.[19]
2. *Secondary qualities*, such as colours, smells, sounds, tastes, etc.[20]

With that he comes to the point of this analysis:[21]

(a) The ideas produced in our minds by the *primary qualities* of external objects, are *resemblances* of them, and their patterns do really exist in the objects themselves.

---

[17] The student should be warned that Locke seems to use the terms 'perception' and 'idea' indiscriminately. Sometimes he speaks as if the sense-impressions made on the mind by external objects are 'perceptions' and 'ideas'. Sometimes he speaks as if the sense-impressions are converted into 'perceptions' and 'ideas' by the mind's reflection on the sense-impressions. Cf. e.g. Essay 2.1.2–4 and 2.8.7–8.

[18] *Essay* 2.8.8.
[19] *Essay* 2.8.9.
[20] *Essay* 2.8.10–14.
[21] *Essay* 2.8.15.

(b) The ideas produced in our minds by the *secondary qualities* do not resemble these secondary qualities at all. There is nothing like our ideas existing in the objects themselves.

He then sums up the practical benefit, as he sees it, of making these epistemological distinctions: 'whereby we may also come to know what ideas are, and what are not, resemblances of something really existing in the bodies we denominate from them'.[22]

The practical issue at stake here is very important. If our senses convey to us from the external world perceptions and ideas that are fallacious and do not correspond to anything in the external world, we need to be made aware of that fact and then correct our ideas. But how shall we correct our false ideas? For if our minds are helplessly dependent on our senses for the information about the external world without which our minds cannot start thinking, how shall we correct our false ideas about the external world? Locke tries to show us by sheer logic that our false ideas are not true; and that they must have been caused in us by qualities in the object that bear no resemblance to our ideas. How helpful is his logic?

> If our senses convey to us from the external world perceptions and ideas that are fallacious and do not correspond to anything in the external world, we need to be made aware of that fact and then correct our ideas.

Evaluation of Locke's snowball

According to Locke our senses convey to our minds three ideas from the snowball: (1) an idea of shape (spherical); (2) an idea of coldness; and (3) an idea of whiteness.

Now shape (extension, or figure) is supposed by Locke to be a primary quality in the snowball. Therefore our idea of the snowball's shape, resembles, or corresponds to, the actual, objective shape of the snowball.

But coldness is said to be a secondary quality of the snowball. Our senses convey to our mind the idea that the snowball is cold. But this time our idea is false: it does not resemble anything objective in the snowball. It is, in fact, caused by certain primary qualities in

---

[22] *Essay* 2.8.22.

the snowball that are not themselves cold. In other words our idea of cold is a subjective idea in our mind, not corresponding to anything in objective reality. And to confirm the fact that our idea is only subjective, Locke points out that to someone whose hands are warm, the snowball will seem very cold; to someone whose hands are already cold, the snowball will not seem very cold. It is solely a matter of subjective impression.

We need not deny that the intensity of the feeling of cold is in part subjective and varies from person to person. Nor do we need to deny that the snowball does not itself experience what we mean by 'feeling cold'. It has no nervous system and does not feel anything. Nor is it self-conscious. But to say that there is no coldness in the snowball answering to our idea of coldness is surely factually inaccurate. Stick a thermometer into a snowball and it will measure its degree of coldness. Do the same with a human body and the thermometer will tell you how hot, or cold, the body is. And in so far as the degree of heat, or cold, depends on the extent of the vibrations of the atoms, snowballs share this feature with human beings. As human beings we give a name to our subjective experience of low temperature: we call it 'cold', or, 'feeling cold.' In this respect the snowball is different from us; it has no subjective experience of cold. It doesn't call it anything. It is not conscious; we are.

Locke's theory about colour raises fascinating questions that have not been completely answered even yet.

Then what about whiteness (colour)? According to Locke colour is a secondary quality. A substance in the snowball creates an impression of whiteness in our mind; but the substance itself is not white—it has no colour. Whiteness is no more in snow than sickness or pain are in a poison that causes sickness and pain in us.[23] If the snowball looks to us to be white, that is merely a subjective sensation that we experience. It is not objectively true of the snowball itself.

Locke's theory about colour raises fascinating questions that have not been completely answered even yet. So let us now debate them.

---

[23] Cf. *Essay* 2.8.17.

First, here are two philosophers who insist that the colours we see when we look at objects in the external world are actually in those objects, and are not merely sensations caused in our heads by those objects.

N. O. Lossky rejects the causal theory of perception, and describes his own intuitive theory thus in his *History of Russian Philosophy*:

> According to the intuitive theory the objects' sensory qualities—colours, sounds, warmth, etc., are transsubjective; i.e., belong to the actual objects of the external world. They are regarded as mental and subjective by the adherents of the *causal* theory of perception according to which the stimulation of sense organs by the light rays, air waves, etc., is the cause that produces the content of perception. Lossky has worked out a *co-ordinational* theory of perception . . . with regard to the part played by physiological processes in perception. The gist of it is that the stimulation of a particular sense organ and the physiological process in the cortex are not the cause producing the content of perception, but merely a stimulus inciting the knowing self to direct its attention and its acts of discrimination upon the actual object of the external world.[24]

Similarly (though from a different philosophical position) Anthony Kenny comments on Locke's account of the secondary qualities (i.e. those qualities in objects that cause sensations of colour in us but have no colour themselves):

> Locke is basically correct in thinking that secondary qualities are powers to produce sensations in human beings, and he has familiar arguments to show that the sensations produced by the same object will vary with circumstances (lukewarm water will appear hot to a cold hand, and cold to a hot hand; colours look very different under a microscope). But from the fact that the secondary qualities are anthropocentric and relative it does not follow that they are subjective or in any way fictional. In a striking image suggested by the Irish chemist Robert Boyle, the secondary qualities are keys which fit particular locks, the

---

[24] *History of Russian Philosophy*, 252.

locks being the different human senses. Once we grasp this, we can accept, in spite of Locke, that grass really is green, and snow really is cold.[25]

Topic for debate: Is the greenness in the grass?

First consideration: It is not enough to consider just two things: (1) our own subjective sense-impressions, and (2) the apparently green grass. We must also consider light, for it conveys to our faculty of sight the impression of the grass that we receive. Obviously, in the dark we don't see either the grass itself or what colour it has (if it has any colour). Is light, therefore, entirely neutral? Does it simply convey the colour green, inherent in the grass itself, to our faculty of sight, without in any way changing the colour? This raises a second question.

Second consideration: What is the nature of light? Scientists all seem to agree on this at least: visible light is 'but a small part of the whole spectrum of electromagnetic radiation, which ranges (with increasing frequency and decreasing wavelength) through radio waves, microwaves, infrared, visible light, ultraviolet, X-rays, and gamma rays.'[26]

Within the whole spectrum of electromagnetic radiation, we are also told that, 'Visible light is electromagnetic radiation whose wavelength falls within the range to which the human retina responds, i.e. between about 390 nanometres (violet light) and 740 nanometres (red). White light consists of a roughly equal mixture of all visible wavelengths, which can be separated to yield the colours of the spectrum, as was first demonstrated conclusively by Newton.'[27]

We should note the implications of this. We cannot see infrared radiation, though we can feel it as radiant heat. At the other end of the visible spectrum we cannot see ultraviolet radiation, though too much exposure to it can cause skin cancer. This obviously implies that what wavelengths, and, therefore, what colours, we see is in part, at least, decided by our subjective, internal mechanisms of sight. This information will be useful later on; for the moment let us turn to another consideration.

---

[25] *Brief History of Western Philosophy*, 212.
[26] Pearsall and Tumble, *Oxford English Reference Dictionary*, 1392.
[27] Pearsall and Tumble, *Oxford English Reference Dictionary*, 829.

Third consideration: Is the colour in the light and not in the grass? If, like Newton, we take a prism and split up white light into the various wavelengths that combine to make white light, what we then see is a whole range of colours just as we do when sunlight is refracted in the water droplets of a rainbow. Is it, then, that the colour is in fact in the light? The water droplets in the rain shower had no colour before the sunlight was refracted in them, any more than Newton's prism did before a beam of light was passed through it.

Or take another example. A lump of iron heated in a forge will emit visible light, the colour of which will change from dull red, to brilliant red, to white, as the temperature of the iron rises. Similarly stars; and from the colour of the light which they emit (red in the case of, say, Betelgeuse, and blue in the case of the Pleiades) astronomers can deduce their temperature, their chemical elements, and the direction of their movement (red-shift or blue-shift).

Is not the colour, then, in the light? After all, if you take a large sheet of white paper and shine a red light on it, the paper will look red; but obviously in this case the red colour is not in the paper, but in the light. But we must not make hasty decisions.

Fourth consideration: Having talked of the spectrum of colours emitted by the various wavelengths of visible light, and having constantly referred to, say, the green wavelength or the violet wavelength, scientists will then turn and define colour as:

> the sensation produced on the eye by rays of light when resolved into different wavelengths, as by a prism, selective reflection, etc. (*black* being the effect produced by no light or by a surface reflecting no rays, and *white* the effect produced by rays of unresolved light) . . . Opaque objects appear coloured according to the wavelengths they reflect (other wavelengths being absorbed).[28]

This explanation is at least unambiguous: the colour is not in the light. When therefore scientists talk of, say, the blue wavelength of visual light, they must be using a kind of shorthand for 'that wavelength, which, while not blue itself, causes a sensation of blue in our head'.

---

[28] Pearsall and Tumble, *Oxford English Reference Dictionary*, 286.

Similarly, when we see, say, grass and to us it looks green, the colour is not in the grass, neither is it in the light. What happens is that the grass contains various pigments. When white light falls on the grass, these pigments reflect only one of the wavelengths in the light, namely the one which, when it enters our eyes, causes us to see green. The rest of the wavelengths are absorbed by the pigments in the grass and are not reflected. The colour, then, is in our head, and not in the grass.

At this, Locke, if he were alive, would perhaps say, 'I told you so; I was right after all.'

Fifth consideration: How, then, and by what mechanisms does a wavelength of light, itself colourless, entering our eye, somehow cause us to see colour? We are told that in the pigmented area of the retina there are thousands of cells called, from their shape, 'rods' and 'cones', which secrete various chemicals; and it is these cells that produce the colours for us to see. But at this point another question arises that we ought to take to the biologists to let them answer it for us.

How do these cells enable us to see colours? Is it that a certain wavelength of light reflected off grass falls on some of these cells and causes the chemicals in *them* to glow with a green hue? And if so, is it that since the retina is part of the eyeball, when we look at grass, the eye is immediately flooded with green colour, and so sees the grass as green? And what causes after images? That is to say, if we look at a bright red colour for half a minute, and then shut our eyes, we shall see a green coloured after image. Does this mean that some chemical reaction in the pigments of the rods and cells is still going on even after we shut our eyes and thus for the time being stops any further light entering the eye, so that our eye is still 'seeing' even when it is shut?

Sixth consideration: Who or what does the seeing? We are told that the cells of the retina transform the incoming radiation into nerve impulses that neural pathways then convey to the visual cortex. But that raises another question at which the quotation from Lossky hints (see above). If 'seeing colours' finally means that nerve impulses arrive on the visual cortex of the brain, and the brain then interprets them as colours, are the nerve impulses themselves coloured? If not, how does the brain, which has never 'seen' colours, but only registered nerve impulses, know to interpret them *as colours*?

And what or who receives this interpretation? Is the visual cortex of the brain the final end of the line? Or does it report its findings to the conscious self, or person, who is simultaneously using his or her eyes, brain, and all the other senses combined along with memory, to look directly at the world and to understand its variegated features? What, finally, is consciousness?

David Hume's epistemology

The Scottish philosopher David Hume was born in 1711 and died in 1776; but still today he is famous and much quoted. Professor Justin Broackes *The Oxford Companion to Philosophy* describes Hume as perhaps the greatest of eighteenth-century philosophers.[29] Professor Ernest C. Mossner prefaces his Introduction with the remark: 'David Hume is the greatest of British philosophers.'[30]

Hume is certainly famous for his scepticism and for his hostility to religion and metaphysics. An atheist himself, he naturally denied that there was, or even could be, any convincing evidence for the existence of God, or for miracles;[31] and he is therefore understandably regarded as an eminent leader of thought by those who find such scepticism attractive. But his scepticism carried him further. He also denied that there is such a thing as the human self; and most famously of all he denied that we can have certain knowledge of causation. If this were true, it would eliminate not only religious belief but a foundational principle of science.

It is the fact, however, that Hume's scepticism arose out of his epistemological theory about how the human mind works. To evaluate his scepticism, therefore, we must first try to understand his philosophy of mind.

Hume's philosophy of mind

Hume was an empiricist in the tradition of Locke. Like Locke (though with a more precise usage of terms) he based his philosophy of mind on what has come in modern times to be known as the Representa-

---

[29] *Oxford Companion to Philosophy*, 377..
[30] David Hume, *A Treatise of Human Nature*, 7.
[31] See our discussion of his views on these things in Book 5: *Claiming to Answer*, Ch. 4.

tive Theory of Perception (RTP). Since we have already studied that theory we need only summarise it briefly here.

With Hume this theory is developed at great length, in great detail and with many subdivisions and subtle distinctions. But its basic principle is as he states it in the opening sentences of his *Treatise of Human Nature* (THN): 'All the perceptions of the human mind resolve themselves into two distinct kinds, which I shall call IMPRESSIONS and IDEAS.'[32] (Note that Hume uses the terms impressions and ideas in a somewhat different sense from Locke.)

Impressions, he goes on to explain, comprise all the sensations that are made upon us by the external world, and also the impressions made on our souls by our passions and emotions.

Ideas are derived from these impressions. The impressions always come first. Ideas are faint images of the impressions; but otherwise they exactly represent those impressions. The intellect then reflects on these ideas and thus it gets its knowledge of the external world and of the soul's emotions and passions.

According to Hume's theory, the mind never has direct cognitive access to the external world, or even to its own passions and emotions.

When he says that ideas are exact images of impressions, the word 'image' seems to imply visual representation. Indeed, the main instance he quotes is the visual impressions his room made on him when he looked at it with his eyes open, and the ideas he formed in his mind of those impressions when he shut his eyes.[33] The ideas, he said, were *exact representations of the impressions* he felt when his eyes were open.

How then, we ask, do ideas provide us with exact images of the impressions that the external world makes on us via the non-visual senses: hearing, feeling, taste and smell? Hume seems not to tell us, though he constantly repeats that 'all our ideas are copied from our impressions'.[34] (At this point it would be worth reading again the quotation from Roger Scruton at the end of Ch. 1.)

According to Hume's theory, then, the mind never has direct

---

[32] THN 1.1.1.1; Norton edn, 7.
[33] THN 1.1.1.1.
[34] THN 1.1.3.4.

cognitive access to the external world, or even to its own passions and emotions. Always between the intellect with its powers of reason and the external world is a screen formed of ideas that are themselves only images or representations or copies of impressions. Modern advocates of RTP do in fact claim that we are like people who never watch a football match directly but only on a television screen. Hume tells us, moreover, that the only true ideas we can have are those which are copies or images of impressions. (It should be noted that, when Hume talks about impressions being made upon the mind, he does not mean 'mind' in the sense of reason or intellect.)

So let us consider what his theory has to say in answer to three test questions.

Question 1 – How do we grasp spoken information?

Suppose a mathematics lecturer sets out to explain to us the abstract idea of ratio and does so merely by speaking without writing anything on the blackboard. He points out that four is two times two, and sixteen is two times eight. Therefore four is to two as sixteen is to eight.

Two questions arise:

(*a*) How do we actually come to hear what he is saying?
(*b*) How do we come to understand it?

How do we hear? Is it that through our ears the sound of his voice makes an impression on our senses? Then an exact copy or recording of this impression is made and becomes an idea; then reason's 'inner ear' listens to this idea, and reason begins to reflect on it? Are there two sets of ears: the external ears and then an internal one? Or do the external ears conduct the sound of the lecturer's voice direct to the listening intelligence?

How do we understand? The crucial thing about the sound of the voice is not the mere sound in itself but the fact that the sound is carrying information. It is that information that we are intent on grasping. On what part of the mind does the information make its impression? Must we think that the information first reaches the mind as a sensation, which becomes an impression, which is then copied and becomes an idea, and only then can the intellect begin to study the information? Or is it not so that our intellect, using hearing as an instrument, involves itself directly in trying to grasp and understand the information as it leaves the lecturer's mouth? In other words, are not the lecturer's voice and our hearing simply the channels that convey the information direct from the lecturer's reasoning mind to ours? What do you think?

Question 2 – What am I myself?

When Hume comes to the question whether or not each human being has a personal self, he tells us that he experimented on himself by introspection:

> For my part, when I enter most intimately into what I call *myself*, I always stumble on some particular perception or other, of heat or cold, light or shade, love or hatred, pain or pleasure. I never can catch *myself* at any time without a perception, and never can observe any thing but the perception. When my perceptions are removed for any time, as by sound sleep, so long I am insensible of *myself*, and may truly be said not to exist. And were all my perceptions removed by death, and I could neither think nor feel, nor see, nor love nor hate after the dissolution of my body, I should be entirely annihilated.[35]

Let us examine the logic of Hume's statement. He tells us that when by introspection he looked inside to discover his 'self', he could never catch his 'self' without a perception; in fact he could never observe anything but a succession, or bundle, of perceptions. His self was non-existent. So there was nothing in which these successions of perceptions could inhere. They were, we may suppose, like a succession of images flitting across a television screen but with no self there to gather and coordinate them in some coherent, meaningful narrative.

But this is very odd, for notice how Hume describes his experiment:

> When *I* enter most intimately into what *I* call myself, *I* always stumble on some particular perception . . . *I* can never catch myself . . . without perception and *I* can never observe anything but the perception.[36]

---

[35] THN 1.4.6.3, emphasis in original.
[36] THN 1.4.6.3, emph. added.

Grant, then, that the self could not be found. But who or what was this 'I' that was trying to find it? Was it too nothing but a bundle of incoherent, un-united perceptions? And who or what was the 'I' that, having discovered that its self did not exist, wrote down its findings in this *Treatise of Human Nature*?

And then this 'I' makes a truly astonishing statement. It now tells us that 'when my perceptions are removed . . . as by sound sleep, so long *I* am insensible of myself and may truly be said not to exist.'[37] So at night, not only are the perceptions removed, but this 'I' itself is non-existent! That's bad enough; but earlier we were told that even during the day the 'I' could never find itself, was never sensible of itself. That must mean that both by night and by day the self that couldn't be found, and the 'I' that couldn't find it, could truly both be said to be non-existent!

Of course, this 'I' that David Hume keeps talking about as not having discovered itself, is none other than David Hume himself. Translated from philosophical language into everyday speech, his statement runs: 'David Hume himself discovered that his self did not exist, and being by night and day insensible of his self, he might have been truly said to have been permanently non-existent.' It sounds implausible.

Now one might regard all this inconsistency as not worthwhile thinking about, were it not for the fact that the question 'What am I?' is fundamental to our significance, dignity, self-esteem and mental health. The Bible insists that we are persons made in the image of a personal God and that we can know ourselves personally loved by that personal God. Hume of course will not have it that there is a God; but here he tries to prove in addition that the human self is non-existent even in life, and at death is annihilated. (He does not appear to explain how an already non-existent thing can be annihilated.)

The trouble lies with the epistemological theory that he uses to demolish the existence of the human self. The Representative Theory of Perception is false. It represents the relation of a thinker to his or her thoughts as that of an internal viewer having perceptions of images on some internal screen in the head. But a human being does not have to search around inside herself to see if her self has made

---

[37] THN 1.4.6.3, emph. added.

an impression on her mind that can then be converted into an idea that her reason is subsequently able to detect. The normal human being is directly aware of herself as a living, thinking, acting, loving, suffering individual person, in direct relation with the external world, other persons, and, we hope, with God himself. Certainly she can think of her reason, sight, hearing, touch, taste, smell, emotions, memory, powers of imagination and body and note their different functions. But the person is not just one more part among all the other parts, any more than the driver of a car is just another part of the car along with the engine, the brakes, the gearbox and the wheels. The person is the whole man, or woman, and being in charge of the wonderful complex of powers that is himself, he can call on any one of them, or any combination of them, reason and senses, mind and body, simultaneously to investigate the external world directly and to get to know it. Hume's epistemology, by contrast, disintegrates the human personality, and eventually dissolves it into nothingness. (Nothingness is, of course, the final destiny that all atheists hope for.)

Question 3 – What causes things?

It is to Hume's credit that he raised the question of causation and forced it on the world's attention ever since. It is a large and complex subject, and we cannot begin to do justice to it here. But there is one aspect of Hume's theory of causation that springs directly out of his theory of perception and therefore deserves study in this context.

Introducing the subject of causation, he first remarks:

> It seems a proposition, which will not admit of much dispute, that all our ideas are nothing but copies of our impressions, or, in other words, that it is impossible for us to *think* any thing, which we have not antecedently *felt*, either by our external or internal senses.[38]

We recognise at once his epistemological theory: we cannot (properly) think of any thing until the external world has first made impressions on us, which have then been copied and turned into ideas that are thus made available to our reason.

He then observes:

---

[38] EHU (*An Enquiry Concerning Human Understanding*) 7.4, emphasis in original.

> When we look about us towards external objects, and consider the operation of causes, we are never able, in a single instance, to discover any power or necessary connexion; any quality, which binds the effect to the cause, and renders the one an infallible consequence of the other. We only find, that the one does actually, in fact, follow the other.[39]

As an illustration of what he means, he cites what we see actually happen, and what we don't see, when one billiard ball strikes another.

> The impulse of one billiard-ball is attended with motion in the second. This is the whole that appears to the *outward* senses. The mind feels no sentiment or *inward* impression from this succession of objects: Consequently, there is not, in any single, particular instance of cause and effect, any thing which can suggest the idea of power or necessary connexion.[40]

Nowadays we should speak of the transfer of energy from the first billiard ball to the second. But energy is invisible, and even advanced science does not know what energy is. It is understandable that Hume in his day should claim that *outward* senses saw only that when one ball hit the other, the other moved: there was nothing else to be *seen*: nothing to 'suggest the idea of power or necessary connexion'.

But then Hume's epistemological theory obliged him to say that if our outward sense did not *see*, or *feel*, that necessary connection, 'it was impossible for our minds to *think* it'. Where, then, we may ask, do we get the idea of this necessary connection from? The answer that he gives is that when we see one event follow another time after time, the sequence becomes so fixed in the imagination that the mind automatically, as though determined, infers that the second event is caused by the first. But, Hume points out, however many times this sequence of events is observed to happen, we still don't actually see any necessary connection between the two events, and cannot logically claim that the first event was the cause of the second.

From this Hume then drew a startling conclusion: when we see the second billiard ball move, it is our mind that infers from the

---

[39] EHU 7.6.
[40] EHU 7.6.

motion of this second ball that the cause of this motion was the first ball. Then our mind transfers this inference to the event in the external world, as though it were a fact in the external world, though we have no right to do so, since we never actually saw the 'cause'. We have, then, no right to infer causes from effects.

Evaluation of Hume's billiard balls

We must not blame Hume for not knowing the results of modern science. But even in his day he was wrong to say that if you could not see in some substance, just by observing it, some power that could necessarily cause some effect, you could not rightly claim that it was the cause of some subsequent event. The ancient world observed that death constantly followed the drinking of certain liquids, and they called them poisons. They could not actually see by observation what it was in the liquid that had this lethal power; nor could they see what exactly it was that this liquid did inside the body to kill it. But reason inferred that death following the drinking of the liquid was *caused* by the liquid. And reason (and common sense) were right! Subsequently chemical analysis has shown exactly what it is in the poisonous liquid that causes death and exactly how it affects the cells in the body.

Nuclear radiation cannot be seen, heard, felt, tasted or smelled. But observing the genetic damage and death that follows exposure to high dosages of radiation, reason infers that radiation is the cause of these effects. To say that reason is wrong in this case to infer cause from effect, because the cause and its essential power cannot be visually observed, would be philosophical pedantry at its worst.

Nuclear radiation cannot be seen, heard, felt, tasted or smelled. But observing the genetic damage and death that follows exposure to high dosages of radiation, reason infers that radiation is the cause of these effects.

In 1764, one of Hume's contemporaries, Thomas Reid (1710–96), an experimental scientist, wrote a critique of Hume's theories in a book deliberately entitled *An Inquiry into the Human Mind on the Principles of Common Sense*. He argued that the notion that we arrive at our conception of things through intermediary ideas in the mind that are themselves images of impressions made on the mind by external objects is altogether contrary to the actual way we come to know things. When we see a tree, for instance, the tree does not give us a mere idea, or image, of a tree; our mind there and then makes the judgment that the tree exists with a certain shape, size and position. And as for Hume's argument that it is invalid to infer a cause, or an object's existence, from its effects, Reid points out that that is precisely what we do in the case of gravity and magnetism.[41]

Similarly E. L. Mascall has likewise pointed out that in addition to sense-data, we have a non-sensory intellectual element in perception which does not consist of inference drawn from the sense-data.[42] Rather it uses sense-data as an instrument through which the intellect grasps in a direct, but mediate, activity, the intelligible extramental reality, which is the real thing.

Bertrand Russell's verdict on Hume's philosophy is:

> Hume's philosophy, whether true or false, represents the bankruptcy of eighteenth-century reasonableness. He starts out, like Locke, with the intention of being sensible and empirical, taking nothing on trust, but seeking whatever instruction is to be obtained from experience and observation. But having a better intellect than Locke's, a great acuteness in analysis, and a smaller capacity for accepting comfortable inconsistencies, he arrives at the disastrous conclusion that from experience and observation nothing is to be learnt. There is no such thing as a rational belief: 'If we believe that fire warms, or water refreshes, 'tis only because it costs us too much pains to think otherwise.' We cannot help believing, but no belief can be grounded in reason. . . . The growth of unreason throughout the nineteenth century and what has passed of the twentieth is a natural sequel to Hume's destruction of empiricism.[43]

Russell's verdict is severe but deserved. The trouble with both Locke and Hume, and those who followed their school of thought, was not empiricism, which rightly teaches that our knowledge of objective reality must be based on that reality, and all the beliefs that we hold about reality must be checked for truth against that reality.

---

[41] See the extended discussion of Reid's work in Kenny, *Brief History of Western Philosophy*, 241-3.
[42] *Words and Images*, 29-45.
[43] Russell, *History of Western Philosophy*, 610-11.

The trouble with Locke and Hume was the screen they erected between reason and reality. Reason was never allowed to have direct perception of reality, not even in association with the senses. Always impressions, copied by ideas, had to come first; reason must be content to come second and try to understand through these ideas what sense impressions had gathered from the external world.

Hume himself puts it this way:

> My intention then . . . is only to make the reader sensible of the truth of my hypothesis, *that all our reasonings concerning causes and effects are derived from nothing but custom; and that belief is more properly an act of the sensitive, than of the cognitive, part of our natures.*[44]

In this way Locke and Hume erected a barrier between reason and external reality. We earlier noticed that Plato divided knowable reality into two utterly distinct worlds: the Sensible World, about which we can form opinions through our senses, and the Intelligible World knowable by the intellect. Aristotle divided the universe into two realms: that from the moon upwards, which was perfect, and that below the moon, which was imperfect. Locke and Hume for their part divide our powers of perception and understanding: our senses, which have direct access to reality and must always have first place, and our reason, which does not have direct access and can only come second. Locke and Hume will not allow us human beings to be integrated persons who can use reason and senses as a cooperative team working simultaneously in unison to perceive and understand reality directly.

A lesser, but still serious, failing in Locke's and Hume's epistemology is what Professor T. F. Torrance has called 'the tyrannical assumption that all knowledge must ultimately rest upon a form of sense-perception', and particularly on visual perception.[45] Hume admittedly speaks of other senses besides sight; but his main emphasis is on visual impressions. Ideas, he says, are 'images', 'copies', 'exact representations' of impressions, and the main illustration he gives of this is that, when he shut his eyes and thought of his room, the

---

[44] THN 1.4.1.8.
[45] *Theological Science*, 21.

ideas he formed of it were exact representations of the impression he felt when he looked at it with his eyes open.[46] But when it comes to conveying information by speech direct from one mind to another, hearing is more important than sight, as we saw earlier, when we considered the case of a school teacher explaining to a class the abstract idea of ratio.

Professor Torrance reminds us that according to the Bible, when God communicated his law to Israel, he commanded them to notice that they saw no form, or image, of God: they only heard his voice (Deut 4:12–15). Since epistemology will eventually involve us in asking how we can know that there is a God, the importance of rational, verbal communication of God's mind to ours without the intervention of visual images will become crucially significant.

But perhaps the final irony of Hume's epistemological system is this. His whole theory is based on the assertion that we gain our knowledge of the external world from the impressions it causes on our minds. But when he comes to discuss causation he admits:

> As to those *impressions*, which arise from the *senses*, their ultimate cause is, in my opinion, perfectly inexplicable by human reason, and it will always be impossible to decide with certainty, whether they arise immediately from the object, or are produced by the creative power of the mind, or are derived from the author of our being.[47]

So for all his empiricism he could not be sure that his impressions of the external world were not mere figments of his own mind—unless perhaps there was a God who created the whole system.

But now we must turn to the famous German philosopher Kant, to see how he attempted to solve the disastrous implications of Locke's and Hume's epistemology.

---

[46] THN 1.1.1.3.
[47] THN 1.3.5.2, emphasis in original.

CHAPTER 3

THE EPISTEMOLOGY OF IMMANUEL KANT

Infancy is the inability to use one's reason without the guidance of another. It is self-imposed, when it depends on a deficiency, not of reason, but of the resolve and courage to use it without external guidance. Thus the watchword of the enlightenment is: *Sapere aude!* Have the courage to use your own reason.

—Immanuel Kant, 'Beantwortung der Frage: Was ist Aufklärung?'

KANT'S METAPHYSICS

Immanuel Kant (1724–1804) is generally regarded as the last and greatest of the Enlightenment philosophers. The book that made him famous is his *Critique of Pure Reason*, first published in 1781, with a second revised edition in 1787.[1]

Paul Guyer and Allen Wood in their edition of the *Critique* say of it that it

> is one of the seminal and monumental works in the history of Western philosophy. . . . In the more than two centuries since the book was first published, it has been the constant object of scholarly interpretation and a continuous source of inspiration to inventive philosophers. To tell the whole story of the book's influence would be to write the history of philosophy since Kant.

To feel the pulse-beat of this philosopher we could do no better than to read again his summary of what the Enlightenment stood for, which we quoted in the previous chapter.

> The emergence of man from his self-imposed infancy. Infancy is the inability to use one's reason without the guidance of another. It is self-imposed, when it depends on a deficiency, not of reason, but of the resolve and courage to use it without external guidance. Thus the watchword of the enlightenment is: *Sapere aude!* Have the courage to use your own reason.[2]

Now metaphysics in Kant's day had for long centuries concerned itself with humankind's major questions: Is there a God, and can it

---

[1] All references are to the English translation by Norman Kemp Smith, first printed in 1929. The letters A and B plus numerals in the margins in this translation indicate passages from the second edition (B) that have been incorporated into the first edition (A).

[2] See 'Beantwortung der Frage: Was ist Aufklärung?', 35.

be proved? Is man really free? Has man an immortal soul? Is there a life to come? Kant's philosophy seeks answers to all these questions.[3]

Naturally, Kant was against mere superstition. He was also impatient with all dogmatism, particularly on the part of philosophers who claimed that by pure reason they could prove God's existence, the immortality of the soul and the reality of the life to come. It is well known that Kant thought that none of these things could be proved on the basis of pure reason; it is less well known, but equally true, that he was a believer in God, in the immortality of the soul and in the reality of the life to come; and he was opposed to all forms of scepticism that held that theology, philosophy and science could not give us any certain answers on these matters.

Moreover, though Kant was an ardent believer in the natural sciences, they raised for him a special problem. Newton had discovered the universal law of gravity and had expressed it mathematically. This suggested to many people that the universe was a gigantic machine working according to relentless mechanical laws. If, then, human beings were part of the universe, and therefore part of this system of unvarying and inexorable causes and effects, how could man be said to be free? How was free thought even possible? And if humans were not free, how could they be held to be morally responsible for their actions? It was a main part of his purpose in writing the *Critique of Pure Reason* to investigate to what extent these questions could be answered by pure reason.

Kant's distinction between pure reason and practical reason

It would be important, therefore, that right from the start we should notice exactly what the book's title is: the book is not about reason in general, but about *pure* reason as distinct from *practical* reason. Subsequently Kant wrote another book entitled *Critique of Practical Reason* (published 1788); but even in the *Critique of Pure Reason* he spends considerable space towards the end of the book emphasising the difference between pure and practical reason. Let us see how this difference affects the answers he gives to the questions he faced about ultimate reality, God, the soul and the life to come.

---

[3] *Pure Reason*, B 7.

Pure reason: it is impossible, he says, to prove by pure reason the existence of God, the immortality of the soul and the life to come.[4]

Practical reason: he asserts his personal *moral belief* thus:

> I must in all points conform to the moral law.... There is only one possible condition under which this end can connect with all other ends, and thereby have practical validity, namely, that there be a God, and a future world.... Since, therefore, the moral precept is at the same time my maxim (reason prescribing that it should be so), I inevitably believe in the existence of God and in a future life, and I am certain that nothing can shake this belief.[5]

And then when it comes to the scientific investigation of nature, though he recognises the order and purposiveness everywhere observable throughout the world and how this seems to point to God the Creator ('the physico-theological argument' as he calls it), his conviction is that on the basis of *pure reason* this argument is unable to give any determinate concept of the supreme cause of the world. It cannot therefore serve as the foundation of a theology that is itself, in turn, to form the basis of religion.[6]

However, on the basis of *practical reason*, he holds that this 'physico-theological', or design argument, is the only satisfactory hypothesis for the investigation of nature:

> Purposive unity is, however, so important a condition of the application of reason to nature that I cannot ignore it, especially as experience supplies me so richly with examples of it. But I know no other condition under which this unity can supply me with guidance in the investigation of nature, save only the postulate that a supreme intelligence has ordered all things in accordance with the wisest ends.[7]

And then Kant goes on to express his personal belief:

> Consequently, as a condition of what is indeed a contingent, but still not unimportant purpose, namely, to have guidance

---

[4] See, e.g. A 592 ff./B 620 ff.
[5] Kant, *Pure Reason*, A 828, B 856.
[6] See Kant, *Pure Reason*, A 628–9, B 656–7.
[7] Kant, *Pure Reason*, A 826, B 854.

in the investigation of nature, we must postulate a wise Author of the world. Moreover, the outcome of my attempts [in explanation of nature] so frequently confirms the usefulness of this postulate, while nothing decisive can be cited against it, that I am saying much too little if I proceed to declare that I hold it merely as an opinion. Even in this theoretical relation it can be said that I firmly believe in God. This belief is not, therefore, strictly speaking, practical; it must be entitled a doctrinal belief, to which the *theology* of nature (physico-theology) must always necessarily give rise. In view of the magnificent equipment of our human nature, and the shortness of life so ill-suited to the full exercise of our powers, we can find in this same divine wisdom a no less sufficient ground for a doctrinal belief in the future life of the human soul.[8]

The question naturally arises: if Kant professes himself bound in actual practice, both in scientific investigation of nature and in the basic presuppositions of the practice of morality, to believe in God, then what does he mean by saying that God's existence cannot be proved by pure reason? What, according to him, is pure reason?

A rough and ready preliminary answer would be that it is the kind of abstract reasoning that we use in arithmetic and geometry, which yields absolutely certain and indisputable, necessary truths, such that their contrary is utterly unthinkable and unimaginable.[9] On the other hand, Kant maintains, for the results of such reasoning to be fruitful, they must demonstrably correspond to real objects of possible experience; otherwise they are empty.[10] You can, for instance, reason in your head according to indisputably correct arithmetic that $10 \times 10 = 100$; and the result is logically true. But such reasoning does not create any money in your bank account. You cannot take the result arrived at by pure reason and on that basis alone argue that it proves that you have, say £100 in the bank. The only way you could prove that £100 actually exist in the bank in your name (or should do, if no one has stolen them) is by experience, that is, by going to the

---

[8] Kant, *Pure Reason*, A 826–7, B 854–5. Bracketed words are in original.
[9] Kant, *Pure Reason*, B ix–x.
[10] See Kant, *Pure Reason*, B xxx.

bank and getting hold of them. Conversely, if such experience were for some reason impossible, and even the possibility of such experience unthinkable, then you could never prove by pure reason that you had money in the bank.

In the same way, Kant maintains, by pure reason you can construct in your head logical arguments for the existence of God, but by itself that would not prove that in actual fact God does exist. (Incidentally, he elsewhere points out that pure reason cannot prove that God does not exist.)[11] Therefore pure reason would advise people to base their faith in God's existence on practical reason, which is, according to Kant, what the mass of people (as distinct from philosophers) do anyway. And rightly so, for 'belief in a wise and great *Author of the world* is generated solely by the glorious order, beauty, and providential care everywhere displayed in nature'.[12]

Knowing God

If we bracket out the adverb 'solely' in the above quotation there is truth in Kant's argument. The Bible likewise says:

> For his invisible attributes, namely, his eternal power and divine nature, have been clearly perceived, ever since the creation of the world, in the things that have been made. (Rom 1:20)

And it is also true, as Kant points out,[13] that when people become too engrossed in abstract, speculative, reasoning as to whether God exists or not, it diverts their attention from the powerful evidence for God's existence that is staring them in the face, if only they allowed practical reason to point them to that evidence.

But let's return to that troublesome adverb 'solely'. Why does Kant say that belief in God is generated solely by the glorious order, beauty and providential care displayed in nature? Is no other experience of God available to us? Kant appears to reply, 'No'. God, he states, is not an object of possible experience, and to argue that he is, is mere speculation. We cannot have certain knowledge of God but only faith that God exists:

---

[11] Kant, *Pure Reason*, A 830/B 858.
[12] Kant, *Pure Reason*, B xxxiii.
[13] Kant, *Pure Reason*, B xxix–xxx.

even the *assumption*—as made on behalf of the necessary practical employment of my reason—of *God, freedom,* and *immortality* is not permissible unless at the same time speculative reason be deprived of its pretensions to transcendent insight. For in order to arrive at such insight it must make use of principles which, in fact, extend only to objects of possible experience, and which, if also applied to what cannot be an object of experience, always really change them into an appearance, thus rendering all *practical extension* of pure reason impossible. I have therefore found it necessary to deny *knowledge*, in order to make room for *faith*.[14]

So according to Kant, we can have faith that God exists; but we cannot know for certain that God exists. We can believe that God exists, but we can have no experience of God. He is beyond all possible experience. If we claim to have experience of God, we are putting our faith in speculation and mere appearances. 'No one, indeed,' he says, 'will be able to boast that he *knows* that there is a God, and a future life.'[15]

At this, of course, the Bible will protest. Admittedly God is not simply an 'object of experience', though he can rightly be experienced as such. He is the Great Subject who has taken the initiative in making it possible for us to get to know and experience him, as in his grace he chooses to 'know' us personally and individually (Gal 4:9). This was the precise purpose of Christ's coming to earth: 'no one knows the Father', he said, 'except the Son and anyone to whom the Son chooses to reveal him. Come to me, . . . and learn from me' (Matt 11:27–29).

Perhaps the most famous of all Christ's parables was the one in which he likened himself to a shepherd and his disciples to sheep. In the course of that parable he says: 'I am the good shepherd. I know my own and my own know me, just as the Father knows me and I know the Father' (John 10:14–15). His mission, indeed, was that people should 'know you the only true God, and Jesus Christ whom you have sent' (John 17:3). And as for experience of God here in this life, Christ asserted that all who receive him and put their faith in him, experience 'being born of God' (John 1:12–13; 3:1–16).

---

[14] Kant, *Pure Reason*, B xxix–xxx.
[15] Kant, *Pure Reason*, A 829/B 857.

In consequence, the constantly repeated affirmation of the early Christians, arising out of their personal experience, was: 'We know that the Son of God has come and has given us understanding, so that we may know him who is true; and we are in him who is true, in his Son Jesus Christ' (1 John 5:20). If Christ, then, says that knowledge and experience of God are possible in this life, and our experience bears that out, Kant's assertion that 'No one indeed will be able to boast that he knows that there is a God' will sound strange indeed. In the first place, it is not a question of boasting. A little child is not boasting when it says that it knows its father, since the relationship with its father was not something that the child has achieved by its good works. The relationship is a result of its birth. Similarly, with the believer in Christ. The relationship with God that allows a believer to know God as Father is not achieved by meritorious works. It is bestowed on the believer as an act of God's grace: 'And because you are sons, God has sent the Spirit of his Son into our hearts, crying, "Abba! Father!" So you are no longer a slave, but a son, and if a son, then an heir through God' (Gal 4:6–7).

> The constantly repeated affirmation of the early Christians, arising out of their personal experience, was: 'We know that the Son of God has come and has given us understanding, so that we may know him who is true; and we are in him who is true, in his Son Jesus Christ' (1 John 5:20).

Denying knowledge to make room for faith

If Kant were alive today he would doubtless shake his head gravely and repeat what he said at the end of the long quotation above: 'I have . . . found it necessary to deny knowledge, in order to make room for faith'; in other words, if it could be logically proved that God exists, then there would be no room left for faith.

This idea is widespread, but it is, in fact, not true. The Bible indicates, somewhat ruefully, that the demons know for certain that God exists. They have no choice whether they shall believe it or not. But that does not stop them believing in God's existence (Jas 2:19), even though they continue to defy him.

It has been indisputably demonstrated according to chemical laws that certain drugs inevitably have a deleterious effect on the brain. Instead of that proven fact eliminating faith, it is faith in that scientifically demonstrated fact that keeps some young people from taking drugs in spite of peer pressure. Lack of faith in the scientifically proved fact is not the inevitable result of its being proved. Lack of faith is perverse and tragically leads some people to yield to peer pressure and to take drugs, with all too often disastrous results. The same is true of smoking, and the proved fact that it damages the lungs.

Kant's Copernican revolution

In his book *Prolegomena to Any Future Metaphysics*[16] Kant confides in us that he was aroused from his dogmatic slumbers by recalling the works of David Hume (which we have just studied). Two things about Hume's philosophy troubled Kant: one was Hume's ideas on causation, the other was Hume's contention that we have no access to knowledge of the external world except through the impressions made by the world on our senses. To understand why these two things troubled Kant we must first take a brief look back to the beginnings of modern science.

Kant's scientific background

Though recognisable as modern science, at its beginning science in Europe was still regarded as a branch of philosophy known as natural philosophy. It still retained many of the basic philosophical ideas and concerns that had been developed by the ancient traditions of Plato and Aristotle. It was these ideas and concerns that motivated the early scientists to debate among themselves what was the true methodology that scientists ought to adopt in their research and what logical principles had to be followed in the interpretation of the results they achieved, if their interpretations were to be regarded as correct and reliable. Let's take some examples.

William Harvey and the circulation of the blood

In 1628 William Harvey published a book, *On the Motion of the Heart and Blood in Animals*, in which he announced his discovery of

---

[16] p. 7.

the circulation of the blood. He had made this discovery largely by what he called 'ocular experiments', that is by actually looking at the heart's behaviour by means of anatomical dissection and vivisections. Descartes announced that as a result of his own study of anatomy he agreed with Harvey that the blood does indeed circulate round the body and that the heart plays a central part in this process. But Descartes disagreed about how the heart did this and what actually caused the blood to circulate.

Harvey maintained that the heart was a muscle and, by regular contractions, acted like a pump to drive the blood around the body. Today we know that Harvey's theory was right. Descartes, however, had a different theory, which we need not stay to consider; it had some plausibility, yet it was wrong. What interests us is the reason Descartes gave for rejecting Harvey's theory.

Harvey, he argued, could not explain how a muscle could have the supposed power to contract on its own in this way. All other muscles, he said, simply control the voluntary movement which humans themselves freely initiate. Merely to point to the fact that in vivisection the heart could be observed to contract regularly did not prove that the heart initiated this contraction, or even that it was this contracting that caused the blood to circulate. Perhaps it was the circulation of the blood that caused the heart to contract. Harvey had observed the contractions; he had observed the blood circulating; he had not observed which of the two was the cause of the other.

Harvey's theory, then, could not be accepted as proven true, unless he could explain what caused the heart to contract in the first place. In other words he would have to explain not merely the material the heart was made of but the form or nature of the heart and the cause of its powers, if his explanation was going to be accepted as a truly philosophical explanation. All agreed that interesting facts and opinions could be obtained by experiment; but to turn these opinions into solid knowledge, they would have to pass the test of strict philosophical reasoning regarding causes.

Newton's theory of gravitation
Newton's famous inverse square law of gravitational attraction was similarly attacked and rejected on several grounds by contemporary scientists and philosophers. Newton claimed that his law was

deduced by mathematical logic from the actual observed phenomena of the behaviour of the moon and the planets. It was not, therefore, an unproven hypothesis.

His critics, however, insisted that it was only a hypothesis, and a very implausible one at that. It involved the idea that some invisible 'gravitational force' could be the cause of one object affecting another at a distance without the objects having any direct or indirect contact. Such an idea, they maintained, was unacceptable to true natural philosophy.

The great and famous Leibniz joined in the criticism. He argued that Newton's inverse square law merely described the fact that planets orbit a fixed point, the sun; but it did not explain what caused this orbital motion. To say that some gravitational force made them orbit the sun did not identify any natural agency that might plausibly be regarded as causing their motion. Obviously Newton did not think it was in the nature of planets to orbit of their own accord in this way: he held that they were being made to do it. By what natural force then? To postulate some external invisible force and simply call it gravity explained nothing. Where did this gravitational force come from? What caused it? Newton, said Leibniz, could not answer the question. His theory, therefore, was tantamount to saying that this gravitational force must be maintained by some constant miraculous, supernatural power—which was not an explanation that would satisfy natural philosophy.

> Obviously Newton did not think it was in the nature of planets to orbit of their own accord in this way: he held that they were being made to do it. By what natural force then? To postulate some external invisible force and simply call it gravity explained nothing. Where did this gravitational force come from? What caused it? Newton, said Leibniz, could not answer the question.

Advances in scientific discovery have shown us that Harvey and Newton were right and Descartes and Leibniz wrong on these points. Science has come down on the side of Harvey's theory, leading to advances in cardiac medicine. And science has come down on the side of Newton's theory, even though not all difficulties in the understanding of gravitation and energy have been resolved. Nevertheless we can admire the caution of the early scientists in refusing to accept a scientific theory, however plausible, until it was fully proved; and we can understand their insistence on the necessity of rigorously explaining the true causes of things.

Kant's objections to Hume's philosophy

Hume had argued, as we have seen, that it is never possible for us to observe causes. He reasoned that our only source of knowledge of events in the external world is through the impressions those events make on our mind. Kant saw at once that if Hume's argument were true, not only would it make knowledge of causation impossible: it would be destructive of all pure philosophy.[17] He felt he had to accept Hume's claim that all the content of our knowledge of the external world must come from the world itself. But he felt equally strongly that the logical principles by means of which we understand and make sense of this knowledge are *not* derived from the external world: they are supplied by the logical powers inherent in the human mind. We do not learn the truths of mathematics and the concept of cause and effect, i.e. that everything that happens has its cause, from experience of the world a posteriori; we know these truths a priori, independently of any experience. In other words, the external world provides us with all the information about itself; but we provide the logical principles and powers necessary for the analysis and understanding of that information.[18]

Sound principles and specific knowledge

There is a key difference to be observed between the principle of cause and effect and knowledge of actual causes and effects. Kant freely admitted, indeed he insisted on the fact, that a priori understanding of the law of cause and effect cannot by itself predict in advance what the actual cause of some particular event will turn out to be. Only empirical investigation can do that—if indeed it is possible to do it at all. But a priori knowledge of the law of cause and effect will assure us that there must have been a cause, whatever it was.[19]

Let's illustrate to ourselves the importance of the distinction that Kant is making here. Take an apple, for example. It starts off being

---

[17] Kant, *Pure Reason*, B 19–20.
[18] See Kant, *Pure Reason*, B 1.
[19] See Kant, *Pure Reason*, B 289–294.

firm and rosy red. Eventually it goes rotten, soft and mushy brown. A priori knowledge of the law of cause and effect cannot tell you what has actually caused this particular change. What it can tell you and insist on, however, is that this change must have been brought about by some cause or causes. This in turn will drive the chemists to look for, and if possible discover, the cause. But even if the cause could not be found, the a priori knowledge of the law that there can be no effect without a cause, would convince people that there must be some cause for the apple's going rotten, even if we cannot discover it.

It is this a priori conviction that drives modern cancer research. The exact cause or causes of many cancers is still not known. But from the a priori law of cause and effect scientists infer that the effect, cancer, must be produced by some cause or causes; and so they continue research to find the cause in the hope that, having found it, they may be able to devise a cure. And when the cure is found, they will regard their medicine as the cause of healing.

Kant's aims in writing the Critique

Kant's belief, then, was that 'though all our knowledge begins with experience, it does not follow that it all arises out of experience'.[20] Some knowledge about things in the external world can be known a priori, that is, before we have experience of them. He thought, however, that he could combine this rationalist view with what he had come to see was the valid element in Hume's empiricism, namely, that all the content of our knowledge of the world must come by experience of the world.

In the *Critique*, therefore, he set out to do two things:

1. rigorously to demonstrate that there is such a thing as a priori synthetic knowledge (what this means we shall see in a moment); and
2. to demonstrate by logical argument the limitations of pure reason.

In his introduction to the second edition of his *Critique*, however, he confessed that to have any hope of achieving the first objective we must be prepared to accept a revolution in our attitude to knowledge

---

[20] Kant, *Pure Reason*, B 1.

of objects in the external world, like the revolution that Copernicus instituted in cosmology.[21]

Before Copernicus's revolution people had tried to explain the movements of the heavenly bodies on the supposition that the heavenly bodies all revolved around the human spectator. Despairing of achieving any success on this basis, Copernicus adopted the hypothesis that the true situation might be the direct opposite: it might be that the human spectators were revolving round the heavenly bodies. Proceeding on this hypothesis Copernicus opened up the way to the eventual establishment of the fundamental laws of the motions of the heavenly bodies and Newton's discovery of the universal law of gravitation.

Similarly, Kant suggested, we must give up asking, as Locke and Hume had done, how our knowledge can conform to objects in the external world. Instead we must adopt the opposite supposition that for true knowledge of objects in the external world to be possible, those objects must conform to our reason and our categories of understanding. On that basis, he argued, it could then be seen that while a posteriori experience of the external world supplies all the content of our knowledge, a priori knowledge is necessary for the understanding of that content. The external world, known by the senses, will still provide the raw material of knowledge, but our knowledge of a priori principles will impose on it the structure of our understanding.

> Kant's suggested Copernican revolution in epistemology was only a heuristic hypothesis adopted in the struggle to reconcile the truth of empiricism with the truths of rationalism. But the suggestion that the universe must conform itself to our preconceived principles of pure reason or else forfeit the possibility of being known, smacks of hubris.

Now scientists frequently adopt an hypothesis as a heuristic tool for investigating nature; and Kant's suggested Copernican revolution in epistemology was only a heuristic hypothesis adopted in the struggle to reconcile the truth of empiricism with the truths of rationalism. But the suggestion that the universe must conform itself to our preconceived principles of pure reason or else forfeit the possibility of being known, smacks of hubris.

---

[21] Kant, *Pure Reason*, B xvi–xvii.

To start with, it raises a fundamental question: what exactly is it that we are seeking to do in science? All agree that, whatever it is we are trying to do, we must bring all our powers of reason to bear upon the task. All agree that we cannot just be passive: we must actively use our reason to design experiments that oblige nature to answer the questions we put to it. But are we using our rational and practical powers to listen to nature in order to discover nature's own inherent intelligibility and order? Or are we seeking to impose our preconceived sense of rational order on nature, thus injecting into nature's material an intelligibility that it did not possess until we forced it to submit to our rational principles?

There are places in the *Critique* where Kant comes perilously near the second of these alternatives. He admits that there are things about nature that reason can learn only from nature, and that these things we must allow nature to teach us and not allow reason fictitiously to invent them. But then in a typical Enlightenment attitude he adds:

> reason has insight only into that which it produces after a plan of its own ... [reason] must not allow itself to be kept, as it were, in nature's leading-strings ... [reason] must adopt as its guide ... that which it has itself put into nature.[22]

Is human reason, then, we ask, so absolutely perfect that it could never be taught a higher order of rationality than it already possesses? It never seems to have occurred to Kant that nature, being the creation of the divine mind, might have an intelligibility of a higher order than he ever conceived of.

To Kant, Euclidean geometry and Newtonian physics were the last word in rationality. Experience has taught us otherwise. Einstein's openness to the possibility that the universe might have a sophistication subtler and more complicated than we had ever thought before, led to the discovery that, at higher levels, Newtonian physics no longer applies and is superseded by quantum physics; and that space-time is not structured according to Euclidean, but non-Euclidean, geometry. The universe's rationality is a hierarchy of levels; we have not yet scaled its utmost heights.

---

[22] Kant, *Pure Reason*, B xiii–xiv.

But Kant's 'Copernican revolution' extends beyond the realm of science. As we have seen, he holds that practical and moral reason assure us that God exists. But then he adds that because pure reason cannot, with its limited powers, prove that God exists, he must remain, as far as pure reason is concerned, beyond all possible experience. This is, as the ancient Greek tragedians might say, the Enlightenment's *hamartia*, its fatal flaw.

The irony of Kant's Copernican revolution

One other thing seems to have escaped Kant's attention: his supposed Copernican revolution in philosophy directed mankind in the opposite direction to what Copernicus's revolution in cosmology did. Before Copernicus, man thought he was the centre; and the sun, the planets and the constellations all circled around him. That supposition severely hindered man's true understanding of cosmology. Copernicus suggested that man was not the centre: the sun was. Before Kant, people thought that for a true understanding of the universe man's ideas had to conform to the universe. Kant's revolution proposed that from now on the universe had to conform to man's understanding, or forfeit the possibility of being known. Man was now the centre and man's own powers of pure reason the final judge of what could be known for certain. We shall find that this attitude dug a deep, arbitrary, unbridgeable chasm between what is potentially knowable and what is not.

KANT'S BASIC PRINCIPLES OF A PRIORI SYNTHETIC KNOWLEDGE

First Principle:
The possibility of a priori synthetic knowledge

To understand what Kant means we must first remind ourselves of the difference between what are called analytic propositions and synthetic propositions.[23]

---

[23] See Kant, *Pure Reason*, A 6–10/B 10–14.

Analytic propositions

All propositions, said Kant, take the form of subject + predicate. In *analytic* propositions, the predicate does not add any information that is not already contained in the subject. Simple examples are:

(a) *A triangle is a figure that has three sides.* The subject is 'a triangle'; the predicate is 'a figure that has three sides'. But the predicate tells us no new information that was not already contained in the subject. The word 'triangle' by itself *means* 'a figure that has three sides'. The predicate merely explains what the term 'triangle' means. It adds no new information. It simply *analyses* the meaning of 'triangle'.

(b) *A widow is a woman whose husband has died.* Once more the predicate adds no new information beyond that involved in the subject (a widow).

(c) *All bodies are extended.* Of course they are extended, for in philosophical terms that is exactly what a body is: something that has size and shape and is not just a mathematical point.

Synthetic propositions

In synthetic propositions the predicate adds information that is not included in the meaning of the subject. The predicate 'puts together' (the meaning of the word synthetic) some new information along with the meaning of the subject. Some examples are:

(a) *This triangle was drawn by Boris.* The fact that this triangle was drawn by Boris could not have been deduced from the meaning of the term 'triangle'. It adds information additional to what is implied in the subject.

(b) *This widow is Hugo's sister.* But you could not have known that she was Hugo's sister simply by knowing what the word widow means. Once more the predicate has supplied new information not necessarily contained in the meaning of the subject.

(c) *This body is heavy.* By definition all bodies are extended, but not all bodies are heavy; some are light. If this particular body is heavy you could not have known it just by thinking about the term 'body' in your head. You must either be told about it or discover it by experience.

Kant's contention

It is Kant's contention, then, that simply by the power of in-built principles of reason we can gain new knowledge—synthetic knowledge—about objects and events in the external world *in advance* of seeing them, and *independently* of experiencing them. He gives examples.

The proposition 'Everything which happens has its cause'

Kant argues as follows:

> In the concept of 'something which happens', I do indeed think of an existence which is preceded by a time, etc., and from this concept analytic judgments may be obtained. But the concept of a 'cause' lies entirely outside the other concept, and signifies something different from 'that which happens', and is not therefore in any way contained in this latter representation.[24]

The predicate, then, 'has its cause', adds information that was not inherent in the subject 'Everything which happens'. It is therefore a synthetic proposition. Moreover, Kant claims, this knowledge is not drawn from experience, which could only give us a contingent truth. The truth we gain in this proposition is necessary ('everything that happens has, and *must have*, a cause') and universal ('*everything* that . . .'). This synthetic knowledge is, therefore, to be recognised as a priori.

Arithmetical propositions

The particular example he quotes is $7 + 5 = 12$.[25] He admits that $7 + 5$ (the subject) is an invitation to add the two numbers together, and hence that the predicate 12 might seem to have been implied in the subject. If so, the proposition would simply be analytic (like 'a triangle is a figure with three sides'). But Kant insists it is not so. What the resultant number is when 7 is added to 5 is not stated in the subject: it must be worked out in the head, and then it supplies a new piece of information. Kant adds that this is seen more clearly with bigger numbers—by which he presumably means something like

---

[24] Kant, *Pure Reason*, A 9/B 13.
[25] Kant, *Pure Reason*, B 15–16.

173 × 5642 = ?, in which the predicate, whatever it turns out to be, is not obviously contained in the subject.

The modern empiricist John Hospers is one among many philosophers who would disagree with Kant here. Write out the subject 7 + 5 as single digits 1 + 1 + 1 + 1 + 1 + 1 + 1 + 1 + 1 + 1 + 1 + 1, he argues, and it is at once evident from the subject that you have 12 digits![26] On the other hand, Bertrand Russell vigorously supported Kant.[27] He admitted that a child learns that 2 + 2 = 4 from experience of, say, two toy bricks and another two toy bricks add up to four toy bricks. He will then come to see that the same applies to all kinds of things. Eventually he will abstract this arithmetical principle from all particular instances of it. He will 'see' that 2 + 2 = 4. Thereafter he will know that the principle applies universally. In consequence, while he cannot know who will be the inhabitants of London a hundred years from now, he will know for certain in advance that any two of them plus another two of them will make four of them. 'This apparent power of anticipating facts about things of which we have no experience', says Russell, 'is certainly surprising.'[28]

This apparent power of anticipating facts about things of which we have no experience is certainly surprising.

–Bertrand Russel, *Problems of Philosophy*

All geometrical propositions

That the straight line between two points is the shortest, is, says Kant, a synthetic proposition.[29] The concept of 'the shortest' is wholly an addition to 'the straight line between two points': it cannot be derived through any process of analysis from the concept of 'the straight line'. Nor, in order to know that this proposition is true, do we have to mark out two points on a piece of paper, measure the length of a straight line between the two points, compare it with the measured length of curved lines between the points and thus, and only thus, from experience gain the a posteriori knowledge that the straight line here is the shortest. We know by intuition that the proposition is true a priori.

---

[26] *Introduction to Philosophical Analysis*, 136–40.
[27] *Problems of Philosophy*, 59–60.
[28] Though he adds: 'Kant's solution of the problem, though not valid in my opinion, is interesting', p. 60.
[29] Kant, *Pure Reason*, B 16–17.

By examples like these, then, Kant felt that he had proved that we have a priori *synthetic* knowledge. Bertrand Russell[30] concluded that likewise our knowledge of the laws of logic is a priori:

1. *The law of identity*: 'Whatever is, is';
2. *The law of non-contradiction*: 'Nothing can both be and not be';
3. *The law of excluded middle*: 'Everything must either be, or not be'.

To use one of his examples, once we know that a tree is a birch tree, we automatically know, without any further information from experience, that it cannot be an oak tree.

On the other hand, N. O. Lossky in his *History of Russian Philosophy* disagrees with Kant. He writes:

> The existence of truths, bearing the character of general and necessary synthetic judgements, unable to be proved either inductively or deductively, does not necessarily lead to Kant's apriorism: it can be established also by a different means, for instance, on the basis of intuitivism, as this is proved in N. Lossky's *Logic* (73–8).[31]

Second Principle: The transcendental aesthetic[32]

Kant loved long words! What he meant by 'aesthetic' is that part of knowledge that we gain through some sensory experience or other. What he meant by 'transcendental' is the understanding of the sensory experience that we derive not from something actually existent in the external world, but from something within us, what he calls 'pure forms of sensory awareness'.

This internal awareness, he argues, makes us see the external world in a framework of space and time. But space and time are not themselves realities, are not actual features of the external world that

---

[30] *Problems of Philosophy*, 57, 59.
[31] Lossky, *History*, 166.
[32] Kant, *Pure Reason*, A 19–49/B 33–73.

exist objectively even when we are not looking at the world. It is as if we could never look at white snow except through red-tinted glasses. We should always see snow as red; we couldn't see it any other way. But the redness is not a quality or property of the snow: it is in the glasses that we cannot help using to look at the snow. As he says: 'Space does not represent any property of things in themselves.'[33]

Kant's argument is this. Suppose I experience some sensation, and I think it was produced by some object outside of me. Even to think that, I have to presuppose the idea of space outside of me and represent that idea of space to myself. This representation of space cannot, therefore, be empirically obtained from the relations of outer appearances. On the contrary, this outer experience is itself possible only through that representation. Time, likewise, he says, is the form of inner sense by which the mind experiences the succession of its inner experiences.[34]

To sum up, then: when we observe the external world, things appear to us to move in space and to change in time. But that is the only way they can appear to our apparatus of perception. In themselves space and time are nothing.

Evaluation of the transcendental aesthetic

These ideas of space and time cannot but appear to us as frankly nonsense. We may wonder, therefore, how Kant ever arrived at them. As we have earlier noticed, Kant held that all geometrical knowledge is a priori (prior to experience of the external world) and synthetic; and to him geometry was the science of space, since figures enclose and define space. Now, unfortunately for him, in his day Euclidean geometry was the only known theory of space, and Kant naturally thought that its basic principles were a priori, necessary, unalterable truths that we bring to bear on the external world as our inherent way of perceiving it.

But not long after Kant, mathematicians began, by abstract reasoning, to discover consistent non-Euclidean geometries. The question then eventually arose whether the structure of space-time is formed according to Euclidean or non-Euclidean geometry. The only

---

[33] Kant, *Pure Reason*, A 26/B 42.
[34] Kant, *Pure Reason*, A 23/B 37–8.

way of settling that was by scientific investigation. But how could that have been possible, if, as Kant claimed, the intuition of spatiality had been built a priori into every scientist's mind in one single inescapable form, that of Euclidean geometry?

Moreover, there is evidence to show that in fact Kant got his ideas of space from Newton. When he remarks, 'Consequently, the original representation of space is an a priori intuition, not a concept',[35] he seems to be restating Corollary V of Newton's *Principia Mathematica*. He certainly accepted Newton's idea of infinite space; but if so, how could it be, as Kant claimed, a necessary intuition built into every human mind? Kant's whole idea of the 'Transcendental Aesthetic' is misconceived.

Third Principle:
The transcendental analytic: pure concepts of the understanding

Under this heading Kant lists the concepts that the understanding contains within itself, and by which alone it can understand anything.[36]

Table of Categories

I. Of Quantity:	Unity, Plurality, Totality.
II. Of Quality:	Reality, Negation, Limitation.
III. Of Relation:	Of Inherence and Subsistence
	Of Causality and Dependence (cause and effect)
	Of Community (reciprocity between agent and patient)
IV. Of Modality:	Possibility — Impossibility
	Existence — Non-existence
	Necessity — Contingency

In other words, these are the basic principles, built into our minds, which we bring to bear on the external world in order to understand it. It is not a question of our understanding conforming to the external, objective world, so that that world may mould

---
[35] Kant, *Pure Reason*, B 40.
[36] Kant, *Pure Reason*, A 80/B 105–6.

our understanding of reality. It is a question of the external world submitting and conforming itself to our categories of understanding. Anything that does not so conform itself to us, forfeits the possibility of ever being understood.

This, then, is the mechanism behind Kant's so-called 'Copernican Revolution'.

THE LIMITS OF KNOWABILITY ACCORDING TO KANT

Having thus established to his satisfaction pure reason's powers of a priori understanding that are in-built into the human mind, Kant turns his attention to what there is for the mind to understand.[37] Here the main question for Kant is: How much of this objective reality can actually be known? His theory is, as we shall now easily recall, that for the content of our knowledge of the external world we depend solely on experience. But for our understanding of that content we depend on our in-built powers of sensibility and pure reason.

But as soon as we ask, 'How much then can we know?' we immediately become aware of the severe limitations that Kant's Copernican revolution imposes on the knowability of things.

Pure reason, so Kant argues, lays it down that some things, like the universe as a whole, the human soul and God himself, lie beyond all possible experience—in this life at least—and because they are beyond all possible experience, they are unknowable to pure reason.

Whatever new knowledge empirical science claims to obtain and however sound it is empirically, if it does not conform to our in-built and unchangeable concepts of rationality, the claim cannot be allowed.

With this in mind we come to the four major areas where Kant in the name of pure reason lays down limits beyond which we cannot rightly lay claim to any knowledge: they are epistemology, psychology, cosmology and theology.

---

[37] Kant, *Pure Reason*, A 293 ff./B 349 ff.

Epistemology

The first impassable gulf that Kant's Copernican revolution digs in the pathway of knowledge lies between how things appear to us (that is, their outward appearance) and what they are really like in themselves (that is, their inner structure, substance, form and nature). Kant divides the whole of reality into two groups:

1. *phenomena*, Greek for 'things that appear', that is, 'appearances'
2. *noumena*, Greek for 'things that are thought'

The second label, noumena, needs some explanation. It can be applied to things we think about in our head; but, in that case, if these things have nothing that answers to them in the external world, they are, from a practical point of view, empty thoughts and imaginations. The label can also apply, however, to things that actually exist in the external world. But in that case the difference between phenomena and noumena is all-important. The phenomena of these actually existent things are their appearances, that is, how they appear to us. These we can know. But the noumena of these things denotes what these things are in themselves. Now we can, if we choose, think about what things-as-they-are-in-themselves might be like. But all that we can validly think about them is that they are a completely unknown something. According to Kant, we can never know what things in themselves are like. Therefore in many contexts in the *Critique* the singular noumenon (plural, noumena), ironically enough, comes to mean a something that cannot be known.[38]

An example: The rainbow

In this passage Kant chides people for thinking that, while the rainbow of colours in a sunny shower is a mere appearance, the rain is 'the thing in itself'. Not so, he insists: 'in the world of sense, however deeply we enquire into its objects, we have to do with nothing but appearances.'[39]

By this he seems to mean that however deeply empirical science enquires into its objects of study, it can never get beyond appearances; for he continues:

---

[38] Kant, *Pure Reason*, B 312.
[39] Kant, *Pure Reason*, A 45–6/B 62–3.

We then realise that not only are the drops of rain mere appearances, but even their round shape, nay even the space in which they fall, are nothing in themselves, but merely modifications or fundamental forms of our sensible intuitions, and that the transcendental object remains unknown to us.[40]

To say that we cannot know what rain-in-itself is by just looking at it would be justifiable. But the idea that however deeply we enquire into it we have to do with nothing but appearances, seems, in the light of scientific discovery, to be a gross exaggeration. We now know, thanks to science, what water vapour is, how it condenses into water droplets, what water is composed of, namely hydrogen and oxygen, what hydrogen and oxygen atoms are made of, and their nuclei, and so on. How much more deeply have we got to enquire into water before we get beyond 'appearances' and know what 'water-in-itself' is like? To insist on this impassable gulf between the outward appearance of objects that can be known and the underlying material and structure, which gives objects their outward shape and appearance and yet supposedly cannot ever be known, is completely false.

In this connection it is informative to trace the unfortunate influence that Kant's theory has had on modern science. T. F. Torrance remarks:

> In every field of enquiry we establish genuine knowledge in terms of its internal relations and intelligibility—the very points that were and still are being denied by Kantian and Heideggerian forms of philosophy. The difference that has come about can be vividly indicated by pointing to the debate between Ernst Mach and Max Planck in quantum theory over the question of the reality of atoms. Mach claimed that atoms do not have any existence in reality and are no more than symbols that we use in the theoretical conventions of physics, for it is impossible to know things in their internal relations. But of course we can, and it is precisely by penetrating into the internal structure of atoms that physics has made such startling advance in our knowledge of nature, but in so doing it destroyed the

---

[40] Kant, *Pure Reason*, A 46/B 63.

Kantian and Machian thesis that phenomenological knowledge was restricted to external relations or appearances.[41]

Psychology

The second impassable gulf that Kant digs lies between our mental and our spiritual powers in the realm of psychology, or as he puts it, between the 'I' and the soul.[42]

Descartes asserted: 'I think, therefore I am.' St. Thomas Aquinas asserted: 'I am, therefore I think.' Descartes made the activity of thinking the basis of his certainty that he existed. Aquinas made the certainty of his existence the ground of his ability to think. It is a fact that no one can logically deny his or her existence. To say 'I deny I exist' is logical nonsense. If I didn't exist, I couldn't even deny I exist (or anything else for that matter).

Kant's interest in this area is to demonstrate that simply by pure reason one cannot prove that the 'I' that thinks, is a real substance, still less that it is an immortal soul. So he fastens on claims like those of Descartes and Aquinas and argues that any statement like, 'Whenever I think, I am conscious that it is I who is thinking', is simply an analytic statement. Necessarily, 'I' is the subject of the sentence all the way through. But the predicate, he maintains, does not tell us any additional information beyond what is contained in the subject, namely that 'I think' and 'I am conscious that I think'. It does not tell us what the 'I' is.[43]

> Descartes asserted: 'I think, therefore I am.' St. Thomas Aquinas asserted: 'I am, therefore I think.' Descartes made the activity of thinking the basis of his certainty that he existed. Aquinas made the certainty of his existence the ground of his ability to think.

Now, says Kant, as we have already seen, we can think in pure thought any number of things; but unless these thoughts correspond to something empirically observable, they are empty; in which case pure reason has inadvertently become mere speculation. The only

---

[41] *Ground and Grammar of Theology*, 42-3.
[42] Kant, *Pure Reason*, B 406 ff.
[43] See Kant, *Pure Reason*, A 348 ff.

way, he maintains, that a person could know that the 'I' was a definite, simplex, substance, like a soul, for instance (and not a mere group of impressions or mental activities), would be for the 'I' to be able to observe this soul empirically as an object. But, even if it could do that, says Kant, all that the 'I' would actually observe would be mere 'appearances' of its soul, mere 'phenomena'. The self, or soul, as 'a thing-in-itself' would, as far as pure reason is concerned, remain a completely unknowable noumenon.

At this point, it must be said, Kant's argumentation borders on the bizarre. In all debates about the human soul or spirit, the issue at stake is whether a human being is nothing but matter, or whether there is a non-material component in man's make-up.[44] By definition this non-material soul or spirit would be invisible. To argue, then, that for pure reason to admit the existence of this invisible component it would have to be empirically observable, and even then all you could observe would be its external *appearances*, is ludicrously beside the point. 'Appearances' is the language of *visual* observation. And if pure reason is going to refuse to believe in the existence of anything that is invisible and has no visual appearance, then it must refuse to believe in gravity, atomic radiation and magnetism.[45]

Practical reason and the soul

Having then proved to his satisfaction that the existence of the soul or spirit cannot be proved by pure reason, Kant proceeds to expound what the attitude of practical reason should be towards this question. At first, it sounds more positive.

At *Critique* B 419 he admits that each one of us has (what he calls) the apperception that 'I think, . . . as identical subject in every state of my thought', and that we know this unity of consciousness because without it we could not make sense of experience. He further admits that one cannot explain this apperception of the 'I' in soulless material terms.[46] He even goes so far as to say that practical reason

---

[44] For a fuller discussion of this topic see the discussion of the Monist/Dualist debate in Book 1: *Being Truly Human*, Ch. 5.

[45] It is only fair to Kant to say that he ran into this absurdity because he allowed himself to be convinced by Locke's and Hume's empiricism and their representative theory of perception. This obsession with visual perception is also to be found in modern continental phenomenology.

[46] Kant, *Pure Reason*, B 420.

would lead us 'to regulate our actions as if our destiny reached infinitely far beyond experience, and therefore beyond this present life'.[47] However, he advises us that practical reason would lead us to concentrate on objects of experience only, and would thus keep us 'from losing ourselves in a spiritualism which must be quite unfounded so long as we remain in this present life.'[48]

Once more we must ask: on what ground or authority does Kant's practical reason assure us that what Kant calls 'spiritualism' must be quite unfounded so long as we remain in this present life? It depends, of course, what he means by spiritualism. Perhaps he was referring to spiritism or occultism or excessive emotionalism masquerading as true spirituality, all of which are unhealthy and some positively dangerous.

But Kant notwithstanding, there is a true spirituality, and one does not have to wait until the life to come before one can experience it. 'God is spirit,' said Christ, 'and those who worship him must worship in spirit and truth' (John 4:24). Christ spoke of our need in this life to be 'born of the Spirit', that is, of the Spirit of God (John 3:1–8). Christ, moreover, has the power to impart to men and women the Spirit of God (John 7:38–39); and those who receive this gracious gift know the practical reality of the experience which Christ's apostle, Paul, describes this way:

> For all who are led by the Spirit of God are sons of God. For you did not receive the spirit of slavery to fall back into fear, but you have received the Spirit of adoption as sons, by whom we cry, 'Abba! Father!' The Spirit himself bears witness with our spirit that we are children of God. (Rom 8:14–16)

> God's love has been poured into our hearts through the Holy Spirit who has been given to us. (Rom 5:5)

Now this New Testament language is the language, not of abstract thinking, whether philosophical or theological; it is clearly the language of experience. Since, then, Kant's own fundamental principle of epistemology is that the content of all our knowledge is provided by experience, we naturally ask by what principle, and

---

[47] Kant, *Pure Reason*, B 421.
[48] Kant, *Pure Reason*, B 421.

by what authority, does he place the possibility of this experience beyond the boundary of this life?

Perhaps he would say that such spiritual experience is not an object of experience such as his practical reason advises us to concentrate on. Admittedly, God, Christ and the Holy Spirit are not an object of experience, if by object is meant a material object. But if Kant is saying that the only things available for our experience in this life are observable material objects, then he is handing us over to the very materialism that he professed to reject.

But then, Kant held, as we shall now see, that pure reason could not prove that God exists; and as for experience, God is not an object of possible experience.[49] We can form a speculative idea of God, but such an idea calls 'for an extension of our knowledge beyond all limits of experience, namely, to the existence of a being that is to correspond to a mere idea of ours, an idea that cannot be paralleled in any experience.'[50] If this is true, we must admit that it would be extremely difficult for anyone to have a personal relationship with a mere speculative idea. Let us now consider, therefore, Kant's reasons for this thesis.

Cosmology and theology

We may take these two areas of knowledge together because they are linked in Kant's thought.

The argument from causation and the argument from design

One of the traditional arguments for the existence of God has always been what Kant calls the cosmological, or the physico-theological, argument. Simply put, it says firstly that everything in the universe is contingent, that is, it has at some stage come into being, and therefore must have been caused by something else. If that is true of everything in the universe, it must be true of the universe as a whole: it too must have a cause. Then, unless there is going to be an infinite regress of causes, the cause of the universe's existence must be a something that

---

[49] See Kant, *Pure Reason*, A 636/B 664.
[50] Kant, *Pure Reason*, A 637–8/B 665–6.

did not owe its existence to anything else. It must be, not merely a first cause, but the uncaused cause of everything else.

The second argument is that the universe shows everywhere overwhelming evidence that it is a vastly complicated mechanism in which each part is deliberately and precisely designed to fulfil its particular function. Therefore the simplest and best possible explanation of it is that the universe is the creation of a divine Creator and Designer.[51]

Kant's objection to the argument from design

Now Kant is impressed by this second argument, as we earlier saw; but nevertheless he holds that it is not sufficient as proof for the existence of God. Why not? It is for two reasons. First, in his own words:

> The purposiveness and harmonious adaptation of so much in nature can suffice to prove the contingency of the form merely, not of the matter, that is, not of the substance in the world. . . . The utmost, therefore, that the argument can prove is an *architect* of the world who is always very much hampered by the adaptability of the material in which he works.[52]

But this argument is based on Kant's own presupposition that we can know the outward form of things but not their inner substance. But in his day no one knew the amazingly complicated engineering of the cell, or the marvels of the inside of an atom. To say that these evidences of design point only to an architect of the outward form of matter, and not a creator of its inner substance is not plausible.

Second, the argument from design, says Kant, points at best only to a designer, perhaps a very wise designer, but not to a being of the character we might suppose an almighty God would have.

The Bible would agree. It never claims that creation reveals God as 'merciful and gracious, slow to anger, and abounding in steadfast love and faithfulness' (Exod 34:6). What creation reveals is the Creator's everlasting power and divinity (Rom 1:20); and that, when Kant is dealing with practical and moral reason, he admits. What the Bible goes on to claim is that the God who revealed part of himself in

---

[51] For a discussion of this evidence see John Lennox's book *God's Undertaker: Has Science Buried God*, Chs. 4 and 5.
[52] Kant, *Pure Reason*, A 626–7/B 654–5.

creation, has fully revealed himself in holy Scripture and supremely in Christ who is God incarnate. By this additional revelation, God has bridged what for us would otherwise be an impassable gulf.

Kant's objections to the argument from causation

The first cosmological argument that we mentioned above, namely that God is the necessary uncaused cause of the universe—this argument Kant rejects entirely, for three reasons.

The first objection is that we can profitably talk of objects in the universe that are objects of observation, or possible observation. But we cannot profitably even think of the universe as a whole because it goes beyond all possible observation.

But modern science would hardly listen to this argument. It seriously attempts to reach justified conclusions about the size, age, rate of expansion and density of the universe as a whole, and even about the 'dark matter' in the universe.

The second objection is that: 'The principle of causality ... is only valid within the field of experience, and outside this field has no application, nay, is indeed meaningless.'[53] The only causes that we can know are either phenomena that we can observe, or, given observable things like stars, we can know that there must have been a cause of those stars in a previous state of affairs that in principle, at least, could have been observed. But God is by definition unobservable. We have no right to infer from some observable thing or event an unobservable cause.

But science constantly explains observable phenomena in terms of unobservable causes. Geiger counters click because they register invisible particles. Lines in cloud chambers indicate the effect of fast moving causes, i.e. electrons, protons, etc.

The third objection is that, if the supreme being were the cause of the series of natural causes of things and events in the universe, he must be part of that natural series. If the supreme being is not part of the series, 'by what bridge can reason contrive to pass over to it? For all laws governing the transition from effects to causes ... refer to nothing but possible experience, and therefore solely to objects

---

[53] Kant, *Pure Reason*, A 636/B 664.

in the sensible world, and apart from them can have no meaning whatsoever.'[54]

The Bible's answer to Kant's problem here is, as Kant must have known well, that God is the uncaused cause of the universe and all its systems of cause and effects, because he created the universe; but that he himself is not part of the universe and its systems because he created the universe not out of himself, but out of nothing by his word.

But, of course, to Kant's pure reason divine revelation was irrelevant. Pure reason would accept that experience of the external world was the sole provider of the content of its knowledge; but pure reason itself was the sole interpreter of that content. And according to his Copernican revolution, anything that did not conform to, or could not be proved by, pure reason was by definition unknowable. God himself could not tell pure reason anything. Practical reason might regard God as a necessary postulate of morality. Practical scientific investigation might regard the Creator as a helpful hypothetical origin of the purposiveness and order in the world. But if pure reason could not prove God's existence or determine his character, God himself must remain unknown and beyond all experience. Any idea that God himself could reveal himself, or anything at all, to pure reason, was out of the question. Human reason must be the sole and central judge of everything.

> Any idea that God himself could reveal himself, or anything at all, to pure reason, was out of the question. Human reason must be the sole and central judge of everything.

A critique of Kant's 'Critique'

The time has come, therefore, to pose a question to Kant. Pure reason owes its powers, so he tells us, to the two Forms of Sensibility and to the Categories of Understanding. Who or what then put these powers in the human mind? What authority stands behind the categories of understanding to give them their validity? If pure reason claims that the law that 'everything that happens has its cause' is an a priori principle of pure reason, from what source or cause did pure reason get

---

[54] Kant, *Pure Reason*, A 621–2/B 649–50.

this principle? If Kant were a modern, he might well reply that pure reason's powers simply evolved out of mindless matter (which would immediately cast doubt on the validity of pure reason). But Kant was not a modern. He professed to believe in God. Then ultimately the divine author of the world, as he called him, must have put these powers in the human mind. If so, how odd it is that God-given pure reason could not provide Kant with any certain knowledge of God, or experience of him—unless it is that Kant's Copernican revolution, which puts man's reason at the centre of the universe, perverts reason's true relation to God.

CHAPTER 4

REASON AND FAITH

In the practical affairs of life wisdom is more important than pure reason, and it is wisdom that regulates reason, rather than reason wisdom. The very word 'philosophy' means (in Greek) not 'love of reason' but 'love of wisdom'; and according to the ancient book of Proverbs (1:7) the beginning of wisdom is not the pursuit of rationality, but the fear of the Lord.

A FOURTH FALSE ALTERNATIVE

So far we have discussed three of four pairs of issues which confront epistemology: idealism and realism, subjective knowledge and objective knowledge, rationalism and empiricism. Now we must tackle the fourth pair: reason and faith. We shall find that, as with the other three pairs, so with this: it is not a question of rejecting one or the other, either reason or faith, but of using both reason and faith, each in its appropriate context.

To many people, however, reason and faith are mutually exclusive terms. Reason, they feel, delivers proved and indubitable facts which everybody who is of sound mind must in the end accept; and these facts, once accepted, constitute genuine, certain knowledge. Moreover, once they have been established by reason, you don't have to try to *believe* them: you *know* them. Not to accept them would be irrational. As examples people often cite the facts established by science, though science is far from being an operation of unaccompanied pure reason.

Faith, by contrast, they feel, has to do with things that, by definition, cannot be known for certain or proved to be true. That is why you have to have faith to believe them. If they could rationally be proved, they say, and thus known for certain, you would not need faith in order to accept them as true. Reason and faith, then, are to their way of thinking mutually exclusive.

This, as we shall remember from our last chapter, was Kant's view. He held that only pure reason could deliver sure and certain knowledge. Since, then, according to him, the existence of God could not be proved by pure reason, no one could know for certain that God exists: 'No one, indeed, will be able to boast that he *knows* that there is a God.'[1] Curiously enough, his idea, that no one could *know* that God exists, seemed to gratify him, because in his view this very

---

[1] Kant, *Pure Reason*, A 828–9/B 856–7.

uncertainty made possible the exercise of faith: 'I have . . . found it necessary to deny *knowledge*, in order to make room for *faith*.'[2] Nevertheless, he held that in the interests of moral behaviour it was necessary to postulate the existence of God, and on those grounds he personally felt morally certain that God exists.

Many people, however, find it impossible to adopt Kant's double stance. They hold that Kant's denial that God's existence can be proved by pure reason effectively removes the topic of God's existence from any rational discussion. They have no objection if other people choose to believe in God; but for themselves they decide that faith in a God whose existence cannot be proved is irrational. The only rational way to live, they feel, is not to believe anything that cannot be proved by pure reason.

REASON

The limitations of pure reason

A moment's reflection, however, will show that all of us do in fact believe in a hundred and one things that have never been proved by pure reason. We must ask ourselves therefore: if it is not irrational to believe in these things, why is it irrational to believe in God?

From childhood, for instance, we have all believed in the existence of the other members of our family, or of our class at school, without their existence having been proved by pure reason. What is more, we believe that other people have minds, as we do ourselves, which is even more difficult to prove by pure abstract reason.

In illness, we are obliged to trust the diagnosis and the treatment given by surgeons—and we are prepared to risk our lives on it, though proving them right in advance by pure reason is out of the question. Our knowledge of history is likewise largely dependent on the opinion of expert historians; and by definition historical events are not necessary, universal truths such as pure reason delivers. They are contingent truths; their contraries are not unthinkable; they

---

[2] Kant, *Pure Reason*, B xxx.

could have been otherwise. They cannot be proved by pure reason. We do not regard it as irrational to be guided here by the principles of high probability and trust in credible authority.

Or take the universe. How did we come to believe in its existence, and on what grounds do we continue to believe that it exists? Was it that at first we did not know if it existed, or were uncertain whether it existed or not, until someone sat down beside us and proved its existence by pure reason; and then, and only then, did we know for certain that the universe existed? No, indeed not. The vast majority of us have known for certain that the universe exists, ever since we have known anything. Its existence did not have to be proved. We were immediately and directly aware of it. It was a given; and we discovered it by experience through our senses.

As any philosopher would point out, it would be very difficult, or even impossible, in fact, to prove the existence of the universe by pure reason. We ourselves are part of the universe. If, then, we did not already exist, and take our own existence for granted, we could not even question whether the universe exists or not, let alone prove it does. In other words, we would first have to *assume* that part of the universe, namely ourselves, exists, before we could even begin to prove its existence. But we surely do not regard ourselves as irrational for believing in the existence of the universe without first proving its existence by pure reason.

Of course, it may well be objected that believing that the universe exists is different from believing in God's existence. We have come to know that the universe—and we ourselves—exist, through experience, through our senses and practical reason; our knowledge, therefore, is based on a large amount of indubitable evidence. But, so the objection goes, we cannot get to know that God exists by such means, can we? Does not belief in God's existence require an act of naked faith without any evidence? No, not really; but we shall deal with that question presently. For the moment we must continue with the limitations of reason.

Human reason did not create the universe

This point is so obvious that at first it might seem trivial; but actually it is of fundamental importance when we come to assess the validity of our cognitive faculties. Let's consider once more the scientific investigation of the universe.

Science, as we know, employs not pure reason alone, but practical reason, intuition, experiment, and heuristic hypotheses, etc. Its goal, however, at least in the opinion of most scientists, is not to impose on the matter and workings of the universe our human sense of order but to unveil and discover the universe's own order and intelligibility. That means, of course, that science has always had to assume, before it started its investigations, that the universe does have an inherent order and intelligibility. If it didn't, scientific research would never discover them, and research would be fruitless and pointless.

Even now, after all their successes, scientists still have to make this basic assumption, if scientific research is to be thought still worth pursuing. The behaviour of elementary particles presents us with quantum phenomena that for the moment outstrip our reason, intuition and powers of imagination. Various theories are proposed; none is universally accepted. The same is true of the question of human consciousness: no one yet understands it; no theory has produced general agreement. In this situation, for research to continue requires faith—faith that nature's intelligibility and order will not peter out into unintelligible chaos (though for all we know they might eventually involve a level of intelligibility higher than we can at present grasp).

Faith, then, in something that has not yet been proved, still is, as it always has been, a prerequisite for scientific investigation of the universe. Shall we therefore accuse science of irrationality? Of course not.

Reason's underlying authority

If we have not already done so, we need to realize that pure reason is not our only cognitive faculty. We have others: intuition, the five senses, practical reason and memory. All agree that among the other faculties, reason, both pure and applied, has an important regulative role. Even so, it would not be true to say that reason should be given the supreme regulative function. In the practical affairs of life wisdom is more important than pure reason, and it is wisdom that regulates reason, rather than reason wisdom. The very word 'philosophy' means (in Greek) not 'love of reason' but 'love of wisdom'; and according to the ancient book of Proverbs (1:7) the beginning of wisdom is not the pursuit of rationality, but the fear of the Lord.

Moreover, in naming their intellectual discipline 'the love of wisdom', the early Greek philosophers, like Plato, pointed to the importance of right motivation in the pursuit of wisdom, namely love. Certainly when it comes to knowledge of our fellow human beings, love and its closely related qualities of empathy and compassion are more likely to arrive at a true diagnosis and understanding of a person's behaviour and actions, than is the cold, dispassionate logic of pure reason. A person who loves her botany, zoology, music, literature or physics is likely to achieve a deeper and richer understanding of her subject than a student who studies these things simply because she is compelled to. And the same thing is true when it comes to knowledge of God: 'If anyone imagines that he knows something, he does not yet know as he ought to know. But if anyone loves God, he is known by God' (1 Cor 8:2–3).

'If anyone imagines that he knows something, he does not yet know as he ought to know. But if anyone loves God, he is known by God' (1 Cor 8:2–3)

But we must return to pure reason and the question of what authority lies behind it. Kant spent many pages describing the 'Categories of Pure Reason' that, according to him, determine what we can and what we cannot know about the universe, about God, the soul and the life to come. Whatever does not conform to our categories of pure reason, he claimed, cannot be known by us. But Kant never told us from what or where the categories of pure reason derive their authority.

Obviously we human beings did not create our own powers of reason. We can develop them by use and practice; but we did not originate them. How can it be, then, that pure reason in our tiny heads can give us anything near a true account of reality? Is pure reason (or any other of our cognitive faculties) an instrument deliberately designed to enable us to discover, recognise and believe the truth? What original authority, and hence what reliability, does pure reason have?

Atheists, of course, deny any deliberate design by a creator. But they still believe that reason does have a proper function and purpose in the same sense as, say, the heart does. The heart's purpose is to pump the blood round the body; whereas a cancerous growth has no proper purpose or function within the human body: it results from purposeless, chaotic growth.

Moreover, atheists reveal their belief that the faculty of reason is in this sense 'designed' to fulfil the purpose of discovering the truth, by asserting that belief in the existence of God results from a misuse of reason. Obviously if reason had no proper function, no one could be accused of misusing it. But many follow Freud's contention that all the apparently rational arguments put forward by believers for the existence of God are in fact driven and perverted by a hidden, subconscious wish-fulfilment-mechanism: the desire to construct for themselves a crutch to help them through life's difficulties; whereas reason, unperverted, would achieve its proper purpose and discover the truth, namely atheism.

The irony of the atheists' position, however, becomes apparent as soon as one enquires about the origin of our human faculty of reason. For atheists hold that the driving force of evolution, which eventually produced our human cognitive faculties, reason included, was not primarily concerned with truth at all, but with survival. And we all know what has generally happened—and still happens—to truth when individuals, or commercial enterprises, or nations, motivated by what Richard Dawkins calls their 'selfish genes', feel themselves threatened and struggle for survival.

How, then, is it *rational* to believe in the theory (not, we note, proved by pure reason) that the evolution of our faculty of reason was not directed for the purpose of discovering the truth; and yet *irrational* to believe that our faculty of reason was designed and created by our Maker to enable us to understand and believe the truth?

THE NATURE OF THEISM'S FAITH

Epistemology, by its very nature, is especially interested in propositions or statements. The reason for that is that it is concerned, not with *whom* we know, so much as with *what* we know and with how we can justify our claim to know what we know. To test our claim it must first get us to state it; and it prefers us to state it in propositional form, i.e. in the form 'I know *that* so-and-so is such and such'. If, for instance, I say 'I know *that* there is life on other planets', I can then set about examining my claim to know this, and how I know it, and whether the fact, which I claim to know, is true.

If, on the other hand, I make a non-propositional statement, as for instance, 'I feel a pain in my stomach', epistemology, with its merely rational analysis, cannot so easily set about examining its truth. A doctor might examine me and decide that I have no reason to feel a pain in my stomach. But if I feel a pain, who is to tell me that I don't? If, moreover, I issue a command, such as 'Please shut the door', the question, 'Is this true or not?' does not arise; epistemologists, as such, would not be interested in it. Similarly epistemology does not concern itself so much with knowledge of persons. If I say 'I know my grandmother as a person', epistemology cannot so easily analyse the truth of this statement.

If, then, epistemologists meet someone who says 'I believe in a kind and loving God', they will tend to rephrase this statement of faith in the form of a proposition: 'I believe that God exists and that he is kind and loving', and then to ask how the speaker knows these facts, and how he can prove that they are true. An atheistic epistemologist is likely to add: 'If you can't first prove that there is a God (and you can't), it's no use your claiming to know that he is kind and loving.'

> A theist's faith does not rest first and foremost in a proposition, or in a number of logical arguments that support that proposition. The theist's faith rests in a person, the living Lord God, who has so revealed himself that the believer is directly aware of him.

A theist (if he understands his faith) might well decline the challenge first to prove that God exists, before saying anything about his qualities. That is not because there are not powerful arguments to support faith in God's existence: there are.[3] But the challenge rests on a false assumption. A theist's faith does not rest first and foremost

---

[3] The 'ontological' argument states that everything we observe in the universe is contingent, that is, it owes its being to something else. The sum total of these contingent beings is what we call the universe. It too, therefore, is a contingent being. There must therefore be a non-contingent, necessary, Being which is the source of all other, contingent, beings but which itself does not owe its existence to any other being. This is what is meant by 'God'. If there were not such a Being, nothing at all would exist. For more on the 'cosmological' argument see John Lennox's book *God's Undertaker: Has Science Buried God*, Chs. 4 and 5. We have dealt with the 'moral' argument in detail in Book 1: *Being Truly Human*, Ch. 3.

in a proposition, or in a number of logical arguments that support that proposition. The theist's faith rests in a person, the living Lord God, who has so revealed himself that the believer is directly aware of him. A believer in God, therefore, being told that he must first prove that God exists before claiming to know anything about God's attributes, might well consider that demand to be like telling a sheep that it must first prove that its shepherd exists before it can know the shepherd and be fed by him.

A believer's basic position, then, is this: his faith in God is grounded objectively in God's self-revelation; and subjectively it is acquired through a God-created and implanted instinct that, when it is not atrophied or repressed, as it can be, naturally perceives and responds to that divine, objective, self-revelation.

God's self-revelation through creation

A biblical passage that expresses this point forcefully runs as follows:

> What can be known about God is plain to them [lit: 'in them', Gk. *en autois*], because God has shown it to them [Gk.: *autois*]. For his invisible attributes, namely, his eternal power and divine nature, have been clearly perceived, ever since the creation of the world, in the things that have been made. So they are without excuse. For although they knew God, they did not honour him as God or give thanks to him. (Rom 1:19–21)

This passage is making a number of points:

1. God has taken the initiative in making himself known to us by first creating us and placing us in a universe designed and created to express, not merely his existence, but something of what he is like.
2. What the visible creation objectively shows us is two of his attributes: his eternal power and divinity.
3. We perceive these things directly, intuitively, not by a long process of discursive, logical reasoning.
4. So that we could perceive the significance of what we see as we contemplate God's creation, he created within us, not

only our cognitive faculties in general, but an instinctive faculty of awareness of God.

The implications of God's self-revelation

Point 1 seems eminently reasonable. If God is the self-existent, transcendent Lord and Creator of all, and if there are going to be creatures capable of recognising and getting to know him, he must take the initiative in making himself known to them and in choosing by what means and to what extent and on what terms he may graciously allow them to get to know him. To that end he must create in them the necessary faculty for receiving that knowledge and set the goal to be aimed at in imparting that knowledge of himself to them. The almighty Creator God could not, without ceasing to be himself, reduce himself to a mere object, not even the biggest object in or outside the universe, which human beings could investigate and get to know in whatever way and by whatever means they might choose. Getting to know something sets up a relationship between the knower and the known. God is the Great Subject, and we human beings are in the first place simply objects that he created, but objects that he so created that by his grace they could themselves become subjects that might come to know him. But obviously the relationship that would thus be formed would be by his initiative and on his terms.

Creation shows God's power and divinity to men and women

Point 2 seems likewise realistic. It does not claim that God's love and mercy can be read off the surface of creation. The two things about God that can be perceived through creation are said to be his eternal power and divinity, that is, his Godhead.

That the universe expresses and exhibits unimaginably vast power is a self-evident fact acknowledged by everyone without exception; and throughout history humankind has also felt and expressed the stark contrast between the brief span of human life and the everlastingness of the universe. Modern science has but increased the contrast. The crucial question is the nature of the source of that power. What the universe shows, according to our passage, is that the source of that power, as to its nature, is deity. That is, it is more than human;

it is, to say the least, supernatural and superhuman. The source is God.

Atheists and agnostics often allege that people who believe in God are guilty of anthropomorphism. They have created God in their own image and think of him in human terms and categories but simply on a larger scale (just as, so it is said, elephants would think of God as an almighty elephant if they ever got round to thinking about it). It is a very ancient criticism, but it is not true. It was long ago answered by Jewish philosophers such as the Alexandrian, Aristobulus, known as 'the Peripatetic' (mid-second century BC). Thoughtful believers know that when the Bible speaks of God's hands and eyes, etc., it is using poetic, metaphorical and analogical language.

The substantive point that our biblical passage is making is this: it is evident from creation that our Creator is, not *less*, but *more*, than we are. If we are persons (and not just matter or machines or mere animals) then our Maker is certainly not less than personal. If we have eyes and can see, he is not blind. If we have tongues and can communicate, he is certainly not dumb. And he who has given us ears to receive communications and minds to understand them, is certainly able to communicate with us, if he so pleases.[4]

It is the atheist, in fact, who is irrational here. He has to believe that humankind's source was something much less than humankind itself, such as mindless matter, or a very clever but abstract set of impersonal, mathematical laws.[5]

But there is more to this prime self-revelation of God to man: it sets out with unmistakable clarity what the basic relationship between man and God, between the creature and the Creator, is and ever must be. It is not a relationship of reciprocal equality. It can never be that. The human race exists and lives in utter dependence on God, whether they acknowledge it or not.

Kant, of course, and a good many others, would claim that it is philosophically unsound to jump to conclusions about the invisible qualities of God on the basis of the visible universe. But the objection is invalid. Faced with a dead body, a detective can rightly conclude on the basis of the visible evidence before him that the death was not natural, nor suicide, but the result of an intention to murder—

---

[4] Cf. the argument of Ps 94:9, 'He who planted the ear, does he not hear? He who formed the eye, does he not see?'

[5] See Paul Davies's theory, Book 2: *Seeking Ultimate Reality*, Ch. 3.

though neither the detective nor anyone else has ever seen an intention. An intention itself is invisible: only its effects are visible.

Creation shows God's power and divinity in men and women

Points 3 and 4 above assert that through creation God has made his eternal power and divinity evident, not only *to* men (Gk. *autois*), but *in* them (Gk. *en autois*). That is to say, that along with all of a human's other cognitive powers, God originally placed in human beings a faculty of direct awareness of God that can be activated by our contemplation of the created universe. This means that we perceive God's power and divinity, not by some logical process, by first laying down some axiom and then deducing each step by careful logic until we prove to ourselves the proposition that God exists. No, we perceive these attributes of God intuitively, in the same way as we perceive that a rose is beautiful or that the universe exists.

> Along with all man's other cognitive powers, God originally placed in human beings a faculty of direct awareness of God that can be activated by our contemplation of the created universe.

This is only fair; for there are multitudes of men and women who have neither the leisure nor the ability to engage personally in sophisticated philosophical argument in order to prove the existence of God. Yet for a man or woman's knowledge of God to be real and living, each man and each woman must come to know God for himself and herself and enter thus into his or her own relationship with God. No one can know God by proxy or at second hand. If therefore, God had so arranged it that one could not begin to know God unless one had first proved by philosophical reasoning that God exists, such elitism would have been grotesquely unfair of God.

And there is yet more to be said about this direct awareness of God. God is not against reason. Reason is one of his own gifts to the human race; and he exhorts people to use it to the full in its proper context (1 Cor 14:20). But God has not given humans reason so that they can, independently of God's self-revelation, decide whether God exists or not. Human reason is not the arbiter in this matter. If men and women pridefully think that the only route to knowing whether God exists is by first using their reason independently of God to prove whether he exists or not, God may well bypass them, while he makes himself directly known to the humble. Christ put it this way: 'I thank you, Father, Lord of heaven and earth, that you have hidden these things from the wise and understanding and revealed them to little children' (Matt 11:25). And the New Testament adds: 'in the wisdom of God, the world did not know God through wisdom' (1 Cor 1:21).

Basic beliefs

In the past few decades there has been a revival of interest among philosophers in the fact that we all believe in various things simply because we are immediately aware of them. Our belief, in these instances, is not dependent on the evidential basis of some other propositions; in other words our belief is not arrived at by logical deduction or inference from some premise. These beliefs are called 'prior beliefs' by some philosophers,[6] or 'properly basic beliefs' by others.[7]

Examples are:

1. **perception**. You pass by a garden and see that some roses have burst into bloom. You do not then begin a logical process: 'I have an impression of redness of a certain shape; from that I construct the idea of a rose; and from that I deduce that it was a rose in bloom that made this impression on my mind; therefore, and on that ground, I finally believe that some roses are now in bloom.' No, we are immediately and directly aware of roses in bloom, and we believe it solely on that basis. We do not require it to be proved to us on some other basis.
2. **memory**. Some memories can be confused or mistaken. But some are so luminous and vivid that we are absolutely sure that they are true. Asked what I had for dinner last night, I might hesitate for a moment, but then the memory comes flooding back so vividly, that I reply with every confidence: 'soup, beef and potatoes'. I require no external evidence to prove it.
3. **a priori truths**. That $1 + 1 = 2$ is not a truth that has to be proved on the basis of some other propositions or by deduction from some premise. I am immediately aware that it is

---

[6] See, e.g. Richard Swinburne, *Faith and Reason*, 36–7, 43.
[7] See, e.g. Alvin Plantinga, *Warranted Christian Belief*, 175 ff.

true. I 'see' it, and I need no other evidence on which to base my belief that $1 + 1 = 2$.

In that same way belief in God's existence is properly basic. It is occasioned by the contemplation of the wonders of creation, from the majesty and awesomeness of the night sky to the perfection of a baby's fingernails, and by the awareness, which wrongdoing brings, of having transgressed the moral law and of being guilty before its Author. Kant, though he argued that God's existence would not be proved by pure reason, yet confessed: 'Two things fill the mind with ever new and increasing admiration and awe the more often and more enduringly reflection is occupied with them: the starry heavens above me and the moral law within me.'[8]

To sum up so far then. A theist's faith is based first and foremost, not in philosophical and logical proofs of God's existence, but in God's self-revelation. Secondly, a theist does not deny the importance of true propositions about God. The Bible itself demands that 'whoever would draw near to God must believe that he exists and that he rewards those who seek him' (Heb 11:6); and there for you are two propositions to start with that have to be believed. At the same time, a theist recognises that a belief in a logically proved proposition, even about God, is not the same thing as a faith in a personal God arising as a response to his personal self-revelation.

AWARENESS OF GOD

The claim that our Creator has made us with an inbuilt awareness of God is liable to be met by an immediate protest: 'It is not true. *I* have no such inbuilt awareness of God.' And if a theist answers: 'That's because there is something wrong, some defect, in you', it will appear to many people, not to strengthen, but to weaken, the theist's case. Anyone, they will say, could prove that there are ten moons circling the earth, if, when people object that they cannot see them, they are told 'that's because there's something wrong with you'. When, therefore, many people claim that they have no awareness of God, a theist

---

[8] Kant, *Pure Reason*, Guyer tr., 1.

will want to investigate their reasons. But they are by no means all the same.

Reasons for claiming no awareness of God

The problem of evil and suffering

This is, perhaps, the most common reason why thoughtful and sensitive people reject faith in God. The existence of widespread, enormous evil, pain and natural disasters seems to them to make the existence of God unthinkable—unless God should turn out to be a monster; in which case they would refuse to believe in him or worship him anyway. Ivan Karamazov, in Fyodor Dostoevsky's classic novel *The Brothers Karamozov*, is typical. Faced with enormous cruelty to children, with the corruption and power politics that he saw in the church, and, above all, God's apparent failure to intervene, he found it morally impossible to maintain faith in God, even though he did not deny God's existence. Dostoevsky makes him say: 'It isn't God I don't accept, Alyosha, it's just his ticket that I most respectfully return to him.'[9] This is a genuine and serious difficulty; we shall try to answer it in one of the later books in this series.[10]

A basic antagonism to God and to the idea of God

One example is Professor Thomas Nagel: 'It isn't just that I don't believe in God and, naturally, hope there is no God! I don't want there to be a God; I don't want the universe to be like that.'[11] Or this from Professor Paul Davies: 'I'm assuming that God did not intervene to make life. I don't want that.'[12]

Peer pressure

In his day, Nietzsche described the suppression of awareness of God by the peer pressure of the political, social and educational establishment of his day:

---

[9] Dostoevsky, *The Karamazov Brothers*, 320.
[10] See Book 6: *Suffering Life's Pain*.
[11] *Last Word*, 130.
[12] Wilkinson, 'Found in space?', 20. Cf. the array of similar sentiments listed in 'The motivation behind dogmatic atheism', Book 1: *Being Truly Human*, Ch. 2 (p. 63).

> Pious or even merely church-going people seldom realise *how much* good will, one might even say wilfulness, it requires nowadays for a German scholar to take the problem of religion seriously; his whole trade . . . disposes him to a superior, almost good-natured merriment in regard to religion, sometimes mixed with a mild contempt . . . The practical indifference to religious things in which he was born and raised is as a rule sublimated in him into a caution . . . which avoids contact with religious people and things . . . how much naivety . . . there is in the scholar's belief in his superiority . . . in the simple unsuspecting certainty with which his instinct treats the religious man as an inferior and lower type which he himself has grown beyond and *above*.[13]

Atrophy

The absent-minded professor is proverbial. He is so totally engrossed in his particular subject that he ceases to be aware of the practicalities of life. In another person an early interest in music, art or poetry can be so overlaid and stifled by business concerns that eventually it atrophies. So is it with awareness of God. Neglect it and overlay it for years with other dominant interests, and, as Christ put it in his famous parable, the thorns grow up and choke it.[14]

Fear

Some people are afraid that if they acknowledge God it will lead to loss of personal freedom and will restrict their lifestyle. Others are loath to accept that there is a God, for the thought of God awakens feelings of guilt that they have tried to repress and forget.

The Bible's answer for why people are not aware of God

Doubtless there are many other causes why people profess not to have any awareness of God—though even atheists have been known in times of acute danger, instinctively to call out to God to save them. But according to the Bible these causes all stem from, and are a continuation of, what happened when the race was young.

---

[13] Nietzsche, *Beyond Good and Evil*, para. 58 (Hollingdale, 65–6).
[14] Matt 13, Mark 4, Luke 8.

If one reads the Bible as a whole, and follows its developing storyline, one discovers that it bears witness to what Bible scholars have called the progress of revelation. God did not reveal everything about himself all at once, as soon as he had created the first man and woman. The Bible records rather what could be called God's progressive education of the human race from its morally innocent babyhood, through its moral childhood, teenage and eventual mature adulthood, each stage being promoted by a further revelation of himself.

The culmination of the Bible in the New Testament, however, makes clear that, right from the very start, God's purpose in the creation of humankind was to have creatures with whom he could have ever increasing, personal relationship. The human race's experience of God, therefore, was never intended to consist merely in knowing certain propositions about God—though they would certainly learn many propositions about him. The human race's experience of God was intended to be an ever growing, conscious, filial relationship. For that purpose men and women were created with such faculties as made them immediately aware of God, as a little child is immediately aware of its human father. At later times the Bible speaks of God treating his people as a father does a growing child and teenager (Gal 4:1-3), by putting them under the firm but loving discipline of the Ten Commandments and many laws beside and, where necessary, chastising their disobediences (Deut 8:1-6). But here again the underlying purpose was to encourage not only developing character and good behaviour but a relational response of love for God and neighbour: 'You shall love the LORD your God with all your heart and with all your soul and with all your might' (Deut 6:5); and 'You shall love your neighbour as yourself' (Lev 19:18).

There is no true knowledge of God outside of some relationship with him. When God makes himself known to us, it is always in some relational situation. He never reveals himself as a merely theoretical proposition.

The culmination of this process was designed to be the sending of the Son of God into the world with authority to effect for all who would receive him their 'adoption as sons of God'. They would remain human still. They would never become God. But they would no longer be merely creatures of God; they would become children of God in a genuine ontological sense.[15]

Knowledge of God, then, in the Bible is relational knowledge. That relationship between God and his people is described in various ways: Creator and creature, God and man, Father and child, Father and grown-up son, Shepherd and sheep, Lover and bride, Husband and wife, Redeemer, Saviour, Friend, Lord, Master, Counsellor, final Judge. There is, indeed, no true knowledge of God outside of some relationship with him. When God makes himself known to us, it is always in some relational situation. He never reveals himself as a merely theoretical proposition.

The original false turn that humanity took in relation to God

This false turn, according to the Bible, was not occasioned by any lack of evidence for God's existence. It arose in the area of man's relationship with God. A relationship that has no boundaries is scarcely a relationship. In human affairs, for example, a marriage that is not bounded is not true marriage. So God set a boundary condition to man's relationship with him, by forbidding him to eat of the tree of the knowledge of good and evil (Gen 3). But man was not content to stay within the boundary. He grasped at knowledge independent of God. Man would be as God, and make up his own mind about what was good and what was evil, as though in this respect man could stand on equal terms with God.

According to the Bible this was the basic lie that Satan insinuated into man's thinking, for no creature can in any absolute sense ever be independent of the Creator (see Gen 3). But the initial temptation to grasp independence of God has spread like a virus down the centuries. Multitudes have suppressed the awareness of God, says the Bible (Rom 1:18–32). One telltale result of it is that they are no longer grateful for the wonderful gifts of life. They are glad of them, and enjoy them. But the lovely natural human instinct to be grateful to the giver for good gifts given has died in them. Denying the Creator, they have no one to be grateful to. It's very difficult to be grateful to a protoplasm or a mindless Big Bang. And denying the true God, men

---

[15] See John 1:11–13; Rom 8:14–17, 26–30; 1 John 3:1–2.

make themselves idols, deifying the forces of nature or human reason or human passion.[16]

But for a man or woman to live as if there were no Creator is to live an unrealistic untruth, and in alienation from the source of his or her being. For a man or woman in that condition to demand that God, in some kind of Kant-like Copernican revolution, submit himself to human reason as the ultimate arbiter as to whether or not he may rightly be thought to exist or not, is both sad and logically absurd. The brains and breath he uses to make his demand depend on the Creator.

Conditions for knowing God

All true knowledge of God, then, is relational and not just theoretical, and it carries lifelong practical implications. On our side, therefore, it depends on our willingness to swallow our pride, give up our independent stance and enter into personal relation with God. And God for his part, of course, lays down the conditions upon which he is prepared to make himself known to us.

1. We must start by acknowledging that he exists and that he rewards those who diligently seek him (Heb 11:6).
2. Our seeking must be in earnest. We may not treat God casually. 'You shall seek me and find me, when you shall search for me with all your heart' (Jer 29:13).
3. We must turn from our idols, whether material or mental. And if we have up until now put our ultimate trust in human reason, and made of it an idol in the place of God, we must repent of that misuse of reason as well (see 1 Cor 1:18–31).
4. We must be prepared to do the will of God, when he shows it to us. In this connection Christ himself said 'If anyone's will is to do God's will, he will know whether the teaching is from God or whether I am speaking on my own authority' (John 7:17).

Anyone who treats the question of God's existence as a matter of mere academic interest with no implications for the way he runs

---

[16] See the longer discussion of this topic in Book 1: *Being Truly Human*, Ch. 2.

his life, will not get far in his knowledge of God. On the other hand Christ has given us his assurance:

> And I tell you, ask, and it will be given to you; seek, and you will find; knock, and it will be opened to you. For everyone who asks receives, and the one who seeks finds, and to the one who knocks it will be opened. (Luke 11:9–10)

The test of genuine knowledge of God

But we must finally return to epistemology's demand that, if we claim to have knowledge, we must be prepared to justify our claim. If then we claim to know God, what kind of justification would be appropriate to validate our claim to have this kind of knowledge? The Bible admits epistemology's demand and replies:

> And by this we know that we have come to know him, if we keep his commandments. Whoever says 'I know him' but does not keep his commandments is a liar, and the truth is not in him, but whoever keeps his word, in him truly the love of God is perfected. By this we may know that we are in him: whoever says he abides in him ought to walk in the same way in which he walked. (1 John 2:3–6)

In other words true knowledge of God will lead to living and loving as Christ lived and loved.

WHAT IS TRUTH?

CHAPTER 5

IN SEARCH OF TRUTH

Great is truth and strongest of all.

1 Esdras 4:35

Buy the truth and do not sell it.

Proverbs 23:23

WHAT WE ARE LOOKING FOR

In this and the following three chapters we set out to examine the question: What is truth? We shall be concerned not merely with the *content* of truth, i.e. what facts, propositions or beliefs are true, but with the *nature* of truth, i.e. what does a belief or a statement have to be in order to qualify as being true? In other words, how should we define truth?

In addition we shall be asking whether there is such a thing as absolute truth, which is objectively true and exists independently of us and of our beliefs or feelings, or whether there is no absolute truth about anything but only various, partial truths which we create for ourselves, or society creates for us, by choosing to accept them or to construct them out of life's experience. In other words, is there such a thing as absolute truth which everybody must accept simply because it is true; or is there only 'truth for us', which we accept because we like it and it suits us, but which is not necessarily true for others if it does not suit them or they don't like it?

Now this is a very far-reaching topic since it affects our lives, not only academically, but practically, individually, socially, commercially, legally, politically and religiously, and carries implications for what we regard as history and art, and for our standards of behaviour in family life, at work and in sport. Since this is so, we ought, perhaps, to begin by considering our own personal attitude to truth.

Our ambivalent attitude to truth

Whatever theoretical philosophy or theology says about the nature of truth, all of us know in our hearts that there is another level to the question of truth besides the academic and intellectual discussion of it. Truth, however we define it, has an uncanny and indisputable authority that silently, yet insistently and undeniably, calls for our submission and loyalty. Not only *our* submission: we expect others to bow to it as well.

Suppose you were brought before a court charged with a serious offence that you had not in fact committed. Suppose further that the prosecution's case was very cleverly contrived and coherent and persuasive but nonetheless false. You would, of course, put forward the true facts, as you knew them, to prove your innocence. But suppose the judge in giving his verdict announced that there was no such thing as objective truth; and therefore he was not interested in trying to decide what the truth of this case was. Each side was entitled to its own story, and it was wrong for either side to claim that the other side's story was wrong. All truth was culturally determined anyway; and he, therefore, was going to decide the case not on the ground of truth, but on the ground that the prosecution's case appealed to his sensibilities and cultural background.

Truth, however we define it, has an uncanny and indisputable authority that silently, yet insistently and undeniably, calls for our submission and loyalty.

You would be outraged, as would all right-minded people, for without regard for objective truth there can be no justice. At one level, therefore, we all believe in truth, and demand that it be upheld. But on other occasions and in different circumstances we find the truth unwelcome and do our best to avoid it, or hide it, or misrepresent it or deny it outright.

The interesting thing, however, is that when we compromise our allegiance to the truth, and substitute some falsehood for it, we still show by our subsequent actions our awareness of the intrinsic authority of truth. None of us would ever say, publicly at least: 'I know that such and such is true, but I hate the truth and am not prepared to accept it. I shall do all I can to oppose and destroy the truth and to propagate in its place what I know to be a lie' (though heaven knows that this has been the hidden inner motive of many individuals and even governments in the course of history).

And yet again, if we succeed in suppressing the truth and propagating a falsehood in its place, we do not of course advertise our version as falsehood. We still call it the truth, thus bearing witness, even in our falsehood, to the authority of truth, which we have now betrayed. There is obviously a reason why we do not call it falsehood:

no one would believe a falsehood—that is, no one would publicly admit to believing a falsehood knowing it to be false, though often people privately and indeed publicly have preferred to go along with a falsehood rather than risk unpopularity or worse by standing up for an embarrassing truth.

Right at the outset, then, as we begin to study what truth is, we need to face this curious ambivalence in our personal attitude to truth and then to ask ourselves what the reason is for this ambivalence. It could affect our decisions as to what truth is.

OBJECTIONS AND REJECTIONS

Objections to the idea of universal objective truth

Perhaps there has never been a period in this last two thousand years like our present one when the idea of universal objective truth has been so widely and thoroughly disputed and denied. Let us briefly list some of the main reasons given for this attitude to truth and then try to understand how they have arisen.

Reason 1 – The limitations of language

All human language consists of symbols, the meaning of which is culturally determined by the particular society that created them. Meaning can be transferred from one person or from one society to another only by conveying the meaning expressed in one set of symbols through another alien set of symbols invented by a different society, and therefore carrying the cultural and emotional connotations of that second different society. In such a process, it is claimed, no universal, objective truth, even if there were such a thing, could survive completely undistorted. What truth survived could not but be relativised by the process.

Reason 2 – The limitations of knowledge

For anyone to claim to possess the total truth about anything in particular or about the universe in general is manifestly false. Neither science nor philosophy could achieve anything like such total knowledge. All knowledge is therefore only relatively true.

Reason 3 – The arrogance of so-called objective truth

All truth is culturally conditioned: what is truth for one culture is not truth for another. In a multicultural world, for one culture to claim that it alone has the truth and all others are false is insufferably arrogant, and leads in the end to violence.

Reason 4 – Objective truth enslaves

The concept of universal objective truth is oppressive. It demands total submission; it pays no regard to individual personality, and it destroys the creativeness of the human spirit. The fact is that each human spirit must be free to create truth for itself. We do not necessarily create the external facts; but we create the truth about them.

Reason 5 – Claims to objective truth are elitist and undemocratic

The philosopher/scientist Roger Bacon (c.1214–92) maintained that 'knowledge is power'. Many thinkers nowadays assert the contrary, that 'power is knowledge'. They hold that it is experts in various disciplines who gain power simply because they are regarded as experts. They then use that power to create knowledge that they proceed to impose on the general populace, even when that 'knowledge' is not in fact true and is subsequently discovered to have been false.

Some underlying reasons for this rejection of objective truth

The past enforcement of ideologies and religions by sheer power

Past and recent history contains notable examples.

In AD 303, for instance, the Roman emperor Diocletian decided to re-impose the universal authority of pagan Rome's state religion. To that end he not only persecuted Christians, as several of his predecessors had done: he decided to uproot and destroy Christianity itself root and branch. All Christian books and Bibles had to be handed in for confiscation, on pain of death. Free thought in religious matters was not to be allowed.

In mediaeval times and for centuries thereafter, Christendom itself—or major sections of it—used its influence with the State not only to persecute Jews and Muslims, and those whom it regarded as heretics, but to forbid individual Christians to possess copies of the

Bible and to read and seek to understand them for themselves. They had to accept as truth whatever the Church declared truth to be. Individual understanding and conscience were not allowed.

In the twentieth century ideologies of the right and of the left were in many countries universally and ruthlessly enforced; and science, philosophy, literature, art and music were rigorously censored and compelled to conform to standards set by the ruling ideology. Possession of the Bible was, of course, made difficult or impossible.

It is understandable, therefore, that nowadays in many quarters great, systematic philosophies, scientific theories, theologies, and ideologies, or 'metanarratives' as they are called, are distinctly out of favour. Hegel's philosophy, for instance, and Marxism, which took over Hegel's idea of dialectic, purported to give an undeniable explanation of the laws of history past, present and future, and of the whole universe, and dominated the mind and behaviour of millions. History itself has discredited them, as we shall later see. Likewise Christianity is often dismissed without a hearing as self-evidently false because it too offers a universal 'metanarrative'.

Christianity will, of course, protest against the charge that the objective and universal truth it proclaims enslaves people either mentally, emotionally or spiritually. Christ himself asserts the opposite, namely that it is knowledge of the truth that sets people free (John 8:31–34). But then the undeniably exclusive claim of Christ—'I am the way, and the truth, and the life. No one comes to the Father except through me' (John 14:6)—offends the multiculturalism of our modern world and is peremptorily dismissed on that ground.

The globalisation of knowledge

This brings us to one more, very potent, reason why the concept of absolute, objective truth goes ever more rapidly out of fashion nowadays: the globalisation of knowledge. The marvels of information technology fill people's minds with a torrent of instantaneous information about every conceivable subject (though not necessarily with genuine understanding of each subject) from every quarter of the globe. People, therefore, become acquainted, if only superficially, with many religions, philosophies, ideologies, scientific theories, etc., in a way and to an extent unthinkable half a century ago. And under the impact of this welter of information they conclude that any one philosophy or religion that claimed itself alone to be true must be either ignorant or arrogant. Truth, if it is to be found at all, must be achieved by judicious selections and combinations taken from all the varied partial truths on offer.

How, then, shall we respond to this situation? Unless we are to abandon all critical thinking and simply absorb uncritically a mixture of bits and pieces of mutually contradictory doctrines, we must attempt to discuss the truth claims of the theories, ideologies, religions and philosophies that we encounter.

But to do that we shall have to use language, and many claim that language by its very nature, being culturally conditioned, can never arrive at, or convey, absolute objective truth. Presently, therefore, we shall examine that claim; but first let us briefly survey the consequences that can arise when people in general come to believe that there is no absolute truth binding on everyone.

LONG-TERM CONSEQUENCES OF THE DEVALUATION OF OBJECTIVE TRUTH

Over two and a half millennia ago the prophet, social critic, and reformer Isaiah gave this description of contemporary society:

> For your hands are defiled with blood
> and your fingers with iniquity;
> your lips have spoken lies;
> your tongue mutters wickedness.
> No one enters suit justly;
> no one goes to law honestly;
> they rely on empty pleas, they speak lies,
> they conceive mischief and give birth to iniquity. . . .
> Their webs will not serve as clothing;
> men will not cover themselves with what they make.
> Their works are works of iniquity,
> and deeds of violence are in their hands. . . .
> The way of peace they do not know,
> and there is no justice in their paths;

> they have made their roads crooked;
>> no one who treads on them knows peace. . . .
> transgressing, and denying the Lord,
>> and turning back from following our God,
> speaking oppression and revolt,
>> conceiving and uttering from the heart lying words.
> Justice is turned back,
>> and righteousness stands far away;
> for truth has stumbled in the public squares,
>> and uprightness cannot enter.
> Truth is lacking,
>> and he who departs from evil makes himself a prey.
>> (Isa 59:3, 4, 6, 8, 13–15)

From his distant century Isaiah is a witness to us of the social disintegration that follows when a society loses its sense of the sacredness and inviolability of objective truth. We notice his repeated charge: 'your lips have spoken lies . . . they speak lies . . . conceiving and uttering from the heart lying words . . . truth has stumbled in the public squares . . . truth is lacking.' What he is describing is not the telling of an occasional untruth in a moment of panic or temptation, but the deliberate adoption of a policy of deceit not only in private life but in the centres of public life.

First to suffer are the law courts, where dishonest pleas and trumped up charges are used intentionally to pervert the very justice that the law courts exist to maintain.

Secondly, he mentions the squares: the centres in the ancient world of public, social and commercial activity. Here too the old standards of truth and truthfulness have decayed: it is thought to be 'mature' and 'clever' and 'astute business practice' for a merchant to misrepresent the quality of his goods in a voice dripping with apparent heartfelt assurances of honesty! And for the city elders to encourage the citizens to believe that they are looking after their interests, and are determined to see justice done, though all the while they have accepted bribes not to prosecute the mafia for corruption.

The result, says Isaiah, is widespread injustice and violence; and the effect on many an individual citizen is to make him feel that if he refuses to play the same game, and dares to act honestly, he will 'make himself a prey', that is, he will become a victim of dishonesty himself.

Now let us hear the verdict of a modern philosopher and social critic. In his book *Truth Decay*, Douglas Groothuis argues vigorously that far from objective truth robbing the individual of his freedom, it is the loss of public respect for the sanctity of objective truth that little by little eats away at the foundations of individual and civic liberty. It is worth quoting him at length:

> Truth decay has ramifications for all religious truth claims ... But truth decay also affects every other area of life, from politics to art, to law to history. If the idea of objective truth falls into disrepute, politics devolves into nothing but image manipulation and power mongering ... Social consensus and the duties of shared citizenship become irrelevant and impossible as various subsets of the population—differentiated by race, ethnicity and sexual orientation—grasp for power by claiming unimpeachable authority on the basis of their cultural particularities ...
>
> If law is not grounded in a moral order that transcends any criminal code or constitution, it becomes a set of malleable and ultimately arbitrary edicts. If no objective facts can be discerned from the past, a novel cannot be distinguished from history, nor mythology differentiated from biography. History becomes a tool for special interest groups who rewrite the past on the basis of their predilections, without the possibility of rational critique from outside the group. If there is no beauty beyond the eye of the beholder, art becomes merely a tool for social influence, political power and personal expression; the category of obscenity is as obsolete as the ideal of beauty.
>
> ... culture wars break out after the breakdown of a consensual understanding of truth as objective and knowable through rational investigation and persuasion. When reasonable debate serves no purpose in achieving a knowledge of truth, all that remains are machinations of power—whether the cause be racial, sexual or religious.[1]

---

[1] See pp. 25–6.

Here, then, is plenty for vigorous, rational debate. But debate can only be carried on by using words. If, then, as some claim, words are so culturally conditioned that they cannot express genuinely objective truth, rational debate can never lead us to truth. All it could do would be to make us aware of irreconcilably different prejudices and opinions. It is, therefore, to a consideration of language as a possible vehicle for truth that we now turn.

CONVENTIONALISM

Conventionalism is a theory of linguistic philosophy associated with such names as Ferdinand de Saussure (1857–1913), Gottlob Frege (1848–1925) and Ludwig Wittgenstein (1889–1951). It holds that all meaning is relative. But if so, then since all truth claims are meaningful statements, it would follow that all truth is likewise relative.

On this view, meaning is arbitrary and relative, since it is determined by culture and context. Language of itself does not possess some inherent, essential meaning. Linguistic meaning derives from the experience of the people whose language it is. Words are symbols, and the same symbol can be used by different people to mean different things. In English, for instance, the sound represented by the letters *g–i–f–t* means 'a present', 'something given', and then 'a special aptitude', 'ability', 'power' or 'talent'. In German the very same sound, represented by the very same letters, means 'poison', and then 'virulence', 'fury', 'malice', 'rage'.

But notice what this does not mean. The fact that the sound (word) 'gift' refers in German to something very different from that same sound (word) in English does not mean that an Englishman can never be brought to understand the reality to which the German sound (word) refers. Nor does it mean that the truth about this reality, namely that it will kill you if you ingest it, is culturally determined, and therefore only relative. It is an absolute truth that holds true in every nation under the sun, whatever symbol/sound/word is used to denote it.

Logically the conventionalist theory is self-contradictory. When a conventionalist says 'All meaning is relative', he has to suppose that he is uttering a meaningful statement, that all people in the world will agree with, when they understand it. His statement, then, is a 'non-conventional' statement that nevertheless purports to claim that all statements are conventional.[2]

THE DEFINITION OF TRUTH

Let's start with what appears to be a simple observation derived from everyday life: each of us has a concept of truth. We say things like:

'I don't think Natasha was telling the truth when she said that she was at Susie's house last night.'

'Tell me the truth, doctor; is this illness terminal?'

'I wish I knew whether he was telling me the truth.'

'It is true that Paris is the capital of France.'

'It is not true that I have a million pounds in the bank.'

These and a thousand and one similar expressions reveal that all of us know what truth and falsehood are and, what is more, we expect others to know it too, and we expect them to tell the truth; we can get very angry if we discover that someone has deliberately told us an untruth.

Yet once we attempt to formulate what exactly we mean by truth, we shall discover, as philosophers have done long since, that clear definition is not as easy as we think. We shall also discover that in recent years the concept of truth has itself been radically questioned. So let us now look at some of the theories of the nature of truth.

The correspondence theory of truth

Aristotle's view of truth

Perhaps the most famous expression of this is that given long ago by Aristotle:

---

[2] We must distinguish, of course, between 'meaning' in the sense of what a word refers to, and 'meaning' in the sense of what the thing referred to means to us, i.e. whether we like it or not, value or detest it, believe in it or not. The word 'God' is a ready example.

> To say of what is that it is not, or of what is not that it is, is false, while to say of what is that it is, and of what is not that it is not, is true; so that he who says of anything that it is, or that it is not, will say either what is true or what is false.[3]

Aristotle's principle applies both to the existence of things and to the qualities of things.

Existence. All agree that the earth exists. If I say of the earth that it exists, then what I say is true because the earth does in fact exist, and my statement corresponds with the fact. If, on the other hand, I were to say that the earth does not exist, then what I said would be false, since my statement would not correspond with the fact.

Qualities. Water not only exists but it has a certain quality, namely, wetness. If I say that water is not wet, then what I say about water is false, for my statement does not correspond with the fact. Conversely, if I say that water is wet, then my statement corresponds with the fact, and it is therefore true.

On the basis of these simple examples we can begin to define the nature of truth according to the correspondence theory. Truth is a property of statements, propositions or beliefs about something that is external to the statements themselves. In other words it is statements, propositions and beliefs that are said to be either false or true; but the criterion by which they are judged to be either false or true lies outside those statements, propositions or beliefs. It lies in the state of affairs to which they refer. If they correspond to that state of affairs, they are true; if not, they are false.

Example 1. If I state that Napoleon was defeated at the battle of Waterloo, my statement is true; and it is true, not because of something intrinsic to that statement which you could discover by investigating the statement itself, but because of something which happened in the past, something entirely outside the statement itself to which nevertheless the statement corresponds.

Example 2. If, on the other hand, I state or believe that Napoleon won the battle of Waterloo, my statement or belief is false, no matter how sincerely or firmly held my belief is. It is false because of something that happened in the past, something outside the statement itself that does not correspond to that statement.

---

[3] *Metaphysics*, IV.7 (Ross trans.).

It is, then, because of this correspondence (or non-correspondence) of statements, propositions or beliefs with the facts, that this theory of truth is called the correspondence theory. A moment's reflection will show that this is the common sense view of truth by which most of us live our lives most of the time.

Bertrand Russell's view

The philosopher and mathematician Bertrand Russell was a staunch defender of the correspondence theory of truth. In his well-known book *The Problems of Philosophy*, he laid down criteria that he regarded as essential for any theory of truth. They are that any such theory:

1. must hold that the very idea of truth implies that its opposite is false;
2. must make truth 'a property of beliefs'; but
3. must make truth 'a property wholly dependent upon the relations of beliefs to outside things'.[4]

This means, according to Russell, that

> The truth of a belief is something not involving beliefs, or (in general) any mind at all, but only the *objects* of the belief. A mind, which believes, believes truly when there is a *corresponding* complex [of facts] not involving the mind, but only its objects. This correspondence ensures truth, and its absence entails falsehood. Hence we account simultaneously for the two facts that beliefs (*a*) depend on minds for their *existence*, (*b*) do not depend on minds for their *truth*. . . .
>
> It will be seen that minds do not *create* truth or falsehood. They create beliefs, but when once the beliefs are created, the mind cannot make them true or false, except in the special case where they concern future things which are within the power of the person believing, such as catching trains. What makes a belief true is a *fact*, and this fact does not (except in exceptional cases) in any way involve the mind of the person who has the belief.[5]

---

[4] *Problems of Philosophy*, 89.
[5] *Problems of Philosophy*, 93–4.

The need to distinguish between objective facts and subjective feelings

The temperature of a room is an objective fact. It can be measured by a thermometer. It is the same for everyone who is in the room, whatever their feelings.

A temperature of 5° centigrade in a room might seem warm to somebody coming in from the outside where the temperature is -20°. It would simultaneously seem cold to a person coming in from an outside temperature of +40°. The different ways in which people feel the temperature is a subjective matter. It does not alter the objective truth of the statement that the temperature of the room is 5°.

If, on the other hand, I say 'I feel cold', my statement refers to an objective state of affairs—my state of feeling cold. If, then, I am really feeling cold, my statement is true, since it corresponds to what I am actually feeling. If, however, I am not feeling cold, but say I am, my statement does not correspond to the actual state of affairs, and is therefore false.

Someone recommends a medicine to his friend, saying it is good for arthritis, and his friend replies: 'It may be true for you, but it isn't true for me: I have arthritis and took that medicine and it did me no good.' What are we to deduce from this? Are we to think that there is no such thing as objective truth: all truth is relative, and what is true for some people is not true for others? No. The fault here was that the original statement, 'This medicine is good for arthritis' was not exact, and therefore, strictly speaking, it was not completely true, because it did not correspond with all the facts. It should have run, 'This medicine is good for some forms of arthritis but not for others'; then it would have corresponded with all the facts.

An objection to the correspondence theory

The correspondence theory has been criticised by the British philosopher P. F. Strawson (1919–2006) in a famous interchange with J. L. Austin (1911–60).[6] Strawson rightly understood the correspondence theory to imply two major things:

---

[6] Austin et al., 'Truth'.

1. facts are actual entities that exist before and independently of any statement made about them; and
2. statements made about facts are true or false to the degree in which they correspond to the facts.

But Strawson held that the theory must be false, because, according to him, we never have access to the bare facts themselves. The only way we can know about facts is by making a statement about them. All we have are statements, our own or other people's, about the facts. All we can do, therefore, is to compare one statement about the facts with another statement about the facts.

Likewise, L. J. J. Wittgenstein (1889-1951), who in his early period had held the correspondence theory, abandoned it later in life. He argued that when we try to test the truth of our judgment about a fact with the fact itself, all that we can really do is to compare our first judgment with some second *judgment*, not with 'the fact itself' independently of any human judgment.

But to argue like that is virtually to deny that we can have any objectively true knowledge of the external world at all—and the denial is false. At one time and for long centuries people believed and stated that the sun orbits the earth. Later people came to believe otherwise and stated that the earth orbits the sun. Modern astronomers insist that the earlier statement was false, the second true. But how can the second statement be judged to be truer than the first, unless we have access to the facts and can assess the comparative truth of the statements by observing how well, or otherwise, they correspond with the facts?

Philosopher John R. Searle argues[7] against Wittgenstein and Strawson that facts are non-linguistic entities, 'because the whole point of having the notion of "fact" is to have a notion for that which stands outside the statement but which makes it true, or in virtue of which it is true, if it is true'.[8] Summing up, Searle says,

> The assignment of 'true' to statements is not arbitrary. In general, statements are true in virtue of conditions in the world that are not parts of the statement. Statements are made true

---

[7] *Construction of Social Reality*, Ch. 9.
[8] *Construction of Social Reality*, 211.

by how things are in the world that is independent of the statement. We need general terms to name these how-things-are-in-the-world, and 'fact' is one such term. Others are 'situation' and 'state of affairs'.[9]

We can see the force of what Searle is saying by reflecting on the fact that the earth was a planet orbiting the sun before there was anyone to make a statement about it. Facts are independent of statements made about them.

The subjective element in knowing the truth

The fact that we have to interpret the knowledge we gain, and that our knowledge is limited, does not mean that there is not an objective truth out there for us to study. The very fact that scientists persist in attempting to get an ever enlarged and increasingly accurate understanding of reality shows that at least they presuppose the correspondence theory of truth, namely, that there is an objective reality which invites our progressive understanding of it.

The coherence theory of truth

Perhaps the most widely held alternative to the *correspondence* theory of truth is the *coherence* theory of truth. Spinoza, Leibniz, Hegel and the British philosopher F. H. Bradley (1846–1924) all subscribed to various versions of it. In this theory the criterion of truth is not whether a given statement, proposition or belief *corresponds* with some *external reality*; it is simply whether that statement, proposition or belief *coheres* with all the other statements, propositions or beliefs *within the system* of which it is a member.

> An incoherent narrative is obviously not true.

The system of thought to which the *coherence* principle most obviously applies is mathematics. A mathematical proposition is regarded as true if it coheres with the axioms and the other propositions in its particular system. In other words, to be true a mathematical theory must be internally coherent.

Similarly many systematic theologians will assess the truth of a

---

[9] *Construction of Social Reality*, 219.

proposed doctrine by whether it coheres with the accepted axioms of their system: if it does, it is true; if it doesn't, it is false.

Likewise in a criminal court one of the first things a judge will look for in the testimony of a witness or of an accused person is whether that testimony is coherent. If the accused person says at the beginning of his statement that he was in Tokyo at the time of the murder, and then later says that he was in Shanghai, his statement is incoherent and will be rejected.

Coherence is also a criterion much used by historians in order to assess the validity of differing accounts of past events. An incoherent narrative is obviously not true.[10]

Evaluation of the coherence theory

It is clear, then, that coherence is a negative test for truth: if a statement is incoherent, it cannot be true. Coherence, therefore, is a necessary condition: all statements must pass this test, if they are to be regarded as true. But while it is a *necessary* condition, it is not by itself a *sufficient* condition for truth.

Russell argues that there are two major reasons for which we must reject the coherence theory as a sufficient condition for truth. First, it is possible to think of two internally coherent theories or stories that are nevertheless mutually contradictory.

Story 1. All life is a dream, and all people and objects we perceive are dream objects with no real existence. Such a story could be presented as internally coherent.

Story 2. Equally coherent internally, as is Story 1: real people and real objects exist in a real world.

These two stories, though both internally coherent, are mutually contradictory. They cannot both be true—and incidentally, we know which one isn't true!

Similarly, while mathematics insists that any theory be internally coherent, mathematical imagination can construct any number of internally coherent systems that are mutually inconsistent. This can happen in mathematics because its theoretical systems do not necessarily correspond with reality.

---

[10] Though if two or three ostensibly independent witnesses were found to give word-for-word exactly the same account of an event, one might suspect collusion of some sort.

The same thing happens in fiction: one could write two novels about the same hero, each novel coherent in itself but completely contradicting the other novel. One can do this because it is fiction; but it shows that internal coherence is not enough to settle the question of truth.

The second problem with the coherence theory is a logical one. In order to be internally coherent a theory or story must observe the law of non-contradiction in logic: one cannot introduce into the theory or the story two contradictory statements about the same thing. A historian, for example, cannot state within one and the same book that Napoleon won the battle of Waterloo and that he lost the battle of Waterloo.

What then, we must ask, is the status of this law of logic? Does it apply simply to a particular story or is it valid and applicable to everything in the whole universe?

Suppose it is valid and universally applicable. Then obviously it exists independently of any particular story and lies not inside but outside each story. That means that to be true, each story has to conform to an *external* law or standard of truth and this principle seems strongly to resemble the correspondence theory of truth.

But suppose this external law of logic is not valid either in the case of some particular story or in the case of any other story throughout the universe. Then each and every story will be coherent with each and every other story, no matter what contradictions and inconsistencies exist between them. In that case the two statements 'I'm a millionaire' and 'I'm completely bankrupt' could be regarded as mutually coherent, and because coherent, simultaneously true. But this is obvious nonsense; and it forces us to conclude that to be a valid criterion of truth, the inner coherence of any story must submit to the external law of truth: the principle of non-contradiction. From the perspective of the correspondence theory of truth, the coherence theory selects a prominent characteristic of truth and mistakenly elevates it to a definition of truth. The same holds for a

> From the perspective of the correspondence theory of truth, the coherence theory selects a prominent characteristic of truth and mistakenly elevates it to a definition of truth.

number of other theories of truth including the next that we will consider.

The pragmatic theory of truth

This theory is associated with the names of American philosophers Charles Sanders Peirce (1839–1914), William James (1842–1910) and John Dewey (1859–1952), who, although they (like all other philosophers!) did not all teach quite the same thing, essentially believed that true beliefs are defined to be those which provoke actions which lead to desirable or successful results. Now, of course, we should all surely agree that true beliefs are a good basis for action, but, as Russell and others have pointed out, we all know also that actions based on true beliefs can sometimes lead to disastrous results, whereas actions based on false beliefs can sometimes lead to good results. A man driving at night in a lonely part of the country might see flames apparently coming from a house. Thinking the house is on fire he goes to investigate and discovers that it is only a harmless fire burning rubbish. However he finds a woman lying by the fire unconscious as a result of a fall, and is able to take her to hospital and save her life. His initial belief was false, but it led to good results.

On the other hand, a man might abandon a ship in the true belief it was sinking and try to swim for the shore only to drown in strong currents, whereas if he had stayed on the ship he would have been rescued by another ship which happened to come by just before the first ship sank. In this case the man's belief was true, but the result of believing it was fatal.

If, then, beliefs are to be judged true if they lead to good results, and false if they lead to bad results, we shall have to conclude that in the first of these two examples an initial false belief (that a house was on fire when in fact it wasn't) was true; and in the second example, a true belief (that the ship was sinking, which in fact it did) was false. But this is nonsense; and it shows that the pragmatic theory of truth is inadequate. In past years crude surgical methods have sometimes saved lives and sometimes hastened death. Nowadays the very best and most modern surgical techniques carry no guarantee of success in every case. Of course, constant bad results will motivate surgeons to devise better techniques. But to make success or failure the absolute and unvarying criterion of truth is false. Many a criminal has successfully, from his point of view, escaped justice by mounting a defence based on persuasive lies.

Finally, it has been frequently pointed out that the correspondence theory of truth is superior to all the others for the simple reason that they all depend on the correspondence theory, even as they attempt to deny it. For to say 'this theory of truth is true' means that it corresponds to the truth about truth.

Questions remain

When we have examined some of the underlying reasons why some people react negatively to the idea of objective truth, examined some of the consequences of rejecting it and tried to understand how truth is defined by those who hold a variety of theories about it there are still issues that we must explore as we consider the nature of truth. Whichever view we adhere to, we all have to wrestle with different levels, and even different kinds, of truth. The question of how particular truths are related to ultimate truth comes into our experience so regularly that we may well cease to think about it. But we must now consider how that question arises, in every area of life, but particularly in relation to the truth about human history.

CHAPTER 6

PARTICULAR TRUTHS AND ULTIMATE TRUTH

Those who start out seriously enquiring for truth will find that at however lowly a level they start, they will not be logically able to resist asking what the Ultimate Truth about everything is.

TRUTH AT DIFFERENT LEVELS

Experience of life soon teaches us that the truth about things is to be found at different levels. Take water once more as a simple example.

Level 1. At this level it is true to say that water can exist as a liquid, as a gas (steam) and as a solid (ice). But even at this level the one truth that water is wet is not equally applicable to all its three possible forms: steam is in fact dry and invisible until it mixes with air.

Level 2. At the level of the constituent elements of water, the truth is that water is composed of two gases, hydrogen and oxygen. But neither of these gases is wet. If, therefore, we wish to consider the truth about the qualities of water at Level 1, we must 'leave behind' the truths of water at Level 2, however true they were at that level.

Level 3. At the atomic and subatomic level the two elements are made up of atoms and particles in the same sense as all elements are; though the distinguishing truth about them would be the particular selection and ratios of their component particles.

Now while all these facts are, each in its turn, true of water, if we wish to think of water *qua* water, we must concentrate on the truth that belongs specially to that level.

But the truth about water is not exhausted by the account of what water is made of: it must take account of what its purpose and functions are in relation to Earth's total system. It has several such functions; but since on Earth water is a substance without which life as we know it would be impossible, modern science understandably seeks to discover whether water is exclusive to our Earth, or whether it exists on any other planets in our solar system, or on any other planets that may be orbiting other suns elsewhere in the universe. But once we start asking about the purpose and function of water within the universe as a whole, it will not be long before we ask what is the truth about the origin, purpose and function of the universe itself. That is the nature of truth. Those who start out seriously enquiring for truth will find that at however lowly a level they start, they will not be logically able to resist asking what the Ultimate Truth about everything is.

This is noticeably true when we begin to ask about ourselves as human beings. At one level the truth is that we are made of the dust of the earth; and if modern cosmologists are right in saying that the heavy elements necessary for life on Earth were produced in the explosions of supernovae, then we are made of stardust. At a higher level it is true that we are made of atoms, molecules, genes, cells. But so are plants, and at another level of truth we are more than plants.

At this higher level we can consider our stomach, liver, kidneys, lungs, heart, limbs, head, tongue, eyes, brain and even intelligence which we have in common with the higher animals, though even in the features we have in common there are significant differences. A human hand is a very different thing from an animal's claw. The truth is that a human is not just a superior animal.

At a higher level still, one thing that uniquely distinguishes humans is the fact that they have minds that can investigate and understand the laws by which the universe works, though there is no evidence that the universe—the stars, the galaxies, etc.—understands how it works. But more than that: the human mind can transcend the universe and ask how the universe began, where its laws came from, what its purpose is, how it will end. And what is more, the human mind instinctively knows itself to be immeasurably superior to mindless matter however vast the quantity of it is.

If, therefore, we ask what is the truth about us human beings, it would be irrational to restrict ourselves to the truth at one or two of the lower levels. Truthfulness itself will demand that we ask what the truth is about humanity at the highest level: our relationship to the universe as a whole—and to what lies behind and beyond the universe. In other words: what is the Ultimate Truth?

Different kinds of truth?

Experience of life seems also to teach us not only that truth is to be sought at different levels, but that there are different kinds of truth. People speak of factual truth, scientific truth, poetic truth, mathematical truth, philosophical truth, moral truth, existential truth, etc. From a practical point of view, at least, these distinctions are helpful.

We need, however, to tread carefully here. C. S. Lewis argued[1] that the difference between so-called factual, scientific and poetic truth was really a question of different kinds of language used to describe the same basic truth. He cited three sentences each describing the same phenomenon, severe cold, but each in a different style of language:

(1) 'It was very cold.'
(2) 'There were 13 degrees of frost.'
(3) 'Ah, bitter chill it was! | The owl, for all his feathers was a-cold; | The hare limped trembling through the frozen grass, | And silent was the flock in woolly fold; | Numb'd were the Beadsman's fingers.'[2]

He then described the first sentence as Ordinary language, the second as Scientific language, and the third as Poetic language. The first sentence aimed to convey the information that it was very cold in ordinary everyday factual language. The second was intended to convey the information about the coldness in precise, scientifically measured terms. The third was intended to convey to our imagination the idea of how cold it was by describing its effects on birds, animals and people. But the truth being conveyed, namely that it was very cold, was the same in all three sentences. Lewis then went on to suggest that there are ideas and concepts that perhaps only poetic language, aimed at the imagination, can convey; but they are nonetheless true for that.

> The interesting thing is that when we speak about these several varieties, scientific truth, poetic truth, moral truth, etc., the word 'truth' is the constant element common to all these varieties.

We could debate Lewis's argument for a long time, but that is not our point here. In ordinary life we can readily see the difference between, say, a necessary universal truth delivered by mathematics, such that $5 \times 5 = 25$, and an existential truth discovered by long experience over many generations and expressed in traditional proverbial form, such as 'Pride goes before a fall'. The interesting thing is that when we speak about these several varieties,

---

[1] 'The Language of Religion', *Christian Reflections*.
[2] Lewis here cited John Keats, *The Eve of St. Agnes*, I, 1–5.

scientific truth, poetic truth, moral truth, etc., the word 'truth' is the constant element common to all these varieties. This surely suggests that there is a basic comprehensiveness about the idea and concept of truth that overarches all these varied areas of human experience and knowledge, though it cannot be confined to any one of them. Christians, at least, would account for it by saying that 'all truth is God's truth', meaning that all truth, at every level, has its ultimate source in the Creator.

Historical truths

It goes without saying that we know numerous indubitable historical facts; and if we choose to refer to these facts as 'historical truths', there is no reason why we shouldn't. That is the way we talk. We commonly say, for instance, that it is true that Alexander the Great defeated the Persians and led his troops into India; or that it is true that Roald Amunsden (1872–1928), the Norwegian explorer, was the first man to reach the South Pole (in 1911); or that Yuri Gagarin was the first to conduct a manned space flight (in 1961).

But in addition to numerous true facts about the past, we can rightly talk about historical truths in the sense of lessons we can learn from a study of history. A knowledge of the past, of the movements of thought, the development of politics, the national and international struggles that have preceded us, can help us to understand the present conditions and attitudes prevalent in our contemporary world. Awareness of understandable, but exaggerated, reactions to one extreme in the past can help us to perceive the reason for an unfortunate tendency in society to go to an opposite extreme in the present.

Secondly, historians can point to the consequences of certain trends in the past, and so warn us not to make the same mistakes in the future. From this knowledge of the past they could even suggest what effect policies being at present adopted are likely to have in the future; though the past is never exactly repeated, and the interpretations put on the past by present historians are often modified by later historians.

But in this context we need to distinguish between genuine history on the one hand, and what may be called historicism on the other.

HISTORICISM AND THE TRUTH ABOUT EVERYTHING

It is common knowledge that some physicists and cosmologists hope one day to be able to construct a 'theory of everything', that is, one unified theory that will describe the workings of the whole universe, regarded as one unified whole. It is an ambitious quest. But while such a theory might explain how the whole universe works, and, conceivably, even how it started, there is something that, by definition, it will never explain simply by studying the universe itself. It will never explain why the universe is there in the first place, that is, why there is something and not nothing. More importantly, it will never explain what the purpose of the universe is. To learn the purpose for the universe's existence you would have to look outside the universe, or at least receive the necessary information from a source outside the universe. To take a simple illustration, if someone were to bake a cake, experts from a variety of disciplines could each tell us something about it, but no one could tell the purpose for which the cake was made, simply by studying the cake. For that we would have to ask the person who baked it.[3]

The same thing is true about history, that is, the history of the human race. If we regard the universe and the history of the human race within it as a closed, self-contained unit and try to work out the truth about human history simply by studying that history without any information from outside, we shall inevitably fail.

There are some obvious additional reasons why this is so. First, if history is defined as everything that everyone who has ever lived has thought, said, done and experienced since the world began, then what we know about history is infinitesimal. How could we discover the truth about the history of the human race so far, simply by studying such a tiny slice of the evidence?

The second obvious reason is even more compelling: the history of the human race has not finished yet, and we cannot tell, simply by looking at human history so far, how it is going to end. We did not join the river at its source. No one has traversed it to its end. How could we, located as we are, simply by looking at history so far,

---

[3] See our further discussion of the principle involved as illustrated by the story of Aunt Olga's cake in the Appendix: 'The Scientific Endeavour', and the section 'Explaining Explanations'.

predict with any certainty how and when and where it will end—still less what the purpose and goal of history as a whole is?

The urge to know the whole story

It is natural for us to look to see if there are any discernible laws in history that might provide some information, at least, as to how the future will develop, so that life ceases to be a purposeless journey to an unknown destination. Some philosophers, indeed, have felt it to be the proper task of philosophy to discover the purpose of the universe. The British philosopher C. E. M. Joad (1891–1953) wrote:

> It is the business of philosophy, as I conceive it, to seek to understand the nature of the universe as a whole, not, as do the sciences, some special department of it, but the whole bag of tricks to which the moral feelings of the Puritan, the herd instinct of the man in the street, the religious consciousness of the saint, the aesthetic enjoyment of the artist, the history of the human race and its contemporary follies, no less than the latest discoveries of science contribute. Reflecting on this mass of data, the philosopher seeks to interpret it. He looks for a clue to guide him through the labyrinth, for a system wherewith to classify, or a purpose in terms of which to make meaningful.[4]

The question remains, however, how could we possibly discover laws that might be thought to have governed universal history so far, simply by studying what we know of history?

We know some things, of course. We know that no empire, however great, has proved permanent. We know that from time to time in different parts of the world brilliant cultures and civilisations have arisen, sometimes for no apparent reason, like the spectacular Greek culture of the fifth century BC. Some have lasted millennia, as did that of ancient Egypt; some for but a comparatively short while, like that of Greece which we have just mentioned. All in the end have petered out, or have been absorbed by some other more powerful civilisation. Some have disappeared without trace, like the Indus Valley, or Harappan, civilisation of northern India; or the brilliant Minoan

---

[4] *Book of Joad*, 213.

civilisation in Crete, which was lost to history until rediscovered at the beginning of the last century.

The progress of science and technology in the last two centuries, and now the astonishing advances in information technology in the last half century and right up to the present, have certainly created the impression in the minds of many that progress is a law of history. But if we choose to look at other areas of life, it is doubtful whether any progress worth speaking of has been made at all. There is no evidence to suggest that our leading experts are any more intelligent than their counterparts in the ancient world, even though they know vastly more than the ancients did; and when it comes to morality there is plenty of evidence to suggest that the modern developed world is no better, perhaps even worse, than the ancient Roman empire in its decadent years. Progress has clearly not marked the whole spectrum of human life.

Progress has clearly not marked the whole spectrum of human life.

Information technology and the activities of multinational commercial complexes are rapidly leading to even greater globalisation. In the West, the Industrial Revolution led eventually to the twentieth century, the bloodiest in the whole of known human history. Is there some law of history that guarantees that globalisation will lead to world peace?

But how could we possibly know what the ultimate goal and meaning of history is, merely by looking at *past* history? History, as Shakespeare reminds us, is like a play, and we human beings have our entrances, and for a while play our different parts on the stage. Then we have our exits.[5] But we are not the author of the play; we are not even spectators looking on from the outside of the play. We are just actors and, simply as actors in the play itself, we don't know exactly whereabouts in the play of world history we are. Only the author knows that; and only the author knows how and when the play will end.

And then there is another question, and that concerns not the whole play, but ourselves as individual players. We do not know when our final exit from the stage will be nor how long the play will go on

---

[5] See Shakespeare's *As You Like It*, Act II, Scene VII, ll. 139–166.

after we have departed. We have a more urgent question, therefore: what is the truth about the purpose, goal, destiny and significance of our individual lives both in relation to the whole play and to its author—if there is one? How could we possibly know that, merely by looking at that tiny amount of past world history that we happen to know about, or by conjecturing about that part of history that has not yet happened? Only someone who stood outside history and could see how it started, and how and when it will end, could tell us that.

According to the Bible, of course, there is such a one who stands outside and above history and sees the end from the beginning. In the Old Testament, he announces himself in this way: 'I am God, and there is no other . . . declaring the end from the beginning and from ancient times things not yet done' (Isa 46:9–10). And in the New Testament he describes himself in these words: '"I am the Alpha and Omega," says the Lord God, "who is and who was and who is to come"' (Rev 1:8). His was the first, and his will be the last, word in human history. He began it all, and he is its goal. He is the one who revealed and expressed himself in the creation of the universe and thus gave it significance; and the full meaning of history will be seen when as its goal God fulfils his purpose 'to bring all things in heaven and on earth together under one head, even Christ' (Eph 1:10 own trans.).

But this is not something that we can read off the surface of human world history. We know these things—if we know them at all—as revealed by God through the law, the prophets, the apostles and supremely through Jesus Christ.

There have been and still are, of course, many who do not accept the Bible as God's revealed truth; and some of these have claimed to have discovered, by their own unaided intellectual powers, the laws of history. On the basis of these laws they have then claimed to tell us the truth about history's development so far and, with undeniable truth, to predict how history will inevitably develop in the future. We call their theories 'historicism' as distinct from history. Historians are content to draw limited lessons from the past and to make sober predictions about where modern trends may eventually lead us in the near future. Historicists are not content with that. They claim to know the truth about the whole of history, past, present and future.

The historicism of Hegel and Marx

The two most famous historicists in comparatively modern times have been G. W. F. Hegel (1770–1831) and Karl Marx (1818–83). In the early nineteenth century, and especially in the so-called 'remarkable decade' of 1838–48, the influence of Hegelianism was powerful and extensive. Alexander Ivanovich Herzen (1812–70) reports that Hegel's works

> were discussed incessantly; there was not a paragraph in the three parts of the *Logic*, in the two of the *Aesthetics*, the *Encyclopaedia* and so on, which had not been the subject of desperate disputes for several nights together. People who loved each other avoided each other for weeks at a time because they disagreed about the definition of 'all-embracing spirit', or had taken as a personal insult an opinion on the 'absolute personality and its existence in itself'.[6]

Commenting on the appeal of Hegelianism at that time, Andrzej Walicki suggests that

> Both as a philosophy of reconciliation and as a philosophy of action, Russian Hegelianism was above all a philosophy of reintegration; a philosophy which helped young intellectuals in overcoming their feeling of alienation and in building bridges between their ideals and reality.[7]

And that is easily understandable in the light of Hegel's dominant idea that the whole of reality, the universe and the human race, in spite of all their apparent differences, are actually One Integrated Whole—or at least, the laws of history are inexorably moving everything on towards that final integration.

A superficial reading of Hegel's works might give the impression that Hegel's philosophy was, broadly speaking, Christian; but as N. O. Lossky observed, 'in his [Hegel's] system God is not the Creator of the world, and his system is not theism, but pantheism.'[8]

---

[6] *Byloe i dumy*, Garnett trans., 398; see further Vol. 2, Ch. 24 for the reception of Hegel in Russia.
[7] Walicki, 'Hegelianism, Russian', 340.
[8] Lossky, *History of Russian Philosophy*, 23. It might be more exact to call it panentheism.

Hegel's basic premise

His philosophical thought (as distinct from his historical theory) starts by postulating pure *being*, which according to him, is contentless. That shows at once that in postulating pure being as his prime concept he is not thinking of the Being of God, which is infinitely far from being contentless. But from this beginning he goes on to illustrate the universal law that according to him controls and guides everything. Since 'being', as he conceives of it, is contentless, and 'contentless' is equivalent to 'nothing', the beginning of things is composed of '*being* and *nothing*'! Thus the beginning of things, he maintains, contains in itself a contradiction—how can 'being' be consistent with 'nothing'? This internal conflict, therefore, by the universal law of dialectic, proceeds to resolve itself by 'becoming' something or other. His words are:

> The beginning contains being and nothing, it is the unity of being and nothing, for it is non-being which is at the same time being, and being which at the same time is non-being.[9]

We notice that Hegel is not content to say that the beginning contains a *combination* or even a *unity* of 'being' and 'non-being'. He insists that 'being' *is* 'non-being' and vice versa. In other words, two opposites are not merely joined together: the two opposites are *identical*. But this is not only nonsense, it is a contradiction of fundamental logic. Lossky comments:

> According to traditional formal logic everything is subject to the laws of identity, contradiction and excluded middle, so that 'every A is A' and 'no A can be non-A'. Hegel regards such logic as an expression of rationalistic abstractions inapplicable to the concrete living reality in which, on the contrary, everything is contradictory and 'every A is B', since the presence of contradictions, conflicts and struggle between opposed principles compels being to progress and develop.... Hegel considers every change to be an embodied contradiction. In truth, however, every change is a unity of opposites, but not their identity violating the law of contradiction.[10]

---

[9] Hegel, *Logic*; or *Wissenschaft der Logik* I:68, 77–80 (Vol. 3, 1833 edn)
[10] Lossky, *History of Russian Philosophy*, 346, 347.

Hegel's philosophy of freedom

The implausibility of Hegel's philosophy of freedom is seen in the way he depicts the climax of historical development:

> The History of the World is the discipline of the uncontrolled natural will, bringing it into obedience to a Universal principle and conferring subjective freedom. The East knew and to this present day knows only that *One* is Free; the Greek and Roman world, that *some* are free; the German World that *All* are free. The first political form therefore which we observe in History is *Despotism*, the second *Democracy* and *Aristocracy*, the third *Monarchy*.[11]

It so happened that at the time when Hegel was extolling monarchy in a free society as the grand climax of world political history, he was living under the recently reformed Prussian monarchy. Though he does not explicitly identify his ideal State with the reformed Prussian monarchy, his description of it is so similar to that monarchy that Schopenhauer (1788–1860) accused him of selling himself to his employer (Hegel was a professor in the national university of Berlin); and after his death his disciples, the so-called Young Hegelians, considered that he had been untrue to the core of his own philosophy. Actually he seems not to have regarded the Prussian monarchy as the last word in political world history, for he considered that the future of the world lay in America 'where . . . the burden of the world's history shall reveal itself'.[12]

On the other hand Hegel maintained that with his own system of philosophy, the history of philosophy had reached its final goal and end! Kenny well sums up Hegel's position:

> In his *Lectures on the History of Philosophy*, he displays earlier philosophies as succumbing, one by one, to a dialectical advance marching steadily in the direction of German Idealism. A new epoch has now arisen, he tells us, in which finite self-consciousness has ceased to be finite, and absolute self-consciousness has achieved reality. The sole task of the history of philosophy is to narrate the strife between finite and infinite

---

[11] *Philosophy of History*, Sibree, 104 (Dover), 121 (Baloche).
[12] Cited from Kenny, *Brief History of Western Philosophy*, 277.

self-consciousness; now that the battle is over, it has reached its goal.[13]

To understand how Hegel came to such extraordinary conclusions we must briefly survey his metaphysics. At the heart of his system stands the German word *Geist*, which can mean either Spirit or Mind.[14]

'Spirit', says Hegel, 'is alone Reality. It is the inner being of the world, that which essentially is, and is *per se*.'[15] Yet to start with, Spirit is empty of content. It is only potential and needs to develop its potential. Hence it creates us, and thus our finite minds, or spirits, are part of the Absolute Spirit. By observing us the Absolute Spirit recognises itself in us. And as we think and develop our philosophies the Absolute Spirit comes to self-consciousness of itself through us! So the finite minds of human beings come to see that the world beyond them is not hostile to them, but part of themselves, since Mind, or Spirit, alone constitutes what is real, and each finite mind is part of Mind. At the same time Mind itself realises the goal of its fully developed potential through us human beings and our thinking.

Professor Peter Singer, himself not altogether unsympathetic with the rest of Hegel's philosophy, comments shrewdly on this feature of it:

> One curious aspect of . . . the *Phenomenology* [*of the Mind*] is that it seeks to understand a process that is completed by the fact that it is understood. The goal of all history is that mind should come to understand itself as the only ultimate reality. When is that understanding first achieved? By Hegel himself in the *Phenomenology*! If Hegel is to be believed, the closing pages of his masterpiece are no mere description of the culmination of everything that has happened since finite minds were first created: they *are* that culmination.[16]

---

[13] Kenny, *Brief History of Western Philosophy*, 278.
[14] Hearing him speak about the Absolute Spirit, Christians might at first think that he meant by it the person of the Holy Spirit, as depicted in the New Testament. But though he uses Christian terminology, Hegel is actually a pantheist or panentheist.
[15] *Phenomenology of the Mind*, 86.
[16] 'Hegel, Georg Wilhelm Friedrich', 342.

So, then, as Anthony Kenny notes, 'the self-awareness of the Absolute comes at the end, not at the beginning ... and is brought into existence by the philosophical reflection of human beings. It is the history of philosophy which brings the Absolute face to face with itself.'[17]

Perhaps the saddest feature of Hegel's system is, as Peter Singer points out, the exaggerated, unwarranted optimism that his dialectic of history spawned. Doubtless he genuinely believed that his dialectic was the law of history that held out the sure prospect of overcoming conflict between human beings and thus bringing about a rational and harmonious community. As an example of how it worked you could start with the ethics and morality of Athens in the days of Socrates. They were built on mere custom. Then Socrates' questioning led eventually to the downfall of customary morality and its replacement during the Reformation by a morality based on the individual conscience. Yet this in turn proves unsatisfactory and unstable; and so it makes way for a synthesis of the two moralities in the formation of the rational State where each citizen sees that he shares reason, or Mind, with every other citizen, and that true freedom consists not in individual isolation but in freely cooperating with all others in the community of the State which is in fact the ideal Self-expression of Absolute Spirit.

So far the theory of dialectic. But Hegel thought he saw it virtually fulfilled in the Prussian monarchy. The German spirit, he held, was the spirit of the new world. Its aim was the realisation of absolute truth as the unlimited self-determination of freedom. Accordingly he divided German history into three periods:

1. the period up to Charlemagne which he called the Kingdom of the Father;
2. the period from Charlemagne to the Reformation which he called the Kingdom of the Son; and
3. the period from the Reformation up to and including the Prussian monarchy which he called the Kingdom of the Holy Spirit.

By what kind of dialectical law of history, we wonder, would he have accounted for Hitler's Third Reich, if he could have foreseen it?

---

[17] *Brief History*, 278.

Marx's historicism

Hegel was a virtual pantheist, or panentheist; Marx was an atheist. Marx rejected Hegel's Idealism and embraced extreme Realism. He took over Hegel's idea of dialectic, however, even though he 'stood Hegel on his head'. He genuinely thought he had discovered a law of history that by its irresistible working, along with man's cooperation, would bring in an eventual utopia. It spawned in him, and in millions of others round the world, an even greater optimism than Hegel's theory had generated—but with what disappointing results we now know.

A final comment on Hegel and Marx

There is, then, one historical truth, at least, that a consideration of Hegel's and Marx's philosophies can teach us. The law that they thought they discovered in history was never in history itself: it was imposed on history by their philosophies. It is, in fact, impossible for human reason to predict what is the ultimate purpose and goal of history simply by studying past history. God alone, who stands above the river of time and sees the end from the beginning, knows that. But according to the Bible he has communicated to us all that we need to know about it (but which we could never have known by reason alone) through his revealed truth. It is to the Bible's concept of truth that we must turn in our next chapter.

CHAPTER 7

THE BIBLICAL VIEW OF TRUTH

Here lies the basic difference between atheism and theism. To the atheist the universe is not a revelation of anything. It is simply a brute fact with nothing to tell us about anything outside itself. . . . The Bible, by contrast, asserts that the universe is the vehicle of God's self-revelation of his power and divine nature; and that to regard the universe itself as the Ultimate Reality, and the matter and forces of nature as the Ultimate Powers, is The Fundamental Falsehood . . .

A PRELIMINARY WORD STUDY

The semantic range of the ancient languages in which the Bible was written allow for a great breadth of meaning. It will be useful, therefore, to examine those original words and how they are used in the biblical context. The Old Testament was for the most part written in Hebrew, and a few chapters in Aramaic. The New Testament was written in Greek.

In Hebrew the main word for truth, $’^emet$, is polysemic, that is, in some contexts it is used to express one meaning, in other contexts another. This is, of course, a common characteristic of words in many languages.

1. $’^emet$ in some contexts means 'truth' as distinct from 'falsehood' or 'lies'.
2. $’^emet$ in other contexts means 'reliability', 'trustworthiness', 'faithfulness'.

In Greek the main words for truth are the noun *alētheia*, the adjectives *alēthēs* and *alēthinos*, and the adverb *alēthēs*. Their meanings cover the range:

1. what is true, as distinct from false
2. what is open and honest as distinct from dishonest concealment
3. what is true as distinct from pretence and hypocrisy
4. what is genuine as distinct from fake
5. what is real as distinct from illusory
6. what is permanently valuable as distinct from only temporarily valuable
7. what is the actual reality as distinct from a symbol of that reality
8. what is the real thing as distinct from a mere copy or model of the real thing.

This group of Greek words does not have the meaning 'reliable', 'trustworthy', or 'faithful' as does the Hebrew word *'emet*. It is not that the Greek language cannot express these meanings that are so closely associated with the idea of 'truth'. It is simply that when Greek wishes to express the idea of reliability, trustworthiness or faithfulness, it uses the noun *pistis* (= both 'faith' and 'faithfulness') and the adjective *pistos* (= 'faithful', or 'worthy of belief and trust'). Here, then, are some examples of the range of meanings of these Hebrew and Greek words as used in the Bible.

Truth as correspondence of words with the facts

Genesis 42:16

Joseph sets his brothers a test 'that your words may be tested, whether there is truth in you'. He has charged them with being spies; they have denied it, and have given him their story. He now insists that they prove that their story corresponds with the actual facts.

John 4:17–18

> Jesus said to her, 'You are right in saying, "I have no husband"; for you have had five husbands, and the one you now have is not your husband. What you have said is true.'

The woman had tried to hide her present marital situation by telling a half-truth. Christ acknowledged that her statement, strictly speaking, corresponded with the truth, but he showed himself aware of the other half of the truth about her actual situation.

Truth as correspondence of deeds and words

The Bible is concerned, not only that our statements should correspond with the facts of the case, but that our attitudes, deeds and behaviour should correspond with what we say we believe and with our promises, both in religious and secular contexts.

1 John 3:17

> If anyone has the world's goods and sees his brother in need, yet closes his heart against him, how does God's love abide in

him? Little children, let us not love in word or talk but in deed and in truth.

Galatians 2:13–14

And the rest of the Jews acted hypocritically along with him . . . But when I saw that their conduct was not in step with the truth of the gospel . . .

This was a case of religious hypocrisy: men who professed to believe the Christian gospel were contradicting by their behaviour what they claimed to believe.

Genesis 32:9–10

And Jacob said, 'O God of my father Abraham . . . who said to me, "Return to your country . . . that I may do you good," I am not worthy of . . . all the faithfulness [truth] that you have shown to your servant.'

What Jacob means by 'truth' here is that God has been true to his promises: he has not made promises and then failed to fulfil them.

Truth as coherence

Mark 14:56–59

For many bore false witness against him, but their testimony did not agree. And some . . . bore false witness . . . 'We heard him say, "I will destroy this temple . . . and in three days I will build another . . ."' Yet even about this their testimony did not agree.

We earlier saw that coherence is not by itself a sufficient test for truth. On the other hand a story that is incoherent cannot possibly be true.

Pragmatic truth

1 Thessalonians 2:13

when you received the word of God, which you heard from us, you accepted it not as the word of men but as what it really is [lit. 'in truth'], the word of God, which is at work in you believers.

We earlier saw that if we define truth as something that produces good results, there will be cases where the definition does not hold, since believing something as true can sometimes lead to bad results. But in practice the mark of what is truly God's word is that it proves to be not just words and theory: it actually works and produces good results in the lives of those who believe it. And they, for their part, are responsible to 'do the truth', that is to practise it. Truth, in the Bible, is not simply a theory that we mentally assent to: it is a belief that has to be practised, as we saw from 1 John 3:17 above.

Truth and true as openness and honesty

Matthew 22:16–17

> They sent their disciples to him [Jesus] . . . saying, 'Teacher, we know that you are true and teach the way of God truthfully, and you do not care about anyone's opinion, for you are not swayed by appearances. Tell us, then . . .'

Mark 5:33

> But the woman, knowing what had happened to her, came in fear and trembling and fell down before him and told him the whole truth.

In other words she concealed nothing, she did not try to get away with telling half-truths.

Truth as integrity

Exodus 18:21–22

> Look for able men . . . who fear God, who are trustworthy [lit. 'men of truth'] and hate a bribe, and place such men over the people . . . And let them judge the people.

Jeremiah 9:3–6

> They bend their tongue like a bow; falsehood and not truth has grown strong in the land . . . Let everyone beware of his neighbour and put no trust in any brother, for every brother is a

deceiver ... and no one speaks the truth; they have taught their tongue to speak lies ... Heaping oppression upon oppression, and deceit upon deceit.

Zechariah 8:16–17

Speak the truth to one another; render in your gates [i.e. in your law courts] judgments that are true and make for peace ... love no false oath.

Truth in all three of these instances is integrity of character, faithfulness, untouched by bribery and corruption, or by partiality and favouritism.

Truth and true as what is real and genuine

John 17:3

that they should know you, the only true God.

1 Thessalonians 1:9

you turned to God from idols to serve the living and true God.

Here truth and true speak of what is real and genuine, as distinct from what is fake or spurious, specifically in consideration of God and idols. The Bible is insistent that there is only one God. He is the true God, i.e. he is the real, the genuine, God. All forms of idol worship are deceptions and falsehoods. Compare how the Old Testament describes a worshipper of an idol: 'he feeds on ashes; a deluded heart has led him astray, and he cannot ... say, "Is there not a lie in my right hand?"' (Isa 44:20). Similarly Romans 1:25: 'they exchanged the truth about God for a lie and worshipped and served the creature rather than the Creator.'

True as what is real and eternal

John 6:27, 32

Do not labour for the food that perishes, but for the food that endures to eternal life ... my Father gives you the true bread from heaven. For the bread of God is he who comes down from heaven and gives life to the world.

Here 'true' is what is real and eternal, as distinct from what is merely physical and temporary. Christ is not denying that we need physical food and must work for it. But the life that physical food maintains is only temporary; the life that the 'real' food maintains is eternal.

Truth as what is ontologically real

John 4:22–24

> You worship what you do not know . . . the true worshippers will worship the Father in spirit and truth . . . God is spirit, and those who worship him must worship in spirit and truth.

Truth in this context is what is ontologically real and distinct from what is merely imaginary and illusory. Christ was here talking to a Samaritan woman. He was not criticising the sincerity of her worship: he was pointing out that she did not really know the God she tried to worship. Her concept of him was not ontologically true, only imaginary and illusory. If someone praised Black Beauty under the impression that it was a painting of a beautiful woman, when in actual fact Black Beauty was the name of a famous horse, his praise of Black Beauty would not be true to the ontological reality that he imagined he was praising. Worship of God must be true to what God is really like.

True as what is the real thing as distinct from its symbol

Hebrews 8:1–2

> We have such a high priest, one who sat down at the right hand of the throne of the Majesty in heaven, a minister in the holy places, in the true tent [or, tabernacle] that the Lord set up, not man.

True here is what is the real thing as distinct from what is merely a symbol of the real thing. The elaborate tabernacle faithfully set up by Moses at God's command was real enough in that it actually existed and was approved by God, as were the subsequent temples built in Jerusalem. But it was only a symbol, a copy and shadow of the true tabernacle that is God's heavenly dwelling place. The writer of Hebrews here encourages his readers to concentrate on reality rather than on mere symbol.

DIFFERENT WAYS OF EXPRESSING TRUTH

It is plain to see that in the Bible there are, in the sense we earlier discussed, different kinds of truth or, better said, different ways of conveying truth.

Poetic truth or truth expressed through poetry

Not only are the books of Job and Psalms written as poetry, but so are major parts of the prophetic books like Isaiah and Jeremiah; and we interpret them accordingly. In the famous shepherd psalm, David says:

> You prepare a table before me in the presence of my enemies;
> you anoint my head with oil; my cup overflows. (Ps 23:5)

The language, taken literally, describes a banquet provided by a host who would anoint the head of each guest with perfumed ointment and see to it that his glass was constantly filled. But no one supposes that David is here talking of a literal banquet. Yet what he says is nonetheless a truthful expression of God's care and provision for him that he had experienced in the desert, when he was being persecuted by King Saul.

Similarly, when the psalmist describes the absolute completeness of God's forgiveness by remarking: 'As far as the east is from the west, so far does he remove our transgressions from us' (Ps 103:12), he is not implying that sin and guilt are entities that can be removed and placed at an enormous physical distance from us. He is expressing in vivid figurative language the truth that when God forgives, he promises never to rake up again the guilt of our sin and haunt us with it (see the same thing said in straightforward language in Heb 10:17).

Propositional truth

In this connection special interest attaches to the so-called 'amen-formula' with which Christ introduced many of his statements. *'āmēn* is a Hebrew word, connected with a verb that carries the idea of affirmation and certainty. So, for instance, if a priest or judge put a person on oath and repeated the terms of the oath and the solemn consequences that would follow perjury, the person concerned would respond with the word *'āmēn*. He or she thus affirmed the oath, and agreed to its terms. Similarly, at the end of a public prayer or confession the congregation would say 'amen', thus affirming their agreement. And since, when people took an oath before God, they were appealing to God to witness their oath, God is sometimes referred to in the Old Testament as 'God of the Amen' (cf. Isa 65:16); translated in many languages as 'God of Truth'.

Faith in the statements, propositions and promises uttered by Christ and God is regarded as being ultimately based on a person's estimate of the moral character and trustworthiness of Christ and God.

Christ was unusual in that when he made solemn statements, whether propositions or promises, he frequently *prefaced* (not ended) those statement with the word *'āmēn*, often repeating it in order to lay double emphasis on their utter truthfulness and certainty. Examples are:

> Amen, amen, I say to you, unless one is born again, he cannot see the kingdom of God. (John 3:3)

> Amen, amen, I say to you, whoever hears my word and believes him who sent me has eternal life. He does not come into judgment, but has passed from death to life. (John 5:24)

Now, as we have said, *'āmēn* is a Hebrew word, and the New Testament was written in Greek. Naturally, therefore, in the New Testament Christ's words are normally translated into Greek. But the apostles were obviously so impressed with Christ's repeated emphatic affirmation of the truthfulness of his statements that, in recording them, they have often simply transliterated the Hebrew word *'āmēn*, rather than translate it. That means that as we now read these words, we are reading the actual words spoken by Christ, as J. Jeremias demonstrated.[1]

Similarly, at Revelation 3:14 Christ applies the term *'āmēn* not only to his statements and promises but to himself: 'The words of the Amen, the faithful and true witness'. Faith, therefore, in the statements, propositions and promises uttered by Christ and God is regarded as being ultimately based on a person's estimate of the moral character and trustworthiness of Christ and God. One cannot separate the truthfulness of the statements from the truthfulness of the persons who make them. So, for instance, in a famous passage the Christian apostle, John, first argues that not to believe a statement made by God is to call into question God's personal truthfulness:

> Whoever does not believe God has made him a liar, because he has not believed in the testimony that God has borne concerning his Son. (1 John 5:10)

And then John cites the statements that God has made and expects people to believe simply on the ground that God has made them:

> And this is the testimony, that God gave us eternal life, and this life is in his Son. Whoever has the Son has the life; whoever does not have the Son of God does not have life. (1 John 5:11–12)

Truths expressed in precise legal language

At various places the Old Testament takes the forms of a legal covenant. When these covenants are interpreted in the New Testament great emphasis is laid on the precise wording of the original covenant and on exact representation of its terms. An example is:

> To give a human example, brothers: even with a man-made covenant, no one annuls it or adds to it once it has been ratified. Now the promises were made to Abraham and to his offspring [lit. 'seed']. It does not say 'And to his offsprings [lit. 'seeds']', referring to many, but referring to one, 'And to your offspring [seed]', who is Christ. This is what I mean: the law, which came

---

[1] *New Testament Theology*, 35–6.

430 years afterwards, does not annul a covenant previously ratified by God, so as to make the promise void. (Gal 3:15-17)

Existential truth

The Bible records not only propositional statements of Christian doctrine, but also the testimony of people who claim to have proved these doctrines to be true in their own practical experience. A good example is that of Paul, the Christian apostle, who first relates his own experience and then on that basis, asserts his conviction of the truth and trustworthiness of Christian doctrine:

> formerly I was a blasphemer, persecutor, and insolent opponent. But I received mercy . . . and the grace of our Lord overflowed for me with faith and love that are in Christ Jesus. The saying is trustworthy and deserving of full acceptance, that Christ Jesus came into the world to save sinners, of whom I am foremost. (1 Tim 1:13-15)

Revealed truth

In a number of places the New Testament uses the term 'the truth' to denote the body of divinely revealed truth in regard to:

Creation

> men, who . . . suppress the truth . . . For what can be known about God is plain to them, because God has shown it to them. For his invisible attributes, namely, his eternal power and divine nature, have been clearly perceived, ever since the creation of the world, in the things that have been made . . . they exchanged the truth about God for a lie and worshipped and served the creature rather than the Creator. (Rom 1:18-20, 25)

Here lies the basic difference between atheism and theism. To the atheist the universe is not a revelation of anything. It is simply a brute fact with nothing to tell us about anything outside itself. One can study what it is made of, how it works, and one can deduce the regular principles its working seems to follow and call these principles laws. But one is not allowed to ask whether the universe reveals a creative Mind behind its existence because by definition, according to atheism, there is no Mind behind the universe for it to reveal.

The Bible, by contrast, asserts that the universe is the vehicle of God's self-revelation of his power and divine nature; and that to regard the universe itself as the Ultimate Reality, and the matter and forces of nature as the Ultimate Powers, is the Fundamental Falsehood in contradistinction to the Fundamental Truth about the universe and our place and significance in it.

The Bible further predicts that when atheism finally produces its fully developed harvest, its fundamental falsehood that there is no God will develop into the further falsehood that man, the highest product of evolution, is God and should act as God (2 Thess 2:3–4, 9–12). It will be the final logical outworking of the deception early instilled, according to the Bible, into mankind's heart and imagination: *'you shall be as God'* (Gen 3:5).

The gospel

> when you heard the word of truth, the gospel of your salvation (Eph 1:13)

> so that the truth of the gospel might be preserved for you (Gal 2:5)

> Who hindered you from obeying the truth? (Gal 5:7)

From these few examples, and many others like them, it is evident in the New Testament that 'the truth of the gospel' and 'the truth' (*tout court*) often refer to the same thing. Truth is essentially the revealed truth of the gospel message. So to believe the gospel and thus become a Christian is 'to come to the knowledge of the truth' (cf. 1 Tim 2:4; 2 Tim 3:7). As to the origin and the communication of this gospel, the New Testament talks in this fashion:

> When the Spirit of truth comes, he will guide you into all the truth. (John 16:13)

> the gospel that was preached by me is not man's gospel. For I did not receive it from any man, nor was I taught it, but I received it through a revelation of Jesus Christ. (Gal 1:11–12)

The gospel, as being truth, is also distinguished from myth and legend. Foreseeing what would happen all too often in the subsequent centuries Paul remarks:

> For the time is coming when people will not endure sound teaching, but . . . will turn away from listening to the truth and wander off into myths. (2 Tim 4:3–4)

Christ is himself the truth

For a true understanding of the Christian gospel, it is important to notice that Christ not only claimed to *teach* the truth: he claimed to *be* the truth. He was the Son of God, in what the theologians call hypostatic union with the Father; and though he became truly human, he never ceased to be God. He was simultaneously God and man. He was, therefore, God revealing himself in human form:

> No one has ever seen God; the only God [or, 'the only One, who is God'], who is at the Father's side, he has made him known. (John 1:18)

> Whoever has seen me has seen the Father. (John 14:9)

> I am the way, and the truth, and the life. No one comes to the Father except through me. (John 14:6)

> He is the radiance of the glory of God and the exact imprint of his nature. (Heb 1:3)

> By him all things were created, in heaven and on earth, visible and invisible . . . all things were created through him and for him. (Col 1:16)

Since everything in heaven and earth was created by God and for God, the ultimate truth about everything—about its origin, maintenance and goal—is God. According to the Bible, Christ is that God incarnate (i.e. in the flesh). In Christ we have eternal truth and historical truth, eternal truth expressed in time and historical truth of eternal significance. The historical facts of the life, death and resurrection of Christ are the truth about God. To know the only true God and Jesus Christ, the Son of the Father, is to experience eternal life already begun here in time (John 17:3). So John, who at the Last Supper reclined at table next to Jesus, subsequently writes:

> And we know that the Son of God has come and has given us understanding, so that we may know him who is true; and we are in him who is true, in his Son Jesus Christ. He is the true God and eternal life. Little children, keep yourselves from idols. (1 John 5:20–21)

Now, of course, not everyone accepts that Jesus is the truth, nor did they when he first made his claims. The opposition to his claims was at times severe, culminating ultimately in his arrest, trial and crucifixion. The issues involved in that trial speak to the question of truth directly and are the subject of our next chapter.

CHAPTER 8

TRUTH ON TRIAL

You have brought about my death in the belief that through it you will be delivered from submitting your conduct to criticism, but I say that the result will be just the opposite. . . . If you expect to stop denunciation of your wrong way of life by putting people to death, there is something amiss with your reasoning. This way of escape is neither possible nor creditable.
—Socrates, in Plato's *Apology*

COMING TO FACE THE TRUTH

It is a characteristic of truth that when we know something to be true we are expected to believe it and, where appropriate, to act accordingly. And so it comes about that when we stand face to face with truth and deliberate what we are going to do with it, it is not the truth that is on trial, it is we ourselves who are being judged by the truth.

Socrates long ago made this point when at the conclusion of his trial he addressed those who had voted for his execution. He had devoted his life to searching for the truth and doubtless had irritated many prominent people by exposing their false beliefs and urging them to join with him in seeking the truth. But they regarded such seeking for the truth as subversive of society and of their power. So they brought him to court on a charge of subverting the young, tried him and sentenced him to death. Of course, it was tacitly understood that if he had been willing to give up his goading of the Athenians to search for the truth, he would have been allowed to escape death by going into voluntary exile. But that he refused to do. His final words to the court about those who voted for his execution have been immortalised by Plato in the *Apology*:

> When I leave this court I shall go away condemned by you to death, but they will go away convicted by truth herself of depravity and wickedness....
>
> I tell you, my executioners, that as soon as I am dead, vengeance shall fall upon you with a punishment far more painful than your killing of me. You have brought about my death in the belief that through it you will be delivered from submitting your conduct to criticism, but I say that the result will be just the opposite. You will have more critics ... If you expect to stop denunciation of your wrong way of life by putting people to death, there is something amiss with your reasoning. This way of escape is neither possible nor creditable. The best and easiest

way is not to stop the mouths of others, but to make yourselves as good men as you can.[1]

Socrates' words have proved more true than he could have known. Millions have read them since and have expressed their condemnation of his executioners. Still today we admire his stand, and that of his many successors who in the course of history have dared, against mighty odds, to believe that 'one word of truth outweighs the world',[2] and that truth in the end will prevail.

And now another trial and, at its heart, the question of truth.

THE TRIAL OF CHRIST

CHRIST For this purpose I was born and for this purpose I have come into the world—to bear witness to the truth. Everyone who is of the truth listens to my voice.

PILATE What is truth? (John 18:37–38)

All four Christian Gospels record the trial of Christ before Pontius Pilate, the Roman procurator of Judaea (AD 26–36),[3] who eventually sentenced him to death by crucifixion. John, however, in the Fourth Gospel, gives brief accounts of two private interviews that Pilate conducted with his prisoner in the course of the trial. For the reader who has first read the whole Gospel, these two accounts pulsate with nuances, ironies and universal implications that turn this local, historical trial into the supreme show trial of all time.

Socrates was put on trial because of his persistent searching for the truth. But according to the Fourth Gospel, Christ never *searched for* the truth: he *was* the truth incarnate, come into our world to express, not only by his words, but by his person, by his life, death and resurrection, what God is really like, and so to dispel the fundamental lie about the character of God insinuated into the human heart by God's inveterate enemy (see John 8:31–47). See the trial of Christ

---

[1] Plato, *Apology*, 39b–d, (Tredennick, 23–4).
[2] A Russian proverb, famously quoted by Alexander Solzhenitsyn in his 1920 address to the Swedish Academy. 'Alexandr Solzhenitsyn—Nobel Lecture'.
[3] While 'procurator' is a more widely known title, 'prefect' may be more accurate, according to Roman inscriptions of that period.

as John intends us to see it and the irony of the situation is awesome: as the ultimate truth, God incarnate submits to being put on trial for his life before one of his creatures.

It will be worthwhile spending time and effort analysing the issues at stake in John's account of the trial. We shall find that as far as Pilate was concerned, there were two major phases in the trial. In the first he discovered the truth of the case before him, namely the innocence of Christ; in the second he discovered the awesomeness of the authority given to him to decide what should be done with the truth.

The background to the trial

The Prosecutors. The case against Christ was led mainly by the aristocratic high priest and the other chief priests. Under the Romans the high priest was a state official in the sense that he was appointed by the Romans. To emphasise that point, the Roman procurator kept the high priest's official robes under lock and key in his own possession, allowing whatever high priest he approved of to wear them on only those occasions that the procurator saw fit.

On the other hand, the high priest had extensive powers. To start with, he was in charge of all matters pertaining to the national temple; and the dues that came to him from the sacrifices offered by the worshippers, and by the hundreds of thousands of the pilgrims at the feasts, made him a very wealthy man. In addition, he was president of the Jewish Council that controlled all civil and commercial activities in the province. Consequently, he had substantial influence both with the procurator and with Rome itself. It was a love-hate relationship.

The charges against Christ. There were two:

1. *A political charge*. Christ, they alleged, was inciting the populace to regard him as the messianic king of the Jews and was fomenting popular uprising against the imperial power of Rome. He was guilty of treason against the emperor (John 19:12).

The priests had their own special reasons for urging this charge against Christ. He had publicly denounced the commercialisation of the temple (2:13–22); and if he succeeded in leading a popular uprising against the Romans (such as others eventually did lead in AD 66–70), the result, they felt, would be disastrous, not only for the nation and their capital city, but for the temple itself. They decided that pre-emptive action must be taken to get Christ executed (John 11:47–53).

2. *A religious charge.* Christ was charged with the extreme blasphemy of claiming to be the Son of God in a unique sense, thus making himself equal with God (5:18; 19:7). This, in Jewish law, was an offence punishable by death.

The first phase of the trial: Pilate discovers the truth

The arrest (John at 18:1–11)

Details of the arrest indicate that the high priest must have had some prior communication with the Roman authorities, informing them that Jesus was a dangerous insurrectionist, and that any attempt at arresting him would be met with armed resistance. For the arresting party, led by Judas to Gethsemane, was made up of two bands of soldiers:

1. Officers and men of the temple-guard, i.e. Jewish men under the command of the captain of the temple, who was one of the chief priests (v. 3). But in addition:
2. A detachment of Roman soldiers.[4]

As things turned out, in making this arrangement the priests were unwittingly laying evidence against their own case; for when the arresting party reached Gethsemane, Jesus made no attempt to use force to avoid arrest. Instead, when one of his hot-headed disciples drew a sword and with bad aim cut an ear (instead of the head) off a servant of the high priest, Jesus immediately commanded him to sheath his sword. And then for all to hear, he announced that he regarded his arrest and all that was to follow as God's will to which he was determined to submit. With that, he voluntarily handed himself up, on the sole condition that his disciples were let go free (v. 8).

---

[4] The Greek word *speiran* in 18:3, is the standard Greek translation of the Latin *cohors*. The soldiers from this cohort are said to have been led by a *chiliarch* (v. 12), which means 'a leader of a thousand men', but which had become the standard Greek translation of the Latin 'military tribune'. He was a commander of a cohort of about 600 men. We are not to think however that the commander took all 600 of his men to arrest Jesus.

It is unthinkable that the officer in charge of the Roman detachment should not have reported this to his captain and he to Pilate himself, which, no doubt, accounts for the way Pilate reacted when the priests brought Jesus before him.

The first formal session of the court (John 18:28–32)

Pilate's first move was to demand a formal statement of the charge against Jesus, which seems to have taken the priests aback, for they answered rather lamely with a vague, non-specific charge: 'If this man were not a criminal, we should not have delivered him up to you' (vv. 29–30). Pilate's brusque response was to order them to take the prisoner away and try him under their own law, which he scarcely would have done if he still thought that the man his soldiers had helped to arrest was involved in fomenting political insurrection against the emperor (v. 31).

> Pilate's first move was to demand a formal statement of the charge against Jesus, which seems to have taken the priests aback.

But under the Romans the Jewish court, as Pilate well knew, had no legal right to inflict the death penalty; and the high priest was determined to get Jesus executed if he could. He therefore insisted that Pilate conduct the case under Roman law. Pilate's response was to adjourn the court as he retired to conduct an interview with the prisoner in private.

Pilate's first interview with Christ (John 18:33–38)

The first thing Pilate wanted to hear from the prisoner's own mouth was whether he regarded himself as the King of the Jews.

But the question could not be answered with a simple yes or no; for the terms 'king' and 'kingdom' meant different things to different people. If 'king' and 'kingdom' were the labels that Pilate, left to himself, was putting on Christ, on his teaching and activity, then Pilate would understand the terms in a political sense; and in this sense Christ must deny that he was a king. Christ was not in political competition with the emperor Tiberius at Rome.

On the other hand, in another sense, he was 'the King of Israel'. Indeed a week earlier, he had allowed himself to be acclaimed by the crowds as 'the King who comes in the name of the Lord'. He had ridden into Jerusalem on a donkey, surrounded by hundreds, if not a few thousands, of followers, deliberately fulfilling an Old Testament prophecy describing the coming of Jerusalem's king (Zech 9:9; John 12:12–19). If it was this incident, among other things, that the Jewish religious authorities had reported to Pilate, Christ had no intention of denying it nor the claim he had thereby made.

But the high priest was misinterpreting this incident (whether in ignorance or deliberately, we shall see in a moment). Christ was not, as they were now making out he was, the leader of an organised band of freedom fighters, ready to fight to the death in a holy war on behalf of their religion, in order to oust the Roman imperialists from their country.[5]

The only way that Christ could answer Pilate's question, therefore, was to explain to him the nature of his kingdom and the power by which he would establish it:

> My kingdom is not of this world. If my kingdom were of this world, my servants would have been fighting[6] that I might not be delivered over to the Jews. But my kingdom is not from this world. (18:36)

As we have earlier suggested, Pilate already knew what happened in the garden. He knew, then, that what Jesus was now saying was the truth. But Jesus had referred to his kingdom. That must imply that he thought of himself as a king. Could it be, then, that his refusal to let his followers fight to avoid arrest was merely pragmatic tactics in view of the presence of armed Roman soldiers? If released now, would he later on, given the right conditions, attempt to set up his kingdom by raising armed insurrection?

Pilate probed further, for he could take no risks: 'You are a king then?'

Jesus' answer put the matter beyond doubt. His refraining from violence in Gethsemane was not temporary pragmatism: it sprang from the nature of his kingdom. Its power to gain people's allegiance was, and could only be, truth:

---

[5] This was the motivating factor behind a band of freedom fighters who made the attempt in the war of AD 66–70 already mentioned.

[6] In Greek the tenses in this hypothetical conditional sentence can refer either to the present, i.e. 'my servants would now be fighting', or to a past process: 'my disciples would have been fighting'. This second translation is to be preferred. Christ is referring to what happened in Gethsemane when he forbade his disciples to fight in order to prevent his arrest by the Jews.

You say that I am a king. For this purpose I was born and for this purpose I have come into the world—to bear witness to the truth. Everyone who is of the truth, listens to my voice. (v. 37)

'What is truth?' said Pilate as he turned and made for the door.

He was not necessarily being cynical. Certainly, truth, in the absolute sense that Jesus obviously intended, may well not have been something that, in Pilate's thinking, had much to do with the military and political affairs in which he was involved. It was the kind of thing that philosophers and religious people talked about. For himself, however, he was now convinced that a man who abjured violence and was concerned only with truth, whatever that was, was no political rival to the emperor. This much, at least, seemed true: Jesus was innocent of the charge brought against him by the priests.

But the priests had been adamant: Jesus was the leader of a potentially violent insurrection. Were not the priests sincere? Were they not also, in their way, concerned with the truth? Pilate decided to test them.

A test for truth (John 18:38–40)

Apparently, it was a custom once a year at the great religious feast of Passover for the Roman procurator to release one Jewish prisoner as a goodwill gesture. So Pilate first announced that he, as the Roman procurator, found Jesus to be completely innocent of the charge of being a revolutionary insurrectionist against Rome. He then proposed to honour the yearly custom and release Jesus. Would they agree? 'No', they shouted; for according to them Jesus *was* an insurrectionist, and they wanted no dealings with such extreme, messianic, and potentially violent, religionists. 'No!' they shouted again and again, 'not this man, but Barabbas!' (v. 40).

It takes only five words (in Greek) for John, the writer of the Gospel, to comment on the priests' choice of Barabbas: 'Now this Barabbas was an insurrectionist'[7] (v. 40 ESV mg). Enough said! But at least Pilate now knew for certain what the truth was and who was telling it. And it wasn't the priests.

---

[7] The Greek word here translated 'insurrectionist' is *lēstēs*. Literally it means 'a robber', or 'a brigand'. But it is used by the historian Josephus to denote political insurrectionists, freedom fighters, among whom Josephus includes Barabbas.

An interval for reflection

Naturally the testimony of Christ before Pilate exercised a powerful influence on the early Christian churches and shaped their concept of their mission to the world and of the only means they must use to spread the Christian faith. Imprisoned by the emperor Nero, the Christian Apostle Paul eventually wrote to a younger colleague:

> I charge you in the presence of God, who gives life to all things, and of Christ Jesus, who in his testimony before Pontius Pilate made the good confession, to keep the commandment unstained and free from reproach until the appearing of our Lord Jesus Christ. (1 Tim 6:13–14)

The kingdom of Christ is not just one more earth-born kingdom among all the others. Its power base is not on earth. It is an invasion of our world from another world. It is not in competition for worldly power with other kingdoms, and it is not in league with any of them. It is not ultimately based, as all other kingdoms are, on physical force. Its mission is to witness to the truth; and genuine acceptance of truth cannot be induced in the human heart by force: it can be achieved only by the power of truth itself. Any attempt to compel people by force either to accept or to retain the Christian faith is a virtual denial of that faith. The sole head of Christ's kingdom is Christ himself (Col 1:18), and its headquarters is where Christ is in heaven (3:1). Therefore, exclusive identification of his kingdom with any particular earthly culture, nation or empire unwarrantably obscures its true universality (Matt 28:18–20). The concern of those who use violence to further any religion whatever has little to do with truth. Truth, by definition, is not something that can be promoted by violence or by the threat of it.

The second phase of the trial: Pilate discovers his own responsibility

Now Pilate must face the awesome responsibility of having to decide what to do with the truth. By this time Pilate has discovered three things:

1. Jesus was telling the truth.
2. The charge brought against him by the priests was false.

3. The priests nonetheless were determined that Jesus be executed.

In spite of it, Pilate was equally determined to release what he considered to be an innocent man. The problem was, how could he pacify the opposition and get them to accept his decision? The priests had gathered an excited crowd behind them, baying for the prisoner's blood (see Luke 23:13–25; Mark 15:10–15). To deny them their quarry could have sparked off a riot—and the emperor in Rome would not have liked that.

Pilate's first attempt to release Christ (John 19:1–6)

He hit upon the tactic of making Jesus' claim to be king look ridiculous, and Jesus himself so forlorn and contemptible a figure, that the priests might see how absurd their accusation was that such a man posed any realistic threat to the emperor.

First, he had Jesus flogged.[8] Then he allowed his soldiers to dress Jesus up as a king with a mock crown of thorns and a robe, ridiculing his supposed kingship with verbal and physical abuse. Then he went out and announced to the priests and people that he was about to bring Jesus out to them so that they might see for themselves that he found no guilt in him. So Jesus came out wearing this mock royal garb, and Pilate cried out 'Look at the fellow'.[9]

But the priests were unmoved and still demanded his crucifixion, at which Pilate bristled and told them to take Jesus and crucify him themselves. He knew they couldn't, of course; they had no legal power to do so. But Pilate was not going to give in to them and use his legal power as a Roman magistrate to execute an innocent man for the sake of gratifying their religious prejudices.

The priests' next move (John 19:7–8)

The priests now saw that they were getting nowhere with the political charge: Pilate had emphatically rejected it twice. How then were they

---

[8] Roman magistrates were allowed to flog non-Roman citizens when they were brought to court, even if they were innocent. They did it just to put the accused 'in the right frame of mind', and as a warning not to create further trouble.

[9] The traditional translation 'Behold the Man' is too majestic. In contexts like this the Greek word for 'man' (*anthrōpos*) carries a mixture of contempt and pity.

to get Jesus executed? They tried their second, and this time, their real, charge against Jesus: 'We have a law, and by that law he ought to die, because he made himself the Son of God' (v. 7).

A religious charge like that, however, was not competent to a Roman civil court; but nevertheless it instilled a certain amount of fear into Pilate (v. 8).

To start with, Jerusalem at Passover time, with thousands of pilgrims joining with the local population, was like a powder keg. Any real or imagined insult to the Jewish religion from the Roman procurator could easily spark off a massive riot. If Jesus' teachings were offensive to Jewish religious sensitivities, Pilate must be careful how he released Jesus.

But secondly, Pilate had another concern. He was not an atheist, but a pagan, who believed in the possibility of god-like men appearing on earth. He would have known ancient myths, like that of the god Dionysus who was said to have visited the city of Thebes in human form. The king of Thebes in his stubborn ignorance had abused and then imprisoned him—and suffered an horrendous fate in consequence.[10] So Pilate retired once more to interview Jesus in private, to discover, if he could, just who this prisoner was that stood before him.

Pilate's second interview with Christ (19:9–11)

The question that now agitated Pilate, as once more he faced the prisoner, was no longer 'What have you done?' but 'Where are you from?' This innocent, yet unusual, man, who talked of his 'coming into the world' as if it had been deliberate and for a deliberate purpose, namely to bear witness to the truth, and who was now alleged to have claimed that he was the Son of God—where in fact was he from?

It is, by the way, a question that eventually arises when anyone starts to think seriously about truth. From where does truth get its authority? Is it merely from human consensus? Is truth the product of each individual's subjective judgment? Or is truth an objective standard that is above and outside our subjective and ever-changing world of thought?

But Jesus made no answer, and that irritated Pilate. After all he was the ultimate authority in this situation, wasn't he?

---

[10] See Euripides, *Bacchae*.

'You will not speak to *me*?' he said impatiently with great emphasis on the 'me'. 'Do you not know that I have authority to release you and authority to crucify you?' (19:10). Pilate was doing his best to get the Jews to accept Jesus' release; but Jesus must cooperate with him for, in the end, Jesus' life or death depended on his decision, and the burden of authority to make this decision lay heavy on Pilate.

But Christ was not denying Pilate's authority as the emperor's appointee with the power of life and death in his hands. Nor was Christ about to refuse to submit to Pilate's authority. But Pilate must be made to consider by whose authority this whole situation had come about.[11]

How and by whose authority had it come about that Pilate had been born into this world, had grown up, entered the Roman army, been appointed procurator of Judaea by the emperor, and now sat here not only with authority from the emperor, but with the human power of free will to decide whether the Son of God should be released or be crucified?

> There is no doubt what Christ meant when he told Pilate that the whole situation had been given him 'from above'. But it meant that the responsibility that Pilate carried was awesome.

As we listen to the story, it is easy enough to see that sooner or later we have to ask the same question about ourselves. The majority of us will never have in our hands the power of life and death over another human being. But we do find ourselves born into this world (not by our own decision), with intelligence to understand the claims of truth in general and the particular claim of Christ to be the truth and above all with the free will to decide whether to believe his claim or to banish both it and him from our lives. And the question still is: by whose authority has this all come about? Anyone's? Or has the whole situation been thrown up by mindless evolutionary chance so that questions about truth are ultimately meaningless?

There is no doubt what Christ meant when he told Pilate that the whole situation had been given him 'from above'. But it meant that

---

[11] When Christ remarked 'You would have no authority over me at all unless it had been given you from above', the word for 'authority', in Greek, is feminine in gender, but the word for 'it (had been given)' is neuter. This means that 'what had been given from above' refers not merely to Pilate's authority, but to the whole situation in which Pilate now found himself with authority to decide whether Jesus should be released or be crucified.

the responsibility that Pilate carried was awesome. He knew beyond doubt what the truth of the case was: Christ was innocent. To hand him over to crucifixion would be to sin against the truth. But if Jesus was the Son of God, to crucify him would be sin against ultimate truth, that is God himself. Even so, said Christ, his sin would be less than that of the Jewish high priest. The priest professed to believe in the God of truth, but he had used the authority of his religious office in the name of God to get Christ executed on the basis of a lie.

Pilate's final attempts to release Christ (John 19:12–15)

From this point on Pilate made repeated effort to release Jesus. But the priests blackmailed him. They had influence in Rome. If they took steps to let Tiberius gain the impression that they had brought a leader of insurrection to Pilate, and Pilate had acquitted him . . . ! Pilate saw the point. He made one last effort to escape their trap by appealing to their patriotism, if not to their religion. 'Shall I crucify your king?' he asked. 'We have no king', replied the chief priests, 'but Caesar' (v. 15). No king at all beside Caesar? To get rid of Jesus they now denied a fundamental tenet of their Jewish faith and all that their inspired prophets had said about their King Messiah.

Questions arising

If Jesus was, as the gospel claims, God incarnate, why did he not tell Pilate so in plain straightforward words?

But if he had said 'I am God incarnate', what could pagan Pilate have made of the claim? And would Pilate have believed his plain statement?

But Christ could have shown himself to Pilate in all his divine majesty and proved to Pilate that he was the Son of God.

Yes, and have frightened Pilate out of his wits, so that he no longer retained any self-control or ability to come to a free decision? The issue at stake was truth, and truth does not behave like that. Moreover, Pilate knew enough truth to know that Christ was not guilty of the charge against him. Pilate must make his decision on the basis of what truth he knew, and he would be held accountable for that and not for what he didn't know.

But there is a far bigger question. How is it credible that the Creator of the universe should endow his human creatures with free will and then become human himself and put himself in a position where his creatures could put him on trial, and, if they chose, use their free will to decide to crucify him?

But that, says the Bible, is precisely what the truth about God is. Away beyond the high priest's machinations, the fears and vacillations of Pilate and the raucous shouting of the fevered mob, the Son of God was 'delivered up according to the definite plan and foreknowledge of God' (Acts 2:23) to achieve four divine purposes:

1. To expose the falsity of his enemy's lie that God is a tyrant and that God's word is meant to enslave man.
2. To demonstrate by the horrors of the Son of God's crucifixion the effect on the human heart of believing the enemy's lie.
3. To demonstrate the truth about God and his attitude even towards his sinfully rebellious creatures so as to win their hearts back by his demonstrated love and to set them free by his truth (1 John 4:10).
4. To induce man's repentance towards God and to make a just and honourable way for man to be reconciled to God through the death of his Son (Rom 5:10–11).

This in true fact is the answer to Pilate's question: *What is Truth?*

POSTMODERNISM

CHAPTER 9

POSTMODERNISM, PHILOSOPHY AND LITERATURE

Truth is what appears true to each individual or community. Facts are not objective entities to which our thinking must conform: it is we who, in discussion with others, decide what the facts shall be. Particularly to be rejected is any theory, ideology or religion that claims to have the 'big story', the metanarrative that gives the universal truth about everything, which everybody must accept.

INTRODUCTION

'Postmodernism', like its philosophical predecessor, 'modernism', is an umbrella term that denotes not a particular theory so much as an attitude shared by many contemporary thinkers in such diverse fields as art, literature, philosophy, social studies, architecture, city planning, science and religion. In this chapter we are to study postmodernism's attitude to literary criticism, chiefly as represented by the work of its most famous exponent, Jacques Derrida (1930–2004), though, of course, some of his views are but extensions of views held by others, whether postmodernists or not.

The question immediately arises, why do that here? This present part of our book is devoted to epistemology, to such topics as, how do we know anything? How do we know that what we claim to know is true; and can we know the ultimate truth about anything? Is there such a thing as objective truth, which is universally true for everybody regardless of whether they recognise it or not, accept it or reject it? What, then, has literary criticism got to do with epistemology?

Literary criticism's search for truth

The answer to the questions we have just raised is that serious literary criticism is a form of search for truth.

At the basic level it seeks carefully to establish exactly what the text before it says; and when that involves translation from a foreign language, and particularly an ancient foreign language, it requires especial care. The question is: do the translation and the exegesis truly represent the original text?

Secondly, it must decide what the text means by what it actually says. What it says and what it means could be two different things. Suppose a character in a novel says: 'Mr Smith must be a master of logic to have come to that conclusion on the basis of this evidence'; he may be speaking ironically. In that case he *means* the very opposite of what he actually *says*. Literary criticism, therefore, involves interpretation of texts, just like science involves interpretation of the physical universe.

Serious literature like, say, Sophocles' *Oedipus Tyrannus*, Euripides' *Bacchae* (or 'Maenads'), Shakespeare's *Hamlet*, or novels by Fyodor Dostoevsky and Jane Austen, are not just interesting stories to be read for their entertainment value only. They discuss fundamental problems of the human condition. Sometimes the discussion is left open-ended; sometimes the author eventually makes his own position clear. In any case, literature of this kind challenges the reader's presuppositions, views and values and raises not only epistemological and aesthetic, but also social, moral and metaphysical questions. Serious literary criticism, therefore, can hardly avoid facing these questions and asking where the truth lies.

In this chapter, then, we examine the philosophy that lies behind postmodernist literary criticism and the effect that that particular philosophy has on postmodernist treatment of literature.

Postmodernism's relation to modernism

The term 'postmodernism' is obviously meant to contrast with 'modernism', though in actual fact postmodernism still shares certain fundamental attitudes with the 'modernism' out of which it developed and against which, in other respects, it is a reaction.

Modernism made human reason the final judge and criterion of all truth in heaven and on earth.[1] If there was a God, and even if it was thought that he might have revealed some truths to humankind, nevertheless God's existence and his revelation must both face the bar of human reason and pass its scrutiny before they could be

---

[1] 'Modernism' in the sense in which we speak of it here is to be distinguished from the term 'modernism' as applied to the period of Russian literature that extended from 1895 to 1925, and is held to have been initiated by a lecture published in 1893 by Dmitry Merezhkovsky, entitled 'On the reasons for the decline and on the new currents in contemporary Russian literature'. Evelyn Bristol characterises this Russian modernism thus: 'The epoch of modernism began as a clear rebellion against the materialist legacy of the 1860s. . . . Where the older generation had rejected supernatural religion, the new intellectuals took a keen interest, not only in Russian Orthodoxy but in religions of all sorts' ('Turn of a Century: Modernism, 1895–1925', 387–8). This Russian modernism then, was very different in its stance from the attitude generally known as modernism in the West.

accepted as true. That said, modernism agreed that there was objective truth 'out there' in the world and in the universe and that with diligent research it could be discovered, understood and defined.

To the postmodernist way of thinking, however, modernism has proved disappointing. Since the Enlightenment, modern man has looked to human reason, and particularly to science, to liberate the human race from the enslavement of superstitions and tyrannies of all kinds, religion included. Instead, for postmodernists, modernism has itself become an enslaver. It has spawned great universal, all-embracing, all-explaining theories—'big stories' or 'metanarratives', as they are called—that have then been tyrannically enforced on people, crushing their spontaneity and creativity and suppressing independence of thought. Moreover, the disastrous world wars of the last century, some brought about by supposedly scientific theories of racial superiority, others by the subjugation of millions under enforced Marxist ideology, and all of them backed up by terrific armaments produced by the progress of science and technology—all this, in postmodernist eyes, leaves modernism self-condemned.

For postmodernists, modernism has itself become an enslaver.

It is understandable, then, that in reaction to this, postmodernism should resent being told how to write, or interpret, literature and should wish to be free to write and interpret without any external constraints or principles imposed from outside the individual's own judgment. Like modernism, postmodernism still makes the human race the centre and arbiter of all things, but not now humankind as a whole, nor any body of so-called experts or 'authorities', but each individual, or at least each individual's community. This means that according to postmodernism there is no objective truth about anything that, once discovered, must be accepted by every rational human being. Truth is what appears true to each individual or community. Facts are not objective entities to which our thinking must conform: it is we who, in discussion with others, decide what the facts shall be.

Particularly to be rejected is any theory, ideology or religion that claims to have the 'big story', the metanarrative that gives the universal truth about everything, which everybody must accept. Marxism in its day was one such metanarrative. Modern science is another. And the claim of Christ—'I am the way, and the truth, and the life.

No one comes to the Father except through me' (John 14:6)—is felt to be especially offensive and intolerable.

Derrida's position in the history and practice of literary criticism

Jacques Derrida (1930–2004) became famous for the 'deconstruction' which he practised on literary texts, and which he recommended that all other critics should likewise practise. His methodology has been widely influential. What it means, we shall consider later on; but a survey of statements about deconstruction taken from some of his followers will give us a preliminary idea of where Derrida stood in relation to other theories of criticism.[2]

> As a mode of textual theory and analysis, contemporary *deconstruction* subverts almost everything in the tradition, putting in question received ideas of the sign and language, the text, the context, the author, the reader, the role of history, the world of interpretation, and the forms of critical writing.[3]

> [Deconstruction] undoes the very comforts of mastery and consensus that underlie the illusion that objectivity is situated somewhere outside the self.[4]

> Deconstruction is the active antithesis of everything that criticism ought to be if one accepts its traditional values and concepts.[5]

From these few descriptions it is clear that deconstruction is nothing if it is not uncompromisingly and deliberately anti-tradition, subversive and revolutionary. Now it is always helpful to be reminded, as we are by deconstructionism, that we must not adopt any theory unthinkingly but must always submit received opinion to careful scrutiny and questioning. But whether all traditions of belief and of criticism throughout history right up until Derrida appeared were all

---

[2] These quotations are cited from Ellis, *Against Deconstruction*, 68–9.
[3] Leitch, *Deconstructive Criticism*, ix.
[4] Johnson, 'Nothing Fails Like Success', 11.
[5] Norris, *Deconstruction*, xii.

so perverse and misguided that they all needed to be totally subverted is, of course, another thing.

Some basic principles of Derrida's theory of literary criticism

We must remind ourselves here that not all of the following principles are peculiar to Derrida. Some were advocated by critics who preceded him and are still held by critics belonging to other schools. On the other hand, where Derrida took over previously held views, he often developed them in his own way and integrated them into his own system:

1. Prohibition of appeal to the intended meaning of the author of a text.
2. The denial of metaphysics in any sense of the term, and the denial that meaning exists before words or that words convey a pre-existent meaning.
3. Assertion that writing precedes speech and that signification creates meaning.
4. Denial that words have any intrinsic meaning. Assertion that the meaning of a word is always deferred, which thus allows unlimited 'play'.
5. The practice of deconstruction. To deconstruct a discourse or text is to show how it, like all other discourses or texts, undermines the very philosophy it asserts.
6. Derrida's ideal writing.

We shall now examine these in turn.

PROHIBITION OF APPEAL TO THE INTENDED MEANING OF THE AUTHOR

For many centuries it was a fundamental principle of literary criticism that to be true an interpretation of a text must discover and then expound the meaning that the author of the text intended. After all, the text would not exist unless the author had decided to write it in order to express the meaning he intended to convey; and the words of the text were those which the author chose in order to express that meaning.

But in 1954 William K. Wimsatt and Monroe Beardsley, under the heading 'The Intentional Fallacy',[6] questioned this basic rule of interpretation. Their thesis was plausible. We ourselves have learned from experience that a living author, whether speaking or writing, can sometimes fail to express himself clearly. He may intend to say one thing but actually say another. He may intend to make one impression on his readers but in fact create an altogether different effect. Moreover, some of his words and sentences can be ambiguous. In addition, the psychological and emotional connotations that a word had for the author might not be the same for his readers. (In standard British English, to say that a woman is 'homely' means that she is unpretentious. It can therefore be a commendation, if not a compliment. In American English to say that a woman is 'homely' would be an insult. It would mean that she is unattractive if not positively ugly.)

As long as an author is still living, he can be asked what meaning he really intended to convey; but once he is dead, he is unavailable for questioning.

Then there is the inevitable limitation of writing compared with speech. A speaker can convey meaning by intonation, tone of voice, pitch, softness or loudness, emphasis, speed or hesitation in delivery, and by gesture of the hands and facial expression, none of which can be satisfactorily indicated in writing.

Furthermore, a world class author, writing in the white heat of his genius, can produce effects beyond what he consciously intends, but which later readers perceive. The Bible itself says that some Old Testament prophets, speaking by the inspiration of God, sometimes spoke more than they knew at the time of their speaking (1 Pet 1:10–12).

As long as an author is still living, he can be asked what meaning he really intended to convey; but once he is dead, he is unavailable for questioning. We are left simply with the text; we must make of it what we can. It has an authority of its own; we do not need to attempt the impossible and reconstruct the thoughts and intentions that the

---

[6] In *Verbal Icon*, 3–20.

author may have had in his head. At least, that is what the Intentional Fallacy Theory says.

Since 1954, then, this theory has gained almost universal acceptance, and is not limited to followers of Derrida. Paul Ricoeur (1913–2005), for instance, is not normally regarded as a deconstructionist, (though Derrida was originally a pupil of his); yet Ricoeur insists that even in the case of texts that originated as a medium of authorial discourse (like, say, the written text of a lecture delivered orally by its author) the interpreter's goal must be to discover the sense of the text, without appeal to the author's intended meaning. Ricoeur states:

> With writing, the verbal meaning of the text no longer coincides with the mental meaning or intention of the text. This intention is both fulfilled and abolished by the text, which is no longer the voice of someone present. The text is mute.[7]

> Writing renders the text autonomous with respect to the intention of the author. What the text signifies no longer coincides with what the author meant; henceforth, textual meaning and psychological meaning have different destinies.[8]

And again:

> The text's career escapes the finite horizon lived by its author. What the text says now matters more than what the author meant to say, and every exegesis unfolds its procedures within the circumference of a meaning that has broken its moorings to the psychology of its author.[9]

As an illustration of the principle of interpretation of literary texts that Ricoeur is arguing for, we may cite the practice that obtains in Britain in regard to the interpretation of legal texts. When Parliament passes an Act, it is Parliament's intention that the wording of the Act shall convey exactly the meaning that Parliament intends. But sometimes it subsequently happens that the meaning of the Act is disputed in the courts, and then a judge is called upon to settle the dispute. In deciding the exact meaning of the Act, the judge does not

---

[7] *Interpretation Theory*, 75.
[8] *Hermeneutics and Human Sciences*, 139.
[9] *Hermeneutics and Human Sciences*, 201.

ask what was the meaning that Parliament had in mind. He decides the meaning of the Act on the basis of the actual words that stand in the text, regardless of what Parliament thought it was saying when the Act was written. It is held that this is the only fair and just way to interpret the Act. How could a citizen conform his practice to the demands of the Act, if he could know what the Act meant only by going behind what its words actually say and imagining what was in the minds of the members of Parliament when they passed the Act perhaps fifty or more years ago?

Limits to the intentional fallacy

The intentional fallacy, then, is certainly valid up to a point; but its validity could be, and often is, exaggerated. Here are some countervailing considerations:

Some texts contain within themselves an explicit statement by the author of his or her intention. The Fourth Gospel in the New Testament is a case in point. It is a mixture of narrative and discourse and certainly invites, and in the course of history has received, multiple interpretations. But towards the end the author explicitly states the purpose and the intended effect he had in mind (John 20:30–31). Granted that an interpreter cannot now consult the author, John, but if he takes the text seriously, how can he not at least take into account the explicit statement of the author's intention that the text contains? (It is of course for the interpreter to decide how well, or otherwise, what the author wrote fulfils the intention he had in writing it).

Some texts contain within themselves an explicit statement by the author of his or her intention.

Second, just because here and there in a text the author's intention may not be indisputably clear, it does not follow that the author's intended meaning is nowhere clear at any point in the text.

Sometimes, even if we cannot be sure of the author's intended meaning, we can be absolutely sure of what he did *not* intend.

As an example of this third point we may cite the ancient Greek myth of Oedipus, which relates that he was fated to murder his father and marry his mother. Freud, as we know, appealed to this myth in support of his theory that young boys get jealous of their father's relationship with their mother, conceive a desire to murder him, then suppress the desire, which later on in life causes them psychological disturbance. Freud called this psychological condition the Oedipus complex.

Now the Greek tragedian Sophocles wrote a play called *Oedipus Tyrannus*. As the play progresses it becomes apparent that, just as the myth relates, earlier in life Oedipus had murdered his father and married his mother. We can, however, be absolutely certain that Sophocles did not intend his play to be a study of the psychological condition that Freud was later to call the Oedipus complex; for in his play Sophocles represents Oedipus as discovering that earlier in his manhood (not in his boyhood) he had murdered a man who he did not even know at the time was his father, and had married a woman who similarly he did not know was his mother. We cannot, of course, consult Sophocles himself; but the details of the text that Sophocles wrote forbid the application of Freud's theory to its interpretation. Oedipus was not jealous of his father, and he killed the old man who he did not know was his father because the old man pushed him off the road and beat him on the head with a rod.

It may not be much to be able to deduce from the text of a play what the author's intended meaning was *not*. But it is a very important something, because it sets a limit to what an interpreter may claim to be the meaning of the play.

Exaggerations of reader-response criticism

Like the intentional fallacy, the reader-response theory of literary criticism that stresses what the text means to a reader, rather than the author's intended meaning, has a certain obvious validity. If any communication of meaning is to take place, a text must have, not only an author, but a reader; and it is no more than might be expected if one and the same text appeals to different readers in different ways. If, then, a reader declares 'this is what the text means to me', we cannot argue that the reader is wrong in saying so. 'This'—whatever 'this' is—is in fact the meaning that this reader takes out of the text.

On the other hand there is a limit to the meanings that can *legitimately* be taken out of the text. If a visitor to the Louvre in Paris stands in front of the Mona Lisa and declares 'This painting appeals to me as the most beautiful family scene that was ever painted', we shall hardly regard it as a valid spectator-response. The Mona Lisa just is not a painting of a family group. The visitor must be dreaming or fantasizing to imagine it is. The same is true of a literary text: the question must be asked whether the meaning which a reader says he takes out of the text, is in fact consistent with what the text itself says.

But just here we need to make an important distinction that some reader-response critics seem to overlook. They seem to think that being free from the necessity to consider the meaning intended by the author of the text is automatically the same as being free from any necessity to be constrained by what the text itself says. But that is false. The interpreter of a text is surely not free to make the text mean anything he or she likes regardless of the language it is written in, its vocabulary, grammar, syntax, and logic. If the reader were so free, there would be no point in starting with the text at all: the reader might as well start with a blank sheet of paper and write his or her own composition without pretending to be interpreting any text.

Yet this is the kind of interpretation that some forms of reader-response theory champion. Here are some examples.

Example 1 – Robert Crosman

> The statement 'authors make meaning', though not of course untrue, is merely a special case of the more universal truth that readers make meaning. . . . a poem really means whatever any reader seriously believes it to mean. . . . the number of possible meanings of a poem is itself *infinite*.[10]

Let's consider this example.

1. *'authors make meaning' . . . is a special case of the more universal truth that readers make meaning. . . . a poem really means whatever any reader seriously believes it to mean.*

What is this saying? We all know, for instance, that a musical score has to be 'interpreted', and one conductor's interpretation of a work by, say, Tchaikovsky can be very different from another conductor's interpretation. But an *interpretation* of Tchaikovsky must still be an interpretation of Tchaikovsky. An interpretation of the *Funeral*

---

[10] Crosman, 'Do Readers Make Meaning?', 151, 154.

March by Tchaikovsky that so disregarded not only Tchaikovsky's intentions but also his score and made it resemble one of Chopin's lighter pieces would not in fact be an interpretation of Tchaikovsky at all, but a different composition altogether. To say that 'a poem means whatever any reader seriously believes it to mean', would imply that a listener who seriously believed that the *Funeral March* was in fact a joyful wedding serenade, would be giving a valid interpretation. It would, however, convince very few people.

2. '*The number of possible meanings of a poem is itself infinite.*'

This surely is an exaggeration. If a poem had an infinite number of possible meanings, it would imply that a poem has no particular meaning at all; it can mean literally anything. And if that were true and applied to all poems, then it would mean that amid all the possible permutations of the infinite number of possible meanings, there would be one, at least, in which the bitterly sarcastic *Satires* of Juvenal, the deadly serious *Il Inferno* of Dante, and any love poem you like, could all be said to mean the same, as long as anyone seriously believed they did.

3. '*A poem really means whatever any reader seriously believes it to mean.*'

Interestingly enough, reader-response-theorists and deconstructionists are not prepared to have this principle applied to their own writings. They protest vigorously if any reviewer misinterprets what they have written. Derrida, for instance, demands that when he writes an article or a book, his critics should take pains to understand it in the sense he intended and not in some other sense. So he comments on a critic's lengthy review of a text of his:

> I can be reproached for being insistent, even monotonous, but it is difficult for me to see how a concept of history as the 'history of meaning' can be attributed to me. . . . I find the expression rather comical. . . . Nor can I go through, line by line, all the propositions whose confusion, I must say, rather disconcerted me.[11]

But how can a literary critic argue for, and expect us to believe in, a principle of literary criticism that he is not prepared to have applied to his own works?

---

[11] Derrida, *Positions*, 45–6.

Example 2 – Stanley Fish

> What we have here then are two critics with opposing interpretations, each of whom claims the same word as internal and confirming evidence. Clearly they cannot both be right, but just as clearly there is no basis for deciding between them. One cannot appeal to the text, because the text has become an extension of the interpretive disagreement that divides them.[12]

This certainly is a striking view, for if it were true, it would spell the end of virtually all literary criticism; and not of literary criticism only, but of all commercial contracts as well. Suppose two businessmen make and sign a contract. Subsequently they disagree about the meaning of a paragraph, sentence or even a word in the contract. Unable to reach a decision themselves, one of them sues the other in court, and the case comes before a judge. According to Fish's theory, the judge could not—or would not be allowed to—appeal to the text of the contract in order to settle the dispute! Why not? Because, so Fish says, the text of the contract is precisely what is in dispute.

But this argument goes against both common sense and legal practice. Just because two people disagree about the interpretation of a sentence or word in a text does not mean that both interpretations must automatically be regarded as equally valid and unquestionable. The judge would have every right to appeal to the text—what else did they appeal to him for?

Upon examination of the text, the judge might conceivably find that the wording of the text was so hopelessly ambiguous and confused, that the two businessmen should drop the case and sue for malpractice the lawyer who drew up the contract for them. But that would by no means be the only possible verdict. The judge might well decide:

(a) that the arguments brought by the plaintiff were completely fallacious, or

(b) that the arguments brought by the plaintiff, while not one hundred percent decisive, were far more cogent than those brought by the defendant, or

(c) that the text of the contract, interpreted strictly, meant

---

[12] Stanley Fish, *Is There a Text in This Class?*, 340.

neither what the plaintiff, nor what the defendant, had taken it to mean, but something altogether different.

The same is true of literary criticism. After centuries of worldwide study there are still many places where Shakespeare's meaning is disputed. It would be foolish for a critic to claim that his interpretation of all these passages was the final truth and altogether beyond correction or improvement. But he might well claim that the arguments for his interpretation were more and stronger than those for any other interpretation on offer (which is what most literary critics normally claim) and that his interpretation should stand until some other critic discovered weaknesses in it and put forward another interpretation supported by more cogent arguments. Just because two critics disagree about the meaning of a line in Shakespeare does not mean that no other critics may examine that line, decide which of the first two critics had the better arguments on his side, or put forward a better interpretation.

This, at any rate, is how not only literary criticism, but all research is practised and makes definite progress. If it had been true a century ago that because scientists sincerely disagreed about the nature and the structure of the atom, one could not appeal to the atom itself in order to settle the dispute, because the atom was the very thing that was in dispute, it would have stopped scientific investigation in its tracks. On the other hand, to have claimed that the nature and structure of the atom were whatever any scientist sincerely believed them to be would have been, as we now know, simply untrue. Some theories have proved more true than others, for the simple reason that their authors have applied themselves more persistently and with more precision to the objective evidence of the atom, instead of accepting that any opinion seriously held is as valid as any other opinion, regardless of the objective evidence. Some interpretations of literary texts are likewise better than others because they are based on closer examination of the text and are argued for with better arguments.

THE DENIAL OF METAPHYSICS

The prohibition of appeal to the intended meaning of the author of a text, is, as we have seen, a doctrine that Derrida shared with other systems of literary criticism besides his own. The denial of any kind of metaphysics is likewise an attitude that is held not only by other literary critics, but also by many linguists and philosophers and others who make no pretension to literary criticism. But with Derrida the denial of metaphysics lies at the very heart of his literary theory, so that it both characterises and motivates his criticism. We shall hardly understand the details of his theory unless we first come to perceive what he meant by denying metaphysics in the context of literary criticism, and why he felt so strongly about it.

Logocentrism

According to Derrida a false idea has for centuries permeated and vitiated not only literary criticism but also a good deal of philosophy and linguistic theory. It is 'logocentrism'. It lies at the heart of metaphysics; and if metaphysics is eventually to be completely got rid of, as Derrida hoped it would be one day, then logocentrism must be demolished. Derrida therefore set out to demolish it.

But what is logocentrism? Unfortunately it is difficult to find in Derrida's writings, or in those of his followers and exponents, any clear, detailed definition of the term. At first sight it might look as if it denoted the mistake of concentrating on words rather than meaning—a fault that any expert in translation from one language to another knows must be avoided. To translate a Russian text into Japanese word for word, as if each particular word in Russian had an exact equivalent word in Japanese to represent it, would result in a very wooden, unidiomatic Japanese, if not in complete gibberish. A translator must first ask what *meaning* the Russian words in a phrase or sentence are being used to convey; and having extracted that meaning, must proceed to choose the Japanese words and phrases that will best convey the *meaning* to the Japanese readers.

Derrida did not believe that there is any such thing as meaning until words are either spoken, or preferably written, by us human beings.

But in Derrida's thought logocentrism is not the fault of concentrating on words rather than meaning. In fact, as we shall later see, he did not believe that there is any such thing as meaning until words are either spoken, or preferably written, by us human beings.

The Stoic understanding of 'logos'

To understand what 'logocentrism' means in Derrida's philosophy we should recall the use of the Greek term *logos* (the first component in 'logocentrism') by the ancient Stoics and then by the New Testament.[13] To the Stoics *logos* was the principle of rationality that lies behind and permeates the whole universe, so giving it rational sense, significance and meaning. Man himself, the Stoics held, is composed of matter and *logos*, that same *logos* that permeates the universe. This principle of rationality in humans is what allows us to perceive the rational purpose and meaning of life and behaviour.

The Christian understanding of 'logos'

In the New Testament Logos is not an impersonal rational principle: it is a title of the second person of the Trinity, by whom the universe was created. He is the one who, in creating the universe, expressed the mind and intentions of God, and created the mathematical, physical, chemical and biological laws by which the universe works; who in addition gave us human beings rational minds so that we can perceive that the universe is not composed simply of brute matter but is the expression of the mind of a personal Creator. Moreover, our rational minds can perceive that the rationality of the universe existed both before, and independently of, us. *We* did not, and do not, create the mathematical laws according to which the universe works by studying and thinking about them. The rationality of the universe expressed the mind of God long before we came on the scene, let alone discovered it.

    It was considerations of this sort that led early philosophers and scientists like Bacon and Leibniz to talk of Nature as one of God's two books (the other being the Bible) in which we can read the laws of the Creator.

Derrida's rejection of 'logos'

It is precisely this idea, then, that Derrida labels *logocentrism* and which he resolutely denies and seeks to abolish. For him there is no meaning, it just does not exist, until we human beings speak, or

---

[13] See the detailed discussion in Book 2: *Finding Ultimate Reality*, Ch. 3.

preferably write: it is our words that create meaning. He complains that in metaphysical thought the idea constantly reoccurs that

> There is only one Book, and this same Book is distributed throughout all books.... there is only one book on earth, that is the law of the earth, the earth's true Bible. The difference between individual works is simply the difference between individual interpretations of one true and established text.[14]

This, to Derrida, is the view of Leibniz, and he protests:

> Nothing is more despairing, more destructive of our books than the Leibnizian Book.[15]

And then he states his own view:

> To write is to know that what has not yet been produced within literality has no other dwelling place, does not await us as prescription in some *topos ouranios* ['heavenly place'], or some divine understanding. Meaning must await being said or written in order to inhabit itself, and in order to become, by differing from itself, what it is: meaning.[16]

What Derrida means by saying that for meaning to become meaning it must differ from itself, we must examine later. For the moment we may sum up Derrida's own meaning so far by quoting the comment of Nicholas Wolterstorff:

> If meaning is not anterior to signification but a creature of signification, of *our* signification, then there is no divine Book on which we are to model our books, no divine thoughts after which to think our thoughts. The God of Leibniz—indeed the Jewish God—will have to go.[17]

Presence

There is yet a third term that in Derrida's thought is connected with the logocentrism and metaphysics and which has had a baneful effect on

---

[14] *Writing and Difference*, 9–10.
[15] *Writing and Difference*, 11.
[16] *Writing and Difference*, 11.
[17] *Divine Discourse*, 161.

literary criticism. That term is presence; and the core error of metaphysics has been to make people regard, or sense, the fundamental concepts of human thinking as a kind of presence. Derrida complains:

> Metaphysics represents 'the determination of Being as *presence* in all senses of this word. It could be shown that all the names related to fundamentals, to principles, or to the center have always designated an invariable presence—*eidos, archē, telos, energeia, ousia* (essence, existence, substance, subject), *aletheia,* transcendentality, consciousness, God, man, and so forth.'[18]

As with other technical terms in Derrida's philosophy so with *presence*: he does not make it clear what exactly he means by the term. We might perhaps illustrate its meaning simply (though Derrida might regard it as an oversimplification) thus: you enter a completely dark room. You sense there is someone else there. You cannot see who it is, or what he or she is like. You simply sense or feel a presence. So it is with us and God. God is not just a concept that people, whether philosophers or not, have built up in their minds. Metaphysics makes people feel that God is a living being, present to himself, that is, self-conscious, aware of himself in all his infinite person, character and power, with no need of anything outside of himself to compare himself with in order to define himself. At the same time he makes people aware of himself, not as an intellectual concept that they have created by their own thinking, but as an independent, self-existent omnipresence, of whom an ancient poet wrote: 'Where shall I go from your Spirit? Or where shall I flee from your presence?' (Ps 139:7).

Simultaneously, metaphysics (of the sort that Derrida doesn't like) has regarded this God, this presence, as the centre, not only of the universe, but of all significance and meaning, without which the universe and all human thought about it and about man himself would be ultimately incoherent. An ancient Greek (perhaps Epimenides) put it: 'In him we live and move and have our being';[19] and the New Testament puts it: 'He is before all things, and in him all things hold together' (Col 1:17).

---

[18] Wolterstorff, *Divine Discourse*, 157, citing Derrida, *Writing and Difference*, 279–80. The Greek words cited here mean: *eidos* = form; *archē* = beginning, or, basic principle; *telos* = end, goal, ultimate form or purpose; *energeia* = actuality; *aletheia* = truth.
[19] Famously quoted by the Apostle Paul in Athens (Acts 17:28).

Similarly, when Derrida says that metaphysics has always represented the fundamental principles, like Form, Purpose, Truth, etc., as an *'invariable presence'*, perhaps he means that metaphysics has regarded them as objective principles which exist independently of us. They would be like the mathematical laws according to which the universe runs and develops. According to many modern mathematical physicists these laws are not created by our thinking but have always existed independently of us, and have, only comparatively recently, been discovered by us.

At any rate, the widely recognised exponent of Derrida's thought, Jonathan Culler, appears to say something very similar. He describes the logocentrism of metaphysics, as Derrida calls it, as: 'the orientation of philosophy toward an order of meaning—thought, truth, reason, logic, the Word—conceived as existing in itself, as foundation.'[20]

Derrida, then, was an implacable foe of metaphysics, as he understood it, with its logocentrism and its 'presence', and he was intent on deconstructing it, and thus doing away with it. In a moment we shall go on to consider the further arguments he raised against it, and what they have to do with literary criticism.

But before we do that, it will help us to see things in due proportion, if we first consider Derrida's final verdict on metaphysics: it is that metaphysics is inescapable! Much as he disliked it, much as he would have liked to get rid of it, not even he could think, speak or write without using its basic concepts and terms.

The inescapability of metaphysics

Faced with the questions: What strategies can be devised for escaping metaphysics? How would language itself work, if one could banish from it all metaphysics? Derrida's constant reply runs: 'I do not believe, that some day it will be possible *simply* to escape metaphysics.'[21]

By this Derrida does not mean that after he has demolished metaphysics with rationally unanswerable arguments some thinkers will still irrationally retain belief in it. He means that to demolish metaphysics one must employ valid arguments, but that the only valid

---

[20] *On Deconstruction*, 92.
[21] *Positions*, 17.

arguments available have to be taken from within metaphysics. One therefore has to assume the validity of metaphysical arguments in order to use them to destroy the validity of metaphysics. For Derrida the concept of a sign and a signified was part and parcel of metaphysics; and he writes:

> But we cannot do without the concept of the sign, for we cannot give up this metaphysical complicity without also giving up the critique we are directing against this complicity . . . And what we are saying here about the sign can be extended to all the concepts and all the sentences of metaphysics [*scilicet* which he needs to use to overturn metaphysics] . . . These concepts are not elements or atoms, and since they are taken from a syntax and a system, every particular borrowing brings along with it the whole of metaphysics.[22]

THE ASSERTION THAT WRITING PRECEDES SPEECH AND THAT SIGNIFICATION CREATES MEANING

Derrida, in his widely read book *Of Grammatology*, sets out to develop a thesis:

> I shall try to show later that there is no linguistic sign before writing.[23]

This to most people is very strange, for spoken language is a system of linguistic signs, and spoken words are still what they always were from the beginning: primarily sounds. By common scholarly consent, moreover, spoken words were linguistic signs long before anyone invented a series of written signs to represent, as best they could, the sounds already in use as words.

We can, in fact, trace the history and development of various systems of writing: pictograms, ideograms, hieroglyphics, cuneiform, alphabets; and it is as clear as anything can be that spoken language was not invented in order to express the meaning of these written signs, but that the written signs were invented to represent, as best as

---

[22] *Writing and Difference*, 355–6.
[23] p. 14.

they could, the spoken signs. In other words, historically speaking, speech came before writing.

It still does. Still today there are spoken languages that have not been reduced to writing. Still today all children (except those unable through disability) speak before they can write. And there are many adults who speak their mother tongue but can neither read nor write it, although it has long since been reduced to writing. Historically and practically speaking it is simply contrary to the facts to say that writing was prior to speech.

Still today there are spoken languages that have not been reduced to writing.

Similarly, when it comes to literature, oral traditions often preceded written traditions. The epic poems that Homer eventually wrote down began life as oral sagas that professional singers sang at the banquets of the heroes. Even as late as the early decades of the nineteenth century men were discovered in Yugoslavia who could recite by memory very long epics that had been handed down orally from father to son for generations without ever having been written down.

It is strange, therefore, to find Derrida setting out to develop a thesis that runs counter to the well-known and long-established facts. One naturally tries to think of possible interpretations of his thesis that would rescue it from this predicament. Could it be, for instance, that he means that writing has, not a temporal priority over speech, but a priority of value or usefulness? He remarks, for instance, that

> If 'writing' signifies inscription and especially the durable institution of a sign (and that is the only irreducible kernel of the concept of writing), writing in general covers the entire field of linguistic signs.[24]

According to this, then, writing has the advantage over speech in that it is durable, whereas speech evaporates, so to speak, as soon as it is spoken.

But even this is not true, or, at least it is no longer true. With the invention of audio-recording devices and computer hard disks speech can be as durable as writing. Moreover, writing as a *visual* representation of speech suffers from its inability satisfactorily to rep-

---

[24] *Grammatology*, 44.

resent the many devices which speech can use (tone, pitch, emphasis, etc.) to convey meaning. Writing, therefore, as a visual medium is inferior to films and videos, which can visually and durably record the gestures of hand, eye and facial expression that accompany speech and enhance its ability to communicate meaning.

But Derrida's thesis only gets stranger still when he continues the paragraph from which we quoted above. He goes on to say:

> writing in general covers the entire field of linguistic signs. In that field a certain sort of instituted signifiers may then appear, 'graphic' in the narrow and derivative sense of the word, ordered by a certain relationship with other instituted—hence 'written', even if they are 'phonic'—signifiers.[25]

Originally when he said 'there is no linguist sign before writing', he seemed to imply that writing was different from speech and predated it. Now in this paragraph he talks about something that he calls 'writing in general' which covers the entire field of linguistic signs. If 'writing' here means what 'writing', as normally understood, means, it is no surprise—it is stating the obvious—to say that in the entire field of linguistic signs covered by 'writing in general' there appear 'graphic' signifiers. How not? For 'graphic' is simply a Greek word meaning 'written'. But it is a surprise to be told that 'writing in general' includes other 'phonic' signifiers; for 'phonic' is a Greek word for 'voiced', that is, 'spoken'. And it is an even greater surprise to be told that these 'voiced' signifiers, that is, orally spoken words, must be classified as 'graphic' (written) signifiers, even though in fact they are 'phonic'. Derrida seems to be redefining the meaning of 'writing' as he goes along.[26]

A possible interpretation of Derrida's meaning

Although Jonathan Culler is a an exponent of Derrida's thought, he nevertheless admits that the traditional ranking of speech *above* writing is true to the actual facts of history and experience. But then he argues that those who adduce these facts do so

---

[25] *Grammatology*, 44.
[26] Could it possibly be that by a 'phonic' sign he means something like italics or underlining, which, though written signs, indicate what would be emphasis in an orally delivered text?

to demonstrate not just a factual or logical priority of speech to writing but a more portentous general and comprehensive priority. Speech is seen as in direct contact with meaning.[27]

According to this interpretation, Derrida's strange claim that writing is prior to speech is not really about that at all: his purpose in making the claim is to deny the view that speech is in direct contact with meaning. If Culler is right and this is the real purpose behind Derrida's argument, then a number of things can be said about it.

Fitting the idea that signification creates meaning

What Culler says fits in with Derrida's contention that signification creates meaning. According to Derrida, meaning is not something that can exist by itself and then be communicated by being put into words and conveyed to others. Meaning does not exist until it is actually signified, that is, either spoken or written.

But it is difficult to convince people that this is true, especially if they are listening to a speaker delivering a speech. They naturally suppose that he thought out what he was going to say and the meaning he wished to convey before he said it. They might admit that he used words to think out in his mind the meaning he wished to convey. But they might also suppose that, having decided in his mind the exact meaning he wanted to convey, he then had to decide what words he must use to convey that meaning precisely to his audience. Suppose, in addition, that the speaker was a Russian philosopher about to address a French audience. He might in his mind first think out his meaning in Russian, and then translate the meaning (not the words) into French, and finally 'signify' his meaning by communicating it in French words.

According to Derrida, meaning does not exist until it is actually signified, that is, either spoken or written.

In all this the average person might well conclude, first, that the speaker's intended meaning was logically prior to the words he eventually spoke; and secondly, that the words he spoke were in more or less direct contact with his meaning. No ordinary person would think that no meaning existed until the French words he used created the meaning.

---

[27] *On Deconstruction*, 100.

Of course, it might happen that some of the French words he used were, unknown to him, ambiguous or carried offensive connotations. At question time, therefore, someone might ask him: 'When you said so-and-so, did you really mean such-and-such?' The speaker would not reply: 'I did not have any meaning in mind before I spoke; like you I had to wait for the words that came out from my mouth to create some meaning or other.' He would rather say: 'No, I did not mean that. I obviously expressed my meaning badly. Let me choose other words to express my meaning more exactly.' That done, the audience would likely comment: 'That makes sense. Now we know what you meant.' They would feel that his words had direct contact with his predetermined meaning, not that the words had created his meaning.

But suppose, like Derrida, you refuse to believe that there exists any such thing as meaning that can then be put into words and communicated to some other person; but rather that meaning does not exist until signification (words) creates it. And suppose you hold, as did Derrida (as we shall presently see), that written words have no intrinsic meaning but are open to an almost infinite number of different interpretations. What literary theory would you prefer?

First of all you would prefer a written text to a living speaker. Then you would accept the intentional fallacy without reserve; for that would excuse you from having to ask what meaning the author was intending to convey by the words he wrote in his text. Thus you would be able to start with written words and be free to extract from those written words an infinite play of meanings just as you pleased. It might then be tempting for you to develop an argument that writing has, and always has had, priority over speech.

The idea is not original to Derrida

The denial that speech is in direct contact with reality is a theory that was advanced by philosophers and language theorists long before Derrida. As we've noted, if Culler is right, Derrida's strange theory that writing is prior to speech is really meant to deny that speech has direct contact with meaning, or indeed with reality. That is a much more serious theory and one that is widely held by distinguished philosophers. Its leading features are:

(*a*) Its advocates tend to hold conventionalism.

(b) It denies that language simply refers to things in the world and labels them.
(c) It denies that concepts expressed in a language are real essences existing independently of language.
(d) In particular it denies that human language can tell us anything objective about God.

We must briefly examine each one of these.

Conventionalism

Conventionalism holds that language has no essential element in itself: language is the creation of the society whose language it is.[28] Linguistic meaning is derived from, and therefore is relative to, the experiences of the particular culture that had those experiences. There are no trans-cultural forms.

There is a certain amount of truth in this view of language; but it is easily exaggerated. It is certainly true that the individual symbols (i.e. words) in any language are mostly conventionally relative. So, for instance, an object which in English is denoted by the symbol tree, is denoted in French by *arbre*, in German by *Baum*, in Greek by *dendron* and in Russian by *derevo*. Similarly, the objects represented in English by 'oak', 'tree', and 'acorns', are represented by different symbols in Russian. But it is important to notice that while the individual symbols are culturally relative, the meaning of a sentence made up of these culturally relative symbols, is not itself culturally relative. The meaning of the English sentence 'Oak trees bear acorns' is exactly the same when expressed in Russian words as it is in English.

It is certainly true that the individual symbols (i.e. words) in any language are mostly conventionally relative.

Conventionalism's first denial

Conventionalism denies that language simply refers to things in the world and labels them. The denial is certainly true to a great extent, and one can readily think up examples of the different ways in which it is true. Consider three examples.

---

[28] See also Ch. 5 on Conventionalism, 169.

1. A word can denote something that does not exist, and never did exist, in the world

The word 'centaur', taken from the Greek *kentauros*, denotes a creature whose body and legs are those of a horse but whose torso and head are those of a man. Such creatures, however, never did exist: they are figments of mythological imagination.

Similarly 'phlogiston' was the word used by eighteenth century scientists to denote a substance that chemists of that time supposed to exist in all combustible bodies, and to be released by combustion. Further research showed that there was no such substance.

2. Different meanings for the same word in different time periods

A word in one and the same language can at one time in history be used as a label for one thing and at a later time as a label for something different. In older English 'closet' meant 'cupboard'; it still means something similar in American English, in the sense of a built-in wardrobe. In later English its meaning became restricted to a 'water closet' (WC). In that sense in today's English 'closet' has gone completely out of fashion, and has been progressively replaced by various euphemisms such as 'lavatory' or 'bathroom', and in American by 'restroom'.

3. Sometimes a word contains an evaluation

Sometimes a word not only labels an objective thing, but also contains an unspoken subjective evaluation of that thing, which is culturally determined. English and German both use the same word 'warm'. But water described as 'warm' in German would normally be many degrees hotter than water described as 'warm' in English. The same word then carries different subjective evaluations.

Now this last example illustrates a point that is immediately relevant to our present discussion. The fact that the word 'warm' carries a different subjective connotation in German from what it does in English does not imply that there is no objective phenomenon in the world denoted by the subjectively neutral word 'temperature'. There is such an objective phenomenon that actually exists in the universe, and it can be measured by objective standards (Celsius, Fahrenheit, Kelvin).

So, then, some words do refer to things in the world and act as labels for them; and it will be instructive to digress for a moment to consider how we get such words.

Animals and plants

The biblical story tells that God brought the animals to Adam and let Adam name them. Adam, then, invented the names, the words, the labels; but Adam did not create the animals by naming them. The animals existed before he did and continued to exist. The names he gave them may have incorporated his personal evaluation of them. But again, that does not imply that the words did not refer to really existent animals. Later scientific classification has given us more exact terms that help us distinguish varieties of the same species; and the same is true of the scientific classification of plants. But in both cases the more precise names have come about by closer study of the actually existent, objective realities. And of this we can be sure: man's naming of the animals did not create the detailed facts about them.

Physical things

The word 'atom' is a good example. When the Greeks first invented the term they used it to describe what at that stage was only a theoretical concept. They had never seen an atom, nor had rigid proof or even indisputable evidence that atoms existed. But from the observation of physical objects they formed the concept that the physical world must be composed of an infinite number of tiny particles, so basic that they could not be further divided. Hence the name they gave to these conjectured particles: atom = something which cannot be split.

We still use the word 'atom' today; but strictly speaking the word is a false label since we now know they can be split. Does this mean that because this word is now an inexact label, it does not refer to any objective reality? No, of course not. We now know that there are such things as atoms, but that they can be subjected to fission or fusion; and the results of atomic fission or fusion are not theoretical concepts but all too real facts.

Observe, therefore, what has happened to the word 'atom'. We still use it, but it no longer means exactly the same as it originally meant. The change in meaning has come about however, not because the word never referred to an objectively real, tiny particle of matter, but because closer study of that objective reality has increased our understanding of that reality, and so the meaning of our word 'atom' has adjusted itself accordingly.

Conventionalism's second denial

Conventionalism denies that concepts expressed in a language are real essences existing independently of language. Let's start with a simple example that shows that sometimes concepts exist before linguistic means are invented to express them. Ancient Greek had two syntactical constructions, each designed to join clauses together and to indicate the logical connection between the ideas in the first clause and the ideas in the second. The one construction was the word *hina* followed by a verb in the subjunctive; the other was the word *hōste* followed by a verb in the indicative.

> Conventionalism denies that concepts expressed in a language are real essences existing independently of language.

These two constructions express two different concepts: one (*hina* + subjunctive) indicates an intended result, brought about by the deliberate premeditated act of some agent. The other (*hōste* + indicative) indicates the simple unintended consequence of some act. The difference in concept is the difference between, for example, deliberate murder on the one hand and accidental homicide on the other.

To understand the difference in meaning of these two constructions you will first have to have clearly in your mind the conceptual difference between a deliberately intended result and an accidental, unintended consequence.

The question arises: did the ancient Greeks first come across these two constructions in their language, then wonder what they could possibly signify, and only subsequently discover the concepts that they expressed? Or was it rather that some one or ones first had the concepts and then invented constructions to express those concepts?

Contrary to many theoretical linguists, Noam Chomsky argues that babies are born with an innate 'language faculty', which among other things specifies a 'universal grammar, that is, a set of constraints on the structural possibilities available in the languages of the world. This enables a child to grasp the logical order and concepts that are presented to it in whatever language it encounters in its early life.[29]

---

[29] *Knowledge of Language.*

Jerry Fodor writes:

> There literally isn't such a thing as the notion of learning a conceptual system richer than the one that one already has; we simply have no idea of what it would be like to get from a conceptually impoverished to a conceptually richer system by anything like a process of learning.[30]

And E. Bates, D. Thal and V. Marchman give their opinion:

> If the basic structural principles of language cannot be learned (bottom-up) or derived (top-down) there are only two possible explanations for their existence: Either universal grammar was endowed to us directly by the Creator, or else our species has undergone a mutation of unprecedented magnitude, a cognitive equivalent of the Big Bang.[31]

We return, then, briefly to the difference in concept between a deliberately intended result, and an unintended consequence. A little child who has thrown a toy brick at his brother and injured him does not have to be very old before it can understand what 'on purpose' means when his mother asks: 'Did you do that on purpose? Did you mean to do it?'

The laws of mathematics

It is the long-held scientific view that the workings of the universe are not haphazard. The universe works according to mathematical laws. Nor does it matter which number system is used, whether the sexagesimal system of ancient Babylonians or the modern decimal system. It is obvious, moreover, that the universe ran according to these principles long before humans used mathematics to describe them. The laws of mathematics, says the mathematician Roger Penrose, are discovered, not invented, by humans.[32] Mathematical concepts and language, then, do refer to self-existent realities. They are the expression of the Creator's rationality imposed on, and through, his creation.

---

[30] J. A. Fodor, 'Fixation of Belief and Concept Acquisition', 149.
[31] 'Symbols and Syntax', 30.
[32] Penrose has long maintained, taught and defended this position. See, for example, his book *The Road to Reality*.

The basic universal moral laws

It is likewise obvious that moral concepts like 'it is wrong to torture children for the fun of it', are not created by human language. They are instinctive, or as the Bible puts it, they are 'the law written . . . on [our] hearts' (Rom 2:15), that is, by the Creator. That is why, as the Intuitionists say, we simply intuit these ethical duties, rather than create them by rational argument.

Conventionalism's third denial

Conventionalism denies that human language can tell us anything objective about God. It is often argued that there is no such thing as a private language. The person who claims to know God, is already using the term 'God' that was invented by the society in which he or she lives; and the word simply expresses ideas that society itself has thought up. By definition, then, it cannot tell us anything objective about what God is like, or indeed whether he exists or not. All it can tell us is what society thinks about itself and about its own feelings about the universe.

Now this view of things might well be true if the assumption on which it is based were true. That assumption is that even if there is a God, it is beyond all doubt that he has left it to our unaided thought to find out what we can about him. But this is only an assumption. The Bible claims the contrary is true, that God our Creator has not left us to find out by our reasoning whether he exists or not and what he is like. God has taken the initiative and spoken through creation, through the moral concepts he has written in our hearts and through the prophets of the Old and New Testaments. Moreover, in speaking to us God has condescended to speak to us in our human languages, though in doing so, he has given some of our human words a fullness of meaning they did not have before. What is more, in order to speak to us finally, he has spoken through the eternal Logos, not only using our human language but becoming human himself.

This, then, is the Bible's assertion; the evidence for its truth will be discussed in a later book in the series.[33] Meanwhile we must get back to Derrida.

---

[33] See Book 5: *Claiming to Answer: How One Person Became the Response to our Deepest Questions*.

THE DENIAL THAT WORDS HAVE ANY INTRINSIC MEANING

The denial that words have any intrinsic meaning corresponds to the assertion that the meaning of a word is always deferred, which thus allows unlimited play:

> This field is in effect that of *play*, that is to say, a field of infinite substitutions ... One could say ... that this movement of play, permitted by the lack or absence of a centre or origin, is the movement of *supplementarity*.[34]

> One could call *play* the absence of the transcendental signified as limitlessness of play, that is to say as the destruction of onto-theology and the metaphysics of presence.[35]

The second quotation above reminds us that at the heart of Derrida's literary criticism is his determination to banish all metaphysics and what he calls onto-theology, that is, the theology of Being. Yet we shall also remember that, contrariwise, he himself admits elsewhere that it is impossible, even for him, to dispense with all metaphysical concepts. But he tries hard. So in order to prove that there is no logos, or fixed centre, or presence, he maintains that words have no intrinsic meaning; and to prove that, he cites the fact that to know what a word means one must wait and see what the next word or words in the sentence mean.

To talk of limitless play of meaning is a wild exaggeration.

One could easily think of thousands of examples of this. Take the word 'operation': it can mean a military operation, a surgical operation, a mechanical operation, etc. If it stood in isolation by itself, one could not tell what kind of operation it signified; only the other words in the context could show us that. Therefore, says Derrida, the meaning of the word is 'deferred' until one arrives at the next word or words, and they then make clear what the first word means in this context.

To say this, of course, is to say nothing new or particularly illuminating. But to say that this shows that the word 'operation' has

---

[34] Derrida, *Writing and Difference*, 365.
[35] Derrida, *Grammatology*, 50.

no intrinsic meaning at all is just not true. It has a core meaning that remains constant in all the connotations that it has acquired in the course of its history (it comes from the Latin *opera/operatio* = work/working). To go further and claim that, because one cannot tell which connotation is intended until one has read the context, this makes possible a *limitless* play of meaning is nonsense. Of course, if one insists on taking each word by itself out of its context and concentrating on its range of possible connotations—as Derrida's technique of deconstruction tends to do—then one can juggle with its several possible meanings. But even so to talk of limitless play of meaning is a wild exaggeration.

But then, confronted with a text, why would any sensible literary critic want to take each individual word by itself in isolation from the context in which it occurs?

This question, however, leads us to the next principle of Derrida's literary criticism.

DECONSTRUCTION

Here again are some quotations from well-recognised adherents of Derrida's system. They describe not only what deconstructive criticism does, but also what it deliberately sets out to do and what its motivation is for doing it.

1. 'To deconstruct a discourse is to show how it undermines the philosophy it asserts.'[36]
2. 'Deconstructive discourse, in criticism, in philosophy, or in poetry itself, undermines the referential status of the language being deconstructed.'[37]
3. 'As a mode of textual theory and analysis, contemporary deconstruction subverts almost everything in the tradition, putting in question received ideas of the sign and language, the text, the context, the author, the reader, the role of history, the work of interpretation, and the forms of critical writing.'[38]

---

[36] Culler, *Deconstruction*, 86.
[37] J. Hillis Miller, 'Deconstructing the Deconstructors', 30.
[38] Leitch, *Deconstructive Criticism*, ix.

4. 'Sooner or later, we learn, deconstruction turns on every critical reading or theoretical construction. When a decision is made, when authority emerges, when theory or criticism operate, the deconstruction questions ... As soon as it does so it becomes subversive ... Ultimately, deconstruction effects revision of traditional thinking.'[39]
5. 'The clearest distinction between traditionalist and deconstructive logic resides in the difference in their attitude toward the exercise of power ... [and] the abdication of the power to dictate taste.'[40]
6. 'A deconstruction, then, shows the text resolutely refusing to offer any privileged reading ... Deconstructive criticism clearly transgresses the limits established by traditional criticism.'[41]

This, then, is how deconstructionism describes itself.

On deconstruction

We see that its aim is negative: It 'undermines', 'subverts', 'transgresses', 'turns on' (i.e. turns round and attacks). But we notice several other things about it.

The first object of its negative, subversive criticism

First and foremost it attacks, undermines and subverts all traditional interpretation. It is, of course, a good and healthy thing to question traditional interpretation and not to take anything on authority, and to adopt only that which proves to be good. But to the deconstructionist there is by definition nothing good in traditional literary criticism and interpretation, for it was all founded on false presuppositions and logic. As Christopher Norris writes:

> Deconstruction is the active antithesis of everything that criticism ought to be if one accepts its traditional values and concepts.[42]

---

[39] Leitch, *Deconstructive Criticism*, 261.
[40] Flieger, 'The Art of Being Taken by Surprise', 57.
[41] Leitch, 'The Book of Deconstructive Criticism', 24–5.
[42] *Deconstruction*, xii.

This is the language of the revolutionary. He can see no good at all in the past. All must be swept aside, and a completely new order brought in.

The other object of its negative, subversive criticism

This is nothing less than the authority of the text itself. The revolution proceeds by 'undermining the referential status of the language [*scil.* of the text] being deconstructed'. No matter what the author intended to refer to, the deconstructionist sets out to show the reference was invalid. And anyway, the legitimacy of even enquiring what the author's intention was has been ruled out in advance.

Its revolutionary opposition to all power and privilege

An interesting psychological feature of deconstructionists is that they do not simply criticise some traditional theories of literary criticism—for we all do that. They, by contrast, feel that all traditional literary criticism is a tyrannical use of power and privilege employed to dictate people's taste; it must be undermined, subverted and completely overturned. This reaction, however, is surely extreme. Suppose, for instance, we are faced with a text in ancient Chinese, and none of us knows ancient Chinese. Then there comes a scholar who knows the language. Is he not in a privileged position to tell us what the text says? Of course we shall wish to check his translation by appealing to other scholars who know ancient Chinese. But how could we dispense with their privileged knowledge and insist on our freedom to interpret the text ourselves even if we don't know the language?

What deconstructionists propose to put in the place of traditional literary criticism

Barbara Johnson points to what this is when she says: Deconstruction 'undoes the very comforts of mastery and consensus that underlie the illusion that objectivity is situated somewhere outside the self'.[43] But if there is no objectivity outside the individual self, where shall we find it? Inside each individual self? But that would mean literary-critical anarchy. Nowhere at all? That would spell the end of literary criticism as a social or academic activity.

---

[43] Johnson, 'Nothing fails like success', 11.

The trouble with deconstructionism's demolition of all traditional literary criticism

Suppose that one day deconstruction manages to abolish all traditional criticism, and itself becomes the universal theory. Fifty or a hundred years from now it will have become the traditional view. How then ought the revolutionary critics of that time to deal with deconstructionism?

Deconstruction theory refuses to have its own principles applied to itself

Derrida writes:

> Justice in itself, if such a thing exists, outside or beyond law, is not deconstructible. No more than deconstruction itself, if such a thing exists. Deconstruction is justice.[44]

And John D. Caputo adds:

> Justice is not deconstructible. After all, not everything is deconstructible, or there would be no point to deconstruction.[45]

These two statements are remarkable. Earlier we saw that according to Derrida there are no objective values, or basic principles, that can be comprehended by us and then expressed in words. The word 'justice' does not refer to some objective 'presence'. To suppose it does is to hold the false idea of logocentrism and transcendental signification. But now Derrida and Caputo wish to assert that there are such objective values: justice and deconstruction; and they are good in themselves, intrinsically and inherently good ('present to themselves', to use Derrida's own technical terms). So here are Derrida and Caputo both contradicting the basic principles on which Derrida based his whole theory of literary and linguistic criticism.

Moreover, we were earlier told that 'to deconstruct a discourse is to show how it undermines the philosophy it asserts'.[46] Now Derrida and Caputo, in the name of deconstructionism, are contradicting

---

[44] Derrida, 'Force of Law', 14–15.
[45] Caputo, *Deconstruction in a Nutshell*, 131.
[46] Culler, *Deconstruction*, 86.

deconstruction theory itself, and then trying to defend deconstruction theory by claiming that while every other text and theory of literary criticism must be deconstructed, deconstruction theory itself must not be deconstructed. What is this but an expression of power and privilege claiming immunity from critical questioning which it applies to everything else? Here, to use Culler's terms, is deconstruction undermining the philosophy of deconstruction which it itself asserts.

Deconstructionism's self-imposed inability to help anyone appreciate any literary text

The first necessity for critiquing a text fairly is not an uncritical acceptance of all it says but a certain positive sympathy or empathy with the author that makes an effort to understand what the author was trying to say. Destructionism's total negativity, its determination to subvert, undermine and deconstruct the text's intended meaning by atomistically concentrating on the supposedly infinite play of meaning of individual words, virtually guarantees that it will never help anyone to appreciate the worth, however imperfect, of any text: not even of the masterpieces.

DERRIDA'S IDEAL WRITING

The question arises: how would Derrida himself go about writing a literary work, if he ever did? Given his own principles, he could not assume that he had an idea, a meaning, that he intended to express by writing a text. Nor could he hope that anyone would ever try to understand what he meant to say anyway. But how can one write words without intending to say anything? Let Derrida himself explain:

> To write is to draw back. Not to retire into one's tent, in order to write, but to draw back from one's writing itself. To be grounded far from one's language, to emancipate it or lose one's hold on it, to let it make its way alone and unarmed. To leave speech. To be a poet is to know how to leave speech. To let it speak alone, which it can only do in written form. To leave writing is to be there only in order to provide its passageway, to be the diaphanous

element of its going forth: everything and nothing. For the work, the writer is at once everything and nothing. Like God.[47]

What he rejects

On the one hand the theological encyclopaedia and, modeled upon it, the book of man.[48]

What he accepts and aims at

On the other a fabric of traces marking the disappearance of an exceeded God or of an erased man.[49]

to retake repossession of his language . . . and to claim responsibility for it against a Father of Logos.[50]

[writing which] runs the risk of being meaningless, and would be nothing without this risk.[51]

[writing which risks] meaning nothing [in order] to start play.[52]

CONCLUDING COMMENT ON DERRIDA

It is clear to see that underlying and motivating Derrida's theory of literary criticism is a certain rebellion against authority whether of the author, or of the text, or of language, or of metaphysics, or of tradition or of power and privilege of any kind. It is a help in understanding this characteristic to know Derrida's academic background. John M. Ellis points out:

> An unusual degree of rigidity and conservatism prevailed in French universities in the mid-sixties when deconstruction

---

[47] *Writing and Difference*, 85. But if a writer is only a passageway for writing to pass through, where does the writing come from in the first place? For further reading on all of Derrida's ideas quoted in this section, see Nicholas Wolterstorff's *Divine Discourse*.
[48] *Writing and Difference*, 371.
[49] *Writing and Difference*, 371.
[50] *Writing and Difference*, 90.
[51] *Writing and Difference*, 90.
[52] *Positions*, 14, cited from Wolterstorff, *Divine Discourse*, 166–7.

emerged.... Nowhere was conservative literary history and biography more pedantic or ossified, and nowhere was there more conformism in what was taught to university students. There was one truth, and it was contained in Gustave Lanson's literary history of France, which students were required to commit to memory. Any deviation from this basic truth provoked a massive, unified reprisal, and that fact constituted a very real repression of any alternative possibilities.[53]

Perhaps only those who have suffered under compulsion to adopt a 'correct' theory of literary criticism enforced by some central authority can understand the resentment of authority that builds up in the minds of students who are not allowed to think for themselves. But it is a pity if, as seems to have happened in Derrida's case, such resentment leads to the other extreme of rejecting all authority of author, text, language, metaphysics, logos and God himself.

---

[53] *Against Deconstruction*, 83–4.

CHAPTER 10

POSTMODERNISM AND SCIENCE

The application of science in some countries has given them simultaneously the most advanced weaponry and the most awful civil wars, poverty and famine. Postmodernism, therefore, not without reason, often openly attacks science as the villain involved in horrific aggression, environmental pollution, alienation and exploitation.

JUST ANOTHER STORY?

Postmodernists tend to hold that the claims that scientists make are exaggerated, because they do not recognise the ways in which their reason is beclouded. For example, some postmodernist thinkers assert that the laws of nature that have been discovered by scientific investigation are nothing but social constructions, that is, they are products of the scientists' own social culture, rather than reflections of how the universe actually works.

Richard Rorty (1931–2007), who was a postmodern pragmatist, wrote:

> The pragmatist tells us that it is useless to hope that objects will constrain us to believe the truth about them, if only they are approached with an unclouded mental eye, or a rigorous method, or a perspicuous language. He wants us to give up the notion that God, or evolution, or some other underwriter of our present world-picture, has programmed us as machines for accurate verbal picturing, and that philosophy brings self-knowledge by letting us read our own program.[1]

For Rorty, the postmodern pragmatist shares

> the Baconian and Hobbesian notion that knowledge is power, a tool for coping with reality. But he carries this Baconian point through to its extreme. . . . He drops the notion of truth as correspondence with reality altogether, and says that modern science does not enable us to cope because it corresponds, it just plain enables us to cope.[2]

Rorty cites Kuhn and Dewey in support: 'Kuhn and Dewey suggest we give up the notion of science travelling towards an end called

---
[1] *Consequences of Pragmatism*, 165.
[2] *Consequences of Pragmatism*, xvii.

"correspondence with reality" and instead say merely that a given vocabulary works better than another for a given purpose.'[3] What they seem to be saying is that we have found a set of (scientific) words which describe the motion of the planets better than any other set of words; but, they maintain, what we cannot say is that these words are getting close to the truth of the real situation.

On the postmodern view, all scientific endeavour to understand the universe is conditioned, and more or less distorted, by the background culture of the scientists themselves. They regard science, therefore, as 'just another set of narratives,' so that when scientists give us an explanation of some feature of the universe, that is just their story about it. Other people could make up another equally valid story. They are all just stories. This inevitably means that we reach the absurdity of not being able to tell the difference between astronomy and astrology. Rorty again:

> It is useless to ask whether one vocabulary rather than another is closer to reality. For different vocabularies serve different purposes, and there is no such thing as a purpose that is closer to reality than another purpose... Nothing is conveyed in saying... that the vocabulary in which we predict the motion of a planet is more in touch with how things really are than the vocabulary in which we assign the planet an astrological significance. For to say that astrology is out of touch with reality cannot explain why astrology is useless: it merely restates that fact in misleading representationalist terms.[4]

However Rorty is inconsistent in his attitude to science:

> The idea that one species of organism is, unlike all the others, oriented not just toward its own increased prosperity but toward Truth, is as un-Darwinian as the idea that every human being has a built-in moral compass—a conscience that swings free of both social history and individual luck.[5]

Rorty's statement is very interesting. He obviously is a Darwinian and holds himself that Darwin's theory is true. But how does he

---

[3] *Consequences of Pragmatism*, 193.
[4] Richard Rorty in his introduction to John P. Murphy's *Pragmatism*, 3.
[5] 'Untruth and Consequences', 36.

come to believe that Darwinism is true, if Darwinism teaches that no organism, not even Rorty himself, is oriented towards the truth? This is simply incoherent.

AN OVERREACTION TO MODERNISM

The strong anti-scientific element in postmodern thinking can easily disguise the fact that postmodernism is in a very real sense an overreaction to a modernism which has overreached itself. This is demonstrated by the modernist doctrine of scientism: that science is the only source of truth and that everything will ultimately yield to scientific analysis. Scientism is based on a true idea: that science is a valid means of gaining knowledge of the universe. However the flaw in scientism is that it exaggerates this truth until it becomes the completely false notion that science is the only valid method of deriving truth.[6]

Another central doctrine of modernism is the idea of progress. Here again this is based on the valid idea that progress is both possible and desirable. However when this doctrine gets elevated to the idea that, by applying science, progress is inevitable, the idea can easily go sour. The application of science in some countries has given them simultaneously the most advanced weaponry and the most awful civil wars, poverty and famine. Postmodernism, therefore, not without reason, often openly attacks science as the villain involved in horrific aggression, environmental pollution, alienation and exploitation.

In order to understand postmodernism, we need to realise that it has (understandably) reacted against these extremes of modernism, dismissing scientism and the myth of progress as the power agenda of the dominant culture. Science, for the postmodernist, is merely the scientists' 'story', a merely human invention whose 'real' purpose is to reinforce and carry forward an agenda of social dominance of the elite scientific culture. Anthropologist Matt Cartmill puts the basic thesis of the postmodern critique like this:

> Anybody who claims to have objective knowledge about anything is trying to control and dominate the rest of us . . . There

---

[6] See the Appendix: 'The Scientific Endeavour.'

are no objective facts. All supposed 'facts' are contaminated with theories, and all theories are infested with moral and political doctrines ... Therefore, when some guy in a lab coat tells you that such and such is an objective fact ... he must have a political agenda up his starched white sleeve.[7]

A RESPONSE TO POSTMODERNISM: IS SCIENCE A SOCIAL CONSTRUCT?

Now whether or not we agree that that science is merely 'their story', to be fair to the postmodern critique we must ask the question: could it be that science and technology are sometimes motivated by a social or political agenda? The answer to that question is yes. Now of course there are good social and political agendas, the obvious one being scientific research for solutions to the problems of disease. Another is for the discovery of alternative energy sources, and we could think of others. But science has been, and is, also used for social and political agendas which are not good: some countries have poured so much of their resources into the production of sophisticated weapons of mass destruction that their citizens live in economic deprivation; and uncontrolled exploitation is ruining the delicately balanced environment of Planet Earth. There is a lot to criticise, and one cannot help but be sympathetic to such criticisms of the abuse of science.

But that brings us to the point: we need here to distinguish things that differ—the abuse of science from science itself. Let us take an extreme case as an illustration. Suppose a clever scientist has a grudge against society and wants to poison a city's water supply. Using his knowledge of chemistry he secretly develops a new and powerful poison but, before he can use it, is fortunately apprehended by the police. The fact that he has developed the poison with an evil motivation arising out of his social situation does not mean that either the chemical laws he uses or the poison he makes have been produced by contemporary theories of society! One taste of the poison would soon show how ridiculous that view is! Thus we need to distinguish between science itself (the chemical laws which the scientist uses to

---

[7] 'Oppressed by Evolution'.

produce his poison) and the ethical question concerning the use to which science is put.

That distinction is vital. For it is certainly true, as the postmodernist claims, that science has given us the technology to produce weapons of mass destruction. But we need to remember that, just as fire both burns and warms, so lasers not only guide missiles, they are also used to repair faulty eyesight. We cannot fairly blame science for the evil ends to which it is sometimes put, but there is no doubt that the use of science is something which needs to be subjected to serious moral analysis. However, science itself is not in a position to give us the necessary moral criteria. As Einstein pointed out: 'What we call science has the sole purpose of determining what *is*. The determination of what *ought to be* is unrelated to it and cannot be accomplished methodically.'[8]

If science is not in a position to give us those moral criteria, neither is postmodernism. How could it conceivably be in a position to produce a moral analysis, if, as postmodernism claims, all truths (and therefore all moral truths) are equally valid! By failing to make the necessary distinctions postmodernism actually knocks the ground from under the valid criticisms it is making.

Postmodernism's confusion of categories

Physicist Alain Sokal maintains that much of the nonsense contained in the postmodern critique of science is in fact generated by confusing two or more of the following levels of analysis:

1. *Ontology*. What objects *exist* in the world? What statements about these objects are true?

2. *Epistemology*. How can human beings obtain *knowledge* of truths about the world? How can they assess the *reliability* of that knowledge?

3. *Sociology of knowledge*. To what extent are the truths *known* (or *knowable*) by humans in any given society influenced (or determined) by social, economic, political, cultural,

---

[8] Einstein, *Letters to Solovine*, 119–21.

and ideological factors? Same question for the false statements erroneously believed to be true.

4. *Individual ethics.* What types of research *ought* a scientist (or technologist) to undertake (or refuse to undertake)?

5. *Social ethics.* What types of research *ought* society to encourage, subsidize, or publicly fund (or, alternatively, to discourage, tax, or forbid)?[9]

Each of these levels of analysis is, of course, important for scientists and others to consider. The postmodern confusion arises, not from the fact that these levels all exist and are important, but from failure to distinguish between them.

Our example involves such confusion of levels. Let us look at it again. The clever chemist has discovered a new poison. At the ontological level he can say that this poison exists and it has such and such properties (level 1). However, it was his social grievance that motivated his research (level 3). This grievance is, in a real sense, a 'social construct', it arises out of the man's experience of society; but his science did not arise in this way.

Note that we are not commenting here on whether his grievance was legitimate or not, simply on the fact that it is a social construct. In other words, the sheer fact of being a social construct is not to be regarded as being necessarily a bad thing. That is a separate issue. There are many grievances arising from social pressures that we all would regard as legitimate—for example, the industrial exploitation of children.

Postmodernism's overestimate of the subjectivity of science

It is fair to say that there is a subjective element in science. The idea of a completely independent observer, free of all preconceived theories, doing investigations and coming to unbiased conclusions that constitute absolute truth, is simply a myth. First of all, there is no such thing as a completely independent observer. In common with the rest of humanity, scientists have preconceived ideas, indeed, worldviews that they bring to bear on every situation. Secondly, we can scarcely ever

---

[9] Sokal, 'Social Text Affair', 14–15.

make an observation without resting on some prior theory; for example, we cannot even take a temperature without having an underlying theory of heat. Thirdly, when we set up our theories they tend to be underdetermined by the data, that is, more than one theory could account for the same set of data. If, for example, we plot our data on a graph as a finite set of points, elementary mathematics will tell us that there is no limit to the number of curves that we can draw through that particular set of points, that is, the data represented by the points on the paper do not determine the curve that we should draw through them (although of course, in any particular case, there may well be physical principles which significantly restrict our choice).

> It is fair to say that there is a subjective element in science. The idea of a completely independent observer, free of all preconceived theories, doing investigations and coming to unbiased conclusions that constitute absolute truth, is simply a myth.

All of this most scientists will freely admit. By its very nature, science possesses an inevitable degree of tentativeness. On the other hand scientists will also want to point out that the degree of tentativeness is extremely small in the overwhelming majority of cases. The fact is that science-based technology has been spectacularly successful in fundamentally changing the face of the world: from radio and television to computers, aircraft, space probes, X-rays and artificial hearts. It is sheer nonsense, therefore, to assert that the elements of tentativeness and subjectivity in science mean that science is a social construct. As physicist Paul Davies says:

> Of course, science has a cultural aspect; but if I say that the planets moving around the sun obey an inverse-square law of gravitation and I give a precise mathematical meaning to that, I think it is really the case. I don't think it is a cultural construct—it's not something we have invented or imagined just for convenience of description—I think it's a fact. And the same for the other basic laws of physics.[10]

It is self-evident, is it not, that if we believed that the science that led to the construction of a jet aircraft was merely a subjective social

---

[10] Wilkinson, 'Found in space?'

construct, none of us would ever get on a plane? Or, to put it another way, one sure method of finding out whether the law of gravity is a social construct or not would be to step off the top of a skyscraper!

The Sokal affair

One consequence of their attitude to language is that postmodernist writers often use scientific terminology in a completely absurd way—at least in the view of the scientists who, after all, invented the terminology in the first place. This was brought to worldwide attention by physicist Alain Sokal whom we have cited. He submitted a cleverly constructed spoof article to a prestigious journal, *Social Text*, which publishes much postmodern literature. In the article, impressively but (to a scientist) nonsensically, entitled 'Transgressing the boundaries: towards a transformative hermeneutic of Quantum Gravity', Sokal appeared to take the postmodern stance and appeared to criticise the modernist 'dogma . . . that there exists an external world, whose properties are independent of any individual human being and indeed of humanity as a whole; that these properties are encoded in "eternal" physical laws; and that human beings can obtain reliable, albeit imperfect and tentative, knowledge of these laws by . . . the "objective" procedures of . . . the (so-called) scientific method.' He then made the startling claim that

> feminist and poststructuralist critiques have demystified the substantive content of mainstream Western scientific practice, revealing the ideology of domination concealed behind the façade of objectivity. It has become apparent that physical 'reality' no less than social 'reality' is at bottom a social and linguistic construct; that scientific 'knowledge', far from being objective, reflects and encodes the dominant ideologies and power relations of the culture that produced it.

The editors of the journal, suspecting nothing, published the article, apparently because it appeared to fit in with their own predilections. However, Sokal then revealed that his article was a parody from beginning to end, full of complete nonsense dressed up in pseudo-scientific language! He had deliberately constructed it in the postmodern fashion in order to reveal the fact that postmodernism was itself largely nonsensical. The resulting storm in the press, particularly in France, the home of many postmodern writers, showed that Sokal had scored a direct hit on a very big nerve.

For Sokal, like most scientists, believes in an objective world which can be studied; and that scientific theories, though not amounting to 'truth' in any absolute sense, give scientists an increasingly firm handle on reality—as exemplified, say, in the development of the understanding of the universe, from Ptolemy to Galileo, to Newton, to Einstein. They believe that they are reaching a better and more accurate understanding, even though they are aware that the advance of science often involves, as in the case just mentioned, a paradigm-shift: that is, a shift in the basic large framework within which science is being carried out at any point in history.[11] For example, Ptolemy's paradigm was that of a universe with the earth at its centre and all the heavenly bodies circling round it. Copernicus and Galileo were responsible for a paradigm-shift to the notion of a solar system. Einstein's discovery of relativity resulted in a further paradigm-shift in the understanding of space-time that had been current since Newton, and so on.

Most scientists are well aware of these issues and take the view that, although paradigm-shifts are involved and the subjective element can never be completely eliminated, nevertheless science is getting a tighter and tighter grip on reality. Lewis Wolpert, FRS, Professor of Biology, University College, London puts it this way: 'Although social processes play a role in science, scientists change theories because the new ones provide a better correspondence with reality.'[12] And again:

> No amount of rhetoric is enough to persuade others of the validity of a new idea, but it can make them take it seriously—that is, follow it up and test it. But persuasion ultimately counts for nothing if the theory does not measure up to the required correspondence with nature. If it does not conform with the evidence, if it is not internally consistent, if it does not provide an adequate explanation, the authority and all the other social

---

[11] The idea of a paradigm was introduced in a famous book by Kuhn (*Structure of Scientific Revolutions*). See the Appendix: 'The Scientific Endeavour', 319.
[12] *Unnatural Nature of Science*, 103.

factors count for nothing: it will fail. Such a failure is undoubtedly culturally determined, the culture being one that adopts a scientific approach.[13]

Nor is Sokal himself unaware of the social dimension to science. Indeed, he regards it as uncontroversial that:

> 1. Science is a human endeavour, and like any other human endeavour, it merits being subjected to rigorous social analysis. . . .
>
> 2. At a more subtle level, even the content of scientific debate—what types of theories can be conceived and entertained, what criteria are to be used to decide among competing theories—is constrained in part by the prevailing attitudes of mind, which in turn arise in part from deep-seated historical factors. . . .
>
> 3. There is nothing wrong with research informed by a political commitment as long as that commitment does not blind the researcher to inconvenient facts. Thus, there is a long and honourable tradition of sociopolitical critique of science, including antiracist critiques of anthropological pseudoscience and eugenics.[14]

However, Sokal goes on to say that over the past two decades certain sociologists and literary intellectuals have become greedier:

> they want to attack the normative conception of scientific inquiry as a search for truths or approximate truths about the world; they want to see science as just another social practice which produces 'narratives' and 'myths' that are no more valid than those produced by other social practices.[15]

And the results are absurd. Take, for example, a front-page article in the *New York Times* of 22 October 1996 concerning the conflict between two views of the origin of certain Native American populations. One view was the archaeological account that humans first came to America across the Bering Strait from Asia; the other was the Zuni myth that native peoples have lived in America ever since

---

[13] *Unnatural Nature of Science*, 118.
[14] Sokal, 'Social Text Affair', 10.
[15] Sokal, 'Social Text Affair', 10.

their ancestors emerged from a subterranean spirit-world. It seems perfectly obvious that both views cannot be correct. And yet, incredible as it may seem, Roger Anyon, a British archaeologist, was quoted as claiming: 'Science is just one of many ways of knowing the world... [The Zunis' worldview is] just as valid as the archaeological viewpoint of what prehistory is about.'[16] However, if we are talking about truth claims, then the two accounts contradict each other. A man who claims the earth is flat and a woman who claims it is spherical cannot both be right!

The absurdity of the postmodern relativisation of truth is also evident from another fact.

The universe is not an intellectual construct

Scientists do not construct by their reason either the universe or the laws by which it works. Theirs is a path of discovery. The universe was there and working long before anyone tried by reason to understand and formulate how it works. Scientists have to allow the universe to impose its nature on them and determine which theories make sense and which do not. That is precisely what distinguishes scientific theories from social constructs. To say, as does the well-known sociologist of science Harry Collins, that 'the natural world has a small or nonexistent role in the construction of scientific knowledge'[17] is sheer nonsense. Scientists are not free to say what they like about the universe and claim it to be true. They are realists and believe in the existence of an objective universe. They put their hypotheses to the test, abandoning or modifying them should the universe not behave in the way they suggest. Many a theory has been slain by an obstinate fact!

> Many a theory has been slain by an obstinate fact!

If we are seeking the truth about the universe and about human beings, our basic assumption clearly is that the truth is already there to be discovered. Our reasoning can create abstract mathematical systems and sometimes those systems can be shown to describe how the universe works. But our mathematical reasoning does not create

---

[16] Quoted in Stolzenberg, 'Reading and relativism', 50, who cites Boghossian, 'Sokal Hoax', 27 who cites 'Indian Tribes' Creationists Thwart Archaeologists', *New York Times*, 22 Oct. 1996.
[17] Collins, 'Stages in the Empirical Programme of Relativism', 3.

the universe or its laws: it merely describes them. This is not a weakness or fault in reason or rationality: it is merely a question of the importance of our recognising what is the proper scope and function of human reason.

This is a very important point. Atoms have to exist in order to be split. If they did not exist then no one could have split them, and nuclear bombs would not exist. The existence of the atom and the motivation for splitting it are two entirely different things (confusion between levels 1, 3, 4 and 5 of Sokal's analysis).

CONCLUSION: THE INTELLECTUAL INCOHERENCE OF THE POSTMODERNIST ILLUSION

In rejecting the notion of objective truth completely, postmodernists themselves are in danger of joining the mythmakers. What is more, common sense tells us that no one actually believes their myths. If you are buying a rope to climb a mountain, you will insist on knowing the truth about the strength of that rope. You would not accept the statement that the rope is strong enough and the statement that the rope is not strong enough as being both equally true. You know that there is a truth about the rope that can be discovered and demonstrated, and you will not be content until you have discovered it because your very life depends on it.

Richard Dawkins, critical of those who pour scorn on the search for truth, writes:

> no philosopher has any trouble using the language of truth when falsely accused of a crime, or when suspecting his wife of adultery. "Is it true?" feels like a fair question, and few who ask it in their private lives would be satisfied with logic-chopping sophistry in response.[18]

Dawkins is right. In everyday life all of us assume that there is ascertainable truth. Suppose, again, just to ram this important point home, that you claim to have two million pounds in the bank and the bank manager claims that you have nothing at all in the bank.

---

[18] *Unweaving the Rainbow*, 21.

Everybody agrees that both claims cannot be true. They will also agree that there is an absolute truth about how much, if anything, you have in the bank. Postmodernism disappears at the bank door!

Moreover, if the presupposition that there is no such thing as absolute truth were itself true, it would have other serious implications far beyond science itself. It would spell the end of true justice—for a judge could not decide between a guilty and a non-guilty verdict on the ground of indisputable truth. Decision would rest on the arbitrary power and authority of the judge. We would then be dependent on totalitarian authority to decide what truth and justice were. That would spell the end of morality—for nothing could be said to be finally right or wrong. It would also spell the end of any sense of human freedom—for if truth is relative then, in the end, truth will be decided by power. Here, once more, postmodernists are inconsistent for in their complaints about the unfairness of various power structures and in their insistence on tolerance and justice, they are appealing to moral absolutes that are independent of themselves. As C. S. Lewis says:

> Whenever you find a man who says he does not believe in a real Right and Wrong, you will find the same man going back on this a moment later. He may break his promise to you, but if you try breaking one to him he will be complaining, 'It's not fair.'[19]

Some people feel positively comforted by postmodern relativism. It makes them feel both free and secure: free, because they are no longer under necessity to seek and to be governed by unyielding authoritative truth; secure, because no one can question the truth of what they have chosen to believe, since the category of truth does not exist. And the uncertainty that they inevitably feel about life's ultimate questions is quietened by the thought that everyone else is in the same boat: no one can be certain about anything. Uncertainty has become their refuge from reality. But their refuge is an illusion: it cannot forever protect them from reality; for the basic principle on which postmodernism rests is not only false, it is self-contradictory. Its basic principle is that there is no such thing as absolute truth; and yet it insists on laying down this principle itself as an absolute

---

[19] *Mere Christianity*, 6.

unquestionable truth. But the statement 'it is an absolute truth that there is no such thing as absolute truth' is self-referential nonsense. For if the statement is true, it declares itself to be false, which is absurd.

However, there is a final note of caution to be sounded. Although much of the postmodern critique of science is absurd as we have seen, there is at least one aspect of it which could have a positive function in alerting our attention to the possibility (although most scientists will be well aware of it anyway) that there are occasions when scientists might be influenced by strong preconceived philosophical or political commitments to give an interpretation to observed facts of nature which is scarcely warranted by those facts (essentially Sokal's point 3 above, warning of the danger of strong commitments blinding the scientist's mind to inconvenient facts). It should be emphasised that these occasions will be rare and are hardly ever likely to occur in the scientific investigation of repeatable processes—of how things work. They are much more likely to occur when scientists are investigating how things came to be, the origins of the universe and of life, or when science is unduly influenced by the financial gain to be made by its application to technology.

Our conclusion, then, is that the postmodern criticism of genuine science fails both in practice and in principle. Genuine science is not a social construct. It attempts to understand a universe that is not of its own invention, and even though it cannot guarantee absolute truth, it believes that there is truth to be found and that it is getting an increasingly accurate picture of that truth. For that reason it is a worthy subject to pursue.

APPENDIX:
THE SCIENTIFIC ENDEAVOUR

The doing of successful science follows no set of cosy rules. It is as complex as the human personalities that are involved in doing it.

THE CLEAR VOICE OF SCIENCE

Science rightly has the power to fire the imagination. Who could read the story of how Francis Crick and James D. Watson unravelled the double helix structure of DNA without entering at least a little into the almost unbearable joy that they experienced at this discovery? Who could watch an operation to repair someone's eye with a delicately controlled laser beam without a sense of wonder at human creativity and invention? Who could see pictures from space showing astronauts floating weightless in the cabin of the International Space Station or watch them repair the Hubble telescope against the background of the almost tangible blackness of space without a feeling akin to awe? Science has a right to our respect and to our active encouragement. Getting young people into science and giving them the training and facilities to develop their intellectual potential is a clear priority for any nation. It would be an incalculable loss if the scientific instinct were in any way stifled by philosophical, economic or political considerations.

But since one of the most powerful and influential voices to which we want to listen is the voice of science, it will be very important for us, whether we are scientists or not, to have some idea of what science is and what the scientific method is before we try to evaluate what science says to us on any particular issue. Our aim, therefore, first of all is to remind ourselves of some of the basic principles of scientific thinking, some of which we may already know. Following this, we shall think about the nature of scientific explanation and we shall examine some of the assumptions that underlie scientific activity—basic beliefs without which science cannot be done.

Then what is science? It tends to be one of those things that we all know what it means until we come to try to define it. And then we find that precise definition eludes us. The difficulty arises because we use the word in different ways. First of all, science is used as shorthand for:

1. sciences—areas of knowledge like physics, chemistry, biology, etc.;
2. scientists—the people who work in these areas;
3. scientific method—the way in which scientists do their work.

Often, however, the word science is used in expressions like 'Science says . . .', or 'Science has demonstrated . . .', as if science were a conscious being of great authority and knowledge. This usage, though understandable, can be misleading. The fact is that, strictly speaking, there is no such thing as 'science' in this sense. Science does not say, demonstrate, know or discover anything—scientists do. Of course, scientists often agree, but it is increasingly recognised that science, being a very human endeavour, is very much more complex than is often thought and there is considerable debate about what constitutes scientific method.

SCIENTIFIC METHOD

It is now generally agreed among philosophers of science that there is no one 'scientific method', so it is easier to speak of the kind of thing that doing science involves than to give a precise definition of science.

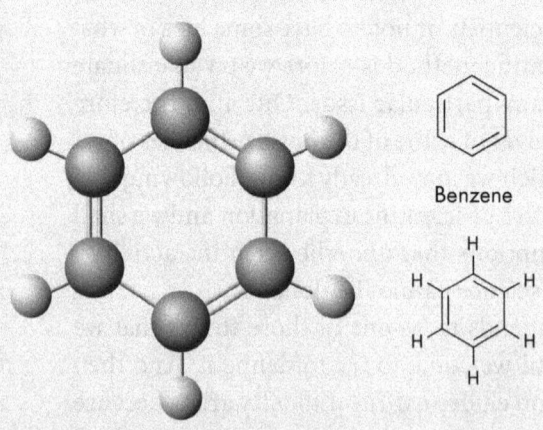

FIGURE Ap.1. Benzene Molecule.

In 1929 crystallographer Kathleen Lonsdale confirmed Kekulé's earlier theory about the flat, cyclic nature of benzene, an important milestone in organic chemistry.

Reproduced with permission of ©iStock/hromatos.

Certainly observation and experimentation have primary roles to play, as well as do the reasoning processes that lead scientists to their conclusions. However, a glance at the history of science will show that there is much more to it than this. We find, for example, that inexplicable hunches have played a considerable role. Even dreams have had their place! The chemist Friedrich August Kekulé was studying the structure of benzene and dreamed about a snake that grabbed its own tail, thus forming itself into a ring. As a result he was led to the idea that benzene might be like the snake. He had a look and found that benzene indeed contained a closed ring of six carbon atoms! The doing of successful science follows no set of cosy rules. It is as complex as the human personalities that are involved in doing it.

Observation and experimentation

It is generally agreed that a revolution in scientific thinking took place in the sixteenth and seventeenth centuries. Up to then one main method of thinking about the nature of the universe was to appeal to authority. For example, in the fourth century BC Aristotle had argued from philosophical principles that the only perfect motion was circular. Thus, if you wanted to know how the planets moved, then, since according to Aristotle they inhabited the realm of perfection beyond the orbit of the moon, they must move in circles. In a radical departure from this approach, scientists like Galileo insisted that the best way to find out how the planets moved was to take his telescope and go and have a look! And through that telescope he saw things like the moons of Jupiter which, according to the Aristotelian system, did not exist. Galileo comes to embody for many people the true spirit of scientific enquiry: the freedom to do full justice to observation and experimentation, even if it meant seriously modifying or even abandoning the theories that he had previously held. That freedom should be retained and jealously guarded by us all.

Data, patterns, relationships and hypotheses

In summary form, the most widespread view, often attributed to Francis Bacon and John Stuart Mill, is that the scientific method consists of:

1. the collection of data (facts, about which there can be no dispute) by means of observation and experiment, neither of them influenced by presuppositions or prejudices;
2. the derivation of hypotheses from the data by looking for patterns or relationships between the data and then making an inductive generalisation;
3. the testing of the hypotheses by deducing predictions from them and then constructing and doing experiments designed to check if those predictions are true;
4. the discarding of hypotheses that are not supported by the experimental data and the building up of the theory by adding confirmed hypotheses.

Scientists collect data, experimental observations and measurements that they record. As examples of data, think of a set of blood pressure measurements of your class just before and just after a school examination, or of the rock samples collected by astronauts from the surface of the moon.

There are, however, many other things that are equally real to us, but which scarcely can count as data in the scientific sense: our subjective experience of a sunset, or of friendship and love, or of dreams. With dreams, of course, heart rate, brain activity and eye movement can be observed by scientists as they monitor people who are asleep and dreaming, but their subjective experience of the dream itself cannot be measured. Thus we see that the scientific method has certain built-in limits. It cannot capture the whole of reality.

Scientists are in the business of looking for relationships and patterns in their data and they try to infer some kind of hypothesis or theory to account for those patterns. Initially the hypothesis may be an intelligent or inspired guess that strikes the scientists from their experience as being a possible way of accounting for what they have observed. For example, a scientist might suggest the (very reasonable) hypothesis that the blood pressure measurements in your class can be accounted for by the fact that examinations cause stress in most people! To test the hypothesis a scientist will then work out what he or she would expect to find if the hypothesis were true and then will proceed to devise an experiment or a series of experiments to check if such is indeed the case. If the experiments fail to confirm expectation, the hypothesis may be modified or discarded in favour of another and the process repeated. Once a hypothesis has been successfully tested by repeated experimentation then it is dignified by being called a theory.[1]

It is now generally agreed by scientists themselves and philosophers of science that our account so far of what the scientific method is, is not only highly idealised but also flawed. In particular, contrary to what is asserted about observation and experimentation above, it is now widely accepted that no scientist, however honest and careful, can come to his or her work in a completely impartial way, without presuppositions and assumptions. This fact will be of importance for our understanding of science's contribution to our worldview. It is easier, however, to consider that topic after we have first had a look at some of the logical concepts and procedures that underlie scientific argumentation and proof.

Induction

Induction is probably the most important logical process that scientists use in the formulation of laws and theories.[2] It is also a process that is familiar to all of us from a very early age whether we are scientists or not, though we may well not have been aware of it. When we as young children first see a crow we notice it is black. For all we know, the next crow we see may well be white or yellow. But after observing crows day after day, there comes a point at which our feeling that any other crow we see is going to be black is so strong that we would be prepared to say that all crows are black. We have taken what is called an inductive step based on our own data—we have seen, say, 435 crows—to make a universal statement about all crows. Induction, then, is the process of

---

[1] The terms *hypothesis* and *theory* are in fact almost indistinguishable, the only difference in normal usage being that a hypothesis is sometimes regarded as more tentative than a theory.

[2] Note for mathematicians: the process of induction described above is not the same as the principle of mathematical induction by which (typically) the truth of a statement $P(n)$ is established for all positive integers n from two propositions:

(1) $P(1)$ is true;

(2) for any positive integer k, we can prove that the truth of $P(k+1)$ follows from the truth of $P(k)$.

The key difference is that (2) describes an infinite set of hypotheses, one for each positive integer, whereas in philosophical induction we are generalising from a finite set of hypotheses.

generalising from a finite set of data to a universal or general statement.

A famous example of the use of induction in science is the derivation of Mendel's laws of heredity. Gregor Mendel and his assistants made a number of observations of the frequency of occurrence of particular characteristics in each of several generations of peas, like whether seeds were wrinkled or smooth, or plants were tall or short, and then made an inductive generalisation from those observations to formulate the laws that now bear his name.

Induction, then, is the process of generalising from a finite set of data to a universal or general statement.

But, as may well have occurred to you, there is a problem with induction. To illustrate this, let's turn our minds to swans rather than the crows we thought about just now. Suppose that from childhood every swan you have seen was white. You might well conclude (by induction) that all swans are white. But then one day you are shown a picture of an Australian black swan and discover that your conclusion was false. This illustrates what the problem with induction is. How can you ever really know that you have made enough observations to draw a universal conclusion from a limited set of observations?

But please notice what the discovery of the black swan has done. It has proved wrong the statement that all swans are white, but it has not proved wrong the modified statement that if you see a swan in Europe, the high probability is that the swan will be white.

Let's look at another example of induction, this time from chemistry.

Particular observations:

Time	Date	Substance	Litmus test result
0905	2015-08-14	sulphuric acid	turned red
1435	2015-09-17	citric acid	turned red
1045	2015-09-18	hydrochloric acid	turned red
1900	2015-10-20	sulphuric acid	turned red

Universal or general statement (law): litmus paper turns red when dipped in acid.

This law, based on induction from the finite set of particular observations that are made of particular acids at particular times in particular places, is claimed to hold for all acids at all times in all places. The problem with induction is, how can we be sure that such a general statement is valid, when, in the very nature of things, we can only make a finite number of observations of litmus paper turning red on the application of acid? The story of the black swan makes us aware of the difficulty.

Well, we cannot be absolutely sure, it is true. But every time we do the experiment and find it works, our confidence in the litmus test is increased to the extent that if we dipped some paper in a liquid and found it did not go red we would be likely to conclude, not that the litmus test did not work, but that either the paper we had was not litmus paper or the liquid was not acid! Of course it is true that underlying our confidence is the assumption that nature behaves in a uniform way, that if I repeat an experiment tomorrow under the same conditions as I did it today, I will get the same results.

Let's take another example that Bertrand Russell used to illustrate the problem of induction in a more complex situation: Bertrand Russell's inductivist turkey. A turkey observes that on its first day at the turkey farm it was fed at 9 a.m. For two months it collects observations and notes that even if it chooses days at random, it is fed at 9 a.m. It finally concludes by induction that it always will be fed at 9 a.m. It therefore gets an awful shock on Christmas Eve when, instead of being fed, it is taken out and killed for Christmas dinner!

So how can we know for certain that we have made enough observations in an experiment? How many times do we have to check that particular metals expand on heating to conclude that all metals expand on heating? How do we avoid the inductivist turkey shock? Of course we can see that the problem with the turkey is that it did not have (indeed could not have) the wider experience of the turkey farmer who could replace the turkey's incorrect inductivist conclusion with a more complicated correct one: namely the law that each turkey will experience a sequence of days of feeding followed by execution!

The point of what we are saying here is not to undermine science by suggesting that induction is useless, nor that science in itself cannot lead us to any firm conclusions. It simply teaches us to recognise the limits of any one method and to found our conclusions, wherever possible, on a combination of them.

The role of deduction

Once a law has been formulated by induction, we can test the validity of the law by using it to make predictions. For example, assuming Mendel's laws to be true, we can deduce from them a prediction as to what the relative frequency of occurrence, say, of blue eyes in different generations of a family, should be. When we find by direct observation that the occurrence of blue eyes is what we predicted it to be, our observations are said to confirm the theory, although this sort of confirmation can never amount to total certainty. Thus deduction plays an important role in the confirmation of induction.

> Deduction plays an important role in the confirmation of induction.

It may be that what we have said about induction has given the impression that scientific work always starts by looking at data and reasoning to some inductive hypothesis that accounts for those data. However, in reality, scientific method tends to be somewhat more complicated than this. Frequently, scientists start by deciding what kind of data they are looking for. That is, they already have in their mind some hypothesis or theory they want to test, and they look for data that will confirm that theory. In this situation deduction will play a dominant role.

For example, as we mentioned above regarding observation and experimentation, in the ancient world, Greek philosophers supposed as a hypothesis that the planets must move in circular orbits around the earth, since, for them, the circle was the perfect shape. They then deduced what their hypothesis should lead them to observe in the heavens. When their observations did not appear to confirm their original hypothesis completely, they modified it. They did this by replacing the original hypothesis by one in which other circular motions are imposed on top of the original one (epicycles, they were called). They then used this more complicated hypothesis from which to deduce their predictions. This theory of epicycles dominated astronomy for a long time, and was overturned and replaced by the revolutionary suggestions of Copernicus and Kepler.

Kepler's work in turn again illustrates the deductive method. Using the observations the astronomer Tycho Brahe had made available, Kepler tried to work out the shape that the orbit of Mars traced against the background of 'fixed' stars. He did not get anywhere until he hit on an idea that was prompted by geometrical work he had done on the ellipse. That idea was to suppose as a hypothesis that the orbit of Mars was an ellipse, then to use mathematical calculations to deduce what should be observed on the basis of that hypothesis, and finally to compare those predictions with the actual observations. The validity of the elliptical orbit hypothesis would then be judged by how closely the predictions fit the observations.

This method of inference is called the deductive or hypothetico-deductive method of reasoning: deducing predictions from a hypothesis, and then comparing them with actual observations.

Since deduction is such an important procedure it is worth considering it briefly. Deduction is a logical process by which an assertion we want to prove (the conclusion) is logically deduced from things we already accept (the premises). Here is an example of logical deduction, usually called a syllogism:

P1: All dogs have four legs.
P2: Fido is a dog.
C: Fido has four legs.

Here statements P1 and P2 are the premises and C is the conclusion. If P1 and P2 are true then C is true. Or to put it another way, to have P1 and P2 true and C false, would involve a logical contradiction. This is the essence of a logically valid deduction.

Let's now look at an example of a logically invalid deduction:

P1: Many dogs have a long tail.
P2: Albert is a dog.
C: Albert has a long tail.

Here statement C does not necessarily follow from P1 and P2. It is clearly possible for P1 and P2 to be true and yet for C to be false.

It all appears to be so simple that there is danger of your switching off. But don't do that quite yet or you might miss something very important. And that is that deductive logic cannot establish the truth of any of the statements involved in the procedure. All that the logic can tell us (but this much is very important!) is that if the premises are true and the argument is logically valid, then the conclusion is true. In order to get this clear let us look at a final example:

P1: All planets have a buried ocean.
P2: Mercury is a planet.

C: Mercury has a buried ocean.

This is a logically valid argument even though statement P1 and statement C are (so far as we know) false. The argument says only that if P1 and P2 were true, then C should be true, which is perfectly valid.

> Logic has to do with the way in which some statements are derived from others, not with the truth of those statements.

This sort of thing may seem strange to us at first, but it can help us grasp that logic can only criticise the argument and check whether it is valid or not. It cannot tell us whether any or all of the premises or conclusion are true. Logic has to do with the way in which some statements are derived from others, not with the truth of those statements.

We should also note that deductive inference plays a central role in pure mathematics where theories are constructed by means of making deductions from explicitly given axioms, as in Euclidean geometry. The results (or theorems, as they are usually called) are said to be true if there is a logically valid chain of deductions deriving them from the axioms. Such deductive proofs give a certainty (granted the consistency of the axioms) that is not attainable in the inductive sciences.

In practice induction and deduction are usually both involved in establishing scientific theories. We referred above to Kepler's use of deduction in deriving his theory that Mars moved in an ellipse round the sun. However, he first thought of the ellipse (rather than, say, the parabola or the hyperbola) because the observations of Brahe led Kepler to believe the orbit of Mars was roughly egg-shaped. The egg shape was initially conjectured as a result of induction from astronomical observations.

Competing hypotheses can cover the same data

But here we should notice that when it comes to interpreting the data we have collected, different hypotheses can be constructed to cover that data. We have two illustrations of this.

Illustration from astronomy. Under the role of deduction above we discussed two hypotheses from ancient astronomy that were put forward to explain the motion of the planets. Successive refinements of the epicyclic model appeared to cover the data at the expense of greater and greater complication in that more and more circles were necessary. Kepler's proposal, by contrast, covered the data by the simple device of replacing the complex array of circles by one single ellipse, which simplified the whole business enormously. Now, if we knew nothing of gravity and the deduction of elliptical orbits that can be made from it by means of Newton's laws, how would we choose between the two explanations?

At this point, scientists might well invoke the principle sometimes called 'Occam's razor', after William of Occam. This is the belief that simpler explanations of natural phenomena are more likely to be correct than more complex ones. More precisely, the idea is that if we have two or more competing hypotheses covering the same data, we should choose the one that involves the least number of assumptions or complications. The metaphorical use of the word 'razor' comes from this cutting or shaving down to the smallest possible number of assumptions. Occam's razor has proved very useful but we should observe that it is a philosophical preference, and it is not something that you can prove to be true in every case, so it needs to be used with care.

Illustration from physics. Another illustration of the way in which different hypotheses can account for the same data is given by a common exercise in school physics. We are given a spring, a series of weights and a ruler and asked to plot a graph of the length of the spring against the weight hanging on the end of it. We end up with a series, say, of 10 points on the paper that look as if they might (with a bit of imagination!) lie on a straight line. We take an inductive step and draw a straight line that goes through most of the points and we claim that there is a linear relationship between the length of spring and the tension it is put under by the weights (Hooke's law). But then we reflect that there is an infinite number of curves that can be drawn through our ten points. Changing the curve would change the relation between spring length and tension. Why not choose one of those other curves in preference to the

> The principle sometimes called 'Occam's razor', after William of Occam . . . is the belief that simpler explanations of natural phenomena are more likely to be correct than more complex ones.

straight line? That is, in the situation just described, there are many different hypotheses that cover the same set of data. How do you choose between them?

Application of Occam's razor would lead to choosing the most elegant or economical solution—a straight line is simpler than a complicated curve. We could also repeat the experiment with 100 points, 200 points, etc. The results would build up our confidence that the straight line was the correct answer. When we build up evidence in this way, we say that we have cumulative evidence for the validity of our hypothesis.

So far we have been looking at various methods employed by scientists and have seen that none of them yields 100% certainty, except in deductive proofs in mathematics where the certainty is that particular conclusions follow from particular axioms. However, we would emphasise once more that this does not mean that the scientific enterprise is about to collapse! Far from it. What we mean by 'not giving 100% certainty' can be interpreted as saying that there is a small probability that a particular result or theory is false. But that does not mean that we cannot have confidence in the theory.

Indeed there are some situations, as in the litmus-paper test for acid where there has been 100% success in the past. Now whereas this does not formally guarantee 100% success in the future, scientists will say that it is a fact that litmus paper turns red on being dipped in acid. By a 'fact', they mean, as palaeontologist Stephen Jay Gould has delightfully put it, 'confirmed to such a degree that it would be perverse to withhold provisional assent to it'.[3]

On other occasions we are prepared to trust our lives to the findings of science and technology even though we know we do not have 100% certainty. For example, before we travel by train, we know that it is theoretically possible for something to go wrong, maybe for the brakes or signalling to fail and cause the train to crash. But we also know from the statistics of rail travel that the probability of such an event is very small indeed (though it is not zero—trains have from time to time crashed). Since the probability of a crash is so small, most of us who travel by train do so without even thinking about the risk.

On the other hand we must not assume that we can accept all

---

[3] Gould, 'Evolution as Fact and Theory', 119.

proposed hypotheses arrived at by scientific method as absolute fact without testing them.

One of the criteria of testing is called falsifiability.

Falsifiability

Karl Popper put the emphasis not on the verifiability of a hypothesis but on its falsifiability. It is unfortunate that Popper's terminology can be a real source of confusion, since the adjective 'falsifiable' does not mean 'will turn out to be false'! The confusion is even worse when one realises, on the other hand, that the verb 'to falsify' means 'to demonstrate that something is false'! The term 'falsifiable' has in fact a technical meaning. A hypothesis is said to be falsifiable if you can think of a logically possible set of observations that would be inconsistent with it.

It is, of course, much easier to falsify a universal statement than to verify it. As an illustration, take one of our earlier examples. The statement 'All swans are white' is, from the very start, falsifiable. One would only have to discover one swan that was black and that would falsify it. And since we know that black swans do exist, the statement has long since been falsified.

However, there can be problems. Most scientific activity is much more complex than dealing with claims like 'All swans are white'!

For example, in the nineteenth century observations of the planet Uranus appeared to indicate that its motion was inconsistent with predictions made on the basis of Newton's laws. Therefore, it appeared to threaten to demonstrate Newton's laws to be false. However, instead of immediately saying that Newton's laws had been falsified, it was suggested by French mathematician Urbain Le Verrier and English astronomer John Couch Adams (unknown to each other) that there might be a hitherto undetected planet in the neighbourhood of Uranus that would account for its apparently anomalous behaviour. As a result another scientist, German astronomer Johann Galle, was prompted to look for a new planet and discovered the planet Neptune.

> The term 'falsifiable' has in fact a technical meaning: a hypothesis is said to be falsifiable if you can think of a logically possible set of observations that would be inconsistent with it.

It would, therefore, have been incorrect to regard the behaviour of Uranus as falsifying Newton's laws. The problem was ignorance of the initial conditions—there was a planet missing in the configuration being studied. In other words, some of the crucial data was missing. This story demonstrates one of the problems inherent in Popper's approach. When observation does not fit theory, it could be that the theory is false, but it could equally well be that the theory is correct but the data is incomplete or even false, or that some of the auxiliary assumptions are incorrect. How can you judge what is the correct picture?

Most scientists in fact feel that Popper's ideas are far too pessimistic and his methodology too counter-intuitive. Their experience and intuition tell them that their scientific methods in fact enable them to get a better and better understanding of the universe, that they are in this sense getting a tighter grip on reality. One benefit of Popper's approach, however, is its insistence that scientific theories be testable.

Repeatability and abduction

The scientific activity we have been thinking of so far is characterised by repeatability. That is, we have considered situations where scientists are looking for universally valid laws that cover repeatable phenomena, laws which, like Newton's laws of motion, may be experimentally tested again and again. Sciences of this sort are often called inductive or nomological sciences (Gk. *nomos* = law) and between them they cover most of science.

However there are major areas of scientific enquiry where repeatability is not possible, notably study of the origin of the universe and the origin and development of life.

Now of course we do not mean to imply that science has nothing to say about phenomena that are non-repeatable. On the contrary, if one is to judge by the amount of literature published, particularly, but not only, at the popular level, the origin of the universe and of life, for example, are among the most interesting subjects by far that science addresses.

But precisely because of the importance of such non-repeatable phenomena, it is vital to see that the way in which they are accessible to science is not the same in general as the way in which repeatable phenomena are. For theories about both kinds of phenomena tend to be presented to the public in the powerful name of science as though they had an equal claim to be accepted. Thus there is a real danger that the public ascribes the same authority and validity to conjectures about non-repeatable events that are not capable of experimental verification as it does to those theories that have been confirmed by repeated experiment.

Physical chemist and philosopher Michael Polanyi points out that the study of how something originates is usually very different from the study of how it operates, although, of course, clues to how something originated may well be found in how it operates. It is one thing to investigate something repeatable in the laboratory, such as dissecting a frog to see how its nervous system functions, but it is an altogether different thing to study something non-repeatable, such as how frogs came to exist in the first place. And, on the large scale, how the universe works is one thing, yet how it came to be may be quite another.

> How the universe works is one thing, yet how it came to be may be quite another.

The most striking difference between the study of non-repeatable and repeatable phenomena is that the method of induction is no longer applicable, since we no longer have a sequence of observations or experiments to induce from, nor any repetition in the future to predict about! The principal method that applies to non-repeatable phenomena is abduction.

Although this term, introduced by logician Charles Peirce in the nineteenth century, may be unfamiliar, the underlying idea is very familiar. For abduction is what every good detective does in order to clear up a murder mystery! With the murder mystery a certain event has happened. No one doubts that it has happened. The question is: who or what was the cause of it happening? And often in the search for causes of an event that has already happened, abduction is the only method available.

As an example of abductive inference, think of the following:

Data: Ivan's car went over the cliff edge and he was killed.

Inference: If the car brakes had failed, then the car would have gone over the cliff.

Abductive conclusion: There is reason to suppose that the brakes failed.

However, an alternative suggests itself (especially to avid readers of detective stories): if someone had pushed Ivan's car over the cliff, the result would have been the same! It would be fallacious and very foolish to assume that just because we had thought of one explanation of the circumstances, that it was the only one.

The basic idea of abduction is given by the following scheme:

Data: A is observed.

Inference: If B were true then A would follow.

Abductive conclusion: There is reason to suppose B may be true.

Of course, there may well be another hypothesis, C, of which we could say: if C were true A would follow. Indeed, there may be many candidates for C.

The detective in our story has a procedure for considering them one by one. He may first consider the chance hypothesis, B, that the brakes failed. He may then consider the hypothesis C that it was no chance event, but deliberately designed by a murderer who pushed the car over the cliff. Or the detective may consider an even more sophisticated hypothesis, D, combining both chance and design, that someone who wanted to kill Ivan had tampered with the brakes of the car so that they would fail somewhere, and they happened to fail on the clifftop!

Inference to the best explanation. Our detective story illustrates how the process of abduction throws up plausible hypotheses and forces upon us the question as to which of the hypotheses best fits the data. In order to decide that question, the hypotheses are compared for their explanatory power: how much of the data do they cover, does the theory make coherent sense, is it consistent with other areas of our knowledge, etc.?

In order to answer these further questions, deduction will often be used. For example, if B in the detective story is true, then we would expect an investigation of the brakes of the wrecked car to reveal worn or broken parts. If C is true we would deduce that the brakes might well be found in perfect order, whereas if D were the case, we might expect to find marks of deliberate damage to the hydraulic braking system. If we found such marks then D would immediately be regarded as the best of the competing explanations given so far, since it has a greater explanatory power than the others.

Thus, abduction together with the subsequent comparison of competing hypotheses may be regarded as an 'inference to the best explanation'. This is the essence not only of detective and legal work but also of the work of the historian. Both detective and historian have to infer the best possible explanation from the available data after the events in which they are interested have occurred.

For more on the application of abduction in the natural sciences, particularly in cosmology and biology, see the books by John Lennox noted at the end of this Appendix. Here we need to consider a few more of the general issues related to the scientific endeavour.

EXPLAINING EXPLANATIONS

Levels of explanation

Science explains. This, for many people encapsulates the power and the fascination of science. Science enables us to understand what we did not understand before and, by giving us understanding, it gives us power over nature. But what do we mean by saying that 'science explains'?

In informal language we take an explanation of something to be adequate when the person to whom the explanation is given understands plainly what he or she did not understand before. However, we must try to be more precise about what we mean by the process of 'explanation', since it has different aspects that are often confused. An illustration can help us. We have considered a similar idea in relation to roses. Let's now take further examples.

Suppose Aunt Olga has baked a beautiful cake. She displays it to a gathering of the world's top scientists and we ask them for an explanation of the cake. The nutrition scientists will tell us about the number of calories in the cake and its nutritional effect; the biochemists will inform us about the structure of the proteins, fats, etc. in the cake and what it is that causes them to hold together; the chemists will enumerate the elements involved and describe their bonding; the physicists will be able to analyse the cake in terms of fundamental particles; and the mathematicians will offer us a set of beautiful equations to describe the behaviour of those particles. Suppose, then, that these experts have given us an exhaustive description of the cake, each in terms of his or her scientific discipline. Can we say that the cake is now completely explained? We have certainly been given a description of how the cake was made and how its various constituent elements relate to each other. But suppose we now ask the assembled group of experts why the cake was made. We notice the grin on Aunt Olga's face. She knows the answer since, after all, she made the cake! But if she does not reveal the answer by telling us, it is clear that no amount of scientific analysis will give us the answer.

Thus, although science can answer 'how' questions in terms of causes and mechanisms, it cannot answer 'why' questions, questions of purpose and intention—teleological questions, as they are sometimes called (Gk. *telos* = end or goal).

However, it would be nonsensical to suggest that Aunt Olga's answer to the teleological question, that she made the cake for Sam's birthday, say, contradicted the scientific analysis of the cake! No. The two kinds of answer are clearly logically compatible.

And yet exactly the same confusion of categories is evidenced when atheists argue that there is no longer need to bring in God and the supernatural to explain the workings of nature, since we now have a scientific explanation for them. As a result, the general public has come to think that belief in a creator belongs to a primitive and unsophisticated stage of human thinking and has been rendered both unnecessary and impossible by science.

Although science can answer 'how' questions in terms of causes and mechanisms, it cannot answer 'why' questions, questions of purpose and intention.

But there is an obvious fallacy here. Think of a Ford motor car. It is conceivable that a primitive person who was seeing one for the first time and who did not understand the principles of an internal combustion engine, might imagine that there was a god (Mr Ford) inside the engine, making it go. He might further imagine that when the engine ran sweetly that was because Mr Ford inside the engine liked him, and when it refused to go that was because Mr Ford did not like him. Of course, if eventually this primitive person became civilised, learned engineering, and took the engine to pieces, he would discover that there was no Mr Ford inside the engine, and that he did not need to introduce Mr Ford as an explanation for the working of the engine. His grasp of the impersonal principles of internal combustion would be altogether enough to explain how the engine worked. So far, so good. But if he then decided that his understanding of the principles of the internal combustion engine made it impossible to believe in the existence of a Mr Ford who designed the engine, this would be patently false!

FIGURE Ap.2. Model T Ford Motor Car.

Introducing the world's first moving assembly line in 1913, Ford Motor Company built more than 15 million Model Ts from 1908 until 1927.

Reproduced with permission of ©iStock/Peter Mah.

It is likewise a confusion of categories to suppose that our understanding of the impersonal principles according to which the universe works makes it either unnecessary or impossible to believe in the existence of a personal creator who designed, made and upholds the great engine that is the universe. In other words, we should not confuse the mechanisms by which the universe works with its Cause. Every one of us knows how to distinguish between the consciously willed movement of an arm for a purpose and an involuntary spasmodic movement of an arm induced by accidental contact with an electric current.

Michael Poole, Visiting Research Fellow, Science and Religion, at King's College London, in his published debate on science and religion with Richard Dawkins, puts it this way:

> There is no logical conflict between reason-giving explanations which concern mechanisms, and reason-giving explanations which concern the plans and purposes of an agent, human or divine. This is a logical point, not a matter of whether one does or does not happen to believe in God oneself.[4]

---

[4] Poole, 'Critique of Aspects of the Philosophy and Theology of Richard Dawkins', 49.

One of the authors, in a debate with Richard Dawkins, noted how his opponent was confusing the categories of mechanism and agency:

> When Isaac Newton, for example, discovered his law of gravity and wrote down the equations of motion, he didn't say, 'Marvellous, I now understand it. I've got a mechanism therefore I don't need God.' In fact it was the exact opposite. It was because he understood the complexity of sophistication of the mathematical description of the universe that his praise for God was increased. And I would like to suggest, Richard, that somewhere down in this you're making a category mistake, because you're confusing mechanism with agency. We have a mechanism that does XYZ, therefore there's no need for an agent. I would suggest that the sophistication of the mechanism, and science rejoices in finding such mechanisms, is evidence for the sheer wonder of the creative genius of God.[5]

In spite of the clarity of the logic expressed in these counterpoints, a famous statement made by the French mathematician Laplace is constantly misappropriated to support atheism. On being asked by Napoleon where God fitted in to his mathematical work, Laplace replied: 'Sir, I have no need of that hypothesis.' Of course, God did not appear in Laplace's mathematical description of how things work, just as Mr Ford would not appear in a scientific description of the laws of internal combustion. But what does that prove? Such an argument can no more be used to prove that God does not exist than it can be used to prove that Mr Ford does not exist.

To sum up, then, it is important to be aware of the danger of confusing different levels of explanation and of thinking that one level of explanation tells the whole story.

This leads us at once to consider the related question of reductionism.

---

[5] Lennox's response to Dawkins's first thesis 'Faith is blind; science is evidence-based', 'The God Delusion Debate', hosted by Fixed Point Foundation, University of Alabama at Birmingham, filmed and broadcast live 3 October 2007, http://fixed-point.org/index.php/video/35-full-length/164-the-dawkins-lennox-debate. Transcript provided courtesy of ProTorah, http://www.protorah.com/god-delusion-debate-dawkins-lennox-transcript/.

Reductionism

In order to study something, especially if it is complex, scientists often split it up into separate parts or aspects and thus 'reduce' it to simpler components that are individually easier to investigate. This kind of reductionism, often called methodological or structural reductionism, is part of the normal process of science and has proved very useful. It is, however, very important to bear in mind that there may well be, and usually is, more to a given whole than simply what we obtain by adding up all that we have learned from the parts. Studying all the parts of a watch separately will never enable you to grasp how the complete watch works as an integrated whole.

Besides methodological reductionism there are two further types of reductionism, epistemological and ontological. *Epistemological reductionism* is the view that higher level sciences can be explained without remainder by the sciences at a lower level. That is, chemistry is explained by physics; biochemistry by chemistry; biology by biochemistry; psychology by biology; sociology by brain science; and theology by sociology. As Francis Crick puts it: 'The ultimate aim of the modern development in biology is in fact to explain all biology in terms of physics and chemistry.'[6] The former Charles Simonyi Professor of the Public Understanding of Science at Oxford, Richard Dawkins, holds the same view: 'My task is to explain elephants, and the world of complex things, in terms of the simple things that physicists either understand, or are working on.'[7] The ultimate goal of reductionism is to reduce all human behaviour, our likes and dislikes, the entire mental landscape of our lives, to physics.

> The ultimate goal of reductionism is to reduce all human behaviour, our likes and dislikes, the entire mental landscape of our lives, to physics.

However, both the viability and the plausibility of this programme are open to serious question. The outstanding Russian psychologist Leo Vygotsky (1896–1934) was critical of certain aspects of this reductionist philosophy as applied to psychology. He pointed out that such reductionism often conflicts

---

[6] Crick, *Of Molecules and Men*, 10.
[7] Dawkins, *Blind Watchmaker*, 15.

with the goal of preserving all the basic features of a phenomenon or event that one wishes to explain. For example, one can reduce water (H_2O) into H and O. However, hydrogen burns and oxygen is necessary for burning, whereas water has neither of these properties, but has many others that are not possessed by either hydrogen or oxygen. Thus, Vygotsky's view was that reductionism can only be done up to certain limits. Karl Popper says: 'There is almost always an unresolved residue left by even the most successful attempts at reduction.'[8]

Furthermore, Michael Polanyi argues the intrinsic implausibility of expecting epistemological reductionism to work in every circumstance.[9] Think of the various levels of process involved in building an office building with bricks. First of all there is the process of extracting the raw materials out of which the bricks have to be made. Then there are the successively higher levels of making the bricks, they do not make themselves; bricklaying, the bricks do not self-assemble; designing the building, it does not design itself; and planning the town in which the building is to be built, it does not organise itself. Each level has its own rules. The laws of physics and chemistry govern the raw material of the bricks; technology prescribes the art of brick making; architecture teaches the builders, and the architects are controlled by the town planners. Each level is controlled by the level above, but the reverse is not true. The laws of a higher level cannot be derived from the laws of a lower level (although, of course what can be done at a higher level will depend on the lower levels: for example, if the bricks are not strong there will be a limit on the height of a building that can be safely built with them).

Consider the page you are reading just now. It consists of paper imprinted with ink or, in the case of an electronic version, text rendered digitally. It is obvious that the physics and chemistry of ink and paper can never, even in principle, tell you anything about the significance of the shapes of the letters on the page. And this is nothing to do with the fact that physics and chemistry are not yet sufficiently advanced to deal with this question. Even if we allow these sciences another 1,000 years of development, we can see that it will make no

---

[8] Popper, 'Scientific Reduction.'
[9] Polanyi, *Tacit Dimension*.

difference, because the shapes of those letters demand a totally new and higher level of explanation than that of which physics and chemistry are capable. In fact, explanation can only be given in terms of the concepts of language and authorship—the communication of a message by a person. The ink and paper are carriers of the message, but the message certainly does not emerge automatically from them. Furthermore, when it comes to language itself, there is again a sequence of levels—you cannot derive a vocabulary from phonetics, or the grammar of a language from its vocabulary, etc.

As is well known, the genetic material DNA carries information. We shall describe this later on in some detail, but the basic idea is simply this. DNA, a substance found in every living cell, can be looked at as a long tape on which there is a string of letters written in a four-letter chemical language. The sequence of letters contains coded instructions (information) that the cell uses to make proteins. Physical biochemist and theologian Arthur Peacocke writes: 'In no way can the concept of "information", the concept of conveying a message, be articulated in terms of the concepts of physics and chemistry, even though the latter can be shown to explain how the molecular machinery (DNA, RNA and protein) operates to carry information.'[10]

In each of the situations we have described above, we have a series of levels, each one higher than the previous one. What happens on a higher level is not completely derivable from what happens on the level beneath it, but requires another level of explanation.

In this kind of situation it is sometimes said that the higher level phenomena 'emerge' from the lower level. Unfortunately, however, the word 'emerge' is easily misunderstood to mean that the higher level properties emerge automatically from the lower level properties. This is clearly false in general, as we showed by considering brick making and writing on paper. Yet notwithstanding the fact that both writing on paper and DNA have in common the fact that they encode a 'message', those scientists committed to materialistic philosophy insist that the information carrying properties of DNA must have emerged automatically out of mindless matter. For if, as materialism insists, matter and energy are all that there is, then it logically follows

---

[10] Peacocke, *Experiment of Life*, 54.

that they must possess the inherent potential to organise themselves in such a way that eventually all the complex molecules necessary for life, including DNA, will emerge.[11]

There is a third type of reductionism, called *ontological reductionism*, which is frequently encountered in statements like the following: The universe is nothing but a collection of atoms in motion, human beings are 'machines for propagating DNA, and the propagation of DNA is a self-sustaining process. It is every living object's sole reason for living.'[12]

Words such as 'nothing but', 'sole' or 'simply' are the telltale sign of (ontological) reductionist thinking. If we remove these words we are usually left with something unobjectionable. The universe certainly is a collection of atoms and human beings do propagate DNA. The question is, is there nothing more to it than that? Are we going to say with Francis Crick, who won the Nobel Prize jointly with James D. Watson for his discovery of the double helix structure of DNA: '"You", your joys and your sorrows, your memories and your ambitions, your sense of personal identity and free will, are in fact no more than the behaviour of a vast assembly of nerve cells and their associated molecules'?[13]

What shall we say of human love and fear, of concepts like beauty and truth? Are they meaningless?

Ontological reductionism, carried to its logical conclusion, would ask us to believe that a Rembrandt painting is nothing but molecules of paint scattered on canvas. Physicist and theologian John Polkinghorne's reaction is clear:

> There is more to the world than physics can ever express.
>
> One of the fundamental experiences of the scientific life is that of wonder at the beautiful structure of the world. It is the pay-off for all the weary hours of labour involved in the pursuit of research. Yet in the world described by science where would that wonder find its lodging? Or our experiences of beauty? Of moral obligation? Of the presence of God? These seem to me

---

[11] Whether matter and energy do have this capacity is another matter that is discussed in the books noted at the end of this appendix.
[12] Dawkins, *Growing Up in the Universe* (study guide), 21.
[13] Crick, *Astonishing Hypothesis*, 3.

to be quite as fundamental as anything we could measure in the laboratory. A worldview that does not take them adequately into account is woefully incomplete.[14]

The most devastating criticism of ontological reductionism is that it is self-destructive. Polkinghorne describes its programme as ultimately suicidal:

> For, not only does it relegate our experiences of beauty, moral obligation, and religious encounter to the epiphenomenal scrapheap. It also destroys rationality. Thought is replaced by electrochemical neural events. Two such events cannot confront each other in rational discourse. They are neither right nor wrong. They simply happen. . . . The very assertions of the reductionist himself are nothing but blips in the neural network of his brain. The world of rational discourse dissolves into the absurd chatter of firing synapses. Quite frankly, that cannot be right and none of us believes it to be so.[15]

BASIC OPERATIONAL PRESUPPOSITIONS

So far we have been concentrating on the scientific method and have seen that this is a much more complex (and, for that reason, a much more interesting) topic than may first appear. As promised earlier, we must now consider the implications of the fact that scientists, being human like the rest of us, do not come to any situation with their mind completely clear of preconceived ideas. The widespread idea that any scientist, if only he or she tries to be impartial, can be a completely dispassionate observer in any but the most trivial of situations, is a fallacy, as has been pointed out repeatedly by philosophers of science and by scientists themselves. At the very least scientists must already

> The widespread idea that any scientist, if only he or she tries to be impartial, can be a completely dispassionate observer in any but the most trivial of situations, is a fallacy.

---

[14] Polkinghorne, *One World*, 72–3.
[15] Polkinghorne, *One World*, 92–3.

have formed some idea or theory about the nature of what they are about to study.

Observation is dependent on theory

It is simply not possible to make observations and do experiments without any presuppositions. Consider, for example, the fact that science, by its very nature, has to be selective. It would clearly be impossible to take every aspect of any given object of study into account. Scientists must therefore choose what variables are likely to be important and what are not. For example, physicists do not think of taking into account the colour of billiard balls when they are conducting a laboratory investigation of the application of Newton's laws to motion: but the shape of the balls is very important—cubical balls would not be much use! In making such choices, scientists are inevitably guided by already formed ideas and theories about what the important factors are likely to be. The problem is that such ideas may sometimes be wrong and cause scientists to miss vital aspects of a problem to such an extent that they draw false conclusions. A famous story about the physicist Heinrich Hertz illustrates this.

Maxwell's electromagnetic theory predicted that radio and light waves would be propagated with the same velocity. Hertz designed an experiment to check this and found that the velocities were different. His mistake, only discovered after his death, was that he did not think that the shape of his laboratory could have any influence on the results of his experiment. Unfortunately for him, it did. Radio waves were reflected from the walls and distorted his results.

The validity of his observations depended on the (preconceived) theory that the shape of the laboratory was irrelevant to his experiment. The fact that this preconception was false invalidated his conclusions.

This story also points up another difficulty. How does one decide in this kind of situation whether it is the theory or the experiment that is at fault, whether one should trust the results of the experiment and abandon the theory and look for a better one, or whether one should keep on having faith in the theory and try to discover what was wrong with the experiment? There is no easy answer to this question. A great deal will depend on the experience and judgment of the scientists involved, and, inevitably, mistakes can and will be made.

Knowledge cannot be gained without making certain assumptions to start with

Scientists not only inevitably have preconceived ideas about particular situations, as illustrated by the story about Hertz, but their science is done within a framework of general assumptions about science as such. World-famous Harvard geneticist Richard Lewontin writes: 'Scientists, like other intellectuals, come to their work with a world view, a set of preconceptions that provides the framework for their analysis of the world.'[16]

And those preconceptions can significantly affect scientists' research methods as well as their results and interpretations of those results, as we shall see.

We would emphasise, however, that the fact that scientists have presuppositions is not to be deprecated. That would, in fact be a nonsensical attitude to adopt. For the voice of logic reminds us that we cannot get to know anything if we are not prepared to presuppose something. Let's unpack this idea by thinking about a common attitude. 'I am not prepared to take anything for granted', says someone, 'I will only accept something if you prove it to me.' Sounds reasonable—but it isn't. For if this is your view then you will never accept or know anything! For suppose I want you to accept some proposition A. You will only accept it if I prove it to you. But I shall have to prove it to you on the basis of some other proposition B. You will only accept B if I prove it to you. I shall have to prove B to you on the basis of C. And so it will go on forever in what is called an infinite regress—that is, if you insist on taking nothing for granted in the first place!

We must all start somewhere with things we take as self-evident, basic assumptions that are not proved on the basis of something else. They are often called *axioms*.[17] Whatever axioms we adopt, we then proceed to try to make sense of the world by building on those

---

[16] Lewontin, *Dialectical Biologist*, 267.
[17] It should be borne in mind, however, that the axioms which appear in various branches of pure mathematics, for example, the theory of numbers or the theory of groups, do not appear out of nowhere. They usually arise from the attempt to encapsulate and formalise years, sometimes centuries, of mathematical research, into a so-called 'axiomatic system'.

axioms. This is true, not only at the worldview level but also in all of our individual disciplines. We retain those axioms that prove useful in the sense that they lead to theories which show a better 'fit' with nature and experience, and we abandon or modify those which do not fit so well. One thing is absolutely clear: none of us can avoid starting with assumptions.

Gaining knowledge involves trusting our senses and other people

There are essentially two sources from which we accumulate knowledge:

1. directly by our own 'hands-on' experience, for example, by accidentally putting our finger in boiling water, we learn that boiling water scalds;
2. we learn all kinds of things from sources external to ourselves, for example, teachers, books, parents, the media, etc.

In doing so we all constantly exercise faith. We intuitively trust our senses, even though we know they deceive us on times. For example, in extremely cold weather, if we put our hand on a metal handrail outside, the rail may feel hot to our touch.

We have faith, too, in our minds to interpret our senses, though here again we know that our minds can be deceived.

We also normally believe what other people tell us—teachers, parents, friends, etc. Sometimes we check what we learn from them because, without insulting them, we realise that even friends can be mistaken, and other people may set out to deceive us. However, much more often than not, we accept things on authority—if only because no one has time to check everything! In technical matters we trust our textbooks. We have faith in what (other) scientists have done. And it is, of course, reasonable so to do, though those experts themselves would teach us to be critical and not just to accept everything on their say-so. They would remind us also that the fact that a statement appears in print in a book, does not make it automatically true!

Gaining scientific knowledge involves belief in the rational intelligibility of the universe

We all take so much for granted the fact that we can use human reason as a probe to investigate the universe that we can fail to see that this is really something to be wondered at. For once we begin to think about the intelligibility of the universe, our minds demand an explanation. But where can we find one? Science cannot give it to us, for the very simple reason that science has to assume the rational intelligibility of the universe in order to get started. Einstein himself, in the same article we quoted earlier, makes this very clear in saying that the scientist's belief in the rational intelligibility of the universe goes beyond science and is in its very nature essentially religious:

> Science can only be created by those who are thoroughly imbued with the aspiration toward truth and understanding. This source of feeling, however, springs from the sphere of religion. To this there also belongs the faith in the possibility that the regulations valid for the world of existence are rational, that is, comprehensible to reason. I cannot conceive of a genuine scientist without that profound faith.[18]

Einstein saw no reason to be embarrassed by the fact that science involves at its root belief in something that science itself cannot justify.

Allied to belief in the rational intelligibility of the universe is the belief that patterns and law-like behaviour are to be expected in nature. The Greeks expressed this by using the word cosmos which means 'ordered'. It is this underlying expectation of order that lies behind the confidence with which scientists use the inductive method. Scientists speak of their belief in the uniformity of nature—the idea that the order in nature and the laws that describe it are valid at all times and in all parts of the universe.

Many theists from the Jewish, Islamic or Christian tradition would want to modify this concept of the uniformity of nature by adding their conviction that God the Creator has built regularities

---

[18] Einstein, *Out of My Later Years*, 26.

FIGURE Ap.3. Milky Way Galaxy.

The Milky Way galaxy is visible from earth on clear nights away from urban areas. Appearing as a cloud in the night sky, our galaxy's spiral bands of dust and glowing nebulae consist of billions of stars as seen from the inside.

Reproduced with permission of ©iStock/Viktar.

into the working of the universe so that in general we can speak of uniformity—the norms to which nature normally operates. But because God is the Creator, he is not a prisoner of those regularities but can vary them by causing things to happen that do not fit into the regular pattern.

Here, again, commitment to the uniformity of nature is a matter of belief. Science cannot prove to us that nature is uniform, since we must assume the uniformity of nature in order to do science. Otherwise we would have no confidence that, if we repeat an experiment under the same conditions as it was done before, we shall get the same result. Were it so, our school textbooks would be useless. But surely, we might say, the uniformity of nature is highly probable since assuming it has led to such stunning scientific advance. However, as C. S. Lewis has observed: 'Can we say that Uniformity is at any rate very probable? Unfortunately not. We have just seen that all probabilities depend on *it*. Unless Nature is uniform, nothing is either probable or improbable.'[19]

---

[19] Lewis, *Miracles*, 163.

Operating within the reigning paradigms

Thomas Kuhn in his famous book *The Structure of Scientific Revolutions* (1962) pictured science as preceding through the following stages: pre-science, normal science, crisis revolution, new normal science, new crisis, and so on. Pre-science is the diverse and disorganised activity characterised by much disagreement that precedes the emergence of a new science that gradually becomes structured when a scientific community adheres to a paradigm. The paradigm is a web of assumptions and theories that are more or less agreed upon and are like the steelwork around which the scientific edifice is erected. Well-known examples are the paradigms of Copernican astronomy, Newtonian mechanics and evolutionary biology.

Normal science is then practised within the paradigm. It sets the standards for legitimate research. The normal scientist uses the paradigm to probe nature. He or she does not (often) look critically at the paradigm itself, because it commands so much agreement, much as we look down the light of a torch to illuminate an object, rather than look critically at the light of the torch itself. For this reason the paradigm will be very resistant to attempts to demonstrate that it is false. When anomalies, difficulties and apparent falsifications turn up, the normal scientists will hope to be able to accommodate them preferably within the paradigm or by making fine adjustments to the paradigm. However, if the difficulties can no longer be resolved and keep on piling up, a crisis situation develops, which leads to a scientific revolution involving the emergence of a new paradigm that then gains the ground to such an extent that the older paradigm is eventually completely abandoned. The essence of such a paradigm shift is the replacing of an old paradigm by a new one, not the refining of the old one by the new. The best known example of a major paradigm shift is the transition from Aristotelian geocentric (earth-centred) astronomy to Copernican heliocentric (sun-centred) astronomy in the sixteenth century.

Although Kuhn's work is open to criticism at various points, he has certainly made scientists aware of a number of issues that are important for our understanding of how science works:

1. the central role that metaphysical ideas play in the development of scientific theories;
2. the high resistance that paradigms show to attempts to prove them false;
3. the fact that science is subject to human frailty.

The second of these points has both a positive and a negative outworking. It means that a good paradigm will not be overturned automatically by the first experimental result or observation that appears to speak against it. On the other hand, it means that a paradigm which eventually proves to be inadequate or false, may take a long time to die and impede scientific progress by constraining scientists within its mesh and not giving them the freedom they need to explore radically new ideas that would yield real scientific advance.

It is important to realise that paradigms themselves are often influenced at a very deep level by worldview considerations. We saw earlier that there are essentially two fundamental worldviews, the materialistic and the theistic. It seems to be the case in science that there is sometimes a tacit understanding that only paradigms which are based on materialism are admissible as scientific. Richard Dawkins, for example, says, 'the kind of explanation we come up with must not contradict the laws of physics. Indeed it will make use of the laws of physics, and nothing more than the laws of physics.'[20] It is the words 'nothing more than' that show that Dawkins is only prepared to accept reductionist, materialistic explanations.

Further reading

Books by John Lennox:
God and Stephen Hawking: Whose Design Is It Anyway? (Lion, 2011)
God's Undertaker: Has Science Buried God? (Lion, 2009)
Gunning for God: A Critique of the New Atheism (Lion, 2011)
Miracles: Is Belief in the Supernatural Irrational? VeriTalks Vol. 2. (The Veritas Forum, 2013)
Seven Days That Divide the World (Zondervan, 2011)

---

[20] Dawkins, *Blind Watchmaker*, 24.

SERIES BIBLIOGRAPHY

See also reading list on p. 321.

BOOKS

A

Abbott, Edwin. *Flatland: A Romance of Many Dimensions*. London, 1884. Repr. Oxford: Oxford University Press, 2006.

Ambrose, E. J. *The Nature and Origin of the Biological World*. New York: Halsted Press, 1982.

Ammon, Otto. *Die Gesellschaftsordnung und ihre natürlichen Grundlagen*. Jena: Gustav Fisher, 1895.

Anderson, J. N. D. (Norman). *Christianity: The Witness of History*. London: Tyndale Press, 1969.

Anderson, J. N. D. (Norman). *The Evidence for the Resurrection*. 1950. Leicester: InterVarsity Press, 1990.

Anderson, J. N. D. (Norman). *Islam in the Modern World*. Leicester: Apollos, 1990.

Andreyev, G. L. *What Kind of Morality Does Religion Teach?* Moscow: 'Znaniye', 1959.

Aristotle. *Metaphysics*. Tr. W. D. Ross, *Aristotle's Metaphysics: A Revised Text with Introduction and Commentary*. Vol. 2. Oxford: Clarendon Press, 1924.

Aristotle. *Nicomachean Ethics*. Tr. W. D. Ross. Oxford: Clarendon Press, 1925. Repr. Kitchener, Ont.: Batoche Books, 1999. Also tr. David Ross. Oxford: Oxford University Press, 1980.

Arnold, Thomas. *Christian Life, Its Hopes, Its Fears, and Its Close: Sermons preached mostly in the chapel of Rugby School, 1841-1842*. 1842. New edn, London: Longmans, 1878.

Ashman, Keith M. and Philip S. Baringer, eds. *After the Science Wars*. London: Routledge, 2001.

Atkins, Peter. *Creation Revisited*. Harmondsworth: Penguin, 1994.

Augustine of Hippo. *Confessions*. AD 397–400. Tr. Henry Chadwick, *The Confessions*. Oxford, 1991. Repr. Oxford World's Classics. Oxford: Oxford University Press, 2008.

Avise, John C. *The Genetic Gods, Evolution and Belief in Human Affairs*. Cambridge, Mass.: Harvard University Press, 1998.

Ayer, A. J., ed. *The Humanist Outlook*. London: Pemberton, 1968.

B

Bacon, Francis. *Advancement of Learning*. 1605. Ed. G. W. Kitchin, 1915. Repr. London: Dent, 1930. Online at http://archive.org/details/advancementlearn00bacouoft (facsimile of 1915 edn).

Bādarāyana, Śankarācārya and George Thibaut. *The Vedānta Sūtras of Bādarāyana*. Vol. 34 of *Sacred books of the East*. Oxford: Clarendon Press, 1890.

Baier, Kurt. *The Moral Point of View: A Rational Basis of Ethics*. Ithaca, N.Y.: Cornell University Press, 1958.

Behe, Michael J. *Darwin's Black Box: The Biochemical Challenge to Evolution*. 1988. 10th ann. edn with new Afterword, New York: Simon & Schuster, 2006.

Bentham, Jeremy. *An Introduction to the Principles of Morals and Legislation*. 1780, 1789. Dover Philosophical Classics. Repr. of Bentham's 1823 rev. edn, Mineola, N.Y.: Dover Publications, 2007.

Berdyaev, N. A. *The Beginning and The End*. Tr. R. M. French. London: Geoffrey Bles, 1952.

Berlinski, David. *The Deniable Darwin and Other Essays*. Seattle, Wash.: Discovery Institute, 2009.

Bickerton, Derek. *Language and Species*. 1990. Repr. Chicago: University of Chicago Press, 1992.

Biddiss, M. D. *Father of Racist Ideology: The Social and Political Thought of Count Gobineau*. New York: Weybright & Talley, 1970.

Bouquet, A. C. *Comparative Religion*. Harmondsworth: Penguin (Pelican), 1962.

Breck, John. *The Sacred Gift of Life: Orthodox Christianity and Bioethics*. Crestwood, N.Y.: St. Vladimir's Seminary Press, 1998.

Bronowski, Jacob. *The Identity of Man*. Harmondsworth: Penguin, 1967.

Brow, Robert. *Religion, Origins and Ideas*. London: Tyndale Press, 1966.

Bruce, F. F. *1 and 2 Corinthians*. New Century Bible Commentary. London: Oliphants, 1971.

Bruce, F. F. *The New Testament Documents: Are They Reliable?* 1943. 6th edn, Nottingham: Inter-Varsity Press, 2000.

Butterfield, Herbert. *Christianity and History*. London: Bell, 1949. Repr. London: Fontana, 1958.

C

Cairns-Smith, A. G. *The Life Puzzle*. Edinburgh: Oliver & Boyd, 1971.

Caputo, John D., ed. *Deconstruction in a Nutshell: A Conversation with Jacques Derrida*. Perspectives in Continental Philosophy No. 1. 1997. Repr. New York: Fordham University Press, 2004.

Cary, M. and T. J. Haarhoff. *Life and Thought in the Greek and Roman World*. 5th edn, London: Methuen, 1951.

Chalmers, David J. *The Conscious Mind: In Search of a Fundamental Theory*. Oxford: Oxford University Press, 1996.

Chamberlain, Paul. *Can We Be Good Without God?: A Conversation about Truth, Morality, Culture and a Few Other Things That Matter.* Downers Grove, Ill.: InterVarsity Press, 1996.

Chomsky, Noam. *Knowledge of Language: Its Nature, Origin and Use.* New York: Praeger, 1986.

Chomsky, Noam. *Language and Mind.* 1972. 3rd edn, Cambridge: Cambridge University Press, 2006.

Chomsky, Noam. *Syntactic Structures.* The Hague: Mouton, 1957.

Cicero, Marcus Tullius. *Cicero, Selected Political Speeches.* Tr. Michael Grant. Harmondsworth: Penguin Books, 1969.

Cicero, Marcus Tullius. *De Natura Deorum.* Tr. H. Rackham, Loeb Classical Library, No. 268. Cambridge, Mass.: Harvard University Press, 1933.

Cicero, Marcus Tullius. *The Nature of the Gods.* Tr. H. C. P. McGregor. London: Penguin, 1972.

Cicero, Marcus Tullius. *Pro Rabirio.*

Clement of Alexandria. Stromata [or, Miscellanies]. In Kirk, G. S., J. E. Raven and M. Schofield. *The Presocratic Philosophers: A Critical History with a Selection of Texts.* 1957. Rev. edn, Cambridge: Cambridge University Press, 1983. Online at http://www.ccel.org/ccel/schaff/anf02.vi.iv.html, accessed 29 Sept. 2015.

Cornford, F. M. *Before and After Socrates.* 1932. Repr. Cambridge: Cambridge University Press, 1999. doi: 10.1017/CBO9780511570308, accessed 29 Sept. 2015.

Craig, Edward, gen. ed. *Concise Routledge Encyclopaedia of Philosophy.* London: Routledge, 2000.

Craig, William Lane. *Reasonable Faith: Christian Truth and Apologetics.* 1994. 3rd edn, Wheaton, Ill.: Crossway, 2008.

Crane, Stephen. *War Is Kind.* New York: Frederick A. Stokes, 1899. Online at http://www.gutenberg.org/ebooks/9870, accessed 11 Sept. 2015.

Cranfield, C. E. B. *A Critical and Exegetical Commentary on the Epistle to the Romans.* Vol. 1. The International Critical Commentary. Edinburgh: T&T Clark, 1975.

Crick, Francis. *The Astonishing Hypothesis: The Scientific Search for the Soul.* New York: Scribner, 1994.

Crick, Francis. *Life Itself: Its Origin and Nature.* New York: Simon & Schuster, 1981.

Crick, Francis. *Of Molecules and Men.* 1966 Jessie and John Danz Lectures. Seattle, Wash.: University of Washington Press, 1966.

Cudakov. A. *Komsomol'skaja Pravda* (11 Oct. 1988).

Culler, Jonathan. *On Deconstruction: Theory and Criticism after Structuralism.* 1982. 25th ann. edn, Ithaca, N.Y.: Cornell University Press, 2007.

D

Darwin, Charles. *The Descent of Man, and Selection in Relation to Sex.* 1871. 2nd edn, New York: A. L. Burt, 1874. Ed. James Moore and Adrian Desmond, Penguin Classics, London: Penguin Books, 2004.

Darwin, Charles. *On the Origin of Species*. 1859. Repr. World's Classics Edition, Oxford: Oxford University Press, 2008. Also cited is the 6th edn (1872) reprinted by New York University Press, 1988. Citations to one or the other edition are indicated as such.

Darwin, Francis. *The Life and Letters of Charles Darwin*. London: John Murray, 1887. doi: 10.5962/bhl.title.1416, accessed 29 June 2015.

Davies, Paul. *The Cosmic Blueprint: New Discoveries in Nature's Creative Ability to Order the Universe*. 1988. Repr. West Conshohocken, Pa.: Templeton Foundation Press, 2004.

Davies, Paul. *The Fifth Miracle: The Search for the Origin and Meaning of Life*. 1999. Repr. New York: Touchstone, 2000.

Davies, Paul. *God and the New Physics*. London: J. M. Dent, 1983. Repr. London: Penguin Books, 1990.

Davies, Paul. *The Mind of God: Science and the Search for Ultimate Meaning*. 1992. Repr. London: Simon & Schuster, 2005.

Davies, Paul and John Gribbin. *The Matter Myth: Dramatic Discoveries that Challenge Our Understanding of Physical Reality*. London, 1991. Repr. London: Simon & Schuster, 2007.

Davis, Percival and Dean H. Kenyon. *Of Pandas and People: The Central Question of Biological Origins*. 1989. 2nd edn, Dallas, Tex.: Haughton Publishing, 1993.

Dawkins, Richard. *The Blind Watchmaker*. 1986. Rev. edn, 2006. Repr. London: Penguin, 2013.

Dawkins, Richard. *Climbing Mount Improbable*. New York: Norton, 1996.

Dawkins, Richard. *Growing Up in the Universe*. The Royal Institution Christmas Lectures for Children, 1991. Five one-hour episodes directed by Stuart McDonald for the BBC. 2-Disc DVD set released 20 April 2007 by the Richard Dawkins Foundation. Available on the Ri Channel, http://www.rigb.org/christmas-lectures/watch/1991/growing-up-in-the-universe. Study Guide with the same title. London: BBC Education, 1991.

Dawkins, Richard. *River Out of Eden: A Darwinian View of Life*. 1995. Repr. London: Phoenix, 2004.

Dawkins, Richard. *The Selfish Gene*. 1976. Repr. 30th ann. edn, Oxford: Oxford University Press, 2006.

Dawkins, Richard. *Unweaving the Rainbow: Science, Delusion and the Appetite for Wonder*. 1998. Repr. London: Penguin Books, 2006.

Dawkins, Richard and John Lennox. 'The God Delusion Debate', hosted by Fixed Point Foundation, University of Alabama at Birmingham, filmed and broadcast live 3 October 2007, online at http://fixed-point.org/video/richard-dawkins-vs-john-lennox-the-god-delusion-debate/. Transcript provided courtesy of ProTorah.com, http://www.protorah.com/god-delusion-debate-dawkins-lennox-transcript/.

Deacon, Terrence. *The Symbolic Species: The Co-Evolution of Language and the Human Brain*. London: Allen Lane, 1997.

Dembski, William A. *Being as Communion: A Metaphysics of Information*. Ashgate Science and Religion. Farnham, Surrey: Ashgate, 2014.

Dembski, William A. *The Design Inference: Eliminating Chance through Small Probabilities*. Cambridge Studies in Probability, Induction and Decision Theory. Cambridge: Cambridge University Press, 1998.

Dembski, William A., ed. *Uncommon Dissent: Intellectuals Who Find Darwinism Unconvincing*. Wilmington, Del.: Intercollegiate Studies Institute, 2004.

Dennett, Daniel. *Darwin's Dangerous Idea: Evolution and the Meanings of Life*. 1995; London: Penguin, 1996.

Denton, Michael. *Evolution: A Theory in Crisis*. 1986. 3rd rev. edn, Bethesda, Md.: Adler & Adler, 1986.

Derrida, Jacques. *Of Grammatology*. 1967 (French). Tr. G. C. Spivak, 1974. Repr. Baltimore, Md.: Johns Hopkins University Press, 1997.

Derrida, Jacques. *Positions*. 1972 (French). Tr. and ed. Alan Bass, 1981. 2nd edn 2002. Repr. London: Continuum, 2010.

Derrida, Jacques. *Writing and Difference*. 1967 (French). Tr. Alan Bass, Chicago, 1978. Repr. London: Routledge Classics, 2001.

Descartes, René. *Discourse on the Method of Rightly Conducting Reason and Reaching the Truth in the Sciences*. 1637. Online at https://www.gutenberg.org/files/59/59-h/59-h.htm, accessed 11 Sept. 2015.

Descartes, René. *Meditations on First Philosophy*. Paris, 1641.

Deutsch, David. *The Fabric of Reality*. London: Penguin, 1997.

Dewey, John. *A Common Faith*. New Haven: Yale University Press, 1934.

Dostoevsky, F. *The Collected Works of Dostoevsky*. Tr. Rodion Raskolnikoff [German]. Munich: Piper, 1866.

Dostoevsky, Fyodor. *The Karamazov Brothers*. 1880 (Russian). Tr. and ed. David McDuff, Penguin Classics, 1993. Rev. edn, London: Penguin Books, 2003.

E

Eastwood, C. Cyril. *Life and Thought in the Ancient World*. Derby: Peter Smith, 1964.

Easwaran, Eknath. *The Bhagavad Gita*. 1985. Berkeley, Calif.: Nilgiri Press, 2007.

Easwaran, Eknath. *The Upanishads*. 1987. Berkeley, Calif.: Nilgiri Press, 2007.

Eccles, John C. *Evolution of the Brain, Creation of the Self*. 1989. Repr. London: Routledge, 2005.

Einstein, A. *Letters to Solovine: 1906–1955*. New York: Philosophical Library, 1987.

Einstein, A. *Out of My Later Years: The Scientist, Philosopher, and Man Portrayed Through His Own Words*. 1956. Secaucus, N.J.: Carol Publishing, 1995.

Eldredge, Niles. *Reinventing Darwin: The Great Debate at the High Table of Evolutionary Theory*. New York: Wiley, 1995.

Eldredge, Niles. *Time Frames: The Evolution of Punctuated Equilibria*. 1985. Corr. edn, Princeton, N.J.: Princeton University Press, 1989.

Ellis, John M. *Against Deconstruction*. Princeton, N.J.: Princeton University Press, 1989.

The Encyclopedia Britannica. 15th edn (*Britannica 3*), ed. Warren E. Preece and Philip W. Goetz. Chicago: Encyclopaedia Britannica, 1974–2012.

Engels, Friedrich. *Ludwig Feuerbach and the End of Classical German Philosophy.* German original first published in 1886, in *Die Neue Zeit.* Moscow: Progress Publishers, 1946.

Erbrich, Paul. *Zufall: Eine Naturwissenschaftlich-Philosophische Untersuchung.* Stuttgart: Kohlhammer, 1988.

Euripides. *The Bacchae.* Tr. James Morwood, *Bacchae and Other Plays.* Oxford World's Classics. 1999. Repr. Oxford: Oxford University Press, 2008.

Evans-Pritchard, E. E. *Nuer Religion.* 1956. 2nd edn, London: Oxford University Press, 1971.

F

Feuerbach, Ludwig. *The Essence of Christianity.* 1841. Ed. and tr. George Eliot (Mary Ann Evans). New York: Harper Torchbooks, 1957.

Feynman, Richard. *Six Easy Pieces.* 1963. Repr. London: Penguin Books, 1995.

Fischer, Ernst. *Marx in His Own Words.* Tr. Anna Bostock. London: Penguin Books, 1973.

Fish, Stanley. *Is There a Text in This Class? The Authority of Interpretive Communities.* Cambridge, Mass.: Harvard University Press, 1980.

Fish, Stanley. *There's No Such Thing as Free Speech, and It's a Good Thing Too.* New York: Oxford University Press, 1994.

Flew, Antony with Roy Abraham Varghese. *There Is a God: How the World's Most Notorious Atheist Changed His Mind.* London: HarperCollins, 2007.

Fox, S. W., ed. *The Origins of Prebiological Systems and of Their Molecular Matrices.* New York: Academic Press, 1965.

Frazer, J. G. *The Golden Bough.* 1890, 1900, 1906–15, 1937.

Fromm, Erich. *You Shall be as Gods: A Radical Interpretation of the Old Testament and its Tradition.* New York: Holt, Rinehart & Winston, 1966.

G

Gates, Bill. *The Road Ahead.* 1995. Rev. edn, Harmondsworth: Penguin, 1996.

Geisler, Norman L., and William E. Nix, *A General Introduction to the Bible* (Chicago: Moody Press, 1986), 475. Gerson, Lloyd P. *Plotinus.* London: Routledge, 1994.

Gilligan, Carol. *In a Different Voice: Psychological Theory and Women's Development.* Cambridge, Mass.: Harvard University Press, 1982.

Goldschmidt, Richard. *The Material Basis of Evolution.* The Silliman Memorial Lectures Series. 1940. Repr. Yale University Press, 1982.

Gooding, David W. and John C. Lennox. *The Human Quest for Significance: Forming a Worldview* [in Russian]. Minsk: Myrtlefield Trust, 1999.

Gould, Stephen Jay. *The Lying Stones of Marrakech: Penultimate Reflections in Natural History.* 2000. Repr. Cambridge, Mass.: Harvard University Press, 2011.

Gould, Stephen Jay. *Wonderful Life: The Burgess Shale and the Nature of History.* 1989. Repr. London: Vintage, 2000.

Grant, Michael. *Jesus: An Historian's Review of the Gospels*. New York: Scribner, 1977.

Grene, Marjorie. *A Portrait of Aristotle*. London: Faber & Faber, 1963.

Groothuis, Douglas. *Truth Decay: Defending Christianity against the Challenges of Postmodernism*. Leicester: Inter-Varsity Press, 2000.

Guthrie, W. K. C. *The Greek Philosophers from Thales to Aristotle*. 1950. Repr. London: Methuen, 2013.

Guthrie, W. K. C. *Plato: the man and his dialogues, earlier period*. Vol. 4 of *A History of Greek Philosophy*. 1875. Repr. Cambridge: Cambridge University Press, 2000.

H

Haldane, J. B. S. *Possible Worlds*. 1927. London: Chatto & Windus, 1945.

Harrison, E. *Masks of the Universe*. 1985. 2nd edn, New York: Macmillan, 2003. Citations are to the first Macmillan edition.

Harvey, William. *On the Motion of the Heart and the Blood of Animals*. 1628. Online at https://ebooks.adelaide.edu.au/h/harvey/william/motion/complete.html, accessed 4 Sept. 2018.

Hawking, Stephen. *A Brief History of Time*. 1988. Updated and expanded 10th ann. edn, London: Bantam Press, 1998.

Hawking, Stephen and Leonard Mlodinow. *The Grand Design*. New York: Bantam Books, 2010.

Hegel, G. W. F. *Hegel's Logic*. Being Part One of the Encyclopaedia of the Philosophical Sciences (1830). Tr. William Wallace, 1892. Repr. Oxford: Clarendon Press, 1984–87.

Hegel, G. W. F. *The Phenomenology of the Mind* (Spirit). 1807. 2nd edn 1841. Tr. J. B. Baillie, London, 1910. Repr. Dover Philosophical Classics, New York: Dover Publications, 2003.

Hegel, G. W. F. *The Philosophy of History*. 1861. Tr. J. Sibree, 1857. Repr. New York: Dover Publications, 1956. Repr. Kitchener, Ont.: Batoche Books, 2001. Online at Internet Archive: https://archive.org/details/lecturesonphilos00hegerich/, accessed 19 Oct. 2018.

Hegel, G. W. F. *Wissenschaft der Logik* [The Science of Logic]. Nurnberg, 1812–16.

Hemer, Colin. *The Book of Acts in the Setting of Hellenistic History*. Tübingen: J. C. B. Mohr, Paul Siebeck, 1989.

Hengel, Martin. *Judaism and Hellenism: Studies in their Encounter in Palestine during the Early Hellenistic Period*. Tr. John Bowden. London: SCM Press, 1974. Repr. Eugene, Oreg.: Wipf & Stock, 2003.

Hengel, Martin. *Studies in Early Christology*. Tr. Rollin Kearns. Edinburgh: T&T Clark, 1995.

Herodotus. *The Histories*. Tr. Robin Waterfield, 1998, Oxford World's Classics. Repr. New York: Oxford University Press, 2008.

Herzen, Alexander Ivanovich. *Byloe i dumy*. London, 1853. Tr. C. Garnett, *My Past and Thoughts, The Memoirs of Alexander Herzen*. Revised by H. Higgens, introduced by I. Berlin, 1968. Repr. London: Chatto and Windus, 2008.

Hesiod. *Theogony.* In Charles Abraham Elton, tr. *The remains of Hesiod.* London: Lackington, Allen, 1812. Also in Dorothea Wender, tr. *Hesiod and Theognis.* Harmondsworth: Penguin, 1973.

Hippolytus, *Refutation of all Heresies.* In Kirk, G. S., J. E. Raven and M. Schofield. *The Presocratic Philosophers: A Critical History with a Selection of Texts.* 1957. Rev. edn, Cambridge: Cambridge University Press, 1983.

Holmes, Arthur F. *Ethics.* Downers Grove, Ill.: InterVarsity Press, 1984; 2nd edn, 2007.

Honderich, Ted, ed. *The Oxford Companion to Philosophy.* Oxford, 1995. 2nd edn, Oxford: Oxford University Press, 2005.

Hooper, Judith. *Of Moths and Men.* New York: Norton, 2002.

Hooykaas, R. *Religion and the Rise of Modern Science.* 1972. Repr. Edinburgh: Scottish Academic Press, 2000.

Hospers, John. *An Introduction to Philosophical Analysis.* 1953. 4th edn, Abingdon: Routledge, 1997.

Houghton, John. *The Search for God—Can Science Help?* Oxford: Lion Publishing, 1995.

Hoyle, Fred. *The Intelligent Universe.* London: Joseph, 1983.

Hoyle, Fred and Chandra Wickramasinghe. *Cosmic Life-Force, the Power of Life Across the Universe.* London: Dent, 1988.

Hoyle, Fred and Chandra Wickramasinghe. *Evolution from Space: A Theory of Cosmic Creationism.* New York: Simon & Schuster, 1984.

Hume, David. *David Hume: A Treatise of Human Nature.* 1739–40. Ed. Lewis Amherst Selby-Bigge and P. H. Nidditch. Oxford: Clarendon Press, 1888. Repr. 1978. Repr. Oxford: Oxford University Press, 2014. doi: 10.1093/actrade/9780198245872.book.1, accessed 11 Sept. 2015; also online at https://davidhume.org/texts/t/, accessed 4 Sept.2018.

Hume, David. *Dialogues Concerning Natural Religion.* 1779. Repr. ed. J. C. A. Gaskin, *Dialogues Concerning Natural Religion, and The Natural History of Religion.* Oxford World's Classics. Oxford: Oxford University Press, 2008. Online at https://davidhume.org/texts/d/, accessed 2 Aug. 2017. (Abbreviated as DNR.)

Hume, David. *An Enquiry Concerning Human Understanding.* London: A. Millar, 1748. Repr. Dover Philosophical Classics, Mineola, N.Y.: Dover Publications, 2012. Online at http://www.davidhume.org/texts/e, accessed 2 Aug. 2017. (Abbreviated as EHU.)

Hume, David. *Treatise of Human Nature.* 1739–40. Eds. David Norton and Mary J. Norton, *David Hume: A Treatise of Human Nature: A critical edition.* Vol. 1 of The Clarendon Edition of The Works Of David Hume. Oxford: Oxford University Press, 2007. Online at http://www.davidhume.org/texts/t/, accessed 2 Aug. 2017. (Abbreviated as THN.)

Hunt, R. N. Carew. *The Theory and Practice of Communism.* Baltimore: Penguin Books, 1966.

Hurley, Thomas. *Method and Results: Collected Essays.* Vol. I. London: Macmillan, 1898.

Husserl, Edmund. *Ideas: General Introduction to Pure Phenomenology.* Ger. orig. *Ideen zu einer reinen Phänomenologie und phänomenologischen Philosophie. Erstes Buch: Allgemeine Einführung in die reine Phänomenologie* (1913). Tr. W. R. Boyce Gibson. London: Macmillan, 1931.

Huxley, Julian. *Essays of a Humanist.* 1964. Repr. Harmondsworth: Penguin Books, 1969.

Huxley, Julian. *Religion Without Revelation.* New York: Mentor, 1957.

I

Isherwood, Christopher, ed. *Vedanta for Modern Man.* 1951. Repr. New York: New American Library, 1972.

J

Jacob, François. *Chance and Necessity: An Essay on the Natural Philosophy of Modern Biology.* Tr. Austryn Wainhouse. New York: Alfred A. Knopf, 1971.

Jacob, François. *The Logic of Life: A History of Heredity.* Tr. Betty E. Spillman. New York: Pantheon Books, 1973.

Jaeger, Werner. *The Theology of the Early Greek Philosophers.* The Gifford Lectures, 1936. Oxford: Oxford University Press, 1967.

James, E. O. *Christianity and Other Religions.* London: Hodder & Stoughton, 1968.

Jaroszwski, T. M. and P. A. Ignatovsky, eds. *Socialism as a Social System.* Moscow: Progress Publishers, 1981.

Jeremias, J. *New Testament Theology: The Proclamation of Jesus.* Tr. John Bowden. New York: Scribner, 1971.

Joad, C. E. M. *The Book of Joad: A Belligerent Autobiography* [= *Under the Fifth Rib*]. London: Faber & Faber, 1944.

Johnson, Phillip E. *Objections Sustained: Subversive Essays on Evolution, Law and Culture.* Downers Grove, Ill.: InterVarsity Press, 1998.

Jones, Steve. *In the Blood: God, Genes and Destiny.* London: Harper Collins, 1996.

Josephus, Flavius. *Antiquities of the Jews.* Tr. William Whiston, *The Works of Flavius Josephus.* 1737. Repr. Grand Rapids: Kregel, 1974. Repr. Peabody, Mass.: Hendrickson, 1995.

K

Kant, Immanuel. *Critique of Practical Reason.* 1788. Tr. and ed. Mary Gregor. Cambridge Texts in the History of Philosophy. 1997. Repr. Cambridge: Cambridge University Press, 2003.

Kant, Immanuel. *Critique of Pure Reason.* 1781. 2nd edn, 1787. Tr. Norman Kemp Smith. London: Macmillan, 1929. Repr. Blunt Press, 2007. Also Paul Guyer and Allen Wood, eds., Cambridge: Cambridge University Press, 1999.

Kant, Immanuel. *Groundwork of the Metaphysics of Morals.* 1785. In H. J. Paton, tr. *The Moral Law.* London: Hutchinson, 1972.

Kant, Immanuel. *The Metaphysics of Morals*. 1797. Tr. and ed. Mary J. Gregor. Cambridge Texts in the History of Philosophy. Cambridge: Cambridge University Press, 1996.

Kant, Immanuel. *Prolegomena to Any Future Metaphysics*. 1783. Tr. and ed. Gary Hatfield, *Prolegomena to Any Future Metaphysics with Selections from the Critique of Pure Reason*. Cambridge Texts in the History of Philosophy. 1997. Rev. edn, Cambridge: Cambridge University Press, 2004.

Kantikar, V. P. (Hemant) and W. Owen. *Hinduism—An Introduction: Teach Yourself*. 1995. Repr. London: Hodder Headline, 2010.

Kaye, Howard L. *The Social Meaning of Modern Biology, From Social Darwinism to Sociobiology*. 1986. Repr. with a new epilogue, New Brunswick, N.J.: Transaction Publishers, 1997.

Kenny, Anthony. *An Illustrated Brief History of Western Philosophy*. Oxford: Blackwell, 2006. First published as *A Brief History of Western Philosophy*, 1998.

Kenyon, D. H. and G. Steinman. *Biochemical Predestination*. New York: McGraw-Hill, 1969.

Kenyon, Frederic. *Our Bible and the Ancient Manuscripts*. 1895. 4th edn, 1938. Repr. Eugene, Oreg.: Wipf & Stock, 2011.

Kilner, J. F., C. C. Hook and D. B. Uustal, eds. *Cutting-Edge Bioethics: A Christian Exploration of Technologies and Trends*. Grand Rapids: Eerdmans, 2002.

Kirk, G. S., J. E. Raven and M. Schofield. *The Presocratic Philosophers: A Critical History with a Selection of Texts*. 1957. Rev. edn, Cambridge: Cambridge University Press, 1983.

Kirk, M. and H. Madsen. *After the Ball*. New York: Plume Books, 1989.

Knott, Kim. *Hinduism: A Very Short Introduction*. Oxford: Oxford University Press, 1998.

Koertge, Noretta, ed. *A House Built on Sand: Exposing Postmodernist Myths About Science*. Oxford: Oxford University Press, 1998.

Kolbanovskiy, V. N. *Communist Morality*. Moscow, 1951.

Krikorian, Yervant H., ed. *Naturalism and the Human Spirit*. 1944. Repr. New York: Columbia University Press, 1969.

Kuhn, Thomas. *The Structure of Scientific Revolutions*. 1962. 3rd edn, Chicago: University of Chicago Press, 1996.

Kurtz, Paul. *The Fullness of Life*. New York: Horizon Press, 1974.

Kurtz, Paul. *The Humanist Alternative*. Buffalo, N.Y.: Prometheus, 1973.

Kurtz, Paul, ed. *Humanist Manifestos I & II*. Buffalo, N.Y.: Prometheus, 1980.

Kurtz, Paul, ed. *Humanist Manifesto II*. Buffalo, N.Y.: Prometheus Books, 1980. Online at https://americanhumanist.org/what-is-humanism/manifesto2/, accessed 11 Sept. 2105.

L

Lamont, Corliss. *A Lifetime of Dissent*. Buffalo, N.Y.: Prometheus Books, 1988.

Lamont, Corliss. *The Philosophy of Humanism*. 1947. 8th edn, Emherst, N.Y.: Humanist Press, 1997.

Lapouge, G. Vacher de. *Les Sélections Sociales*. Paris: Fontemoing, 1899.

Leakey, Richard. *The Origin of Humankind*. London: Weidenfeld & Nicolson, 1994.

Leitch, Vincent B. *Deconstructive Criticism: An Advanced Introduction*. New York: Columbia University Press, 1982.

Lenin, V. I. *Complete Collected Works*. Tr. Andrew Rothstein. 4th Eng. edn, Moscow: Progress Publishers, 1960-78. Online at http://www.marx2mao.com/Lenin/Index.html (facsimile), accessed 11 Sept. 2015. Repr. Moscow: Progress Publishers, 1982.

Lenin, V. I. *Materialism and Empirico-Criticism*. New York: International Publishers, 1927.

Lennox, John C. *Determined to Believe: The Sovereignty of God, Freedom, Faith and Human*. Oxford: Monarch Books, 2017.

Lennox, John C. *God and Stephen Hawking: Whose Design is it Anyway?* Oxford: Lion, 2010.

Lennox, John C. *God's Undertaker: Has Science Buried God?* Oxford, Lion Books, 2007, 2009.

Leslie, John. *Universes*. London: Routledge, 1989.

Levinskaya, Irina. *The Book of Acts in its First Century Setting*. Vol. 5. Diaspora Setting. Grand Rapids: Eerdmans, 1996.

Lewis, C. S. *The Abolition of Man*. London, 1945. Repr. London: Collins, Fount, 1978.

Lewis, C. S. *Christian Reflections*. London, 1967. Repr. New York: HarperCollins, 1998.

Lewis, C. S. *God in the Dock*. London, 1979. Repr. Grand Rapids: Eerdmans, 2014.

Lewis, C. S. *Mere Christianity*. London, 1952. Rev. edn with new introduction and foreword by Kathleen Norris, New York: HarperCollins, 2001.

Lewis, C. S. *Miracles*. 1947. Repr. London: Collins, 2012.

Lewis, C. S. *The Problem of Pain*. 1940. Repr. London: Collins, 2009.

Lewis, C. S. *Transposition and other Addresses*. London: Geoffrey Bles, 1949.

Lewontin, Richard. *The Dialectical Biologist*. Cambridge, Mass.: Harvard University Press, 1987.

Locke, John. *An Essay Concerning Human Understanding*. London, 1689. Ed. Peter H. Nidditch, Oxford: Oxford University Press, 1975.

Long, A. A. *Hellenistic Philosophy*. 1974. 2nd edn, Berkeley, Calif.: University of California Press, 1986.

Lossky, N. O. *History of Russian Philosophy*. London: Allen & Unwin, 1952.

Lucretius (Titus Lucretius Carus). *De Rerum Natura*. 50 BC. Tr. A. E. Stallings as *The Nature of Things*. London: Penguin, 2007. Also tr. and ed. William Ellery Leonard. 1916. Online at: http://www.perseus.tufts.edu/hopper/text?doc=Lucr or http://classics.mit.edu/Carus/nature_things.html.

Lumsden, Charles J. and Edward O. Wilson. *Promethean Fire: Reflections on the Origin of Mind*. Cambridge, Mass.: Harvard University Press, 1983.

M

Mabbott, J. D. *An Introduction to Ethics*. Hutchinson University Library. London: Hutchinson, 1966.

McKay, Donald. *The Clockwork Image: A Christian Perspective on Science*. London: Inter-Varsity Press, 1974.

Majerus, Michael. *Melanism: Evolution in Action*. Oxford: Oxford University Press, 1998.

Margenau, Henry and Roy Abraham Varghese, eds. *Cosmos, Bios, and Theos: Scientists Reflect on Science, God, and the Origins of the Universe, Life, and Homo Sapiens*. La Salle, Ill.: Open Court, 1992.

Marx, Karl. *Marx's Theses on Feuerbach*. 1845.

Mascall, E. L. *Words and Images, a study in the Possibility of Religious Discourse*. London: Longmans, 1957.

Mascaró, Juan, tr. *The Upanishads*. Harmondsworth: Penguin, 1965.

Maslow, Abraham. *Towards a Psychology of Being*. New York: Van Nostrand Reinhold, 1968.

Masterson, Patrick. *Atheism and Alienation*. Harmondsworth: Pelican Books, 1972.

May, Rollo. *Psychology and the Human Dilemma*. Princeton, N.J., 1967. Repr. New York: Norton, 1996.

Medawar, Peter. *Advice to a Young Scientist*. New York: Harper & Row, 1979.

Medawar, Peter. *The Limits of Science*. Oxford: Oxford University Press, 1985.

Medawar, Peter and Jean Medawar. *The Life Science*. London: Wildwood House, 1977.

Metzger, Bruce. *The Text of the New Testament, its Transmission, Corruption and Restoration*. 1964. 3rd edn, Oxford: Oxford University Press, 1992.

Mill, John Stuart. *Utilitarianism*. 1861, 1863. Repr. Mineola, N.Y.: Dover Publications, 2007.

Millard, Alan. *Reading and Writing in the Time of Jesus*. Sheffield: Sheffield Academic Press, 2000.

Miller, David, Janet Coleman, William Connolly, and Alan Ryan, eds. *The Blackwell Encyclopaedia of Political Thought*. 1987. Repr. Oxford: Blackwell, 1991.

Monod, Jacques. *Chance and Necessity: An Essay on the Natural Philosophy of Modern Biology*. 1970 (French). Tr. Austryn Wainhouse, 1971. Repr. London: Penguin Books, 1997. Citations are from Vintage Books 1972 edn.

Monod, Jacques. *From Biology to Ethics*. San Diego: Salk Institute for Biological Studies, 1969.

Morris, Simon Conway. *The Crucible of Creation: The Burgess Shale and the Rise of Animals*. 1998. New edn, Oxford: Oxford University Press, 1999.

Mossner, Ernest C., ed. *David Hume, A Treatise of Human Nature*. London: Penguin Classics, 1985.

Moule, C. F. D. *The Phenomenon of the New Testament: An Inquiry into the Implications of Certain Features of the New Testament*. London: SCM, 1967.

Murphy, John P. *Pragmatism: From Peirce to Davidson*. Boulder, Colo.: Westview Press, 1990.

N

Nagel, Thomas. *The Last Word*. Oxford: Oxford University Press, 1997.

Nagel, Thomas. *Mortal Questions*. Cambridge: Cambridge University Press. 1979.

Nahem, Joseph. *Psychology and Psychiatry Today: A Marxist View*. New York: International Publishers, 1981.

Nasr, Seyyed Hossein, and Oliver Leaman, eds. *History of Islamic Philosophy*. Part 1, Vol. 1 of *Routledge History of World Philosophies*. 1996. Repr. London: Routledge, 2001.

Nettleship, R. L. *Lectures on the Republic of Plato*. London: Macmillan, 1922.

Newton, Isaac. *Principia Mathematica*. London, 1687.

Nietzsche, Friedrich. *Beyond Good and Evil: Prelude to a Philosophy of the Future*. Leipzig, 1886. 1973. Repr. tr. R. J. Hollingdale, Harmondsworth: Penguin, 1975.

Noddings, Nel. *Caring: A Feminine Approach to Ethics and Moral Education*. 1984. Repr. Berkeley, Calif.: University of California Press, 2013.

Norris, Christopher. *Deconstruction: Theory and Practice*. 1982. 3rd edn, London: Methuen, 2002.

O

Olivelle, Patrick. *The Early Upanishads: Annotated Text and Translation*. 1996. Repr. Oxford: Oxford University Press, 1998.

O'Meara, Dominic J. *Plotinus: An Introduction to the Enneads*. Oxford: Clarendon Press, 1993.

P

Paley, William. *Natural Theology on Evidence and Attributes of Deity*. 1802. Repr. Oxford: Oxford University Press, 2006.

Patterson, Colin. *Evolution*. 1978. 2nd edn, Ithaca, N.Y.: Cornstock Publishing Associates, 1999.

Peacocke, Arthur. *The Experiment of Life*. Toronto: University of Toronto Press, 1983.

Pearsall, Judy and Bill Trumble, eds. *The Oxford English Reference Dictionary*. 2nd edn, Oxford: Oxford University Press, 1996.

Pearse, E. K. Victor. *Evidence for Truth: Science*. Guildford: Eagle, 1998.

Penfield, Wilder. *The Mystery of the Mind*. Princeton, N.J.: Princeton University Press, 1975.

Penrose, Roger. *The Emperor's New Mind*. 1986. Repr. with new preface, Oxford: Oxford University Press, 1999.

Penrose, Roger. *The Road to Reality: A Complete Guide to the Laws of the Universe*. London: Jonathan Cape, 2004.

Peterson, Houston, ed. *Essays in Philosophy*. New York: Pocket Library, 1959.

Pinker, Steven. *The Language Instinct: How the Mind Creates Language*. New York: Morrow, 1994.

Plantinga, Alvin. *Warranted Christian Belief.* Oxford: Oxford University Press, 2000.

Plato. *Apology.* Tr. Hugh Tredennick, 1954. Repr. Harmondsworth: Penguin Books, 1976. Also in *The Collected Dialogues of Plato including the letters.* 1961. Repr. with corrections, Princeton, N.J.: Princeton University Press, 1973.

Plato. *The Euthyphro.*

Plato. *The Last Days of Socrates.* Tr. Hugh Tredennick. Harmondsworth: Penguin Books, 1969.

Plato. *Phaedo.*

Plato. *Republic.* Tr. Desmond Lee. 2nd edn, Harmondsworth: Penguin, 1974. Also tr. Paul Shorey, Loeb Classical Library. Cambridge, Mass.: Harvard University Press, 1930. Also in *The Collected Dialogues of Plato including the letters,* 1961. Repr. with corrections, Princeton, N.J.: Princeton University Press, 1973.

Plato. *Timaeus.*

Pliny the Younger. *Letters.* Tr. Betty Radice as *The Letters of the Younger Pliny.* Harmondsworth: Penguin Books, 1963.

Plotinus. *Enneads.* Tr. Stephen MacKenna, 1917–30. Repr. London: Penguin, 2005.

Polanyi, Michael. *The Tacit Dimension.* New York: Doubleday, 1966.

Polkinghorne, John. *One World: The Interaction of Science and Theology.* London: SPCK, 1986.

Polkinghorne, John. *Reason and Reality: The Relationship between Science and Theology.* 1991. Repr. London: SPCK, 2011.

Polkinghorne, John. *Science and Creation: The Search for Understanding.* 1988. Rev. edn, West Conshohocken, Pa.: Templeton Foundation Press, 2009.

Polkinghorne, John. *Science and Providence: God's Interaction with the World.* 1989. Repr. West Conshohocken, Pa.: Templeton Foundation Press, 2011.

Popper, Karl R. *The World of Parmenides.* London: Routledge, 1998.

Popper, Karl R. and John C. Eccles. *The Self and Its Brain: An Argument for Interactionism.* 1977. Repr. Springer Berlin Heidelberg, 2012.

Pospisil, Leopold J. *Kapauku Papuans and their Law.* Yale University Publications in Anthropology 54. New Haven, 1958.

Pospisil, Leopold J. *The Kapauku Papuans of West New Guinea.* Case Studies in Cultural Anthropology. 1963. 2nd edn, New York: Holt, Rinehart and Winston, 1978.

Powers, B. Ward. *The Progressive Publication of Matthew.* Nashville: B&H Academic, 2010.

Poythress, Vern S. *Inerrancy and the Gospels: A God-Centered Approach to the Challenges of Harmonization.* Wheaton, Ill.: Crossway, 2012.

Pritchard, J. B., ed. *Ancient Near Eastern Texts Relating to the Old Testament.* Princeton, 1950. 3rd edn, Princeton, N.J.: Princeton University Press, 1969.

Putnam, Hilary. *Reason, Truth and History.* Cambridge: Cambridge University Press, 1981.

R

Rachels, James. *Elements of Moral Philosophy*. New York: McGraw-Hill, 1986.

Ragg, Lonsdale and Laura Ragg, eds. *The Gospel of Barnabas*. Oxford: Clarendon Press, 1907.

Ramsay, William. *St. Paul the Traveller and the Roman Citizen*. London: Hodder & Stoughton, 1895.

Randall, John H. *Cosmos*. New York: Random House, 1980.

Raphael, D. D. *Moral Philosophy*. 1981. 2nd edn, Oxford: Oxford University Press, 1994.

Rawls, John. *A Theory of Justice*. Cambridge, Mass.: Harvard University Press, 1971.

Redford, Donald B., ed. *The Oxford Encyclopaedia of Ancient Egypt*. Oxford: Oxford University Press, 2001. doi: 10.1093/acref/9780195102345.001.0001.

Reid, Thomas. *An Enquiry Concerning Human Understanding*. Oxford: Clarendon Press, 1777.

Reid, Thomas. *An Inquiry into the Human Mind on the Principles of Common Sense*. 1764. Repr. Cambridge: Cambridge University Press, 2011.

Renfrew, Colin. *Archaeology and Language: The Puzzle of Indo-European Origins*. 1987. Repr. Cambridge: Cambridge University Press, 1999.

Ricoeur, Paul. *Hermeneutics and the Human Sciences*. 1981. Ed. and tr. J. B. Thompson. Repr. Cambridge: Cambridge University Press, 1998.

Ricoeur, Paul. *Interpretation Theory: Discourse and the Surplus of Meaning*. Fort Worth, Tex.: Texas Christian University Press, 1976.

Ridley, Mark. *The Problems of Evolution*. Oxford: Oxford University Press, 1985.

Rodwell, J. M., tr. *The Koran*. Ed. Alan Jones. London: Phoenix, 2011.

Rorty, Richard. *Consequences of Pragmatism: Essays, 1972–1980*. Minneapolis, Minn.: University of Minnesota Press, 1982.

Rose, Steven. *Lifelines: Biology, Freedom, Determinism*. 1998. Repr. New York: Oxford University Press, 2003.

Ross, Hugh. *The Creator and the Cosmos*. Colorado Springs: NavPress, 1995.

Ross, W. D. *The Right and the Good*. Oxford: Clarendon Press, 1930. Repr. 2002.

Rousseau, Jean Jacques. *The Social Contract*. 1762.

Russell, Bertrand. *The Autobiography of Bertrand Russell*. 1967–69. Repr. London: Routledge, 1998.

Russell, Bertrand. *History of Western Philosophy*. 1946. New edn, London: Routledge, 2004.

Russell, Bertrand. *Human Society in Ethics and Politics*. New York: Mentor, 1962.

Russell, Bertrand. *The Problems of Philosophy*. 1912. Repr. New York: Cosimo Classics, 2010.

Russell, Bertrand. *Religion and Science*. Oxford: Oxford University Press, 1970.

Russell, Bertrand. *Understanding History*. 1943. New York: Philosophical Library, 1957.

Russell, Bertrand. *Why I Am Not a Christian and Other Essays on Religion and Related Subjects*. New York: Simon & Schuster, 1957.

Russell, L. O. and G. A. Adebiyi. *Classical Thermodynamics*. Oxford: Oxford University Press, 1993.

Ryle, Gilbert. *The Concept of Mind*. London, 1949. Repr. London: Routledge, 2009.

S

Sagan, Carl. *The Cosmic Connection: An Extraterrestrial Perspective*. New York: Anchor Press, 1973.

Sagan, Carl. *Cosmos: The Story of Cosmic Evolution, Science and Civilisation*. 1980. Repr. London: Abacus, 2003.

Sagan, Carl. *The Demon-Haunted World: Science as a Candle in the Dark*. London: Headline, 1996.

Sandbach, F. H. *The Stoics*. 1975. Rev. edn, London: Bloomsbury, 2013.

Sartre, Jean-Paul. *Being and Nothingness: An Essay on Phenomenological Ontology*. 1943. Tr. Hazel E. Barnes. 1956. Repr. New York: Pocket Books, 1984.

Sartre, Jean-Paul. *Existentialism and Human Emotions*. Tr. Bernard Frechtman. New York: Philosophical Library, 1957.

Sartre, Jean-Paul. *Existentialism and Humanism*. Tr. and ed. P. Mairet. London: Methuen, 1948.

Sartre, Jean-Paul. *The Flies*. 1943 (French). Tr. Stuart Gilbert. New York: Knopf, 1947.

Schaff, Adam. *A Philosophy of Man*. London: Lawrence and Wishart, 1963.

Scherer, Siegfried. *Evolution. Ein kritisches Lehrbuch*. Weyel Biologie, Giessen: Weyel Lehrmittelverlag, 1998.

Schmidt, W. *The Origin and Growth of Religion*. Tr. J. Rose. London: Methuen, 1931.

Scruton, Roger. *Modern Philosophy*. 1994; London: Arrow Books, 1996.

Searle, John R. *The Construction of Social Reality*. London: Penguin, 1995.

Searle, John R. *Minds, Brains and Science*. 1984 Reith Lectures. London: British Broadcasting Corporation, 1984.

Selsam, Howard. *Socialism and Ethics*. New York: International Publishers, 1943.

Sen, Amartya and Bernard Williams, eds. *Utilitarianism and Beyond*. Cambridge: Cambridge University Press, 1982. 8th repr. in association with La Maison Des Sciences De L'Homme, Paris, 1999.

Shakespeare, William. *As You Like It*.

Sherrington, Charles S. *The Integrative Action of the Nervous System*. 1906. Repr. with new preface, Cambridge: Cambridge University Press, 1947.

Sherwin-White, A. N. *Roman Society and Roman Law in the New Testament*. The Sarum Lectures 1960–61. Oxford: Clarendon Press, 1963. Repr. Eugene, Oreg.: Wipf & Stock, 2004.

Simplicius. *Commentary on Aristotle's Physics* [or, Miscellanies]. In Kirk, G. S., J. E. Raven, and M. Schofield. *The Presocratic Philosophers: A Critical History with a Selection of Texts*. 1957. Rev. edn, Cambridge: Cambridge University Press, 1983.

Simpson, George Gaylord. *The Meaning of Evolution: A Study of the History of Life and of Its Significance for Man*. The Terry Lectures Series. 1949. Rev. edn, New Haven, Conn.: Yale University Press, 1967.

Singer, Peter. *Practical Ethics*. 1979. 2nd edn, Cambridge: Cambridge University Press, 1993.

Singer, Peter. *Rethinking Life and Death: The Collapse of Our Traditional Ethics*. Oxford: Oxford University Press, 1994.

Singer, Peter and Helga Kuhse. *Should the Baby Live?: The Problem of Handicapped Infants* (Studies in Bioethics). Oxford: Oxford University Press, 1985.

Sire, James. *The Universe Next Door*. Downers Grove, Ill.: InterVarsity Press, 1988.

Skinner, B. F. *Beyond Freedom and Dignity*. 1971; Harmondsworth: Penguin, 1974.

Skinner, B. F. *Lectures on Conditioned Reflexes*. New York: International Publishers, 1963.

Skinner, B. F. *Science and Human Behaviour*. New York: Macmillan, 1953.

Sleeper, Raymond S. *A Lexicon of Marxist-Leninist Semantics*. Alexandria, Va.: Western Goals, 1983.

Smart, J. J. C. and Bernard Williams. *Utilitarianism For and Against*. 1973. Repr. Cambridge: Cambridge University Press, 1998.

Smith, Adam. *An Enquiry into the Nature and Causes of the Wealth of Nations*. 1776. With introduction by Mark G. Spencer, Ware, UK: Wordsworth Editions, 2012.

Smith, John Maynard and Eörs Szathmary. *The Major Transitions in Evolution*. 1995. Repr. Oxford: Oxford University Press, 2010.

Smith, Wilbur. *Therefore Stand*. Grand Rapids: Baker, 1965.

Sober, E. *Philosophy of Biology*. 1993. Rev. 2nd edn, Boulder, Colo.: Westview Press, 2000.

Social Exclusion Unit. *Teenage Pregnancy*. Cmnd 4342. London: The Stationery Office, 1999.

Sophocles. *Antigone*. Tr. F. H. Storr, *Sophocles* Vol. 1. London: Heinemann, 1912.

Spencer, Herbert. *Social Statics*. New York: D. Appleton, 1851.

Stalin, Joseph. *J. Stalin Works*. Moscow: Foreign Languages Publishing House, 1953.

Stam, James H. *Inquiries into the Origin of Language: The Fate of a Question*. New York: Harper & Row, 1976.

Starkey, Mike. *God, Sex, and the Search for Lost Wonder: For Those Looking for Something to Believe In*. 1997. 2nd edn, Downers Grove, Ill.: InterVarsity Press, 1998.

Stauber, Ethelbert. *Jesus—Gestalt und Geschichte*. Bern: Francke Verlag, 1957.

Storer, Morris B., ed. *Humanist Ethics: Dialogue on Basics*. Buffalo, N.Y.: Prometheus Books, 1980.

Stott, John R. W. *The Message of Romans*. Leicester: Inter-Varsity Press, 1994.

Strabo. *Geography*. Tr. with introduction Duane W. Roller as *The Geography of Strabo*, Cambridge: Cambridge University Press, 2014. Tr. H. C. Hamilton and W. Falconer, London, 1903. Online at Perseus, Tufts University, http://www.

perseus.tufts.edu/hopper/text?doc=Perseus%3Atext%3A1999.01.0239, accessed 11 Sept. 2015.

Strickberger, Monroe. *Evolution*. 1990. 3rd edn, London: Jones and Bartlett, 2000.

Strobel, Lee. *The Case for Christ: A Journalist's Personal Investigation of the Evidence for Jesus*. Grand Rapids: Zondervan, 1998.

Suetonius. *Lives of the Caesars*. Tr. Catharine Edwards. 2000. Repr. Oxford World's Classics. Oxford: Oxford University Press, 2008.

Sunderland, Luther D. *Darwin's Enigma*. Green Forest, Ark.: Master Books, 1998.

Swinburne, Richard. *The Existence of God*. 1979. Repr. Oxford: Oxford University Press, 2004.

Swinburne, Richard. *Faith and Reason*. 1981. Repr. Oxford: Clarendon Press, 2002.

Swinburne, Richard. *Is There a God?* Oxford: Oxford University Press, 1996.

Swinburne, Richard. *Providence and the Problem of Evil*. Oxford: Oxford University Press, 1998.

T

Tacitus, Cornelius. *Annals*. Tr. Alfred John Church and William Jackson Brodribb as *Complete Works of Tacitus*. New York: Random House, 1872. Repr. 1942. Online at Sara Byrant, ed., Perseus Digital Library, Tufts University, Medford, MA: http://www.perseus.tufts.edu/hopper/text?doc=Perseus:text:1999.02.0078, accessed 2 Aug. 2017.

Tada, Joni Eareckson and Steven Estes. *When God Weeps: Why Our Sufferings Matter to the Almighty*. Grand Rapids: Zondervan, 1997.

Tax, Sol and Charles Callender, eds. *Issues in Evolution*. Chicago: University of Chicago Press, 1960.

Thaxton, Charles B., Walter L. Bradley and Roger L. Olsen. *The Mystery of Life's Origin*. Dallas: Lewis & Stanley, 1992.

Thibaut, George, tr. *The Vedānta Sūtras of Bādarāyana* with the Commentary by Śankara, 2 Parts. New York: Dover, 1962.

Torrance, T. F. *The Ground and Grammar of Theology*. Belfast: Christian Journals Limited, 1980; and Charlottesville: The University Press of Virginia, 1980. Repr. with new preface, Edinburgh: T&T Clark, 2001.

Torrance, T. F. *Theological Science*. Oxford: Oxford University Press, 1978.

U

Unamuno, Don Miguel de. *The Tragic Sense of Life*. Tr. J. E. Crawford. 1921. Repr. Charleston, S.C.: BiblioBazaar, 2007.

V

Von Neumann, John. *Theory of Self-Reproducing Automata*. Ed. and completed by Arthur W. Burks, Urbana: University of Illinois Press, 1966.

W

Waddington, C. H., ed. *Science and Ethics: An Essay*. London: Allen & Unwin, 1942.

Wallis, R. T. *Neoplatonism*. 1972. Repr. London: Duckworth, 1985.

Ward, Keith. *God, Chance and Necessity*. 1996. Repr. Oxford: Oneworld Publications, 2001.

Warner, Richard, and Tadeusz Szubka. *The Mind-Body Problem*. Oxford: Blackwell, 1994.

Weiner, Jonathan. *The Beak of the Finch*. London: Cape, 1994.

Welch, I. David, George A. Tate and Fred Richards, eds. *Humanistic Psychology*. Buffalo, N.Y.: Prometheus Books, 1978.

Wenham, John. *Easter Enigma—Do the Resurrection Stories Contradict One Another?* Exeter: Paternoster Press, 1984. Repr. as *Easter Enigma: Are the Resurrection Accounts in Conflict?*, Eugene, Oreg.: Wipf & Stock, 2005.

Wesson, Paul. *Beyond Natural Selection*. 1991. Repr. Cambridge, Mass.: Massachusetts Institute of Technology Press, 1997.

Westminster Shorter Catechism. 1647. [Widely available in print and online.]

Wetter, Gustav A. *Dialectical Materialism*. Westport, Conn.: Greenwood Press, 1977.

Whitehead, Alfred North. *Process and Reality*. Gifford Lectures 1927–28. London: Macmillan, 1929. Repr. New York: The Free Press, 1978.

Wilson, Edward O. *Consilience*. London: Little, Brown, 1998.

Wilson, Edward O. *Genes, Mind and Culture*. Cambridge, Mass.: Harvard University Press, 1981.

Wilson, Edward O. *On Human Nature*. Cambridge, Mass.: Harvard University Press, 1978.

Wilson, Edward O. *Sociobiology: The New Synthesis*. Cambridge, Mass.: Harvard University Press, 1975.

Wimsatt, William K. and Monroe Beardsley. *The Verbal Icon: Studies in the Meaning of Poetry*. 1954. Repr. Lexington, Ky.: University of Kentucky Press, 1982.

Wippel, John F., ed. *Studies in Medieval Philosophy*. Vol. 17 of *Studies in Philosophy and the History of Philosophy*. Washington D.C.: Catholic University of America Press, 1987.

Wittgenstein, L. *On Certainty*. Ed. G. E. M. Anscombe and G. H. von Wright; tr. Denis Paul and G. E. M. Anscombe. Oxford, 1969. Repr. New York: Harper & Row, 1972.

Wolpert, Lewis. *The Unnatural Nature of Science*. London: Faber & Faber, 1992.

Wolstenholme, Gordon, ed. *Man and His Future*. A Ciba Foundation Volume. London: J. & A. Churchill, 1963.

Wolters, Clifton, tr. *The Cloud of Unknowing*. 1961. Repr. London: Penguin, 1978.

Wolterstorff, Nicholas. *Divine Discourse: Philosophical Reflections on the Claim that God Speaks*. 1995. Repr. Cambridge: Cambridge University Press, 2000.

X

Xenophon. *Memorabilia*. Tr. E. C. Marchant. *Memorabilia. Oeconomicus. Symposium. Apology.* Vol. 4. Loeb Classical Library, Vol. 168. 1923. Repr. Cambridge, Mass.: Harvard University Press, 1997.

Y

Yancey, Philip. *Soul Survivor: How my Faith Survived the Church.* London: Hodder & Stoughton, 2001.

Yockey, Hubert. *Information Theory and Biology.* Cambridge: Cambridge University Press, 1992.

Z

Zacharias, Ravi. *Jesus Among Other Gods: The Absolute Claims of the Christian Message.* Nashville, Tenn.: Thomas Nelson, 2000.

Zacharias, Ravi. *The Real Face of Atheism.* Grand Rapids: Baker, 2004.

Zaehner, Z. C., ed. *The Concise Encyclopedia of Living Faiths.* 1959. 2nd edn, 1971. Repr. London: Hutchinson, 1982.

ARTICLES, PAPERS, CHAPTERS AND LECTURES

A

Adams, R. M. 'Religious Ethics in a Pluralistic Society.' In G. Outka and J. P. Reeder, Jr., eds. *Prospects for a Common Morality*. Princeton, N.J.: Princeton University Press, 1993.

Alberts, Bruce. 'The Cell as a Collection of Protein Machines: Preparing the Next Generation of Molecular Biologists.' *Cell* 92/3 (6 Feb. 1998), 291–4. doi: 10.1016/S0092-8674(00)80922-8.

Almond, Brenda. 'Liberty or Community? Defining the Post-Marxist Agenda.' In Brenda Almond, ed. *Introducing Applied Ethics*. Oxford: Wiley Blackwell, 1995.

Alpher, R. A., H. Bethe and G. Gamow. 'The Origin of Chemical Elements.' *Physical Review* 73/7 (Apr. 1948), 803–4. doi: 10.1103/PhysRev.73.803.

Anscombe, G. E. M. 'Modern Moral Philosophy.' *Philosophy* 33 (1958), 1–19.

Asimov, Isaac (interview by Paul Kurtz). 'An Interview with Isaac Asimov on Science and the Bible.' *Free Enquiry* 2/2 (Spring 1982), 6–10.

Auer, J. A. C. F. 'Religion as the Integration of Human Life.' *The Humanist* (Spring 1947).

Austin, J. L., P. F. Strawson and D. R. Cousin. 'Truth.' *Proceedings of the Aristotelian Society, Supplementary Volumes, Vol. 24, Physical Research, Ethics and Logic* (1950), 111–72. Online at http://www.jstor.org/stable/4106745. Repr. in Paul Horwich, ed. *Theories of Truth*. Aldershot: Dartmouth Publishing, 1994.

B

Bada, Jeffrey L. 'Stanley Miller's 70th Birthday.' *Origins of Life and Evolution of Biospheres* 30/2 (2000), 107–12. doi: 10.1023/A:1006746205180.

Baier, Kurt E. M. 'Egoism.' In P. Singer, ed. *A Companion to Ethics*. Oxford: Blackwell, 1991. Repr. 2000, 197–204.

Baier, Kurt E. M. 'Freedom, Obligation, and Responsibility.' In Morris B. Storer, ed. *Humanist Ethics: Dialogue on Basics*. Buffalo, N.Y.: Prometheus Books, 1980, 75–92.

Baier, Kurt E. M. 'The Meaning of Life.' 1947. In Peter Angeles, ed. *Critiques of God*, Buffalo, N.Y.: Prometheus Books, 1976. Repr. in E. D. Klemke, ed. *The Meaning of Life*. New York: Oxford University Press, 1981, 81–117.

Baker, S. W. 'Albert Nyanza, Account of the Discovery of the Second Great Lake of the Nile.' *Journal of the Royal Geographical Society* 36 (1866). Also in *Proceedings of the Royal Geographical Society of London* 10 (13 Nov. 1856), 6–27.

Bates, Elizabeth, Donna Thal and Virginia Marchman. 'Symbols and Syntax: A Darwinian Approach to Language Development.' In Norman A. Krasnegor, Duane M. Rumbaugh, Richard L. Schiefelbusch and Michael Studdert-Kennedy, eds. *Biological and Behavioural Determinants of Language Development*. 1991. Repr. New York: Psychology Press, 2014, 29–65.

Behe, Michael J. 'Reply to My Critics: A Response to Reviews of *Darwin's Black Box: The Biochemical Challenge to Evolution*.' *Biology and Philosophy* 16 (2001), 685–709.

Berenbaum, Michael. 'T4 Program' In *Encyclopaedia Britannica*. Online at https://www.britannica.com/event/T4-Program, accessed 2 Nov. 2017.

Berlinski, David. 'The Deniable Darwin.' *Commentary* (June 1996), 19–29.

Bernal, J. D. 'The Unity of Ethics.' In C. H. Waddington, ed. *Science and Ethics: An Essay*. London: Allen & Unwin, 1942.

Black, Deborah L. 'Al-Kindi.' In Seyyed Hossein Nasr and Oliver Leaman, eds. *History of Islamic Philosophy*. Part 1, Vol. 1 of *Routledge History of World Philosophies*. 1996. Repr. London: Routledge, 2001, 178–97.

Boghossian, Paul A. 'What the Sokal hoax ought to teach us: The pernicious consequences and internal contradictions of "postmodernist" relativism.' *Times Literary Supplement*, Commentary (13 Dec. 1996), 14–15. Reprinted in Noretta Koertge, ed. *A House Built on Sand: Exposing Postmodernist Myths about Science*. Oxford: Oxford University Press, 1998, 23–31.

Briggs, Arthur E. 'The Third Annual Humanist Convention.' *The Humanist* (Spring 1945).

Bristol, Evelyn. 'Turn of a Century: Modernism, 1895–1925.' Ch. 8 in C. A. Moser, ed. *The Cambridge History of Russian Literature*. 1989. Rev. edn, 1992. Repr. 1996, Cambridge: Cambridge University Press, 387–457.

C

Caputo, John D. 'The End of Ethics.' In Hugh LaFollette, ed. *The Blackwell Guide to Ethical Theory*. Oxford: Blackwell, 1999, 111–28.

Cartmill, Matt. 'Oppressed by Evolution.' *Discover* Magazine 19/3 (Mar. 1998), 78–83. Reprinted in L. Polnac, ed. *Purpose, Pattern, and Process*. 6th edn, Dubuque: Kendall-Hunt, 2002, 389–97.

Cavalier-Smith, T. 'The Blind Biochemist.' *Trends in Ecology and Evolution* 12 (1997), 162–3.

Chaitin, Gregory J. 'Randomness in Arithmetic and the Decline and Fall of Reductionism in Pure Mathematics.' Ch. 3 in John Cornwell, ed. *Nature's Imagination: The Frontiers of Scientific Vision*. Oxford: Oxford University Press, 1995, 27–44.

Chomsky, Noam. 'Review of B. F. Skinner.' *Verbal Behavior. Language* 35/1 (1959), 26–58.

Chomsky, Noam. 'Science, Mind, and Limits of Understanding.' Transcript of talk given at the Science and Faith Foundation (STOQ), The Vatican (Jan. 2014). No pages. Online at https://chomsky.info/201401__/, accessed 3 Aug. 2017.

Coghlan, Andy. 'Selling the family secrets.' *New Scientist* 160/2163 (5 Dec. 1998), 20–1.

Collins, Harry. 'Introduction: Stages in the Empirical Programme of Relativism.' *Social Studies of Science* 11/1 (Feb. 1981), 3–10. Online at http://www.jstor.org/stable/284733, accessed 11 Sept. 2015.

Collins, R. 'A Physician's View of College Sex.' *Journal of the American Medical Association* 232 (1975), 392.

Cook, Sidney. 'Solzhenitsyn and Secular Humanism: A Response.' *The Humanist* (Nov./Dec. 1978), 6.

Cookson, Clive. 'Scientist Who Glimpsed God.' *Financial Times* (29 Apr. 1995), 20.

Cottingham, John. 'Descartes, René.' In Ted Honderich, ed. *The Oxford Companion to Philosophy*. Oxford, 1995. 2nd edn, Oxford: Oxford University Press, 2005.

Crick, Francis. 'Lessons from Biology.' *Natural History* 97 (Nov. 1988), 32–9.

Crosman, Robert. 'Do Readers Make Meaning?' In Susan R. Suleiman and Inge Crosman, eds. *The Reader in the Text: Essays on Audience and Interpretation*. Princeton, N.J.: Princeton University Press, 1980.

D

Davies, Paul. 'Bit before It?' *New Scientist* 2171 (30 Jan. 1999), 3.

Dawkins, Richard. 'Put Your Money on Evolution.' Review of Maitland A. Edey and Donald C. Johanson. *Blueprint: Solving the Mystery of Evolution*. Penguin, 1989. *The New York Times Review of Books* (9 Apr. 1989), sec. 7, 34–5.

Dembski, William. 'Intelligent Design as a Theory of Information.' *Perspectives on Science and Christian Faith* 49/3 (Sept. 1997), 180–90.

Derrida, Jacques. 'Force of Law: The "Mystical Foundation of Authority".' In Drucilla Cornell, Michel Rosenfeld and David Gray Carlson, eds. *Deconstruction and the Possibility of Justice*. 1992. Repr. Abingdon: Routledge, 2008.

Dirac, P. A. M. 'The Evolution of the Physicist's Picture of Nature.' *Scientific American* 208/5 (1963), 45–53. doi: 10.1038/scientificamerican0563-45.

Dobzhansky, Theodosius. 'Chance and Creativity in Evolution.' Ch. 18 in Francisco J. Ayala and Theodosius Dobzhansky, eds. *Studies in the Philosophy of Biology: Reduction and Related Problems*. Berkeley, Calif.: University of California Press, 1974, 307–36.

Dobzhansky, Theodosius. Discussion of paper by Gerhard Schramm, 'Synthesis of Nucleosides and Polynucleotide with Metaphosphate Esters.' In Sidney W. Fox, ed. *The Origins of Prebiological Systems and of Their Molecular Matrices*, 299–315. Proceedings of a Conference Conducted at Wakulla Springs, Florida, on 20–30 October 1963 under the auspices of the Institute for Space Biosciences, the Florida State University and the National Aeronautics and Space Administration. New York: Academic Press, 1965.

Dobzhansky, Theodosius. 'Evolutionary Roots of Family Ethics and Group Ethics.' In *The Centrality of Science and Absolute Values*, Vol. I of *Proceedings of the Fourth International Conference on the Unity of the Sciences*. New York: International Cultural Foundation, 1975.

Documents of the 22nd Congress of the Communist Party of the Soviet Union. 2 vols. Documents of Current History, nos. 18–19. New York: Crosscurrents Press, 1961.

Dose, Klaus. 'The Origin of Life: More Questions Than Answers.' *Interdisciplinary Science Reviews* 13 (Dec. 1988), 348–56.

Druart, Th.-A. 'Al-Fārābī and Emanationism.' In J. F. Wippel, ed. *Studies in Medieval Philosophy*. Vol. 17 of Studies in Philosophy and the History of Philosophy. Washington D.C.: Catholic University of America Press, 1987, 23–43.

Dyson, Freeman. 'Energy in the Universe.' *Scientific American* 225/3 (1971), 50–9.

E

Eddington, Arthur. 'The End of the World: From the Standpoint of Mathematical Physics.' *Nature* 127 (21 Mar. 1931), 447–53. doi: 10.1038/127447a0.

Edwards, William. 'On the Physical Death of Jesus Christ.' *Journal of the American Medical Association* 255/11 (21 Mar. 1986), 1455–63.

Eigen, Manfred, Christof K. Biebricher, Michael Gebinoga and William C. Gardiner. 'The Hypercycle: Coupling of RNA and Protein Biosynthesis in the Infection Cycle of an RNA Bacteriophage.' *Biochemistry* 30/46 (1991), 11005–18. doi: 10.1021/bi00110a001.

Einstein, Albert. 'Physics and Reality.' 1936. In Sonja Bargmann, tr. *Ideas and Opinions*. New York: Bonanza, 1954.

Einstein, Albert. 'Science and Religion.' 1941. Published in *Science, Philosophy and Religion, A Symposium*. New York: The Conference on Science, Philosophy and Religion in Their Relation to the Democratic Way of Life, 1941. Repr. in *Out of My Later Years*, 1950, 1956. Repr. New York: Open Road Media, 2011.

Eysenck, H. J. 'A Reason with Compassion.' In Paul Kurtz, ed. *The Humanist Alternative*. Buffalo, N.Y.: Prometheus Books, 1973.

F

Feynman, Richard P. 'Cargo Cult Science.' Repr. in *Engineering and Science* 37/7 (1974), 10–13. Online at http://calteches.library.caltech.edu/51/2/CargoCult.pdf (facsimile), accessed 11 Sept. 2015. (Originally delivered as Caltech's 1974 commencement address in Pasadena, Calif.)

Fletcher, J. 'Comment by Joseph Fletcher on Nielsen Article.' In Morris B. Storer, ed. *Humanist Ethics: Dialogue on Basics*. Buffalo, N.Y.: Prometheus Books, 1980, 70.

Flew, Anthony. 'Miracles.' In Paul Edwards, ed. *The Encyclopedia of Philosophy*. New York: Macmillan, 1967, 5:346–53.

Flew, Anthony. 'Neo-Humean Arguments about the Miraculous.' In R. D. Geivett and G. R. Habermas, eds. *In Defence of Miracles*. Leicester: Apollos, 1997, 45–57.

Flieger, Jerry Aline. 'The Art of Being Taken by Surprise.' *Destructive Criticism: Directions. SCE Reports* 8 (Fall 1980), 54–67.

Fodor, J. A. 'Fixation of Belief and Concept Acquisition.' In M. Piattelli-Palmarini, ed., *Language and Learning: The Debate Between Jean Piaget and Noam Chomsky*. Cambridge, Mass.: Harvard University Press, 1980, 143–9.

Fotion, Nicholas G. 'Logical Positivism.' In Ted Honderich, ed. *The Oxford Companion to Philosophy*. 2nd edn, Oxford: Oxford University Press, 2005.

Frank, Lawrence K. 'Potentialities of Human Nature.' *The Humanist* (Apr. 1951).

Frankena, William K. 'Is morality logically dependent on religion?' In G. Outka and J. P. Reeder, Jr., eds. *Religion and Morality*. Garden City, N.Y.: Anchor, 1973.

G

Genequand, Charles. 'Metaphysics.' Ch. 47 in Seyyed Nossein Nasr and Oliver Leaman, eds. *History of Islamic Philosophy*. Vol. 1 of *Routledge History of World Philosophies*. London: Routledge, 1996, 783–801.

Genné, William H. 'Our Moral Responsibility.' *Journal of the American College Health Association* 15/Suppl (May 1967), 55–60.

Gilbert, Scott F., John Opitz and Rudolf A Raff. 'Resynthesizing Evolutionary and Developmental Biology.' *Developmental Biology* 173/2 (1996), 357–72.

Ginsburg, V. L. *Poisk* 29–30 (1998).

Gould, Stephen Jay. 'Evolution as Fact and Theory.' In Ashley Montagu, ed. *Science and Creationism*. Oxford: Oxford University Press, 1984.

Gould, Stephen Jay. 'Evolution's Erratic Pace.' *Natural History* 86/5 (May 1977), 12–16.

Gould, Stephen Jay. 'Evolutionary Considerations.' Paper presented at the McDonnell Foundation Conference, 'Selection vs. Instruction'. Venice, May 1989.

Gould, Stephen Jay. 'In Praise of Charles Darwin.' Paper presented at the Nobel Conference XVIII, Gustavus Adolphus College, St. Peter, Minn. Repr. in Charles L. Hamrum, ed. *Darwin's Legacy*. San Francisco: Harper & Row, 1983.

Gould, Stephen Jay. 'The Paradox of the Visibly Irrelevant.' *Annals of the New York Academy of Sciences* 879 (June 1999), 87–97. doi: 10.1111/j.1749-6632.1999.tb10407.x. Repr. in *The Lying Stones of Marrakech: Penultimate Reflections in Natural History*. 2000. Repr. Cambridge, Mass.: Harvard University Press, 2011.

Gribbin, John. 'Oscillating Universe Bounces Back.' *Nature* 259 (1 Jan. 1976), 15–16. doi: 10.1038/259015c0.

Grigg, Russell. 'Could Monkeys Type the 23rd Psalm?' *Interchange* 50 (1993), 25–31.

Guth, A. H. 'Inflationary Universe: A Possible Solution to the Horizon and Flatness Problems.' *Physical Review D* 23/2 (1981), 347–56.

Guttmacher Institute. 'Induced Abortion in the United States', Fact Sheet. New York: Guttmacher Institute, Jan. 2018. Online at https://www.guttmacher.org/fact-sheet/induced-abortion-united-states, accessed 1 Feb. 2018.

H

Haldane, J. B. S. 'When I am Dead.' In *Possible Worlds*. [1927] London: Chatto & Windus, 1945, 204–11.

Hansen, Michèle; Jennifer J. Kurinczuk, Carol Bower and Sandra Webb. 'The Risk of Major Birth Defects after Intracytoplasmic Sperm Injection and in Vitro Fertilization.' *New England Journal of Medicine* 346 (2002), 725–30. doi: 10.1056/NEJMoa010035.

Hardwig, John. 'Dying at the Right Time: Reflections on (Un)Assisted Suicide.' In Hugh LaFollette, ed. *Ethics In Practice*. Blackwell Philosophy Anthologies. 2nd edn, Oxford: Blackwell, 1997, 101–11.

Hawking, S. W. 'The Edge of Spacetime: Does the universe have an edge and time a beginning, as Einstein's general relativity predicts, or is spacetime finite without boundary, as quantum mechanics suggests?' *American Scientist* 72/4 (1984), 355–9. Online at http://www.jstor.org/stable/27852759, accessed 15 Sept. 2015.

Hawking, S. W. Letters to the Editors. Reply to letter by J. J. Tanner relating to article 'The Edge of Spacetime'. *American Scientist* 73/1 (1985), 12. Online at http://www.jstor.org/stable/27853056, accessed 15 Sept. 2015.

Hawking, S. W. and R. Penrose. 'The Singularities of Gravitational Collapse and Cosmology.' *Proceedings of the Royal Society London A* 314/1519 (1970), 529–48. doi: 10.1098/rspa.1970.0021.

Hocutt, Max. 'Does Humanism Have an Ethic of Responsibility?' In Morris B. Storer, ed. *Humanist Ethic: Dialogue on Basics*. Buffalo, N.Y.: Prometheus Books, 1980, 11–24.

Hocutt, Max. 'Toward an Ethic of Mutual Accommodation.' In Morris B. Storer, ed. *Humanist Ethics: Dialogue on Basics*. Buffalo, N.Y.: Prometheus Books, 1980, 137–46.

Hookway, C. J. 'Scepticism.' In Ted Honderich, ed. *The Oxford Companion to Philosophy*. Oxford, 1995. 2nd edn, Oxford: Oxford University Press, 2005.

Hoyle, Fred. 'The Universe: Past and Present Reflections.' *Annual Reviews of Astronomy and Astrophysics* 20 (1982), 1–35. doi: 10.1146/annurev.aa.20.090182.000245.

Hursthouse, Rosalind. 'Virtue theory and abortion.' *Philosophy and Public Affairs* 20, 1991, 223–46.

Huxley, Julian. 'The Emergence of Darwinism.' In Sol Tax, ed. *The Evolution of Life: Its Origins, History, and Future*. Vol. 1 of *Evolution after Darwin*. Chicago: University of Chicago Press, 1960, 1–21.

Huxley, Julian. 'The Evolutionary Vision: The Convocation Address.' In Sol Tax and Charles Callender, eds. *Issues in Evolution*. Vol. 3 of *Evolution after Darwin*. Chicago: University of Chicago Press, 1960, 249–61.

I

Inwood, M. J. 'Feuerbach, Ludwig Andreas.' In Ted Honderich, ed. *The Oxford Companion to Philosophy*. Oxford, 1995. 2nd edn, Oxford: Oxford University Press, 2005.

J

Jeeves, Malcolm. 'Brain, Mind, and Behaviour.' In Warren S. Brown, Nancey Murphy and H. Newton Malony, eds. *Whatever Happened to the Soul: Scientific and Theological Portraits of Human Nature*. Minneapolis: Fortress Press, 1998.

Johnson, Barbara. 'Nothing Fails Like Success.' *Deconstructive Criticism: Directions*. SCE Reports 8 (Fall 1980), 7–16.

Josephson, Brian. Letters to the Editor. *The Independent* (12 Jan. 1997), London.

K

Kant, Immanuel. 'Beantwortung der Frage: Was ist Aufklärung?' *Berlinische Monatsschrift* 4 (Dec. 1784), 481–94. Repr. in *Kant's Gesammelte Schriften*. Berlin: Akademie Ausgabe, 1923, 8:33–42.

Khrushchev, Nikita. *Ukrainian Bulletin* (1–15 Aug. 1960), 12.

Klein-Franke, Felix. 'Al-Kindī.' In Seyyed Hossein Nasr and Oliver Leaman, eds. *History of Islamic Philosophy*. Vol. 1, Part 1 of *Routledge History of World Philosophies*. 1996. Repr. London: Routledge, 2001, 165–77.

Kurtz, Paul. 'A Declaration of Interdependence: A New Global Ethics.' *Free Inquiry* 8/4 (Fall 1988), 4–7. Also published in Vern L. Ballough and Timothy J. Madigan, ed. *Toward a New Enlightenment: The Philosophy of Paul Kurtz*. New Brunswick, N.J.: Transaction Publishers, 1994 (ch. 3, 'The Twenty-First Century and Beyond: The Need for a New Global Ethic and a Declaration of Interdependence').

Kurtz, Paul. 'Does Humanism Have an Ethic of Responsibility?' In Morris B. Storer, ed. *Humanist Ethics: Dialogue on Basics*. Buffalo, N.Y.: Prometheus Books, 1980, 11–24.

Kurtz, Paul. 'Is Everyone a Humanist?' In Paul Kurtz, ed. *The Humanist Alternative*. Buffalo, N.Y.: Prometheus Books, 1973.

L

Lamont, Corliss. 'The Ethics of Humanism.' In Frederick C. Dommeyer, ed. *In Quest of Value: Readings in Philosophy and Personal Values*. San Francisco: Chandler, 1963, 46–59. Repr. from ch. 6 of Corliss Lamont. *Humanism as a Philosophy*. Philosophical Library, 273–97.

Larson, Erik. 'Looking for the Mind.' (Review of David J. Chalmers. *The Conscious Mind: In Search of a Fundamental Theory*.) *Origins & Design* 18/1(34) (Winter 1997), Colorado Springs: Access Research Network, 28–9.

Leitch, Vincent B. 'The Book of Deconstructive Criticism.' *Studies in the Literary Imagination* 12/1 (Spring 1979), 19–39.

Lewis, C. S. 'The Funeral of a Great Myth.' In Walter Hooper, ed. *Christian Reflections*. Grand Rapids: Eerdmans, 1967, 102–116.

Lewis, C. S. 'The Weight of Glory.' In *Transposition and other Addresses*. London: Geoffrey Bles, 1949. Repr. in *The Weight of Glory and Other Addresses*. HarperOne, 2001.

Lewontin, Richard C. 'Billions and Billions of Demons.' *The New York Review of Books* 44/1 (9 Jan. 1997).

Lewontin, Richard C. 'Evolution/Creation Debate: A Time for Truth.' *BioScience* 31/8 (Sept. 1981), 559. Reprinted in J. Peter Zetterberg, ed. *Evolution versus Creationism*. Phoenix, Ariz.: Oryx Press, 1983. doi: 10.1093/bioscience/31.8.559, accessed 15 Sept. 2015.

Lieberman, Philip and E. S. Crelin. 'On the Speech of Neanderthal Man.' *Linguistic Inquiry* 2/2 (Mar. 1971), 203–22.

Louden, Robert. 'On Some Vices of Virtue Ethics.' Ch. 10 in R. Crisp and M. Slote, eds. *Virtue Ethics*. Oxford: Oxford University Press, 1997.

M

Mackie, J. L. 'Evil and Omnipotence.' *Mind* 64/254 (Apr. 1955), 200–12.

McNaughton, David and Piers Rawling. 'Intuitionism.' Ch. 13 in Hugh LaFollette, ed. *The Blackwell Guide to Ethical Theory*. Oxford: Blackwell, 2000, 268–87. Ch. 14 in 2nd edn, Wiley Blackwell, 2013, 287–310.

Maddox, John. 'Down with the Big Bang.' *Nature* 340 (1989), 425. doi: 10.1038/340425a0.

Marx, Karl. 'The Difference between the Natural Philosophy of Democritus and the Natural Philosophy of Epicurus.' In *K. Marx and F. Engels on Religion*. Moscow: Foreign Languages Publishing House, 1955.

Marx, Karl. 'Economic and Philosophical Manuscripts.' In T. B. Bottomore, tr. and ed. *Karl Marx: Early Writings*. London: Watts, 1963.

Marx, Karl. 'Theses on Feuerback.' In Frederick Engels, *Ludwig Feuerback*. New York: International Publishers, 1941.

May, Rollo. 'The Problem of Evil: An Open Letter to Carl Rogers.' *Journal of Humanistic Psychology* (Summer 1982).

Merezhkovsky, Dmitry. 'On the Reasons for the Decline and on the New Currents in Contemporary Russian Literature.' 1892 lecture. In Dmitry Merezhkovsky. *On the reasons for the decline and on the new currents in contemporary Russian literature*. Petersburg, 1893.

Meyer, Stephen C. 'The Explanatory Power of Design: DNA and the Origin of Information.' In William A. Dembski, ed. *Mere Creation: Science, Faith and Intelligent Design*. Downers Grove, Ill.: InterVarsity Press, 1998, 114–47.

Meyer, Stephen C. 'The Methodological Equivalence of Design and Descent.' In J. P. Moreland, ed. *The Creation Hypothesis*. Downers Grove, Ill.: InterVarsity Press, 1994, 67–112.

Meyer, Stephen C. 'Qualified Agreement: Modern Science and the Return of the "God Hypothesis".' In Richard F. Carlson, ed. *Science and Christianity: Four Views*. Downers Grove, Ill.: InterVarsity Press, 2000, 129–75.

Meyer, Stephen C. 'The Return of the God Hypothesis.' *Journal of Interdisciplinary Studies* 11/1&2 (Jan. 1999), 1–38. Online at http://www.discovery.org/a/642, accessed 3 Aug. 2017. Citations are to the archived version, which is repaginated, and online at http://www.discovery.org/scripts/viewDB/filesDB-download.php?command=download&id=12006, accessed 3 Aug. 2017.

Miller, J. Hillis. 'Deconstructing the Deconstructors.' Review of Joseph N. Riddel. *The Inverted Bell: Modernism and the Counterpoetics of William Carlos Williams*. *Diacritics* 5/2 (Summer 1975), 24–31. Online at http://www.jstor.org/stable/464639, accessed 3 Aug. 2017. doi: 10.2307/464639.

Monod, Jacques. 'On the Logical Relationship between Knowledge and Values.' In Watson Fuller, ed. *The Biological Revolution*. Garden City, N.Y.: Doubleday, 1972.

N

Nagel, Ernest. 'Naturalism Reconsidered.' 1954. In Houston Peterson, ed. *Essays in Philosophy*. New York: Pocket Books, 1959. Repr. New York: Pocket Books, 1974.

Nagel, Thomas. 'Rawls, John.' In Ted Honderich, ed. *The Oxford Companion to Philosophy*. 1995. 2nd edn, Oxford: Oxford University Press, 2005.

Nagler, Michael N. 'Reading the Upanishads.' In Eknath Easwaran. *The Upanishads*. 1987. Repr. Berkeley, Calif.: Nilgiri Press, 2007.

Neill, Stephen. 'The Wrath of God and the Peace of God.' In Max Warren, *Interpreting the Cross*. London: SCM Press, 1966.

Newing, Edward G. 'Religions of pre-literary societies.' In Sir Norman Anderson, ed. *The World's Religions*. 4th edn, London: Inter-Varsity Press, 1975.

Nielsen, Kai. 'Religiosity and Powerlessness: Part III of "The Resurgence of Fundamentalism".' *The Humanist* 37/3 (May/June 1977), 46–8.

O

The Oxford Reference Encyclopaedia. Oxford: Oxford University Press, 1998.

P

Palmer, Alasdair. 'Must Knowledge Gained Mean Paradise Lost?' *Sunday Telegraph*. London (6 Apr. 1997).

Penzias, Arno. 'Creation is Supported by all the Data So Far.' In Henry Margenau and Roy Abraham Varghese, eds. *Cosmos, Bios, Theos: Scientists Reflect on Science, God, and the Origins of the Universe, Life, and Homo Sapiens*. La Salle, Ill.: Open Court, 1992.

Pinker, Steven, and Paul Bloom. 'Natural Language and Natural Selection.' *Behavioral and Brain Sciences* 13/4 (Dec. 1990), 707–27. doi: 10.1017/S0140525X00081061.

Polanyi, Michael. 'Life's Irreducible Structure. Live mechanisms and information in DNA are boundary conditions with a sequence of boundaries above them.' *Science* 160/3834 (1968), 1308–12. Online at http://www.jstor.org/stable/1724152, accessed 3 Aug. 2017.

Poole, Michael. 'A Critique of Aspects of the Philosophy and Theology of Richard Dawkins.' *Christians and Science* 6/1 (1994), 41–59. Online at http://www.scienceandchristianbelief.org/serve_pdf_free.php?filename=SCB+6-1+Poole.pdf, accessed 3 Aug. 2017.

Popper, Karl. 'Scientific Reduction and the Essential Incompleteness of All Science.' In F. J. Ayala and T. Dobzhansky, ed. *Studies in the Philosophy of Biology, Reduction and Related Problems*. London: MacMillan, 1974.

Premack, David. '"Gavagai!" or The Future History of the Animal Controversy.' *Cognition* 19/3 (1985), 207–96. doi: 10.1016/0010-0277(85)90036-8.

Provine, William B. 'Evolution and the Foundation of Ethics.' *Marine Biological Laboratory Science* 3 (1988), 27–8.

Provine, William B. 'Scientists, Face it! Science and Religion are Incompatible.' *The Scientist* (5 Sept. 1988), 10–11.

R

Rachels, James. 'Naturalism.' In Hugh LaFollette, ed. *The Blackwell Guide to Ethical Theory*. Oxford: Blackwell, 2000, 74–91.

Randall, John H. 'The Nature of Naturalism.' In Yervant H. Krikorian, ed. *Naturalism*, 354–82.

Raup, David. 'Conflicts between Darwin and Palaeontology.' *Field Museum of Natural History Bulletin* 50/1 (Jan. 1979), 22–9.

Reidhaar-Olson, John F. and Robert T. Sauer. 'Functionally Acceptable Substitutions in Two α-helical Regions of λ Repressor.' *Proteins: Structure, Function, and Genetics* 7/4 (1990), 306–16. doi: 10.1002/prot.340070403.

Rescher, Nicholas. 'Idealism.' In Jonathan Dancy and Ernest Sosa, eds. *A Companion to Epistemology*. 1992. Repr. Oxford: Blackwell, 2000.

Ridley, Mark. 'Who Doubts Evolution?' *New Scientist* 90 (25 June 1981), 830–2.

Rogers, Carl. 'Notes on Rollo May.' *Journal of Humanistic Psychology* 22/3 (Summer 1982), 8–9. doi: 10.1177/0022167882223002.

Rorty, Richard. 'Untruth and Consequences.' *The New Republic* (31 July 1995), 32–6.

Ruse, Michael. 'Is Rape Wrong on Andromeda?' In E. Regis Jr., ed. *Extraterrestrials*. Cambridge: Cambridge University Press, 1985.

Ruse, Michael. 'Transcript: Speech by Professor Michael Ruse,' Symposium, 'The New Antievolutionism', 1993 Annual Meeting of the American Association for the Advancement of Science, 13 Feb. 1993. Online at http://www.arn.org/docs/orpages/or151/mr93tran.htm, accessed 3 Aug. 2017.

Ruse, Michael and Edward O. Wilson. 'The Evolution of Ethics.' *New Scientist* 108/1478 (17 Oct. 1985), 50–2.

Russell, Bertrand. 'A Free Man's Worship.' 1903. In *Why I Am Not a Christian*. New York: Simon & Schuster, 1957. Also in *Mysticism and Logic Including A Free Man's Worship*. London: Unwin, 1986.

Russell, Colin. 'The Conflict Metaphor and its Social Origins.' *Science and Christian Belief* 1/1 (1989), 3–26.

S

Sanders, Blanche. *The Humanist* 5 (1945).

Sanders, Peter. 'Eutychus.' *Triple Helix* (Summer 2002), 17.

Sayre-McCord, Geoffrey. 'Contractarianism.' In Hugh LaFollette, ed. *The Blackwell Guide to Ethical Theory*. Oxford: Blackwell, 2000, 247–67. 2nd edn, Wiley Blackwell, 2013, 332–53.

Scruton, Roger. *The Times* (Dec. 1997), London.

Searle, John. 'Minds, Brains and Programs.' In John Haugeland, ed. *Mind Design*. Cambridge, Mass.: Cambridge University Press, 1981.

Sedgh, Gilda, et al., 'Abortion incidence between 1990 and 2014: global, regional, and subregional levels and trends.' *The Lancet* 388/10041 (16 July 2016), 258–67. doi: 10.1016/S0140-6736(16)30380-4.

Shapiro, James A. 'In the Details ... What?' *National Review* (16 Sept. 1996), 62–5.

Simpson, George Gaylord. 'The Biological Nature of Man.' *Science* 152/3721 (22 Apr. 1966), 472–8.

Singer, Peter. 'Hegel, Georg Wilhelm Friedrich.' In Ted Honderich, ed. *The Oxford Companion to Philosophy*. Oxford, 1995. 2nd edn, Oxford: Oxford University Press, 2005.

Skorupski, John. 'Mill, John Stuart.' In Ted Honderich, ed. *The Oxford Companion to Philosophy*. Oxford, 1995. 2nd edn, Oxford: Oxford University Press, 2005.

Slote, Michael. 'Utilitarianism.' In Ted Honderich, ed. *The Oxford Companion to Philosophy*. Oxford, 1995. 2nd edn, Oxford: Oxford University Press, 2005.

Slote, Michael. 'Virtue Ethics.' In Hugh LaFollette, ed. *The Blackwell Guide to Ethical Theory*. Oxford: Blackwell, 2000, 325–47.

Sokal, Alan D. 'Transgressing the boundaries: towards a transformative hermeneutic of Quantum Gravity.' *Social Text* (Spring/Summer 1996), 217–52.

Sokal, Alan D. 'What the Social Text Affair Does and Does Not Prove.' In Noretta Koertge, ed. *A House Built on Sand: Exposing Postmodernist Myths About Science*. Oxford: Oxford University Press, 1998, 9–22.

Solzhenitsyn, Alexander. 'Alexandr Solzhenitsyn—Nobel Lecture.' *Nobelprize.org*. Nobel Media AB 2014. Online at https://www.nobelprize.org/nobel_prizes/literature/laureates/1970/solzhenitsyn-lecture.html, accessed 15 Aug. 2017.

Spetner, L. M. 'Natural selection: An information-transmission mechanism for evolution.' *Journal of Theoretical Biology* 7/3 (Nov. 1964), 412–29.

Stalin, Joseph. Speech delivered 24 April 1924. New York, International Publishers, 1934.

Stolzenberg, Gabriel. 'Reading and relativism: an introduction to the science wars.' In Keith M. Ashman and Philip S. Baringer, eds. *After the Science Wars*. London: Routledge, 2001, 33–63.

T

Tarkunde, V. M. 'Comment by V. M. Tarkunde on Hocutt Article.' In Morris B. Storer, ed. *Humanist Ethics: Dialogue on Basics*. Buffalo, N.Y.: Prometheus Books, 1980, 147–8.

Taylor, Robert. 'Evolution is Dead.' *New Scientist* 160/2154 (3 Oct. 1998), 25–9.

W

Walicki, Andrzej. 'Hegelianism, Russian.' In Edward Craig, gen. ed. *Concise Routledge Encyclopedia of Philosophy*. London: Routledge, 2000.

Wallace, Daniel, "The Majority Text and the Original Text: Are They Identical?," *Bibliotheca Sacra*, April-June, 1991, 157–8.

Walton, J. C. 'Organization and the Origin of Life.' *Origins* 4 (1977), 16–35.

Warren, Mary Ann. 'On the Moral and Legal Status of Abortion.' Ch. 11 in Hugh LaFollette, ed. *Ethics in Practice: An Anthology*, 1997, 72–82. 4th edn, Oxford: Blackwell, 2014, 132–40.

Watters, Wendell W. 'Christianity and Mental Health.' *The Humanist* 37 (Nov./Dec. 1987).

Weatherford, Roy C. 'Freedom and Determinism.' In Ted Honderich, ed. *The Oxford Companion to Philosophy*. Oxford, 1995. 2nd edn, Oxford: Oxford University Press, 2005.

Wheeler, John A. 'Information, Physics, Quantum: The Search for Links.' In Wojciech Hubert Zurek. *Complexity, Entropy, and the Physics of Information*. The Proceedings of the 1988 Workshop on Complexity, Entropy, and the Physics of Information, held May–June, 1989, in Santa Fe, N. Mex. Redwood City, Calif.: Addison-Wesley, 1990.

Wigner, Eugene. 'The Unreasonable Effectiveness of Mathematics in the Natural Sciences', Richard Courant Lecture in Mathematical Sciences, delivered at New York University, 11 May 1959. *Communications in Pure and Applied Mathematics*, 13/1 (Feb. 1960), 1–14. Repr. in E. Wiger. *Symmetries and Reflections.* Bloomingon, Ind., 1967. Repr. Woodbridge, Conn.: Ox Bow Press, 1979, 222–37.

Wilford, John Noble. 'Sizing Up the Cosmos: An Astronomer's Quest.' *New York Times* (12 Mar. 1991), B9.

Wilkinson, David. 'Found in space?' Interview with Paul Davies. *Third Way* 22:6 (July 1999), 17–21.

Wilson, Edward O. 'The Ethical Implications of Human Sociobiology.' *Hastings Center Report* 10:6 (Dec. 1980), 27–9. doi: 10.2307/3560296.

Y

Yockey, Hubert. 'A Calculation of the Probability of Spontaneous Biogenesis by Information Theory.' *Journal of Theoretical Biology* 67 (1977), 377–98.

Yockey, Hubert. 'Self-Organisation Origin of Life Scenarios and Information Theory.' *Journal of Theoretical Biology* 91 (1981), 13–31.

STUDY QUESTIONS FOR TEACHERS AND STUDENTS

PART 1: HOW DO WE KNOW ANYTHING?

CHAPTER 1: HOW WE PERCEIVE THE WORLD

The problem stated

1.1 Are our senses always reliable? Can any of them mislead us?

1.2 Are there things which reason, by itself, cannot decide? If so, what kinds of things are they?

1.3 What is epistemology? How does it come by its name?

1.4 What is meant by saying that epistemology is a second-order discipline? Why is that important?

1.5 What is the difference between a scientist's approach to the external world, and a philosopher's?

1.6 Do you think we can know anything for certain about the external world?

1.7 What is scepticism? How did it first arise?

Forms of scepticism

1.8 Would you classify Socrates as a sceptic? If so, on what grounds?

1.9 How did some of Socrates' admirers misinterpret the purpose of his philosophical method?

1.10 How did Pyrrhonian sceptics try to prove that it was impossible to know anything for certain? Were their arguments sound?

1.11 Consider the example of the tower. Were the sceptics right in deducing from it that eyesight is always unreliable?

1.12 What were the motives behind the scepticism of philosophers like Sextus Empiricus? Do you approve?

1.13 Does the fact that we cannot know everything about everything mean that we cannot know anything for certain about anything?

Examples of extreme scepticism

1.14 Why was Descartes interested more in science than in philosophy?

1.15 In what respects did Descartes' assumptions about the universe differ from the Aristotelian tradition?

1.16 How did Descartes regard the information we get from our senses?

1.17 What was Descartes trying to achieve by doubting all he possibly could?

1.18 What for Descartes was the final guarantee of the possibility of reliable knowledge?

QUESTIONING OUR KNOWLEDGE

1.19 Put in your own words the sceptic's 'brain-in-a-vat' argument. What is he seeking to prove by this analogy?

1.20 Why do some philosophers say that the sceptic's challenge is unanswerable?

1.21 Have we any reason for supposing that our human brains are anything like a 'brain in a vat wired up to a computer'?

1.22 Do you agree that there is a fatal flaw in the sceptic's analogy that forbids our taking it seriously? If so, what is it?

1.23 What do you think is the source of human rationality? What gives it its validity?

1.24 How did G. E. Moore try to establish that we can know that the external world exists? Are you convinced by his demonstration?

How do we perceive the external world?

1.25 What do you understand by the terms Direct Realism and the Representative Theory of Perception?

1.26 If the Representative Theory were true, what would its implication be for the possibility of our perceiving what the external world is really like?

1.27 What are the different connotations of the verbs 'seeing' and 'perceiving'?

1.28 What is the difference between seeing an event and seeing a fact?

1.29 What are the main kinds of argument brought against Direct Realism?

1.30 What is a mirage? Is it true to say that when a person sees a mirage, he or she is actually seeing a real objective phenomenon? If so, what phenomenon?

1.31 Why does a straight stick, partly submerged in water, look bent?

1.32 What is meant by the laws of perspective?

1.33 Why is it important not to depend on one sense alone?

1.34 What does the thought experiment with the train teach us?

1.35 What are the strengths and weaknesses of
   (a) the Representative Theory of Perception;
   (b) Direct Realism?

1.36 Explain Roger Scruton's argument in your own words.

1.37 Do you think that we can have direct perception of at least some things in the external world?

CHAPTER 2: FALSE ALTERNATIVES AT THE EXTREMES

Idealism and realism

2.1 What do you understand by the philosophical term 'Idealism'?

2.2 How would you describe the difference between 'Idealism' and 'Realism'?

2.3 What is meant by saying that if there were no minds, there would be no pain?

2.4 How would you refute George Berkeley's views?

2.5 Would a flower in a remote valley have any fragrance if no one ever smelt it?

2.6 Is it true to say that when we study nature we can understand only what fits in with our preconceived concepts?

STUDY QUESTIONS FOR TEACHERS AND STUDENTS

2.7   Cite examples of the way that modern scientific discoveries have changed previously held concepts.

2.8   Are you an idealist or a realist?

Knowledge is subjective and knowledge is objective

2.9   In what sense is the term 'subject' used in epistemology?

2.10 What is meant by saying that in solving problems or in getting to know the world of physics, botany, biology or cookery we have to use creative thinking?

2.11 Do the constellations in the sky have any significance beyond what we give them? Or do they provide an objective way of marking the seasons, whether we notice them or not?

2.12 By what processes did John Locke think that we human beings gain knowledge of the external world?

2.13 Why did N. A. Berdyaev reject Locke's view?

2.14 How different is the Bible's view of the material world from that espoused by Hinduism and Neoplatonism?

2.15 What is meant by saying that, to be true, our knowledge of the external world must always be checked against objective reality?

Rationalism and empiricism

2.16 What is the meaning of the actual words 'Rationalism' and 'Empiricism'?

2.17 What is the difference between Rationalism and Empiricism as positions in epistemology?

2.18 What was the Enlightenment and why was it so named?

2.19 What slogan did Kant give to the Enlightenment thinkers? What did it mean in its historical context?

2.20 In what sense was Aristotle's view of the universe dualistic?

2.21 What effect did Galileo's and Newton's discoveries have on Aristotle's cosmology?

Locke's epistemological theory

2.22 According to Locke by what means and processes do we acquire our knowledge of the external world?

2.23 Did Locke, the empiricist, disagree with Descartes, the rationalist? What similarities were there between their views?

2.24 What was the basic difference between empiricism and rationalism?

2.25 What did Leibniz mean by 'necessary truths' and 'contingent truths'? Give examples of the difference between them.

2.26 What, according to Leibniz, was the basic weakness in Locke's empiricism?

2.27 What validation did Locke say was necessary for abstract mathematical theories? What is the significance of N. O. Lossky's work?

2.28 What kind of ideas have always to be checked for validity by reference to the external world?

2.29 Do you think human beings are born with certain innate ideas already in their mind? What would you say about Noam Chomsky's suggestion?

A serious weakness in Locke's epistemology

2.30 What does Locke mean by the term 'ideas'? From what two sources do we acquire them and how?

2.31 What, according to Locke, are primary qualities and what are secondary qualities?

2.32 What difference does Locke see between ideas caused in our minds by primary qualities in an object, and ideas caused by secondary qualities in that object?

2.33 Locke says that a snowball has the power to produce in us three ideas. What are they? And which of them is a primary quality in the snowball, and which a secondary quality?

2.34 What would you say to someone who said that our idea that a snowball is cold is false, and that there is no coldness in the snow?

2.35 What is happening when we see a lump of iron in a furnace glow red and then white? What is the cause of this phenomenon?

2.36 Are some stars really red, and some really blue? Or is that merely how they look to us?

2.37 Is grass really green?

2.38 What is visible light?

2.39 Is it true to say that colour is in the light?

2.40 What are the rods and cones in the eye? What is their function?

2.41 Would you say:
  (a) it is my eyes that see? or
  (b) it is my brain that sees? or
  (c) it is I who see?

David Hume's epistemology

2.42 What, according to Hume, are impressions and ideas?

2.43 What does Hume think is the process by which we come to know things?

2.44 How do we grasp spoken information?

2.45 How do you answer the question: What am I? Are you conscious of yourself as a distinct, individual personality?

2.46 Would you say that when you are asleep you are non-existent?

2.47 What would you say is the significance of the human self? What is a human being? What do you mean by a 'person'?

2.48 What does Hume try to prove by his example of two billiard balls?

2.49 Was Hume right to say that we cannot rightly infer causes from effects? Give examples to support your view.

2.50 Do you think that something can begin to exist without a cause?

2.51 What is meant by saying that Hume's epistemology disintegrates the human personality?

2.52 What is meant by saying that nothingness is the final destiny that all atheists hope for? Is it true?

2.53 Why is communication by spoken word superior to visual communication?

STUDY QUESTIONS FOR TEACHERS AND STUDENTS

CHAPTER 3: THE EPISTEMOLOGY OF IMMANUEL KANT

Kant's metaphysics

3.1   What is meant by calling Kant an Enlightenment philosopher?
3.2   What is the gist of his description of what the Enlightenment stood for?
3.3   What according to Kant is the difference between pure reason and practical reason?
3.4   What effect did this distinction have on Kant's philosophy?
3.5   Kant says that in order to engage in profitable investigation of nature, he had to assume a divine Author of the universe. What led him to that assumption? Would you agree with him?
3.6   On what moral grounds did Kant believe it was necessary to believe in God?
3.7   Would you agree with Kant that in order to make room for faith in God, you must deny the possibility of rationally proving God's existence?
3.8   What does Christ say about the possibility of knowing God in this present life?

Kant's Copernican revolution

3.9   Why was the question of causation so important to Kant?
3.10 On what ground did Descartes reject Harvey's explanation of the circulation of the blood?
3.11 What was Leibniz's argument against Newton's theory of gravitation?
3.12 Why did Hume say that our ideas of causation are invalid?
3.13 How did Kant try to reconcile Hume's empiricism with his own rationalism?
3.14 Where did Kant say that we get our idea of causation?
3.15 What lesson is the example of the rotten apple meant to illustrate?
3.16 What change in the process of our getting to know the external world did Kant propose by his 'Copernican revolution'?
3.17 What is meant by saying that nature has its own created intelligibility?
3.18 What should our true attitude to nature be in scientific research?
3.19 In what sense was Kant's proposed Copernican revolution in philosophy the very opposite of Copernicus's revolution in cosmology?
3.20 What did the Greeks mean by 'hubris'?

Kant's First Principle of a priori synthetic knowledge

3.21 What is the difference between analytic propositions and synthetic propositions?
3.22 Which of the following propositions are analytic and which synthetic?
   (a) The sun rose at 6 a.m.
   (b) The moon is the body that circles the earth.
   (c) Tuesday comes after Monday.
   (d) Tuesday was a wet day.
3.23 Would you agree that 7 + 5 = 12 is a synthetic proposition? If not, why not?
3.24. What are the laws of logic? How can we know for certain in advance that they will always be true?

3.25 What logical law forbids us to think that a birch tree is also an oak tree?
3.26 How does Kant seek to prove that our knowledge that 'a straight line between two points is the shortest' is a priori synthetic? Are you convinced by his argument?
3.27 Does it strike you as strange that we can know some things about objects in advance without having first experienced them, met them, or heard about them?

Kant's Second Principle of a priori synthetic knowledge

3.28 What does Kant mean by the 'Transcendental Aesthetic'?
3.29 What did Kant think that space is? Did he think that it really exists? If not, how do we come to imagine it does?
3.30 Do you think that space is something? Or is it just nothing? And if it is nothing, how can it be said to exist?
3.31 What, according to Kant, is time?
3.32 What is the difference between Euclidean and non-Euclidean geometries?
3.33 If Kant got his ideas of space from Newton, what does that show us about Kant's 'Transcendental Aesthetic'?
3.34 Would a modern astronaut have the same idea of space and time as Kant?

The limits of knowability according to Kant: epistemology and psychology

3.35 What does Kant mean by the term phenomena?
3.36 What does Kant mean by the term noumena?
3.37 What did Kant say about the possibility of our knowing what a rainbow is, and what rain is?
3.38 Would science agree that we cannot know what rain is in itself? Would you?
3.39 How were the views of Ernst Mach about the question of the reality of atoms influenced by Kant's theories?
3.40 What is meant by saying that Kant put an impassable gulf between our mental and spiritual powers?
3.41 What do you understand by the terms 'soul' or 'spirit'?
3.42 On what ground did Kant say that we cannot know by pure reason that we have a soul? Does it make sense to you?
3.43 What, according to Kant, is the attitude that practical reason has towards the existence of the soul?
3.44 Did Kant think that a human being is composed of nothing but soulless matter?
3.45 Why did Kant say that we ought to concentrate on objects of experience only rather than on spiritualism?
3.46 What kind of spiritual experience does the Bible offer for our enjoyment?

The limits of knowability according to Kant: cosmology and theology

3.47 What is the first traditional argument, given here, for the existence of God?
3.48 What is the second traditional argument, given here, for the existence of God?

3.49 What was Kant's objection to the argument from design?

3.50 What does Kant mean by saying that the purposiveness and order of the universe could only prove the existence of an architect of the universe, not a Creator? And why does he say it? Would you agree?

3.51 What does the Bible say we can learn about God from creation?

3.52 What would modern science say about Kant's claim that we should not infer non-observable causes from observable effects?

3.53 What do you think about Kant's argument that if God were the cause of the series of all the causes and effects in the universe, God would have to be part of the series? What does the Bible say about it?

3.54 What is meant by saying that Kant's Copernican revolution perverts the true relation between reason and God?

3.55 What would you say is the source of man's power of reason?

3.56 When Kant said that God's existence cannot be proved by pure reason, what did he mean by pure reason; and how is pure reason different from practical reason?

CHAPTER 4: REASON AND FAITH

A fourth false alternative

4.1 Why do some people regard 'faith' and 'reason' as mutually exclusive terms?

4.2 What kinds of things do we all believe in without their first having been proved by pure reason?

4.3 In what sense is science dependent on faith?

4.4 What is the difference between knowledge and wisdom?

4.5 In what way does love affect the success of our cognitive faculties?

4.6 Do you think that our cognitive faculties are designed for a purpose just like the heart is? If so, in what sense are they designed and for what purpose?

4.7 Would you say that it is, strictly speaking, irrational to believe that God created our faculty of reason? If so, why? What alternative origin of reason would you suggest?

The nature of theism's faith

4.8 Why is epistemology concerned with our knowledge of facts rather than our knowledge of persons? What is the difference between the two?

4.9 If an atheist were to argue that you must first prove philosophically that God exists, before you are justified in saying anything about his qualities, how might a theist reply?

4.10 What is meant by 'the ontological argument for God'?

4.11 What is meant by 'the cosmological argument for God'?

4.12 What is meant by 'the moral argument for God'?

4.13 Read again the passage cited from Romans 1:19–21. What would you say are the major points it is making?

The points raised by Romans 1:19–21

4.14 What is meant by saying that God must take, and has taken, the initiative in making himself known to us?

4.15 Is it true to say that if someone lets us get to know him personally it sets up a relationship between the known and the knower? Would that be true of our being allowed to get to know God?

4.16 What two things about the Creator are said to be made evident to us through creation?

4.17 What is meant by anthropomorphism? Do you think that humans have created God in humanity's image?

4.18 'Theists believe that the human race's Source is greater than the human race is. Atheists believe that the human race's Source was less than the human race is.' Discuss.

4.19 Give examples of what is meant by intuition. What is meant by claiming that we perceive God's power and divinity in the same way as we perceive a rose is beautiful?

4.20 Christ said that God hides some things from the wise. What things? And why?

4.21 What do modern epistemologists mean by 'prior beliefs' or 'properly basic beliefs'? Give some examples. What has this got to do with belief in God?

4.22 Do you feel the same as Kant did, when he contemplated 'the starry heavens'?

4.23 What would you say is the difference between mental assent to the proposition that God exists, and personal faith in God?

Objections and answers

4.24 In your experience what are the main reasons that people give for not being aware of God?

4.25 Which of those reasons in your judgment is the strongest?

4.26 What do Bible scholars mean by the progress of divine revelation?

4.27 What is meant by saying that knowledge of God is relational and not just theoretical?

4.28 By what analogies and terms does the Bible describe God's relation with those who believe in him?

4.29 What false turn did early humanity take in relation to God according to the Bible?

4.30 'To live as if there were no Creator is to live an unrealistic untruth.' Discuss.

4.31 How would someone who claims to know God, justify his claim?

PART 2: WHAT IS TRUTH?

CHAPTER 5: IN SEARCH OF TRUTH

Our ambivalent attitude to truth

5.1 Do you agree that our attitude to truth is ambivalent? If so, why is it ambivalent?

5.2 Would you ever be prepared to say publicly 'I hate the truth, and shall do all I can to suppress it'? If not, why not?

5.3 In what way does the question of truth affect:
   (a) sport;
   (b) business;
   (c) history;
   (d) marriage and family life;
   (e) justice?

5.4 Consider the five objections listed, which are sometimes given for rejecting the idea of objective, universal truth. Argue for and against any one (or all) of them.

5.5 State what you understand by the term 'metanarrative'. Why have metanarratives fallen out of fashion?

5.6 To what extent, if at all, is it justifiable to impose intellectual acceptance of:
   (a) an ideology; or,
   (b) a religion,
   by force?

5.7 Why, do you think, has the Bible been suppressed at various times in the course of history by such diverse elements as paganism, atheism and Christendom?

5.8 What worldwide effects do you foresee will result from the globalisation of knowledge?

Long-term consequences of the devaluation of objective truth

5.9 What has the pursuit of truth got to do with education?

5.10 If social cohesion depends ultimately on mutual trust, on what basis can trust be built if not on truth?

5.11 Is there any real difference between a history book and a novel? If so, what is it?

5.12 What should be the aim of a historical documentary film? Is it to convey the truth, or to entertain? Some producers of documentaries have changed the historical facts in some places in order to gain the sympathy and therefore the better interest of the viewers. Is it right to mix fiction with history?

5.13 Is it possible for a businessman always to tell the truth? Is falsehood acceptable, or is it always wrong, even in business?

5.14 On what grounds, or by what standard, would you be prepared to say that something is a true work of art?

5.15 If in the course of some dispute you said 'the truth is on my side', what exactly would you mean by the truth?

Conventionalism and the definition of truth

5.16 What is 'conventionalism'? Do you think that its basic contention is true? Give your reasons.

5.17 What is meant by saying that languages are merely sets of symbols whose meanings are culturally determined? Give examples from any two languages you know. Does it mean that all truth conveyed by language is only relative?

5.18 Do you agree with the contention that we all have an idea of what truth is? Give examples from everyday life that illustrate your view.
5.19 What is the correspondence theory of truth? How valid are the objections made against it?
5.20 What is the coherence theory of truth?
5.21 What is meant by saying that coherence is a necessary but not a sufficient condition for truth?
5.22 What is the pragmatic theory of truth? Cite arguments for and against the pragmatic theory.
5.23 Which theory of truth makes most sense to you?

CHAPTER 6: PARTICULAR TRUTHS AND ULTIMATE TRUTH

6.1 What is meant by talking about different levels of truth?
6.2 Do you think that there are different kinds of truth? If so, give examples.
6.3 What do Christians mean by saying that all truth is God's truth?
6.4 What kind of lessons can we learn from history?
6.5 What is the difference between history and historicism?
6.6 Is it possible by studying past history to predict how the future will turn out? If not, why not? If yes, on what basis?
6.7 What does Hegel mean by dialectic?
6.8 Why does Lossky say that Hegel's theory breaks a fundamental law of logic? Do you agree?
6.9 What is there about Hegel's thought that leads people to say that he was a pantheist or a panentheist?
6.10 What did Hegel mean by 'Spirit' or 'Mind'?
6.11 Does Hegel's theory about the development of human freedom match the facts of history? Is there no slavery and slave trade anywhere in the world today?
6.12 Is the morality of the modern world better than, say, that in the Roman Empire?

CHAPTER 7: THE BIBLICAL VIEW OF TRUTH

A preliminary study of the word and its usage

7.1 In light of the Hebrew word *ᵉmeṯ* do you see any relation between the idea of 'truth' on the one hand, and of 'faithfulness' and 'reliability' on the other?
7.2 Read 1 John 3:17, Galatians 2:13–14 and Genesis 32:9–10 again and then discuss:
   (a) What is hypocrisy?
   (b) Why does it matter if, in religious contexts, someone acts inconsistently with his professed beliefs? Can the same thing happen in other walks of life?
   (c) What damage do I do to other people if I constantly break promises that I have made to them? What damage do I do to myself?

7.3 Read Exodus 18:21 again. In light of the fact that in some countries bribery is endemic and is almost a way of life, discuss the following:
   (a) If you had been unjustly defrauded, would you see nothing wrong if the fraudster bribed the judge and jury to deliver a verdict in his favour?
   (b) Is it wrong for a government official to demand and accept bribes?
   (c) What exactly is wrong with bribery?
7.4 Read Jeremiah 9:3–5 and Zechariah 8:16 again. Discuss: what are the social, commercial and political effects if people come to accept that misrepresentation, deceit, falsehoods, lies, broken promises and agreements are the normal and only-to-be-expected way of life?
7.5 Read John 4:22–24 again; then discuss the question: is religious worship true, provided only that the worshipper is sincere and finds worship aesthetically and emotionally satisfying?

Different ways of expressing truth

7.6 Read Psalm 23 and then discuss its poetic imagery:
   (a) Attempt to express its meaning in modern prose. Can it be done successfully?
   (b) What is meant by 'the valley of the shadow of death'?
   (c) What does 'dwelling in the house of the Lord' mean?
7.7 Of what relevance and importance is the truth or otherwise of the propositions of the marriage contract for the successful development of a secure personal relationship between husband and wife?
7.8 If someone asked you your name, and you told him truthfully what it was, and the person refused to believe you and implied that you were a liar, how would you feel?
7.9 'Experience is worth a ton of theory.' Do you agree? Or is true theory important for validating experience?
7.10 'For an atheist the universe is not a revelation of anything. It simply means what human reason decides it means.' Explain and discuss.
7.11 'Truth is exclusive; by its very nature it must deny its contrary.' Do you agree?
7.12 Some philosophers have maintained that the contingent facts of history can never teach us eternal, necessary truths. Do you suppose that Christians would agree? If not, why not?
7.13 What, according to the Bible, does 'eternal life' mean?

CHAPTER 8: TRUTH ON TRIAL

Coming to face the truth

8.1 What is meant by saying that when we stand in front of the truth and decide what to do with it, it is we who are on trial?
8.2 Why, do you think, did the citizens of ancient Athens regard Socrates as a subversive influence?

8.3 What other famous trial scenes do you know of in history or in literature? Cite any you know.

8.4 Is the proverb true that 'one word of truth outweighs the world'?

The trial of Christ, its background and first phase

8.5 When Constantine the Great converted to Christianity, he is said to have put the sign of the cross on the military standards of his armies. Was that a good thing for Christianity, or a bad thing?

8.6 Can genuine belief in an ideology, or a religion, be produced by force?

8.7 Why, do you think, did the Jewish high priests choose Barabbas rather than Jesus?

Pilate discovers his own responsibility

8.8 Do you feel sorry for Pilate?

8.9 What would you have done if you had been Pilate? Would you have had the courage to release Jesus?

8.10 What was it about Jesus that so antagonised the Jewish priests?

8.11 What in your mind does the Christian symbol of the cross stand for?

8.12 When Jesus said that he came into the world to bear witness to the truth, what do you think he meant by 'truth'?

8.13 In what way was there more to the death of Jesus than, say, the death of Socrates or of any other martyr for truth in the course of history?

8.14 Study the painting by Nikolai Ge (in 1890) entitled 'What is truth? Christ and Pilate'.[1] How do you interpret the gesture that Ge has given to Pilate? Is it meant to express cynicism, impatience or something else?

PART 3: POSTMODERNISM

CHAPTER 9: POSTMODERNISM, PHILOSOPHY AND LITERATURE

Introduction

9.1 What fields of thought does postmodernism cover?

9.2 What reasons have we for discussing in the context of epistemology postmodernism's attitude to literary criticism?

9.3 How would you describe the relation of postmodernism to modernism? What are the similarities and the dissimilarities between them?

9.4 Why do postmodernists tend to resent any external constraints on their freedom to interpret literature in any way they please?

9.5 What do postmodernists mean by the term 'metanarratives'? Why don't they like them?

9.6 What are Jacques Derrida's position and significance in the history and practice of literary criticism?

---

[1] [online] http://www.dartmouth.edu/~russ15/russia_PI/Russian_art.html.

Prohibition of appeal to the intended meaning of the author

9.7 What do you understand by 'The Intentional Fallacy Theory' in literary criticism?

9.8 What reasons can you adduce in favour of this theory?

9.9 What attitude does Ricoeur take to this theory?

9.10 How does the way a judge interprets an Act of Parliament support the theory?

9.11 What obvious limits must be put to the theory?

9.12 What use did Freud make of the Oedipus myth? What did he mean by the Oedipus complex?

9.13 The ancient Greek tragedian wrote a play based on the Oedipus myth. To what extent can we, on the basis of the text of this play, be sure of what the author did *not* intend the play to mean? Why is that important?

Exaggerations of reader-response criticism

9.14 What do you understand by the reader-response theory of literary criticism?

9.15 To what extent can we say that the meaning of a literary text is simply the meaning that any reader sees in it? Are there any limits to this point of view?

9.16 What point is the reference to the Mona Lisa meant to illustrate?

9.17 What is meant by saying that being free from having to consider the intentions of a text's author does not imply that we are free not to take the text itself seriously?

9.18 What features of a text constrain our interpretation of it?

9.19 'A poem really means whatever any reader seriously believes it to mean.' Do you agree? Derrida does not like it when this principle is applied to his writings. What conclusion do you draw from that?

9.20 Are there any limits to the different interpretations that various conductors put upon a musical score?

9.21 'The number of possible meanings of a poem is itself infinite.' What would the implications be if this were true?

Questions raised by the quotation from Stanley Fish

9.22 Read again the quotation from Stanley Fish on page 244. On what ground does Fish say that if two people disagree about the meaning of a text, you cannot appeal to the text in order to decide which of them is right?

9.23 Is it true to say that if Fish's principle were true it would spell the end of literary criticism? Why would it?

9.24 What would a judge do if two businessmen disagreed about the interpretation of a business contract, and one of them sued the other in court? Would the judge refuse to consult the text of the contract in order to reach his decision? If not, why not?

9.25 What possible decisions could the judge come to over the two men's conflicting interpretations of the contract?

9.26 No one can say that his or her interpretation of a large literary work is the final truth. But does that mean that any one interpretation is just as good as another? If not, why not?

9.27 Would it be true to say that the nature and structure of the atom are whatever any scientist seriously believes them to be?

9.28 Would it be right to say that, if two scientists disagreed about the interpretation of nuclear particles, there would be no point in continuing to study nuclear particles?

The denial of metaphysics

9.29. Why cannot a translator of a Russian text into Japanese translate word for word?

9.30 'Translate meaning, not words.' What does this mean, and how does one go about it? Is 'meaning' somehow different from words?

9.31 What did the ancient Stoics mean by the term 'logos'? What relation did this logos have to the universe and to man?

9.32 What does the New Testament mean by the term Logos? What relation does the Logos have to creation and to man (see John 1:1–4)?

9.33 What does the term 'logocentrism' mean in Derrida's philosophy and literary theory? What does his rejection of it imply?

9.34 What does Derrida mean by 'the Leibnizian Book'? And why does he repudiate it?

9.35 'Meaning must await being said or written in order to become what it is: meaning.' What do you think Derrida means by this?

9.36 Read again Wolterstorff's comment on Derrida's theory. Is Wolterstorff's conclusion logically true?

Presence

9.37 Have you ever been in a dark room and sensed that there was someone present, although you could not see or hear him or her?

9.38 What do you think Derrida means by presence as applied
   (a) to God in himself?
   (b) to God in relation to us?
   (c) in relation to the names related to fundamentals, principles and to the centre of all things?

9.39 How does Jonathan Culler explain the logocentrism of metaphysics in Derrida's thought?

9.40 Derrida is the implacable foe of metaphysics. Why then does he say that it is logically impossible, (a) to escape metaphysics, and (b) to disprove it?

9.41 In light of that, why do you think he persists in trying to escape it?

The assertion that writing precedes speech and that signification creates meaning

9.42 'Words are primarily sounds.' What does this mean?

9.43 What evidence is there that speech preceded writing?

9.44 What various forms of writing have there been in the course of history?

9.45 What do you think Derrida means by claiming that 'there is no linguistic sign before writing'?

STUDY QUESTIONS FOR TEACHERS AND STUDENTS

9.46 Do you agree with Derrida's claim? If not, why not?
9.47 Why, do you think, may Derrida have found the idea attractive that writing has priority over speech?
9.48 What advantages has writing over speech?

Conventionalism's first denial

9.49 What do philosophers and language theorists mean when they deny that language has direct contact with reality?
9.50 What does conventionalism hold about language?
9.51 To what extent is conventionalism true?
9.52 In what respects is it not true?
9.53 'A word can denote something that does not exist, and never did exist, in the world.' Cite examples of this.
9.54 Cite examples of words in your own language that over the centuries have changed their meaning.
9.55 What is the difference in meaning between the English word 'warm' and the German word 'warm'?
9.56 What does this difference *not* imply?
9.57 If, as Derrida holds, signification creates meaning, did our word 'dinosaur' create the dinosaurs?
9.58 What is meant by saying that the word 'atom' originally referred only to a theoretical concept?
9.59 Has this concept proved wholly, or in part, true to reality?
9.60 Why has the meaning of the word 'atom' changed over the course of history?

Conventionalism's second and third denials

9.61 What logical concepts do the two Greek syntactical constructions mentioned in the text express?
9.62 Why would you have to have these logical concepts clear in your mind in order to understand what these two constructions express?
9.63 What is the logical difference between murder and accidental homicide? How important is the difference?
9.64 What does Noam Chomsky mean by claiming that a child has an innate language faculty? Do you think he could be right?
9.65 Read again the quotation from Bates, Thal and Marchman. What alternative explanations of universal grammar do they give? Which do you think is more likely to be true?
9.66 Do you think a child of five could understand what 'doing something on purpose' means as distinct from doing something without intending to do it?
9.67 Do you think that scientists create the principles according to which the universe runs? Or do they just discover them?
9.68 How, do you think, people come to feel that torturing children for fun is wrong?

9.69 On what supposition does the idea rest that human language cannot tell us anything about God? Do you think that the supposition has been proved true?

The denial that words have any intrinsic meaning

9.70 What does Derrida mean by saying that the meaning of a word is always deferred? Give examples to show in what sense that is true.

9.71 Does this mean:
  (a) that no word has any core meaning?
  (b) that this deference of meaning makes possible an infinite play of meanings?

9.72 What does Derrida mean by 'deconstructing' a text?

9.73 'Deconstruction is negative, and the terminology it uses is that of a revolutionary.' What does this mean? Is it a fair judgment of Derrida's theory?

9.74 What are the objects of deconstruction's negative, subversive criticism?

9.75 'Derrida's literary criticism is motivated by opposition to all forms of power and privilege.' Comment.

9.76 'What deconstruction wishes to put in place of traditional literary criticism would lead to literary-critical anarchy.' What does this mean? Is this true?

9.77 'In refusing to have deconstruction applied to his own theory, Derrida contradicts his own theory.' How?

9.78 'Derrida's theory offers no real positive help towards understanding a literary text.' Is this true? If so, why?

9.79 What do you understand by the ideal that Derrida sets before him in writing a literary work? What sense does it make to you?

9.80 Do you think that Derrida's experience as a student in the French universities in the 1960s helps us to understand his own attitude to literary criticism? Does it engender in you any sympathy for him?

CHAPTER 10: POSTMODERNISM AND SCIENCE

10.1 Does the fact that science can be motivated by political or social considerations invalidate its truth claims?

10.2 What evidence would you advance for the idea that science, though influenced by culture, gives us results that are independent of culture?

10.3 Why can science not give us the moral apparatus with which to criticise its activities? Where are such moral criteria to be found?

10.4 Explain the 'Sokal affair' in your own words. What do you deduce from it about the validity of the postmodern critique of science?

10.5 Should scientists be free to say what they like about the universe regardless of any facts? In your opinion, are there any objective facts about the universe?

10.6 What are some of the consequences of rejecting the idea of absolute truth?

10.7 Subject for a debate: 'This house believes that postmodernism is intellectually incoherent.'

APPENDIX: THE SCIENTIFIC ENDEAVOUR

Scientific method

A.1 In what different ways have you heard the word 'science' used? How would you define it?

A.2 How is induction understood as part of our everyday experience and also of the scientific endeavour?

A.3 In what ways does deduction differ from induction, and what role does each play in scientific experiments?

A.4 Do you find the idea of 'falsifiability' appealing, or unsatisfactory? Why?

A.5 How does abduction differ from both induction and deduction, and what is the relationship among the three?

Explaining explanations

A.6 How many levels of explanation can you think of to explain a cake, in terms of how was it made, what was it made from, and why was it made? What can scientists tell us? What can 'Aunt Olga' tell us?

A.7 In what ways is reductionism helpful in scientific research, and in what ways could it be limiting, or even detrimental, to scientific research?

A.8 How do you react to physicist and theologian John Polkinghorne's statement that reductionism relegates 'our experiences of beauty, moral obligation, and religious encounter to the epiphenomenal scrapheap. It also destroys rationality'?

The basic operational presuppositions of the scientific endeavour

A.9 What is meant by the statement 'Observation is dependent on theory'?

A.10 What are some of the axioms upon which your thinking about scientific knowledge rests?

A.11 What does trust have to do with gaining knowledge?

A.12 What does belief have to do with gaining knowledge?

A.13 According to physicist and philosopher of science Thomas Kuhn, how do new scientific paradigms emerge?

SCRIPTURE INDEX

OLD TESTAMENT

Genesis
1:31   75
3   153
3:5   209
32:9–10   201
42:16   200

Exodus
18:21–22   202
34:6   131

Leviticus
19:18   152

Deuteronomy
4:12–15   99
6:5   152
8:1–6   152

Job
book   205

Psalms
book   205
23:5   205
94:9   146 n. 4
103:12   205
111:2   19
139:7   249

Proverbs
1:7   140–1

Isaiah
book   205
44:20   203
46:9–10   190
59:3, 4, 6, 8   166–7
59:13–15   166–7
65:16   206

Jeremiah
book   205
9:3–6   202–3
29:13   154

Zechariah
8:16–17   203
9:9   219–20

NEW TESTAMENT

Matthew
11:25   147
11:27–29   108
13   151
22:16–17   202
28:18–20   222

Mark
4   151
5:33   202
14:56–59   201
15:10–15   223

Luke
8   151
11:9–10   154
23:13–25   223

John
1:11–13   152 n. 15
1:12–13   108
1:18   210
2:13–22   217
3:1–16   108
3:1–8   129
3:3   206
4:17–18   200
4:22–24   204
4:24   129
5:18   218
5:24   206
6:27   203–4
6:32   203–4
7:17   154
7:38–39   129
8:31–47   216
8:31–34   165
10:14–15   108
11:47–53   217–8
12:12–19   219–20
14:6   165, 210, 235–6
14:9   210
16:13   209
17:3   108, 203, 210–11
17:28   249 n. 19
18:1–11   218–19
18:12   218 n. 4
18:28–32   219
18:33–38   219–21
18:37–38   216
18:38–40   221
19:1–6   223
19:7–8   223–4
19:7   218
19:9–11   224–6
19:12–15   226
19:12   217
20:30–31   240

Acts
2:23   227
17:28   249 n. 19

Romans
1:18–32   153
1:18–20   208
1:19–21   144–5
1:20   131
1:25   203, 208
2:15   261
5:5   129

Romans
5:10–11	227
8:14–17	152 n. 15
8:14–16	129
8:26–30	152 n. 15

1 Corinthians
1:18–31	154
1:21	147
8:2–3	141
14:20	147

Galatians
1:11–12	209
2:5	209
2:13–14	201
3:15–17	207–8
4:1–3	152
4:6–7	109
4:9	108
5:7	209

Ephesians
1:10	190
1:13	209

Colossians
1:16	210
1:17	249
1:18	222
3:1	222

1 Thessalonians
1:9	203
2:13	201

2 Thessalonians
2:3–4	209
2:9–12	209

1 Timothy
1:13–15	208
2:4	209
6:13–14	222

2 Timothy
3:7	209
4:3–4	210

Hebrews
1:3	210
8:1–2	204–5
10:17	205
11:6	149, 154

James
2:19	109

1 Peter
1:10–12	238

1 John
2:3–6	155
3:1–2	152 n. 15
3:17	200, 202
4:10	227
5:10–12	207
5:20–21	211
5:20	109

Revelation
1:8	190
3:14	207

OTHER ANCIENT LITERATURE

Aristotle
Nicomachean Ethics 11
Metaphysics
iv.–7 170–1

Euripides
Bacchae 224, 234

Lucian of Samosata
Vera Historia 25

Plato
Apology
39b–d 215–6
Timaeus 11

Sophocles
Oedipus Tyrannus 234, 240–1

Theophrastus
On Stone 32

GENERAL INDEX

A
abduction 303–5
Adams, John Couch 301
adoption (thrology) 129, 152–3
aesthetic, transcendental 121–3
afterlife 14–15, 108. *See also* DEATH; HEAVEN
agency 305–8
alētheia 199, 249
alēthēs 199
alēthinos 199
'āmēn 206–7
analytic, transcendental 123–4
anthropomorphism 146
anthrōpos 223 n. 9
antithesis 51
Anyon, Roger 283
appearance 125–7
Aquinas, Thomas 127
archē 249
Aristobulus 146
Aristotle 11, 21, 77, 98, 110, 170–1, 291
arithmetic 106, 119–20
astronomy 28, 77, 111–13, 296–7, 298–9, 301–2, 319–20
ataraxia 51–2
atheism 141–2, 208–9, 306. *See also* INDEPENDENCE FROM GOD
and God as Creator 24
Austen, Jane 234
Austin, J. L. 173–4
authorial intent 237–45
authority 217, 224–5 235, 285, 290, 291, 302–3, 316
and deconstruction 264, 265, 269
of reason 140–2
ultimate/supreme xii
axioms 79, 315–16

B
Bacon, Francis 26, 247, 273, 291–2
Bacon, Roger 164

basic beliefs 148–9
Bates, E. 260
Beardsley, Monroe 238
being, pure 192
Berdyaev, Nicolai Alexandrovitch 73, 74–5
Berkeley, George 70
Big Bang theory 36, 153–4, 260
biology 305, 309
Bradley, F. H. 175
Brahe, Tycho 296–7, 298
'brain in a vat' analogy 54–6
Bristol, Evelyn 234 n. 1
Broackes, Justin 89
Bronowski, Jacob 38
business, dishonesty in 167–8

C
Caputo, John D. 266–7
Cartmill, Matt 275–6
causation 85, 89, 94–9, 110–14, 130–1, 132–3, 307
chiliarch 218 n. 4
Chomsky, Noam 80 n. 15, 259
Christ *See* JESUS CHRIST
Christianity 14
civilisation
 Egyptian 188
 Greek 188
 Harappan 188
 Indus Valley 188
 Minoan 188–9
'cogito, ergo sum' 54
coherence theory of truth 175–7
cohors 218 n. 4
Collins, Francis S. 28
Collins, Harry 283
colour 84–9
consciousness in direct experience 34
contingency 81, 130, 131, 143 n. 3
contradiction 169–70, 192
conventionalism 169–70, 255–61

Copernican revolution 110, 115, 117, 124, 125, 133–4, 154, 319, 320
Copernicus, Nicolas 114–15, 117, 281, 296
correspondence theory of truth 170–5, 177, 273–4
cosmology 53, 77, 130–3
counterfeit vs. reality 30–3
creation 78, 208–9
  biblical view of 74–5
Crick, Sir Francis 289, 309, 312
Crosman, Robert 242–3
Culler, Jonathan 250, 253–4, 255, 263, 267

D
Darwin, Charles 26–7
data
  collection 291–3, 298–301
  sense 97
Davies, Paul 150, 279
Dawkins, Richard 142, 284, 307–8, 309, 320–1
death 14, 15. *See also* LIFE AFTER DEATH
deception 53–5, 56
deconstruction 236–7, 263–7
  and authority 264–5
  and literary appreciation 267
  and objectivity 265–7
  and power 265
  and privilege 265
deduction/inference 292, 296–8, 303–5
  defined 291–2
Derrida, Jacques 233, 236–7, 239, 243, 245–51, 261–3, 266–9
  and logocentrism 246–50
Descartes, René 52–4, 78, 80–1, 111, 112, 127
design in nature 13, 105, 130–2
determinism 17, 34
Dewey, John 178, 273–4
dialectic 192, 195, 196
dialectical materialism 23
Diocletian 164
Direct Realism 58–61
dishonesty in business 167–8
divine revelation 24–9, 131–2, 133, 143–9, 196, 208–11, 261
DNA 28, 289, 311–12

dogmatism 48, 51, 52, 104, 110, 150
Dostoevsky, Fyodor 150, 234
dualism 77
duty/duties xiii, 7, 9, 14

E
education 3–4
Egyptian civilisation 188
Greek civilisation 188
eidos 249
Einstein, Albert 28, 277, 281, 317
Ellis, John M. 236, 268–9
emergence 311–12
'emet 199, 200
empeiria 75
empiricism 70 n. 2, 75–99
  compared to rationalism 75–8
  defined 75–6
  and Hume, David 89–99
  and Locke, John 78–99
energeia 249
Enlightenment, the 76–7, 103–34, 116, 117, 235
Epimenides 249
epistēmē 46
epistemology 46–8, 125–7, 277
  defined 46
epochē 51
equilibrium 49
ethics 278
Euripides 224, 234
evil, problem of 150
evolution (organic) 13–14, 28, 142
existentialism 38
experience xi, xii, xiv, 4, 9, 26, 34, 75–8, 80–1, 114, 292, 302, 312, 314, 315–16
  of God 108–9, 117
  a posteriori 113, 115
  a priori 113
  consciousness in direct 34
  spiritual 128–30
experimentation 110–11, 291, 292, 295, 320
explanation 305–13

F
facts 258
  nature of 173–5
  objective 173
faith 107–8, 109–10, 316–17

and reason 137–55
and science 140
and theism 142–9
fallacy, the intentional 238, 240–1, 255
falsifiability 301–2
feelings (subjective) 173
Fish, Stanley 244–5
Flieger, Jerry Aline 264
flux 49
Fodor, Jerry 260
Forms (Plato) 70 n. 1, 77
Fotion, Nicholas 23
free will 17, 34, 225, 226–7, 312
freedom 108–9, 163, 168, 193–5, 235
Frege, Gottlob 169
Freud, Sigmund 142, 240–1

G
Galileo Galilei 17, 53 n. 7, 77, 281, 291
Galle, Johann 301
Geist 194
genes 142, 184
geometry 106, 120–1
    Euclidean 116, 122–3
    non-Euclidean 116, 122–3
globalisation of knowledge 165–6
Gnosticism 74–5
God. *See also* GOD AS CREATOR
    awareness of 149–53, 249
    belief in 105–9
    character of 54, 204, 207, 216
    dependence on 146
    existence of 54, 56–7, 89, 105–8, 109, 117, 130–4, 137–9, 142, 147–8, 154, 306–8
        cosmological argument for 105, 130–3, 143 n. 3
        moral argument for 143 n. 3
        proof of 107, 147–9, 153
        ontological argument for 143 n. 3
        physico-theological (design) argument for 105, 130–3, 143 n. 3
    experience of 108–9, 117
    gratitude to 153
    and history 196
    image of 14
    independence from 153
    knowledge of 107–10, 133–4, 141, 154–5, 261
    love of 145, 152, 155
    mercy of 145
    as personal 143–4, 145–6
    power of 145
    relationship with 152–5
    and revelation 24–9, 131–2, 133, 143–9, 196, 261
    will of 154
    wisdom of 148
God as Creator 26–7, 28, 46, 191, 306–7. *See also* GOD
    atheism and 24
    of humanity 14–15, 26
    of rationality 14
    and science 26–9
    of universe 317–18
gospel 209–10
Grootuis, Douglas 168
guilt 34
Guyer, Paul 103

H
hallucinations 59–60, 61–2
hamartia 117
Hamlet (Shakespeare) 234
Harappan civilisation 188
Harvey, William 110–11, 112
heaven 15
Hegel, Georg Wilhelm Friedrich 23, 175, 191–6
Hegelianism 191
Heraclitus 49
Hero of Alexandria 22
Hertz, Heinrich Rudolf 315
Herzen, Alexander Ivanovich 191
high priest 217, 218, 220
hina 259
Hinduism 74–5
historicism 186–96
history 22–4, 33, 176, 186, 196
    and God 196
    and reality 33
    of philosophy 193–5
    purpose of 196
Hobbes, Thomas 273
Holy Spirit 129–30, 194 n. 14, 195
Hookway, C. J. 55, 57
Hospers, John 120
hōste 259
human

freedom 108-9, 163, 168, 193-5
mind 51-2, 70-2, 79, 81-2 89-91, 172, 194-5
progress 189, 275
reason 234-5
human
rights 14-15, 17
spirit 75
humanity. *See also* MAN
individual significance 35-6
nature of 14-15
origin of 36, 302
purpose of 14, 15, 36-8
rights of 14-15, 17
superior to non-personal beings 34-5
Hume, David 78, 89-99, 110, 113, 114, 115, 128 n. 45
and causation 94-9
and ideas 90-1
and impressions 90-1, 93-5
philosophy of mind 89-91
and Representative Theory of Perception 89-91
and self 92-4
Husserl, Edmund 48
hypotheses 111-12, 291-3, 296-7, 298-301, 304-5
hypothetico-deductive method 292, 296-8, 303-5

I
idealism 69-70
defined 69-70, 71
ideas (Hume) 90-1
defined 90
validation of (Locke) 79-80
idolatry 154, 203
ignorance 50
illusion 29-30, 49
image of God 14
immortality 78, 104, 105, 108, 127
impressions (Hume) 90-1, 93-5
defined 90
independence from God 153
induction 292, 293-5, 296, 298, 317
Indus Valley civilisation 188
inference/deduction 292, 296-8, 303-5
defined 291-2
information 91-2, 310-12
Intelligible World 77, 98

intent, authorial 237-45
interpretation 110-11, 242-3, 255, 263
legal 239-40, 244-5
of literary texts 239-40
intuition 17-18, 34-5, 121
irrationality 138-9, 146
Islam 14, 317-8

J
James, William 178
Jesus Christ
arrest of 218-20
and ethics xiv
and human rationality 26
influence of 23-4
kingdom of 219-21, 222
as revealer of God 24, 26
trial of 216-27
as truth 210-11
Joad, C. E. M. 188-90
Johnson, Barbara 236, 265
Judaism 14, 317-8
judgment 174, 235
analytic 119
final/eternal 206
legal 203
subjective 75, 224,
suspension/reservation of 49, 51
value 74
justice 167, 285

K
Kant, Immanuel 76, 78, 103-34, 146-7, 149
basic principles of a priori synthetic knowledge 117-24
his Copernican revolution 110-17
and cosmology 130-3
critique of 133-4
epitemology of 125-7
and Hume 110, 113, 114, 115
and knowing God 107-10
and limits of knowability 124-34
practical reason 104-7, 128-30, 133
and psychology 127-30
pure reason 104-7, 115, 124, 127-8, 130, 133-4
his scientific background 110-17
and theology 130-3

Kekulé, Friedrich August 290-1
Kenny, Anthony 85-6, 193-4
kentauros 257
Kepler, Johannes 296-7, 298-9
knowability, limits of 124-34
  in cosmology 130-3
  in epistemology 125-7
  in psychology 127-30
  in theology 130-3
knowledge 4-8, 57
  globalisation of 165-6
  innate 78-9, 80-1
  objective 72, 74-5
  phenomenological 125-7
  a priori (synthetic) 81, 113-14, 117-24
  sociology of 277-8
  subjective 72-4
  and truth 163
Kuhn, Thomas 273-4, 281 n. 11, 319-21

L

language 166, 169-70, 185, 205, 263, 280-1
  Aramaic 199
  Greek 199-200
  Hebrew 199
  and intrinsic meaning of words denied 262-3
  limitations of 163
  legal 207-8
  and truth 163-4, 169-70
  universal grammar 259-60
Laplace, Pierre-Simon 308
Lanson, Gustave 269
law(s)
  of contradiction 192
  of dialectic 192
  of excluded middle 121, 192
  of identity 121, 192
  of logic 79, 121, 192
  of mathematics 247, 260
  moral 261
  of nature 247
  of non-affirmability 34
  of non-contradiction 121, 177
Leibniz, Gottfried Wilhelm (von) 78, 81, 112, 175, 247-8
Leitch, Vincent B. 236, 263-4
lēstēs 221 n. 7
Le Verrier, Urbain 301

Lewis, C. S. 185, 285, 318
Lewontin, Richard 315
life
  after death 14-15, 108. *See also* DEATH; HEAVEN
  origin of 36
literary criticism 233-69
  denial of metaphysics 245-51
  Derrida, Jacques 236-7
  logocentrism 246-50
  and truth 233-4
literature, Russian 234 n. 1
Lobachevski, Nikolai Ivanovich 80 n. 14
Locke, John 70 n. 2, 73, 78-89, 97-8, 115, 128 n. 45
  evaluation of epistemology 80-4
  and innate knowledge 78-9
  theory of colour 84-9
  validation of ideas 79-80
logic 113
  laws of 79, 121
logical positivism 23
logocentrism 246-50, 266-7
Logos 14, 26, 46, 247-8, 268, 269. *See also* REASON/REASONING
Lonsdale, Kathleen 290
Lossky, N. O. 85, 121, 191, 192
Lucian of Samosata 25

M

Maenads 234
man. *See also* HUMANITY
  at centre of universe 117, 235
  as machine 37-8, 312
  as subject 73-4
Marchman, V. 260
Marx, Karl 23, 191, 196
Marxism 165, 235
Mascall, E. L. 97
materialism 12-13, 75 n. 7, 320-1
  dialectical 23
mathematics 53, 176
  laws of 260
matter 70 n. 2
  as bad/evil 74
meaning 246-8, 254-5, 256-7
  deferred 262
  intrinsic 262-3
  of life 247

metaphysics and 262
mechanism 305-8
Medawar, Sir Peter B. 20
memory 34, 64-5, 66, 89, 140, 148, 312.
   See also MIND
Mendel, Gregor 294, 296
Merezhkovsky, Dmitry 234 n. 1
metanarrative(s) 165, 235-6, 274, 275-6
metaphysics 89, 103-34, 320
metaphysics
   denial of 245-51
   and meaning 262
Mill, John Stuart 291-2
Miller, J. Hillis 263
mind (human) 51-2, 70-3, 79, 81-2, 172, 194-5. *See also* MEMORY
   philosophy of 89-99
Minoan civilisation 188-9
miracles 89
mirages 60, 62
modernism 233, 275-553
   defined 234 n. 1
   relation to postmodernism 234-6
Moore, G. E. 57
moral laws 261
morality 277, 285
Mossner, Ernest C. 89
myth 282-3, 284

N

Nagel, Thomas 150
Naive Realism 58-61
nature, design in 105, 130-2
necessity 176
Neoplatonism 74-5
Newton, Isaac 77, 86-7, 111-13, 123, 281
Newtonian physics 116
Nietzsche, Friedrich 150-1
nomos 302
Norris, Christopher 236, 264-5
non-rationality/the non-rational 14, 35, 36. *See also* RATIONALITY
noumenon/noumena 125, 128

O

object, defined 72-3
objective values 266
objectivity 266

observation 132, 291, 293-4, 296, 314, 320
'Occam's razor' 299, 300
'ontological' argument for existence of God 143 n. 3
ontology 262, 277, 278
onto-theology 262
opinion 49
organic evolution 13-14, 28, 142
ousia 249

P

panentheism 191 n. 8, 194 n. 14, 196
pantheism 191, 194 n. 14, 196
paradigm shift 114-17, 281, 291, 319-21
Parmenides 49
peace of mind 51-2
Peacocke, Arthur 311
Peirce, Charles Sanders 178, 303
Penrose, Roger 260
perception 70, 73, 79, 82, 92-4, 97-8, 148.
   See also REPRESENTATIVE THEORY OF PERCEPTION (RTP)
   causal theory of 85
   co-ordinational theory of 85
   defined 59
   perceptual error 60, 62-3
persecution 164-5
perspectival relativity perspectival relativity and 61, 63
phenomena 125
Phillips, William D. 28
philosophy 15, 16, 20-2, 23, 263
   history of 193-4
   of mind 89-99
   natural 110-13
physico-theology 105-6
physics 53, 299-300, 309-11
   Newtonian 116
   quantum 116
pistis 200
pistos 200
Plantinga, Alvin 148
Plato 11, 21, 49, 98, 110, 141
   theory of Forms 70 n. 1, 77
poetry 205, 242-3, 263
Polanyi, Michael 303, 310
Polkinghorne, John 312-3
Pontius Pilate 216-27
Poole, Michael 307

Popper, Karl R. 23, 301-2, 310
postmodernism 233-69
　relation to modernism 234-6
　and science 273-86
power
　and truth 164
pragmatic theory of truth 178-9, 273-4
Prance, Ghillean 28
prediction(s) 22-3, 292, 296-7, 301, 303, 314
presence 248-50
preference(s) 7, 37, 299
presuppositions 14-16, 21, 278-9, 292, 293, 313-21
　and axioms 315-16
　and intelligibility of universe 317-18
　and observation 314
　and paradigms 319-21
prior beliefs 148
privilege 265
probability 300, 318
progress, human 189, 275
properly basic beliefs 148
propositions 206-7
　analytic 117-18, 127
　arithmetical 119-20
　geometrical 120-1
　synthetic 117, 118-19
psychology 127-30
purpose
　of humanity 14, 15, 36-8
　of universe 188-90
Putnam, Hilary 55
Pyrrho 51

Q

qualities (Locke) 82-5, 171
quantum physics 116

R

Raphael (Raffaello Sanzio da Urbino) 11
ratio 75
rationalism 75-8
　defined 75-6
rationality 14, 25-7, 34-5, 56, 247, 317. *See also* NON-RATIONALITY; REASON/REASONING
reader-response theory 241-5
　Crosman, Robert 242-3
　Fish, Stanley 244-5

realism 70-2, 196
　naive/direct 58-61
reality 29-35
　definition/meaning 29
　external 29-30
　and history 33
　ultimate 34-5
　vs. counterfeit 30-3
reason/reasoning 17, 21-2, 24-5, 64-5, 79-80, 116, 147. *See also* RATIONALITY
　authority of 140-2
　and evolution 142
　and faith 137-55
　human 133, 234-5
　limitation(s) 46
　practical reason 104-7, 117, 128-30, 133
　pure reason 104-7, 115, 117, 124, 127-8, 130, 133-4, 137-9
　　atheism and 141-2
　　categories of 115, 123-4, 133, 141, 146
　　limitations of 114, 117, 138-9
redemption 15
reductionism 309-13, 320-1
Reid, Thomas 96-7
religion 15, 89, 105, 235
repeatability 302-5
Representative Theory of Perception (RTP) 58, 59-65, 82, 89-91, 93
　evaluated 61-3
　hallucinations 59-60, 61-2
　mirages and 60, 62
　perceptual error and 60, 62-3
　perspectival relativity and 61, 63
Rescher, Nicholas 71, 72
revelation
　divine 24-9, 131-2, 133, 143-9, 190, 196, 208-11, 261
　progressive 151-2
　Two Book view of 26-7
revolution
　in scientific thinking 291, 296
Ricoeur, Paul 239
rights, human 14-15, 17
RNA 311
Rorty, Richard 273-5
rules xii, 8, 21, 37, 291, 310

Russell, Bertrand 20, 97, 120, 121, 172, 176, 178, 295

S

Sagan, Carl 28
'Sapere aude!' 76, 103
Saussure, Ferdinand de 169
scepticism 48-56, 89, 104
    and 'brain in a vat' analogy 54-6
    Descartes and 52-4
    Pyrrho and 51
    rise of 48-9
    Sextus Empiricus and 51-2
    Socrates and 50
Schaff, Adam 36-7
Schopenhauer, Arthur 193
science 4, 15-16, 18-20, 26-9, 105, 110, 287-321. *See also* SCIENTIFIC METHOD
    abuse of 276-7
    defined 289-90
    explanation 305-13
    and faith 140
    and God as Creator 26-9
    limitation of 19-20, 36-7, 292, 306, 317, 320
    and postmodernism 271-86
    and morality 277
    presuppositions 313-21. *See also* PRESUPPOSITIONS
    as a social construct 276-84
    subjectivity of 278-80
scientific method 110, 139-40, 245, 290-305. *See also* SCIENCE
    abduction 303-5
    axioms 315-16
    data collection 291-3
    deduction/inference 292, 296-8, 303-5
    experimentation 291, 292, 295
    explanation 305-13
    falsifiability 301-2
    hypotheses 283, 291-3, 296-7, 298-301
    induction 293-5, 296, 298
    observation 291, 294, 296, 314
    paradigm shift 291, 319-21
    repeatability 302-5
    trust and 316
scientism 275
Scruton, Roger 65

Searle, John R. 174-5
self 92-4
self-consciousness 34
sense (experience, perception) 29-30, 45-6, 48, 53-6, 57-63, 79, 98, 110, 113, 115, 121, 139, 316
sense-data 58-9, 60, 61, 63-4, 65, 73, 82, 97
senses (five) 64, 79, 82, 83, 98
Sensible World 77, 98
SETI 28
Sextus Empiricus 51-2
Shakespeare, William 189, 234, 245
significance, individual 35-6
signification 251-61, 266
Singer, Peter 194-5
skeptomai 48-9
sociology 4, 309
    of knowledge 277-8
Socrates 9, 21, 50, 195, 215-16
Sokal, Alan 277-8, 280-1, 282, 284, 286
soul. *See also* SPIRIT
    human 106, 127-30
    immortality of 78, 104, 105
    World 74-5
space 121-3
speech 251-61
speiran 218 n. 4
Spinoza 78, 175
spirit 75, 194-5. *See also* SOUL
    Absolute Spirit 194-5
    Holy Spirit 129-30, 194 n. 14, 195
    World 74-5
spiritualism 129
spirituality 129
State, the 17
Stoicism 247
Strawson, P. F. 173-4
subject, defined 72-3
subjectivity 175, 278-80
suffering, problem of 150
sufficiency 176
summum bonum 21
supernatural, the 112, 145-6, 234 n. 1, 306
Swinburne, Richard 148
syllogism 297-8

T

technology 286

telos 249, 306
Ten Commandments. 152
Thal, D. 260
'the intentional fallacy' 238, 240–1, 255
theism xiii, 13, 16, 24–9, 191, 317–18, 320–1. *See also* ATHEISM; PANTHEISM
and faith 142–9
theology 130–3
and knowability 130–3
onto- 262
physico- 105–6
theory/theories/theorems 79, 245, 278–9, 282, 292–3, 296, 298, 314–15
'theory of everything' 187
Theophrastus 32
time 121–3
Torrance, T. F. 98–9, 126–7
touchstone 32–3
trust 138, 316
truth 46, 50, 137, 142–3, 159–180, 181–96, 197–211, 213–27, 233–4
authority of 224
biblical view of 197–211
Christ himself as 210–11
as coherence 201
coherence theory of 175–7
contingent 81, 119, 138
as correspondence of deeds and words 200–1
as correspondence of words with facts 200
correspondence theory of 170–5, 177, 273–4
defined 170, 171
and existence 171
existential 208
and freedom 165, 168
and gospel 209–10
in Greek language 199–200
in Hebrew language 199
historical 186
incarnate 216
as integrity 202–3
and justice 167
kinds of 184–86
and knowledge 163
and language 163–4, 169–70, 205–8
levels of 183–4
and mind 172

necessary 81, 119
objective (absolute) 161–3, 169, 173, 235, 275–6, 284–6
attitude to 161–3
consequences of rejecting 166–8
objections to 163–4
oppresses 164
as openness and honesty 202
poetic 205
and power 164
pragmatic 201–2
pragmatic theory of 178–9
a priori 148
propositional 206–7
and qualities 171
as real and eternal 203–4
as real and genuine 203
relative 169
revealed 190, 208–10
source of 186
ultimate 183–4, 210–11, 216–17
universal 119
as what is ontologically real 204
as what is the real thing as distinct from its symbol 204–5
Two Book view of revelation 26–7, 247

U

ultimate reality and individuals 34–5. *See also* REALITY
uniformity 317–18
universal grammar 259–60
universe 187, 283–4
intelligibility of 317–18
origin of 286, 302, 317–18
purpose of 188–90
utopia 14–15, 23, 196

V

validation of ideas 79–80
Verification Principle 23, 301
Vygotsky, Leo 309–10

W

Walicki, Andrzej 191
Watson, James D 289, 312
Whitehead, Sir Alfred North 27
Wimsatt, William K. 238
wisdom 140–1, 148
Wittgenstein, Ludwig J. J. 57, 169, 174

Wolpert, Lewis 281–2
Wolterstorff, Nicholas 248, 268 n. 47
Wood, Allen 103
world (external) 57–65
  Representative Theory of Perception and 58–65
  sense perception and 57–63
World Soul (or Spirit) 74–5
worldview 3–9, 15–29, 320–1
  defined 8–9
worship 19, 129, 150, 203, 204, 208, 217
writing 251–61, 267–8

ABOUT THE AUTHORS

David W. Gooding is Professor Emeritus of Old Testament Greek at Queen's University Belfast and a Member of the Royal Irish Academy. He has taught the Bible internationally and lectured on both its authenticity and its relevance to philosophy, world religions and daily life. He has published scholarly articles on the Septuagint and Old Testament narratives, as well as expositions of Luke, John, Acts, Hebrews, the New Testament's use of the Old Testament, and several books addressing arguments against the Bible and the Christian faith. His analysis of the Bible and our world continues to shape the thinking of scholars, teachers and students alike.

John C. Lennox is Professor Emeritus of Mathematics at the University of Oxford and Emeritus Fellow in Mathematics and the Philosophy of Science at Green Templeton College. He is also an Associate Fellow of the Saïd Business School. In addition, he is an Adjunct Lecturer at the Oxford Centre for Christian Apologetics, as well as being a Senior Fellow of the Trinity Forum. In addition to academic works, he has published on the relationship between science and Christianity, the books of Genesis and Daniel, and the doctrine of divine sovereignty and human free will. He has lectured internationally and participated in a number of televised debates with some of the world's leading atheist thinkers.

David W. Gooding (right) and John C. Lennox (left)

Photo credit: Barbara Hamilton.

Myrtlefield Encounters

Key Bible Concepts
How can one book be so widely appreciated and so contested? Millions revere it and many ridicule it, but the Bible is often not allowed to speak for itself. Key Bible Concepts explores and clarifies the central terms of the Christian gospel. Gooding and Lennox provide succinct explanations of the basic vocabulary of Christian thought to unlock the Bible's meaning and its significance for today.

The Definition of Christianity
Who gets to determine what Christianity means? Is it possible to understand its original message after centuries of tradition and conflicting ideas? Gooding and Lennox throw fresh light on these questions by tracing the Book of Acts' historical account of the message that proved so effective in the time of Christ's apostles. Luke's record of its confrontations with competing philosophical and religious systems reveals Christianity's own original and lasting definition.

Myrtlefield Encounters

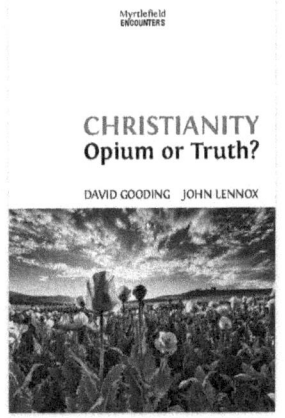

Christianity: Opium or Truth
Is Christianity just a belief that dulls the pain of our existence with dreams that are beautiful but false? Or is it an accurate account of reality, our own condition and God's attitude toward us? Gooding and Lennox address crucial issues that can make it difficult for thoughtful people to accept the Christian message. They answer those questions and show that clear thinking is not in conflict with personal faith in Jesus Christ.

The Bible and Ethics
Why should we tell the truth or value a human life? Why should we not treat others in any way we like? Some say the Bible is the last place to find answers to such questions, but even its critics recognize the magnificence of Jesus' ethical teaching. To understand the ethics of Jesus we need to understand the values and beliefs on which they are based. Gooding and Lennox take us on a journey through the Bible and give us a concise survey of its leading events and people, ideas, poetry, moral values and ethics to bring into focus the ultimate significance of what Jesus taught about right and wrong.

Clear, simple, fresh and highly practical—this David Gooding/John Lennox series is a goldmine for anyone who desires to live Socrates' 'examined life'.

Above all, the books are comprehensive and foundational, so they form an invaluable handbook for negotiating the crazy chaos of today's modern world.

Os Guinness, author of *Last Call for Liberty*

These six volumes, totalling almost 2000 pages, were written by two outstanding scholars who combine careers of research and teaching at the highest levels. David Gooding and John Lennox cover well the fields of Scripture, science, and philosophy, integrating them with one voice. The result is a set of texts that work systematically through a potpourri of major topics, like being human, discovering ultimate reality, knowing truth, ethically evaluating life's choices, answering our deepest questions, plus the problems of pain and suffering. To get all this wisdom together in this set was an enormous undertaking! Highly recommended!

Gary R. Habermas, Distinguished Research Professor & Chair, Dept. of Philosophy, Liberty University & Theological Seminary

David Gooding and John Lennox are exemplary guides to the deepest questions of life in this comprehensive series. It will equip thinking Christians with an intellectual roadmap to the fundamental conflict between Christianity and secular humanism. For thinking seekers it will be a provocation to consider which worldview makes best sense of our deepest convictions about life.

Justin Brierley, host of the *Unbelievable?* radio show and podcast

I would recommend these books to anyone searching to answer the big questions of life. Both Gooding and Lennox are premier scholars and faithful biblicists—a rare combination.

Alexander Strauch, author of *Biblical Eldership*

www.ingramcontent.com/pod-product-compliance
Lightning Source LLC
Chambersburg PA
CBHW071733150426
43191CB00010B/1555